# Resilient Universities

# Resilient Universities

## Confronting Changes in a Challenging World

Edited by

Jan Erik Karlsen and Rosalind M.O. Pritchard

PETER LANG
Oxford · Bern · Berlin · Bruxelles · Frankfurt am Main · New York · Wien

Bibliographic information published by Die Deutsche Nationalbibliothek.
Die Deutsche Nationalbibliothek lists this publication in the Deutsche Nationalbibliografie; detailed bibliographic data is available on the Internet at http://dnb.d-nb.de.

A catalogue record for this book is available from the British Library.

Library of Congress Control Number: 2013948168

Cover image © Galyna Andrushko.

ISBN 978-3-0343-1716-0


Hochfeldstrasse 32, CH-3012 Bern, Switzerland
info@peterlang.com, www.peterlang.com, www.peterlang.net



This publication has been peer reviewed

Printed in Germany

*We wish to dedicate this book to family and friends.*

*Jan Erik to Bjørg, Hanne, Tonje and Ketil*
*Rosalind to Jennifer, Liz, Petra, Rae and Vincent*

# Contents

Preface ix

List of Figures xi

List of Tables xiii

List of Abbreviations xv

JAN ERIK KARLSEN AND ROSALIND M.O. PRITCHARD

1 Resilience – The Ability to Adapt 1

JAN ERIK KARLSEN

2 Reframing University Adaptation 17

ELLEN HAZELKORN

3 Higher Education's Future: A New Global Order? 53

JOUNI KEKÄLE

4 Megatrends Affecting Resilient Universities in Europe 91

ROSALIND M.O. PRITCHARD

5 Higher Education in a Competitive World: The New British Regime 115

STIG A. SELMER-ANDERSSEN

6 Robustness in Organized Anarchies: Efficient Composting in the Organizational Garbage Cans? 149

LISE DEGN

7 Making Sense of Management: A Study of Department Heads' Sensemaking Processes in a Changing Environment 191

CELIA WHITCHURCH AND GEORGE GORDON

8 Universities Responding to Change: Implications for Roles and Staffing Practices 213

MARIA HINFELAAR AND MICHAEL O'CONNELL

9 Shall We Dance? Dynamic Collaborations, Alliances and Mergers in the Shifting Irish Higher Education Landscape 239

PÅL BAKKEN AND INGRID STORM

10 Academic Drift and Diversity: Institutional Dynamics in Norwegian Higher Education 261

MATTHIAS KLUMPP

11 Higher Education Efficiency: Questions, Methods, Results and Implications 283

CARMEN PÉREZ-ESPARRELLS AND EVA M. TORRE

12 Fundraising in European Higher Education Institutions: A Strategy for University Enhancement 323

JAN ERIK KARLSEN

13 Backcasting European University Governance 2042+ 349

GUDMUND HERNES

14 Super-Resilient Organizations 381

Notes on Contributors 403

Index 405

# Preface

Resilience is ostensibly acknowledged as a cross-disciplinary issue, yet resilience analysis has seldom been applied to understand universities and the academic world. Indeed, this book aims to compensate for such theoretical and empirical scarcity.

The title for the collection of contributions reflects our best desire to stretch debates in new directions and to assemble a fresh set of models and tools for thinking about resilient universities. Bringing together a range of domain experts, this book marks a novel departure within the social sciences and, we hope, acts as a first step towards establishing a holistic approach to future university governance and adaptation.

It all started in Warsaw in August 2011. The Organizing Committee for the European Association for Institutional Research 2012 conference to be held in Stavanger, Norway, decided to push for a publication on the deep changes that confronted European universities. The Committee nominated Jan Erik Karlsen and Rosalind M.O. Pritchard to compile contributions and edit the book. As editors we owe the committee members, Ingvild Marheim Larsen, Ole-Jacob Skodvin, Janis Stonis, Jannecke Wiers-Jensen and Dag Gjerløw Aasland, many thanks for their initial support and enthusiasm. The authors who have contributed to this text have been generous with their time and thoughts. Some of the chapters are elaborated and extended versions originating from the European Association for Institutional Research 2012 Stavanger conference, but most contributions are written exclusively for this publication. The authors, who come from different countries and many walks of life, have made this publication possible. We offer thanks and appreciation to all. Sincere thanks also to the Director of Academic Affairs at the University of Stavanger, Kristofer Rossmann Henrichsen, who provided us with the financial resources to finish the publication.

JAN ERIK KARLSEN, Stavanger, Norway and
ROSALIND M.O. PRITCHARD, Coleraine, Northern Ireland,
May 2013

# List of Figures


| | | |
|---|---|---|
| Figure 2.1 | The Governance Triangle | 27 |
| Figure 2.2 | Typology of Institutional Changes | 29 |
| Figure 2.3 | Characteristics of Good Governance | 37 |
| Figure 2.4 | Resilience, Anticipation and Mindfulness | 40 |
| Figure 2.5 | A Conceptual Model of Future University Adaptation | 47 |
| Figure 6.1 | The Overlap Model | 170 |
| Figure 6.2 | Organizational Resilience Theoretical Framework | 174 |
| Figure 6.3 | The Three Decision Structures in the Garbage Can Model | 184–185 |
| Figure 10.1 | Proportion of the Total Student Population in Each Institutional Category | 275 |
| Figure 11.1 | Comparison of Performance and Productivity Measurement Schemes | 289 |
| Figure 11.2 | Efficiency-THE-Score Matrix | 296 |
| Figure 11.3 | Efficiency-THE-Position Matrix | 298 |
| Figure 11.4 | Graduate Number-Cost-Relation | 300 |
| Figure 11.5 | Efficiency-Volume-Relation (Assumption) | 302 |
| Figure 11.6 | DEA Frontier Graph – CCR and BBC Model | 312 |
| Figure 13.1 | The 'Greek Triangle' | 355 |
| Figure 13.2 | Principal Ways of Linking Present and Future | 357 |
| Figure 13.3 | Backcasting the Vision 2042+ | 358 |
| Figure 13.4 | University Conceptual Model 2042+ | 366 |

# List of Tables


Table 2.1 Core Elements in HEI Governance Models 25

Table 3.1 Increasing Stratification 76

Table 4.1 Summary of the Megatrends' Estimated Influence on Higher Education Institutions and Potential Institutional Responses 104–105

Table 6.1 Decision Structures in Single and Triple Authority Garbage Can Simulations 159

Table 6.2 Proportion of Choices that Resolve Problems by Load and Single Authority Decision Structure 161

Table 6.3 Proportion of Choices that Resolve Problems by Load and Triple Authority Decision Structure 162

Table 6.4 Effects of Variations in Load on Single and Triple Authority Garbage Can Simulations 163

Table 6.5 Effects of Variations in Load on MAGCM Simulations with Three Identical Authorities 164

Table 6.6 Effects of Variations in Load for the UHS Variety of Triple Authority MAGCM Simulations 169

Table 6.7 Effects of Variations in Load for the USS Triple Authority Variety of the MAGCM Simulations 171

Table 6.8 Two Specific Triple Authority Varieties of the MAGCM Simulations, Means Over All Load Levels 172

Table 6.9 Energy Distributions in the Garbage Can Model 187

Table 9.1 A Two-Way Typology of CAM Rationale and Activity 245

Table 9.2 Two-Way CAM Typology Applied to Limerick Institute of Technology 257

Table 11.1 Management Questions and Management Decisions Regarding Efficiency 286

| | | |
|---|---|---|
| Table 11.2 | Top 10: University Dataset from THE WRU and Budget Data (2011/2012) | 293 |
| Table 11.3 | Top 10: Simple Productivity Analysis Budget-Outcome-Indicators (Score per 1 mil. €) | 294 |
| Table 11.4 | Top 17: Complex Productivity Analysis: Data Envelopment Analysis Results | 295 |
| Table 11.5 | University Dataset from THE WRU and Budget Data (2011/2012) | 313–315 |
| Table 11.6 | Simple Productivity Analysis: Budget-Outcome-Indicators (Score per 1 mil. €) | 316–318 |
| Table 11.7 | Complex Productivity Analysis: Data Envelopment Analysis Results | 319–321 |
| Table 12.1 | Expectations on Income Streams Evolution in European Universities | 329–330 |
| Table 12.2 | Main Higher Education Stakeholders in European Universities and their Function in a Fundraising Strategy | 336 |
| Table 12.3 | First Steps in Promoting University Fundraising: Instilling a 'Culture of Giving' | 337 |
| Table 12.4 | First Steps in Promoting University Fundraising: Creating an 'Asking Institution' | 340 |
| Table 13.1 | Backcasting University Adaptation Actions | 363 |

# List of Abbreviations

| | |
|---|---|
| ARWU | Academic Ranking of World Universities |
| AUA | Association of University Administrators |
| BIS | Department for Business, Innovation and Skills |
| CAM(s) | Collaborations, Alliances and Merger |
| CARO | Cambridge Alumni Relations Office |
| CUC | Committee of University Chairs |
| CUDO | Cambridge University Development Office |
| EHEA | European Higher Education Area |
| EIE | Education Industry in Europe |
| ERA | European Research Area |
| ETH | Eidgenössische Technische Hochschule |
| ETTO | Efficiency Thoroughness Trade Off |
| EU | European Union |
| FE | Further Education |
| FEI | Further Education Institution |
| HE | Higher Education |
| HEA | Higher Education Authority of Ireland |
| HEFCE | Higher Education Funding Council for England |
| HEI | Higher Education Institution (see also university below) |
| HESA | Higher Education Statistics Agency |
| HUMANE | Heads of University Management and Administration Network in Europe |

| | |
|---|---|
| IESE | Business School Instituto de Estudios Superiores de la Empresa |
| IOT | Institute of Technology |
| ITT | Institute of Technology Tralee |
| JISC | Joint Information Systems Committee |
| JNCHES | Joint Negotiating Committee for Higher Education Staff |
| KE | Knowledge Exchange |
| LFHE | Leadership Foundation for Higher Education |
| LIT | Limerick Institute of Technology |
| LMU | London Metropolitan University |
| MIC | Mary Immaculate College of Education |
| MTU | Munster Technological University |
| OECD | Organization for Economic Cooperation and Development |
| OFFA | Office for Fair Access |
| PSL | Paris Sciences et Lettres |
| QAA | Quality Assurance Agency |
| RPE | Research Prioritization Exercise |
| SFC | Scottish Funding Council |
| SIF | Strategic Innovation Fund |
| STEM | Science, Technology, Engineering and Mathematics |
| TGE | Transnational Giving Europe |
| TI | Tipperary Institute |
| TRAC | Transparency Approach to Costing |
| TU | Technological University |
| UCAS | Universities and Colleges Admissions Service |
| UCEA | Universities and Colleges Employers Association |
| UCU | University and College Union |

| | |
|---|---|
| UK | United Kingdom |
| UL | University of Limerick |
| UNAV | University of Navarra |
| University | Refers to all HEIs undertaking research and awarding higher degrees, irrespective of their name and status in national law |
| UUK | UniversitiesUK |
| WSAN | Winter School Alumni Network |

JAN ERIK KARLSEN AND ROSALIND M.O. PRITCHARD

# 1 Resilience – The Ability to Adapt

## Building Blocks of Institutional Resilience

Academe has been allocated more functions and responsibilities than ever before. In many countries, though, it has not been provided with the resources necessary to do the job, and funding has been constantly decreasing. Hence, academic institutions need to reorganize themselves in order to strengthen (or even preserve) their societal legitimacy as producers, assessors and distributors of relevant knowledge and competences. Planning, designing and innovating for the future inevitably involves considering multiple alternatives, assessing potential risks and coping with damaging setbacks. The ability to bounce back is often regarded as a critical resource for individuals, groups or organizations when facing untoward events. It is a question of resilience. The aim of the book is to explore ways in which universities can achieve this resilience in a wide variety of domains.

Basically, resilience points to the capacity of individuals or social/technical systems to handle boundary conditions and interpret early warnings and weak signals of change. Being resilient entails the ability to guard against something dysfunctional happening, to prevent something damaging from worsening and to recover from adversity once it has happened. Few governments would take the view that what they impose is dysfunctionality, but the conditions that they impose often create severe challenges for their higher education institutions (HEIs). The capacity to respond to dysfunctionality resides in the expertise, strategies, tools and plans that people in various roles can deploy to respond to change. So, resilience can be conceived as a person's and/or system's capacity to manage the unexpected and to cope with surprises.

'Latent pathogens' tend to be present in social systems, just as they exist in our bodies and in the environment. Such potential time bombs combine and interact to breach defences and boundaries. We may say that resilience, as a form of adaptive capacity, is a system's potential for adaptive action in the future when conditions change and previous models and assumptions are no longer viable. The challenge for today's HEIs is how to make the institutions resilient in a longer term perspective. This ambition implies that they must be able to adjust their functioning so that they can sustain required operations under both expected and unexpected conditions. Furthermore, institutional resilience must not be limited to dysfunctional conditions or to things going wrong. It must encompass both threats and opportunities. Thus, there is a need to include and improve the anticipative capacity of the HEIs as an imaging of plausible and preferable HEI futures.

The concept of resilience has been taken from the seminal works of Weick et al. (1999) and is now seen in different contexts, i.e. in physical, biological, psychological, social and cultural systems, and at different levels of analysis (Aguirre, 2006), i.e. micro (individual), meso (organizational) and macro levels (systemic). Although the concept of resilience may need some theoretical refinement (Välikangas and Romme, 2012), it is still applicable for both practical and political purposes. In our university context, resilience is a metaphor related to institutional viability and governance structure, as well as a measurable quantity related to the swiftness and strength necessary to adapt to and thrive on change. According to Bruijne et al. (2010: 23), organization and management literature has listed a range of strategies and measures conducive to resilience: structural flexibility, redundancy or slack, high-performance relationships, sense-making, a culture of reliability and improvisation. Resilient organizations not only re-establish a status quo, they also improve their institutional capacity as a result of the effort to adapt.

For our analysis of university adaptation, we mainly see resilience as the institutional capability to effectively absorb, respond to and recover from an internally or externally induced set of extraordinary demands. Hamel and Välikangas (2003: 3) discuss resilience as one of three forms of organizational innovation, the other two being revolution and renewal. In their vocabulary, resilience is the capacity for continuous reconstruction.

To be resilient an organization needs to meet cognitive, strategic, political and ideological challenges. Cognitive means becoming free of 'denial, nostalgia, and arrogance', strategic 'requires alternatives as well as awareness', political means diverting accumulated resources to 'support a broad portfolio of breakout experiments', and ideological implies that 'renewal has to be continuous and future oriented'.

Välikangas (2010: 99–110) introduces a set of criteria conducive to building such an innovative, institutional resilience, the defining dimensions being resourcefulness, robustness and adaptiveness. Resourcefulness may be gained in several ways, though it requires foresight to obtain internal reserves, both financial and human. Organizational robustness is more or less a structural or design affair. 'The more varied and intense the challenges which the organization can cope with, the more robust it is. Robustness is also the capacity to accommodate multiple, different futures' (ibid.: 104). So, robustness can be structural as well as strategic. Adaptation is about the ever vibrating relationship with the environment, the markets, the stakeholders and the systemic arrangements. Change requires intelligence applied to the environment, and it takes timing and capacity to achieve. Survival depends on the capacity to respond to market signals, whether strong and visible or incipient and weak.

In addition to these three dimensions, Välikangas (2010: 113–120) introduces an extra dimension, 'sisu', a concept derived from Finnish and well-known to Nordic people as the ability to endure pain and adversity. It is seen as strength of will, determination, perseverance and the capacity to act rationally in the face of hardship. It is not short-lived bravery: rather it is an inner ability to sustain an action against the odds. As such it resembles the perseverance and coping capability of psychological resilience. This is assumed to reflect the internal strength and 'guts' of the institution, and is to be understood as some cultural capacity, supporting resilience by corporate humour and jesting. Applying it to the university sector, the notion of institutional resilience seems like a tall order: it is no mean feat to transform universities – in Välikangas' wording – into 'adaptive cultures which may thrive on change'.

Resilience may also be seen as a dynamic, but invisible non-event (Weick, 2001: 235–236). It is dynamic in the sense that it is an on-going condition in which problems are momentarily under control due to compensating changes in components. It is invisible in the sense that it does not reveal the worst case scenarios (how many mistakes and breakdowns could possibly happen) and in the sense that reliable outcomes are constant (there is nothing to pay attention to since nothing is happening).

How do we recognize resilience in ontological terms as long as we do not expect a person or a social system to have a total breakdown? Subsequently, how do we perceive the ontological and epistemological aspects of resilience to be visualized and presented? Resilience is not a technological device; rather it is an organizational or an individual capacity meant to prevent dysfunctions emerging and to appear if something unwanted and (relatively) unforeseen happens. We may say that resilience is a phenomenon which is not intended or even expected to be activated. However, if a breakdown happens it is expected to serve as a safety net restoring the capacity of the system or the individual. As such resilience is a sort of organizational redundancy, an extra capacity to capitalize on when needed. Failures and successes are outcomes of normal performance variability; however they represent opposite hopes for the future (Hollnagel, 2008). This goes for universities as for businesses.

Kaufmann (2012) writes that 'self-organization' and 'flexibility' are the keys to cultivating resilience. Pertaining to institutions, self-organization means that an institution can take action in the absence of external direction (e.g. lack of governmental regulation), thus innovating to find its own solutions to the change. Flexibility on its part could include diversity and plurality in applying measures and solutions, as well as stimulating in-house creativity and connectivity. However (ibid.: 3):

> Understanding how self-organization and flexibility can be facilitated requires comprehensive assessments not only of interrelated problems and vulnerabilities, but also of human and systematic capacities and potential collaborations between different societal stakeholders.

Resilience is realized when a disruption is unfolding or cannot be avoided. It is the system's potential for adaptive action in the future when information varies, conditions change, or new kinds of events (even external shocks) occur. Thus, the concept of resilience does not include prevention measures as such; however learning from resilience processes may strengthen prevention policies (ibid.: 3). Hence, we expect resilient higher education institutions to demonstrate an ability to detect emerging challenges, to confront and handle problems when they must be faced and to recover from damage once the dysfunctionality has happened. Resilience is thus the process of being mindful of errors and disruptions, abating and correcting them before they worsen or cause more serious harm.

The concept of resilience is contested and debated, but we may think about it as a form of adaptive capacity. If resilience is meant to encompass the capability to respond, to monitor and to anticipate and by the end of the day also to learn both from success and failure, the present situation of European universities illustrates the necessity of linking these aspects when building institutional resilience. Resilience is mostly displayed in (re) action, rather than in strategic vision. However, it does not exclude forward planning or emergency preparedness. One may argue that today's mergers and alliances, shared governance, bureaucratic rule and use of ICT mostly are examples of such (re)active strategies, although apparently anticipative tactical and strategic reasoning are also connected to such organizational adaptations. However, if we accept that the concept of resilience incorporates the notion of adaptation, then complex dynamic systems like universities are subject to processes of restructuring and adaptation, due to intramurally as well as extramurally generated change.

## How the Text is Organized

The book has a European framing, and it places this framing into an international context by factoring in the enormous potential of emerging world powers like China, India and Korea; it also demonstrates consciousness of the demand from the Middle East and North-African countries. It addresses the serious competition that all these countries pose to a Europe that is sometimes characterized by complacency and over-attachment to past eminence, and is often critical of developments within the home countries from which the contributors emanate. Contributions come from Denmark, Finland, Germany, Ireland, Norway, Spain and the United Kingdom, thus connecting with reality in a range of key countries. They deal with issues confronting higher education on a number of different levels: globally, internationally and nationally. The authors grapple with new ways of sharing governance and managing. They address the re-configuration of institutions through mergers, linkages and growing diversification. New forms of academic identity are identified, arising from the fact that specialized administrative functions continue to increase, some say at the expense of the traditional faculty. New ways are proposed of raising funding and of testing efficiency within European universities. Foresight management methods are used to produce images of a future which may help to illuminate the present situation. The question is addressed: What harbingers of the future can we identify in the present, and how can we develop the resilience to deal with the challenges that it will inevitably pose?

The present chapter by Jan Erik Karlsen and Rosalind M.O. Pritchard outlines the theory of resilience, gives the motivation for the book, and signposts its content for the reader.

In Chapter 2 Jan Erik Karlsen outlines the conceptual baseline of the book. He discusses theoretical aspects of resilience, shows how new concepts of university adaptation are emerging, and with them the need to strike a better balance between all the parties concerned. The core concepts are summarized in a functional-historicist model, depicting trends, key drivers, governance, institutional responses and adaptive goals as main blocks of change in the operations of current and future European universities. Shared governance, robustness and resilience are concepts that are gradually being put forward on universities' front stages along with the pursuit of traditional academic values. Shared university governance is perceived as an open and inclusive authority platform. Resilience is the capability to cope with both sudden and creeping changes, instigating adaptations conducive to the university's long term robustness and survival.

Chapters 3, 4 and 5 proceed from global through European towards national perspectives. Ellen Hazelkorn's contribution in Chapter 3 views the challenges facing the modern university in global terms. Over the last decades, access to higher education has expanded from being a privilege of birth or talent or both (the elite phase, according to Martin Trow) to a right for those with certain qualifications (the mass phase) to being an obligation for the vast majority of society and occupations (universal). However, adjustment to the global economic crisis is putting great pressure on higher education to demonstrate increased relevance to, and better value for, individuals and society. The continuing shift to the knowledge-based economy, and the rising demand for and costs of higher education, are occurring at the same time that many governments face serious financial strain – with knock-on effects on higher education budgets. Many of these challenges were manifest decades ago; but the confluence of factors associated with the new economic reality has intensified their impact. Many people argue that the modern university has remained largely unchanged for 1000 years; but are recent developments a sign of a profound paradigm shift in our model for mass higher education or simply a transitory moment? While each country and university faces particular and often unique challenges, there are some common factors which affect most countries around the world today – issues which have become more acute since 2008. The chapter focuses on the three big challenges of the moment: 1) ensuring sustainable higher education systems at the same time that public funding is decreasing and competitiveness increasing; 2) improving the quality of the total student experience at the same time that the demand for participation is growing; 3) strengthening knowledge and innovation as drivers of growth while ensuring that multi- and cross-disciplinary critical inquiry is maintained. This chapter reviews some of the key challenges facing higher education, and hypothesizes some possible scenarios.

Jouni Kekäle (Chapter 4) discusses major trends in the European context. It can be claimed that the operational environment for universities in Europe is fundamentally changing, and in this chapter, key trends affecting the sector will be discussed. First, there is a major change going on in demography: the proportion of young age cohorts entering the age of university enrolment is diminishing whilst the older age groups will come to represent an increasing part of the age pyramid in relative terms. Secondly, the EU is going through an economic crisis which is by no means over yet. It is possible that for years to come public budgets will diminish or stagnate due to recession and increased debts. Thirdly, there appear to be rising educational markets in China and the so-called Third World, whereas in the 'old Europe' the demand for education is not necessarily increasing in a similar manner; more effort must be devoted to find growing market segments. Fourthly, the new educational technology – eLearning, web-teaching – appears to challenge traditional forms of instruction. And finally, it appears that the post-modern western culture is characterized by hastiness and a shortened time-span in decision making, business and politics. Apparently increasing superficiality, overflow of information and commercialism all add to the challenges for higher education institutions which once built their operations around long term, if not eternal, truths and slow accumulation of knowledge during the widely shared project of Enlightenment.

Rosalind M.O. Pritchard (Chapter 5) uses resilience theory to analyse recent developments in one specific higher education system: that of the United Kingdom which has long been in the vanguard of change. The chapter begins by outlining major features of resilience theory, and proceeds to apply it to recent developments in British higher education. The raising of fees has led to a decline in student numbers in England and Wales. Middle class parents are increasingly sending their children abroad to study where fees are lower. Institutions are more reliant than ever upon the international students who bring premium fees, but the UK Border Agency makes it difficult for such students to obtain visas. The under-representation of male students has increased, thereby exacerbating an existing and unwelcome trend. Subject choice has diminished, thereby leading to a certain level of homogenization, and reducing institutional competition based on academic profile. The government will no longer give block funding to Arts or Social Science subjects, favouring instead STEM subjects. The proportion of GDP spent on British HE is one of the lowest in all OECD countries – a fact which may jeopardize its high quality. Large tracts of time are spent on satisfying quality assurance requirements which are, however, not applied at present to all private institutions; this is felt by many publicly-funded institutions to be inequitable. Latent pathogens affect mental health and human relationships. Surveys show that British academics are one of the most stressed professional groups in the country, and several Vice-Chancellors have resigned before completing their terms of office. In circumstances of great challenge, the institutions make extensive use of 'harm absorbers' and compensatory strategies in order to achieve resilience. Above all, the government exploits their intrinsic motivation to do more with less.

No sector of higher education is immune to the implications of change, and the next four chapters (Chapters 6–9) deal with governance, management and academic identity. Stig A. Selmer-Anderssen's Chapter 6 tests governance models according to common resilience criteria; during the last two decades, there has been a shift in governance to new modes for European public organizations generally and for HEIs specifically, as certain significant forces affecting the sector have changed. A number of observers comment that these changes 'all add up to regimes appropriate to a stakeholder organization' (Bleiklie and Kogan, 2007: 480). Among the dimensions of the new governance modes, at least three (and in many cases several more) sources of *de jure* as well as *de facto* power can be found. In this chapter, Cohen, March and Olsen's Garbage Can Model (GCM) is revised. It was originally created to simulate an organization run through three different authority schemes, but only one at a time. Selmer-Anderssen expands it to simulate several powers operating *simultaneously*. The robustness of multiple stakeholder power is assessed in terms of how it relates to resilience and how it produces decisions under varying circumstances. It is shown that a multi authority version of the Garbage Can Model could be particularly useful in coming to grips with decision making in universities that have adapted to stakeholders. A significant finding is that Norwegian universities have 'organized anarchy' as their fundamental form, and that far from being counter-productive, this actually contributes to their resilience. The GCM is useful in understanding organizational resilience work generally in universities and other organizations with similar characteristics.

In Chapter 7, Lise Degn focuses upon the important layer of middle management, pressurized from many directions. The European higher education sector is changing – and especially the governance and management structures of the higher education institutions are subject to reform all across Europe. The chapter illustrates how a particular group of managers (Department Heads) within higher education institutions make sense of the changing demands, the organizational rearrangements and the new responsibilities of the job as a university manager. This investigation illuminates how the resilience of academic ideas and institutions affect the individuals who fill the roles in the new governance and management structures. They are faced with the task of navigating between demands of strategic capacity, flexibility and accountability, and the ideas that have characterized academia for centuries and are held in high regard by the academic staff. This is done while at the same time balancing between their identity as managers and as academic researchers. The chapter presents results of a study from two Danish universities where the sensemaking processes of 16 Department Heads have been studied. Three distinct categories, or 'types' of Department Heads are introduced: the shielder, the co-ordinator and the agenda setter. The action-patterns and consequences of identifying with each of these Department Head types are highlighted and the implications for other research areas, e.g. questions of organizational identity, are discussed.

Both Selmer-Anderssen in Chapter 6 and Whitchurch and Gordon deal with new identities. In Chapter 8 Celia Whitchurch and George Gordon show how such pressures are leading to the redefinition of academic identities. Change and challenge go beyond management and organization within institutions, and extend to the relationships between them; based on recent research, the chapter will reflect on the relationship between institutions and a diversifying range of staff who may have academic, non-academic or split contracts, and/ or undertake roles with both academic and professional components. It will explore roles that are new or undergoing redefinition, focussing upon how these affect traditional ideas of spaces and identities in higher education, and consequences for institutions and individuals. Discussion will include the implications of, for instance, differentiated contracts that reflect teaching, research and service in different ways, as well as the emergence of cross-boundary activity between academic and professional spheres.

In both England (as addressed by Pritchard in Chapter 5) and in Ireland, government policy lurches and incoherence greatly intensify the need for resilience. Chapter 9, by Maria Hinfelaar and Michael O'Connell, portrays a shifting landscape in Ireland in which there is institutional re-alignment. Within these parameters, the Irish national strategy has changed in a way that poses a strong challenge to institutional leadership. At first the prospect was dangled in front of the Institutes of Technology (IOTs) that they should prepare themselves for and seek status as Technical Universities. Those that failed in the endeavour feared that they might be downgraded to further education colleges. In the circumstances, the Limerick Institute of Technology signed a Memorandum of Understanding with two other IOTs that was intended to lead to the establishment of the Munster Technological University (MTU). About a year afterwards, the government distanced itself from that position, and declared a preference for regional cross-binary clusters involving strong, autonomous institutions. When it became doubtful that there would be political will and or resource allocation for the IOT sector to upgrade to TUs, LIT was one of the IOTs that decided to slam on the brakes as fast as possible, whereas other IOTs made different choices. In this case, resilience required that it demonstrate speed of response and agility in reversing its earlier decision to go for the MTU. Its leadership response had to be fluid and anticipatory in responding to external drivers, with the steering core repeatedly drawn into revisiting decisions taken earlier. Both this chapter and Chapter 5 (Pritchard on the United Kingdom) demonstrate the need for resilience to cope with government unpredictability and arbitrariness.

Pål Bakken and Ingrid Storm in Chapter 10 attend to similar issues within the Norwegian scenario. Economic stringency is at the heart of the need for change. Not alone must universities make the best use of the resources available to them, but they must also try to access new sources of funding; the higher education sector in Norway is organized in a binary system of research-oriented universities on the one hand, and university colleges offering vocational education on the other hand. However, this distinction is becoming increasingly blurred as university colleges can also offer postgraduate degrees, may apply for university status and are permitted to merge with a university. In recent years, the Ministry has implemented reforms and new incentives in order to stimulate more cooperation and mergers between institutions. One reason for this is the need to make small institutions more resilient. The paper analyses the general forces contributing to academic drift and the institutions' own motives for advancement as well as the effects that these developments have on diversity. Mergers can be seen as a tool that the institutions use to achieve university status. In addition, both the institutions themselves and the government consider this a measure to make small institutions more resilient. Academic drift has only reduced diversity in some aspects and to a very limited degree. While there are more institutions in Norway using the name 'university', there continues to be a great deal of functional differentiation at study programme level and reputational stratification at institutional level. In addition, most new universities maintain their disciplinary specializations. The processes of academic drift tend to make the institutions more resilient: this is partly because some of them are growing (via mergers), and partly because many institutions are offering a greater variety of courses.

Matthias Klumpp in Chapter 11 studies how to measure the efficiency of European university functioning; higher education efficiency has been a long standing research issue, especially in relation to research productivity. But this very narrow and qualitative field of analysis within universities is currently being broadened in terms of methods and comparative international views as well as implications for HE management in practice. Tight budgets impel the public stakeholders as well as university leadership cadres to demand effective instruments for accountability. This chapter gives an overview of a particular approach to efficiency analysis in higher education; it reports on some distinguished international findings and outlines the implications for higher education research and management.

In Chapter 12, Carmen Pérez-Esparrells and Eva M. Torre provide important indications of how European institutions can begin to emulate the success of their American equivalents in private fundraising. The European higher education sector is facing problems in relation to financial sustainability: its institutions have to navigate increasing international competition whilst their core public funding is dropping. This situation is leading European universities to diversify their income sources as a risk-mitigation measure. They need to seek new means of raising supplementary private funds in addition to relying on traditional private sources such as student contributions and contracts with business sector. One of the tools for change is the promotion of university fundraising. The chapter proposes a fundraising model: firstly, institutions need to create a brand image and to strengthen their bonds with their social and economic environment (involvement of stakeholders); secondly, a professional management of fundraising activity is required, with the support and commitment of the university leaders; and thirdly, communicative and petitionary actions are needed in which the entire university community is engaged. A new higher education social contract in Europe is necessary in order to implement this theoretical model and to develop in each HEI the culture of 'asking' that American universities have already established. The chapter concludes with a set of recommendations on how to develop university fundraising as a component of a comprehensive funding strategy in order to build resilient universities prepared for a '*transition management*'.

Arguably, institutional resilience must not be limited to dysfunctional circumstances nor to things going wrong. It must encompass both threats and opportunities. Thus, there is a need to improve the anticipative (foreseeing, foresighting) capacity of the universities. In Chapter 13, Jan Erik Karlsen pursues the idea of 'European university governance 2042' as an imaging of plausible and preferable university futures. The challenge for today's universities is how to make the institutions resilient in a longer term perspective. Such an ambition implies that universities must be able to adjust their functioning prior to, during, or following changes and disturbances, so that they can sustain required operations under both expected and unexpected conditions. Backcasting is used to produce images of a future which in turn may help illuminate the present situation. By thinking and debating how the development of academe and universities may evolve during the next generation as some sort of foreseeing, we project our imaginations into a preferred image of the future. Then we look backwards from the future at how we proceeded to solve the challenges of university adaptation in our own time.

The book concludes with Gudmund Hernes' concept of 'super-resilient organizations' in Chapter 14, pointing at universities which have the capacity to adapt and thrive in times of rapid and deep change. They have been able to transit learning and advance knowledge for nearly a thousand years. While meeting the Darwinian survival criterion of the fittest, super-resilient universities of today develop and nurse talent, discover and engage in important themes, and instigate life-long obsessions of learning and knowledge in students, staff and faculty.

## Conclusion

European universities are confronted with unprecedented challenges that have been identified by some observers as a paradigm shift. Falling demographic trends, stagnating economies, government debts and pressure for certain outcomes are making it difficult for some institutions to achieve sustainability, let alone prosperity. Presently higher education institutions restructure due to declining and meagre funding, implying strategies for lean thinking (in procedures, teaching, costs, etc.), and implementing new pedagogic as well as managerial technologies. Universities are competing for top ranked faculty and talented students to keep their 'market value'. The owners (state/private) are keeping the institutions on a tighter leash than previously, demanding new kinds of reporting and auditing. In addition to the growth in overall student population in many countries, universities are recruiting new professionals holding university degrees of much the same kind and quality as the faculty. Both the number of administrators and the variety of specialized administrative functions continue to increase, some say at the expense of the faculty.

The scenario calls for development of resilience in many domains. Variations of shared governance models have been introduced as a more open and inclusive authority platform; alongside the traditional academic values, robustness and resilience are concepts that are gradually moving to the universities' core agenda. The book discusses changes in governance, management, academic identity and fundraising; it challenges concepts of organized anarchies; it highlights megatrends and current drivers of global reorientation; it advances innovative approaches to efficiency analysis in higher education. It also uses images produced by foresight management to envisage university models set in the future – a generation from now.

## References

Aguirre, B.E. (2006). 'On the Concept of Resilience'. University of Delaware Disaster Research Center, Preliminary Paper Number 356.

Bleiklie, I. and Kogan, M. (2007). 'Organization and Governance of Universities', *Higher Education Policy* 20 (4): 477–493.

Bruijne, M., de, Boin, A., and van Eeten, M. (2010). 'Resilience. Exploring the Concept and its Meanings', In L.K. Comfort, A. Boin, and C. Demchak (eds), *Designing Resilience: Preparing for Extreme Events*, pp. 12–32. Pittsburg, Pa.: University of Pittsburgh Press.

Hamel, G. and Välikangas, L. (2003). 'The Quest for Resilience', *Harvard Business Review*, September, pp. 52–63.

Hollnagel, E., Nemeth, C.P., and Dekker, S. (2008). *Resilience Engineering Perspectives: Remaining Sensitive to the Possibility of Failure*. Volume 1 of Ashgate Studies in Resilience Engineering, pp. 9–17. Aldershot, Hampshire UK and Burlington, USA: Ashgate.

Kaufmann, M. (2012). *Resilience: a Stock-Taking. Key Characteristics and Implications for Human and Societal Security Policy*. Oslo: Prio Policy Brief 01|2012.

Välikangas, L. (2010). *The Resilient Organization. How Adaptive Cultures Thrive Even When Strategy Fails*. New York: McGraw-Hill.

Välikangas, L. and Romme, A.G.L. (2012). 'Building Resilience Capabilities at "Big Brown Box, Inc."', *Strategy and Leadership*, 40 (4), 43–45.

Weick, K. (2001). *Making Sense of the Organization*. Oxford: Blackwell Business.

Weick, K., Sutcliffe K.M., and Obstfeld D. (1999). 'Organizing for High Reliability: Processes of Collective Mindfulness', *Research in Organizational Behavior*, 21, 81–123.

JAN ERIK KARLSEN

# 2 Reframing University Adaptation

In an increasingly interconnected and a rapidly changing world of knowledge, universities have to be adaptive to endure. Resilience pre-assumes that disruption will occur or that a major change is already emerging. It is about survival, return to a pre-disruptive state, and it includes future progress to establish a new normality. What should universities do to foster resilience? Literature points to self-organization and flexibility as key approaches to institutional resilience; however achieving this may be easier said than done.

## Why Institutional Resilience?

Consider university resilience. Basically, resilience points to the capacity of individuals, social and technical systems to handle boundary conditions. Being resilient entails the ability to prevent something dysfunctional from happening, or prevent something damaging from worsening, or to recover from adversity once it has happened (Hollnagel et al., 2006: 59; Westrum, 2008: 1–2). Dysfunctional events occur because technology, plans and procedures have fundamental limits, or because the environment changes, or because the object itself adapts, given the changing pressures and expectations for performance (Woods, 2009: 499–501). The capacity to respond to dysfunctionalities resides in the expertise, strategies, tools and plans that people in various roles can deploy to prepare for and respond to specific classes of change. So resilience can be a person's and/or system's capacity to manage the unexpected and cope with surprises. Woods (2009: 500) states that:

> Resilience, as a form of adaptive capacity, is a system's potential for adaptive action in the *future* when information varies, conditions change, or new kinds of events occur, any of which challenge the viability of previous adaptations, models, or assumptions.

Institutional resilience is what a system does, not what it has. In some sense these actions are always in the present sense, but what is done is dependent on what has happened in the past and what is expected to happen in the future. Indeed, any action is taken because it is assumed to conduct the organization to a certain outcome, hence lead to a certain future state.

The contemporary university sector is a melting pot of emerging events, external and internal, calling for vigorous institutions. Not every attempt to merge or find a networking solution among partner universities will be robust, and what are the reasons for that? Wrong decisions by the management, weak partners, market decline, new stakeholder claims etc.? How do universities plan a success and avoid a permanent failure? Experiences from the business sector show that mergers are risky transformations and often they result in fiascos rather than in healthy enterprises (Gulati, 2006; Koenig and Mellewigt, 2006). Still, there is a recent flow of mergers amongst European universities.

Hamel and Välikangas (2003) point out that resilience is a form of institutional innovation conducive to continuous reshaping and adaptation of an organization. We may say that resilience is not limited to dysfunctional conditions or to things going utterly wrong. Resilience is also the ability to function in both expected and unexpected conditions, where the latter may include both threats and opportunities (Välikangas, 2010). An example of the former would be long term decline in state block grants and the latter would be to deliver low cost 'massive open online courses' to counteract sudden drops in student admissions/entrants. So, resilience is about functioning and governance, and pertains to more than crisis intervention. It is about the intrinsic ability of an institution to adjust its operative functioning prior to, during or following changes and disturbances to the established order, and the capability to act strategically in a situation of unexpected or sudden change. Välikangas and Romme (2012) argue that training for resilience involves mastering three strategic management practices: cultivating foresight, rehearsing non-routine behaviours and building an experimentation-oriented community. Thus, anticipation, i.e. the capability of expecting and imagining future situations, is part of resilience.

Weick and Sutcliffe (2001: 67–68) claim that resilience and anticipation reside side by side in an organization. Together they constitute collective mindfulness. In resilient organizations both employees and managers act mindfully. Organizations committed to resilience develop knowledge and skills to cope with and respond to errors, capability for swift feedback and learning, speed and accuracy in communication, flexible role structures, quick sizing-up, experiential variety, skill at re-combining existing response repertoires and comfort with improvisation. Such organizations allocate decision making rapidly to those with the necessary expertise. A wide range of academic disciplines, from physics and biology to psychology and the various social sciences, address the issue of anticipation but without drawing out the distinction between the capacity to anticipate and the nature of the systems that make such anticipation possible (Poli, 2010). Arguably, when analysing adaptations in the European university sector we need to understand the nature of resilience, anticipation and the structure and processes of the higher education institutions themselves.

## *The Core is…?*

Then, consider institutional governance. Governance is a frequently used concept when describing organizational responses to internal and external conditions, reframing university operations. However, there is no single or generally accepted definition of governance, whether applied to the higher education institutions or to other sectors. Rather, it concerns a series of issues. At the institutional level, which is our principal focus, it relates to organizational structures, legal relationships, patterns of authority and power distribution, rights and responsibilities and, of course, decision making. Arguably, university governance encompasses the way policy issues affect the whole institution or its organizational components (divisions, departments, faculties, institutes, centres, programmes, projects, etc.) and how they are initialized, decided and put into action by formal and informal significant actors. Often governance can be distinguished from administrative decisions and implementation since it is more about the creation of ideas, strategies and policies which usually run prior to the administrative effectuation and implementation of these issues.

However, there is no organization whatsoever that can prevail without relating to its technical and its institutional environment, i.e. to its various markets and cultures, norms and judicial systems. Besides, formal organizations must have objectives (teleological), structures (hierarchical or other,) rules of action (e.g. policies) and are subject to drivers (e.g. threats or opportunities) causing a particular path of development. Such ideas are baseline assumptions in present neo-institutional organization theory (Greenwood and Hinings, 1996). So a university is affected by global trends and drivers, as well as by changes in national policies and education markets, as amply exemplified by Hazelkorn in Chapter 3, by Kekäle in Chapter 4 and by Hernes in Chapter 14.

An organization (including a university) is constituted by its exchange of resources with its external environment, and it must master different governance models to influence and adapt to the environmental contingencies. University governance is about how universities are formally organized and managed at the institutional level. It is the set of policies, roles, responsibilities and processes established to guide, direct and control how the university accomplishes its objectives.

University governance focuses on the formal and informal actors involved in decision making and implementing the decisions made, including the formal and informal structures that have been set in place to arrive at and implement the decisions (Olson, 2009). Effective governance anticipates the needs and goals of the institution and its sub-units. Every university has unique needs and goals that will affect its approach to governance. No single approach will fit the structures, cultures or requirements of all universities. Probably, larger universities will require more formal governance than smaller ones, and probably also apply a wider variety of governance techniques.

Organizations, herein also universities, go through change all the time. The organizational responses vary considerably in nature, scope and intensity. Different kinds of organizational change will presumably require different kinds of leadership behaviour in initiating, energizing and implementing the change. And, at least in theory, the leadership responses will vary whether the driver is mainly external (push) or internal (pull). The leadership of the university has to analyse and act upon the need for changes, including the external pressure and the internal adjustments. For example, alliances and networking between different universities are just one governance response amongst several possible choices of institutional structure. However, it is not the outcome of an 'invisible hand', but is probably due to tough discussions and prompt decisions on behalf of both parties.

## *Stampede to Shared Governance?*

Models of shared university governance have been practised for a long time (Tierney and Lechuga, 2004), but are currently being more rigorously tested than before (Crellin, 2010). However, a novel governance model will not grow up from the soil without distinctive fertilizers. Assumptions that the first decades of the twenty-first century will be much harsher than the last three decades of the twentieth century are blooming in the literature. The principal reasons why change might be more pervasive than before are a tighter economic climate, melting of higher education into business and industry and widespread use of information technology.

In his literature review Skolnik (1998: 638–644) points to seven distinctive, early twenty-first-century 'scenarios', which in turn influence the governance responses from the universities at the present time. There is pressure for both institutional and employee survival. Institutional strategies encompass deregulation, re-engineering, downscaling and rightsizing – all strategies emanating from the business sector. Then comes economizing on the use of time spent by employees: professional staff and faculty. Survival-conscious institutions reduce the number of academic staff, and increase the monitoring and control of those retained. They also practise dis-aggregated time allocation through role specialization and 'just-in-time' assignments for faculty. Pervasive assessments of learning outcomes are introduced. The challenge is how to find optimal targets and indicators which in turn could serve as basis for institution-wide assessments and benchmarks.

Also, there is a transition from instruction to a learning paradigm. The 'new' university will deliver 'learning' rather than teaching or instruction. Measuring learning outcomes is like watching a Janus face: the pretty side demonstrates what works, its ugly side narrows the curriculum down to what can be measured. Maybe the most obvious driver is the extensive use of ICT. The internet removes former constraints on time and space, and enhances the ability to match individual interests (in all users/stakeholders) to institutional capability (i.e. 'The Me University'). A learning (research) network may replace the intramural institution with an inter-university set of connections. Disciplinary specialization replaces the natural work group with networks; evaluation of research is done by external bodies, e.g. research councils and scientific journals. Also the evaluation and certification of courses from different higher education suppliers (universities, university colleges, specialized universities, technical institutes, etc.) may come from agencies outside the university. Finally, a client-user orientation or a consumer-centrism is pointed out. The learner is seen as a consumer of educational packages and no longer as a 'student'. This indicates a fundamental change in the educational perspective. Emphasis is put on a seller-buyer relationship, not a teacher-student relationship. Customer satisfaction (pleasing the student) becomes the core, not knowledge acquisition and institutional care for student learning.

Further, Skolnik (1998: 648) argues that most probably faculty will be the only constituency that will oppose some of these drivers. At least, many academics will resist the automation of their jobs and a degradation of their institutional status. However, traditional university teaching is not a good defence against novel learning platforms or against a new role for students in the governance process. Moreover, the effect for the student will possibly be the most decisive factor supporting or opposing the seven scenarios and their likely impact on university governance (ibid.: 648).

Universities have a long history of not always reflecting the emerging ideas of their surrounding societies. However, gradually during recent decades the university governance model has responded to the general societal patterns for decision making in a democracy, where representative or collective decision making prevails. Present shared governance practice refers to those structures and processes through which faculty, professional staff, administration, governing boards, often students and sometimes external stakeholders participate in the development of policies and in the decision making processes that affect the institution (Christopher, 2012). Shared governance has become a cornerstone of the university decision making process though in many shapes and forms. However, it is not convincingly documented that it always 'delivers the goods'. Lachs (2011), having experience as Chair of the Vanderbilt University Faculty Senate, claims that shared governance is a myth. Although there are decision making arenas at different levels in a university, power resides at the top, i.e. with the Vice-Chancellor and her tribe (ibid.: 2):

> Decision-making about the future of colleges and universities is vested in (vice) chancellors or presidents, who hire a circle of more or less professional managers.

Thus, distributed governance looks like a conundrum not yet well explained by organizational theorists or fully trusted by the university stakeholders. So, particularly since the student revolt in the 1960s, why was there this 'stampede' towards sharing institutional authority? And even if there is no such rush, the somewhat impertinent question to ask is whether shared governance is possible, plausible and preferable?

Smith (2009: 9) claims that in the US there has been a decline of shared governance in higher education. His point is that shared governance in its real sense requires a collegial university model on which faculty can operate 'in a climate of reason and persuasion as opposed to a centralized command and control'. Such a model has declined in American universities, he argues. Shaw, commenting on 'things' that work in European higher education governance (2012: 17), states:

> For administrators, faculty, university staff, and students, institutional governance is not an absorbing theoretical model, but the scaffolding of their daily activities and interactions.

Thus, higher education research should focus more on the strengths and weaknesses of different scaffolding, giving European academic institutions insight to thrive according to their own ideas and qualifications.

*Principal Models of Institutional Structuring*

Olsen (2005) describes four 'visions' of current universities: (A) as a community of scholars, (B) as an instrument for national purposes, (C) as a representative democracy, and (D) as a service enterprise embedded in competitive markets as shown in Table 2.1 below. Olsen argues that within each 'ideal type' we find different constitutive logics, criteria of assessment, reasons for autonomy and modes of change. Two general dimensions shape the typology: a distinction is drawn between those universities governed mainly by internal or by external factors, and those whose actors share or have conflicting norms and objectives. Thus the self-governing and the instrumental type of universities involve actors sharing norms and objectives; however the first type is internally and the latter is externally administered. Likewise, the democracy and the market models have actors with conflicting norms and objectives, whether governed by internal or by external factors, respectively.

Minksova and Pabian (2011) rephrase the Olsen typology (cf. Table 2.1, row 1) as a baseline when discussing the students' role in university governance. They point to the paradox of students being recognized as major stakeholders within all university institutions, but having varying participation in governance depending on the ideal institutional type. However, departing from such a typology of 'the European university' as Olsen puts it, we added some general characteristics (rows 6–10; incentives, communication, control, decision making and strategic focus) pertaining to the concept of university structuring. Universities are stimulated by incentives of different sorts and they communicate their core messages using different kinds of codes and signifiers. Also, the sources and means of control vary from expertise of the few to self-control of the many, encompassing both authority and pecuniary aspects. And arguably a core dimension – decision making models and practices – varies widely. Finally the universities' strategic focus differs between the major ideal types, illustrating the point that modern universities are no longer seen as single objective institutions: they serve different masters and markets.

Table 2.1 Core Elements in HEI Governance Models
1) Source: Olsen (2005: 9). 2) Source: Minksova and Pabian (2011: 184–186).

| *Dimensions* | *Core Elements in Higher Education Institutional Governance Models* | | | |
|---|---|---|---|---|
| *Institutional type*[1] | *A. Self-governing community of scholars* | *B. Instrument for national purposes* | *C. Representative democracy* | *D. Competitive service market provider* |
| *1. Governance form*[2] | Academic oligarchy | Hierarchy and bureaucracy | Distributed governance | Diversified enterprise |
| *2. Constitutive logic*[1] | Internal truth finding | Administrative procedures | Bargaining and majority votes | Market prices and deliverables |
| *3. Criteria for assessment*[1] | Academic quality | Effective and efficient goal attainment | Accommodating internal interests of core players | Consumer demands |
| *4. Reasons for autonomy*[1] | Authority to the best qualified | Delegated, provisional concession depending on achievement | Democratic rules and functional competence | Survival and stakeholder responsiveness |
| *5. Modes of change*[1] | Incremental except with performance crises | External shifts in political regimes | Tug-of-war game between opponents | Competitive selection, adaptive learning |
| *6. Incentive form* | Academic reputation | Political and social acknowledgement | Contribution-reward balance | Commercial and pecuniary |
| *7. Communication form* | Peer reviewed codes | Routines | Relations | Prices (tuitions/fees, etc.) |
| *8. Control form* | Expertise | Authority | Self-control | Bottom line (results) |
| *9. Decision making form* | Informal, intramural consensus | Top down, multi-level, mostly extramural | Formal, intramural, weighted and shared | Formal, stakeholder checks-and-balances |
| *10. Strategic focus* | Excellence | Serving the political agenda | To each his own | Preferred service provider |

In Olsen's typology just one ideal type resembles what we so far have deemed 'practising shared governance': type C – representative democracy – is based on distributed governance. Type A accumulates power at the top of the faculty pyramid, i.e. an academic oligarchy; type B is a sort of multi-level governance institution where both hierarchy and bureaucracy apply, bowing to the king only when necessary, and type D may mix different distributions (enterprise models) of in-house authority, but be submissive to the needs and whims of market actors. In the eyes of some scholars, type A is the old and type D is the new university ideal. Lachs (2011: 3) claims there is a simple way to judge whether the old or the new idea reigns in a university; 'If education is primarily business, managers hire faculty. If universities are communities of students and scholars, faculty members hire the managers'. Of course, this distinction may be too simple to encompass every type of regime, however it points at polar ends of present administrative reasoning.

Taken together all these dimensions characterize the basic ideal types of European universities, tentatively illustrating that governance takes on different organizational 'liveries'. Shared governance (e.g. representative democracy) is not the only possible model of administration and leadership for current universities. Besides, the concept of shared governance resides 'like chalk and cheese' inside quite different institutional university structures.

## A Theoretical Puzzle

### *The Governance Triangle*

Contrary to Lachs' (2011) opinion of shared governance as a myth, Clark (1983) in his classical study describes governance systems in the higher education sector as a triangle of state authority, the market and the academic oligarchy. Clark's model is relevant to the whole sector, but will need adjustments when addressing the intra-organizational structure and processes of university governance. Why is shared governance crucial to the intramural operations of universities? What are its institutional functions? Operations of most universities are regulated by law, so we have to look at the governance from a *de jure* perspective.

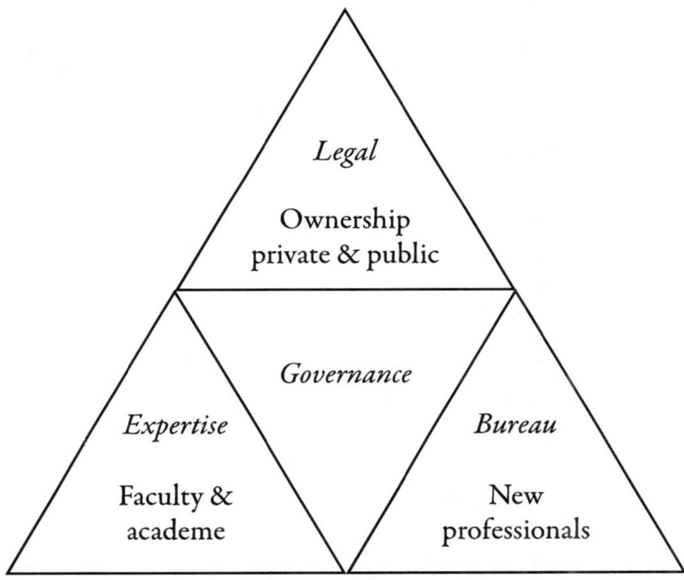


Figure 2.1 The Governance Triangle

Usually we will find three different principles embedded in the laws and regulations pertaining to this sector. Firstly, the right to manage is closely linked to the ownership aspect. Public universities are administrative bodies granted particular rights, but the government may instruct the institution both in administrative and financial matters. Secondly, the university is given institutional autonomy where the board sets the principles of internal governance in relation to the state and the society at large. The leeway may thus be expanded for both the board and the university administration, and management may make sense of this latitude to develop different strategies and leadership roles, as described by Degn in Chapter 7. Thirdly, also the principle of academic freedom comes into action. The professional expertise, i.e. that of the faculty, is granted latitude and room for manoeuvre, both intra- and extramurally. This scope may, ceteris paribus, restrict some of the room for manoeuvre initially granted for the board and management. Chapter 8, by Whitchurch and Gordon, shows how such, mostly externally induced, responses to change are leading to the redefinition of academic identities, roles and staffing practices.

For the purpose of our book, a modern higher education institution such as a university is seen as a multi-authority system. We have owners with authority to instruct, but also institutional and academic authority within the institution itself. This tripartite authority system is depicted as 'the governance triangle' in Figure 2.1. None of these three authorities will on its own be able obstruct or veto the others in the long run. However, any of the sets of actors may apply the *de jure* legitimated power to impact on decisions. The field of tension evolving out of such interactions will be a characteristic connected to the governance of academic institutions. They do not guarantee an equilibrium or steady state at any moment. Arguably, we may see this field as the shared governance 'centre court'; a long enduring fight will prevail. Such a model indicates that it is the interface or overlap between the three sources of authority that constitute the operative arena for university governance. To be productive the university institution has to seek approval and consent from all three parties. The political authority attached to the ownership axis seems to be relatively unified and common to most universities. The expertise does also have long history and wide experience in building networks and alliances across institutions as well as along disciplinary affiliations and agendas. The intramural institutional bureaucratic authority is presumably the most vulnerable and unstable authority. It has a short history, often submitted both to the legal ownership or the expertise factions, and is more tenuously linked across institutions or unified within a single university.

Outside the triangle are market actors like employers and students, their funders and supporters. Arguably, the influence from the external actors has increased during the last generation. It is no longer up to the universities to 'dictate' their environment. Referring to the present British HEI regime, Pritchard in Chapter 5 discusses vital aspects of this exchange of interests in a time of heightened competition.

## *Challenges to University Leadership*

Now, consider leadership and organizational change. Nadler and Tushman (1989, 1990) point to the observation that all organizations are subject to change, but that various changes require different 'frame bending' and actions from management (1990: 94):

> In a world characterized by global competition, deregulation, sharp technological change and political turmoil, discontinuous change seems to be a determinant of organization adaptation.

The management and the executive leadership are a critical factor in the initiation and implementation of major system changes in organizations in general. Increasing external constraints, such as presently experienced by European universities, require management to focus precisely on leadership and its ability to act strategically. Whether an organization survives and how well it thrives depends on the ability of management to manoeuvre through the troubled waters of the ever-changing environment. Nadler and Tushman discuss how the management structure can be built to succeed in the face of organizational changes of varying size and character.

In all organizations, there are both promoting and inhibiting forces that trigger change. A key strategy may be to exploit the sustaining forces, i.e. create and take advantage of the energy that occurs around these forces. Another strategy is to try to overcome the retarding forces, i.e. combat organizational resistance. The authors propose a taxonomy for understanding these changes and the responses to them along two dimensions: extent of change measures (strategic versus incremental), and timing or re-working (reactive versus anticipatory/proactive), as depicted in Figure 2.2.

| | *Incremental* | *Strategic* |
|---|---|---|
| *Anticipatory* | Tuning | Re-orientation |
| *Reactive* | Adaptation | Re-creation |

Figure 2.2 Typology of Institutional Changes
Source: Nadler and Tushman, 1990.

Some organizational changes affect only certain parts of the organization, and intend to maintain and improve efficiency. Such changes take place within the framework, structure and values of the current organization; they are incremental and take place in small steps, but are not always small in effect and extent. Strategic changes are deemed necessary and are usually driven by the environmental factors such as competitiveness, technology and regulation. They are often large transformation projects that directly affect the organization's strategic position and core values: e.g. rising from the status of university college to university. Examples and analysis of such academic drift are given by Bakken and Storm in Chapter 10. Presumably, incremental change can be devolved down the organization, while strategic changes must be run by the top management.

Other organizational changes are direct responses to external events. Such events, e.g. novel funding and auditing regimes, which are forced upon it, are named reactive. Changes that are initiated by management and not justified by external factors, but because management believes that changes at this stage will give the organization a competitive advantage, are called *proactive* changes. Such changes come in advance of an anticipated challenging event. Therefore gearing the organization to cope with external and internal pressures or to exploit opportunities it assumes or knows will come is the main task.

Incremental changes are taking place all the time in universities because of new structures, technological improvements and shifts, internal administrative processes, new study programmes, etc. Typically such changes do not affect the strategic positioning of the institution. They can be delegated as opposed to strategic change which must be driven by senior management. Taken together, incremental and proactive change is called tuning, or harmonization. Such changes affect only specific in-house components and are intended to make the organization better able to serve its stakeholders. The changes do not imply new and essential structural adaptations. Rather they constitute a modification of certain parts of the organization and will be implemented in advance of any corrective or preventive action. Reactive and incremental changes, termed adaptation, are smaller adjustments corresponding to changes in the environment. Examples of adaptive changes may be novel kinds of fundraising to strengthen the finances of the university, and are broadly described by Pérez-Esparrells and Torre in Chapter 12.

Strategic changes affect and redefine in a fundamental way the university's goals and purposes. They are necessary because the environment is constantly changing. When the university is forced to do a complete strategic revision, we call it re-creation. Strategic changes implemented by expectations of future events or opportunities are termed re-orientation. Mergers between higher education institutions may be of either kind, depending on the motive and timing of the amalgamation. Hinfelaar and O'Connell present examples of re-creative actions in Chapter 9, while Bakken and Storm discuss re-orientation in Chapter 10. However, re-creation strategy is riskier because it is often initiated during a crisis and, under urgent time constraints, fast timing is essential (Nadler and Tushman, 1990: 80). It may also imply changes in core values which in turn can create great intramural resistance. Besides, re-creation could mean changing the core values of the organization; e.g. engaging in third mission activities, i.e. entrepreneurship and business-related affairs (Gulbrandsen and Slipersæter, 2007) like research transfer, regional cooperation and other stakeholder interaction. Klumpp in his Chapter 11 points to the assumption that third mission operations have higher operation costs than teaching, especially since it takes more time to establish extramural interaction. Moreover, core values are difficult to change, and can mobilize opposition to the proposed innovation. Success may also involve changes in management, which may be replaced with resources from outside.

Re-orientation is more often associated with success than thoroughgoing re-creation. A re-orientation strategy is more robust and resilient. It can be successful because it often implies more extensive time buffers. In turn this allows for stronger coalition bargaining, empowerment of employees, time to implement measures, build coalitions and change management structures in the 'new' organization. This strategy also gives leaders time to formulate and polish the core values to adapt to the new structures and processes. Yet re-orientation is also associated with risk. Such changes are dependent on a visionary and charismatic leader who can create enthusiasm and support for the modifications, since strategic changes are taking place when the organization is in a stable working mode.

Nadler and Tushman (1990: 94) argue that vision and charisma within top management are not sufficient for the organization to effect large-scale, long-term alterations. In times of radical changes, the competitive edge is conferred by the ability to initiate changes proactively. Therefore, the organization must have a top management model that is focused on re-orientation, i.e. on discontinuous change implemented prior to a competitive challenge or an assumed performance crisis. It takes time to implement strategic changes, whether they constitute a proactive re-orientation or a reactive re-creation. Since many universities are large and complex, the responsibility for large scale change must be institutionalized through the entire management system. This calls for resilient and anticipative leadership.

## *The Intramural Governance Game*

There has been a rapid expansion in number of administrators and their governance functions. In the US the number of administrators for every 100 college students increased by 39 per cent from 1993 to 2007, while the number of professors and researchers rose by 18 per cent during that period (Fishman, 2010). By virtue of their sheer number and their managerial rather than academic orientation, Ginsberg (2011) argues, these administrators have served to marginalize the faculty in carrying out tasks related to personnel and curriculum that once sat squarely in their domain. These structural and cultural conflicts are both manifest and latent, and there is still a lack of research on certain aspects of shared governance.

A paradox seems to have emerged. Why has there been a hypertrophy of university administrators? Have the ideas of lean management (i.e. reducing middle manager layers), outsourcing and focusing on core tasks, become less prominent in the university sector than in business life? At present we have to admit that the relationship between faculty members and administrators in universities is still contentious. Favero and Bray (2010: 478) state:

> On the structural side, the number of administrators, as well as the variety of specialized administrative functions, continue to increase with the professionalization of administrators (Rosenzweig, 1994; Waugh, 1998), raising the perception among some that this comes at the expense of the faculty.

During the period 2003–2010 the number of faculty at the writer's Norwegian university increased by 15 per cent, while the administration increased by 36 per cent. Is this structural shift necessarily good or bad, productive or contra-productive to the mission of the universities? Larsen (2003: 86) pointed to shifting roles and models a decade ago:

> Since a more extended leadership role than what can be implied by the traditional governance model is observed, we could ask whether this can be regarded as support for a leadership role based on a model for universities as knowledge-based enterprises. [...] It could also be argued that training programmes for academic leaders mean a professionalisation of the role. Consultations about staff development, responsibilities for external funding and promoting more group-oriented research are all elements that point in the direction of a more extensive leadership role in line with the enterprise model.

Does this change towards Olsen's 'service enterprise' university type indicate a role shift or role extension, a movement towards heightened or lowered resilience? Two major institutional responses to the assumed 'structural slide' are recognizable, both concurrent with similar industry reorganization efforts. First, lean thinking. Some public and private universities are presently testing out new ways of doing more with less. This is a direct response to the reduction in funding taking place in most countries. This topic links to the issues of access, cost, quality and institutional effectiveness in higher education, as discussed by Klumpp in Chapter 11. Lean education is a tool which enables practitioners of education to achieve more with less. What change agents, skills and techniques can reduce costs and improve outcomes? It remains true that administrative staff is increasing more than faculty and students, so apparently these cost reduction strategies are not all-encompassing.

Subsequently come new technologies to assist teaching, administration and research. A basic contribution of technology development is to offer higher speed, higher precision, lower cost and solution of more complex problems. Increasingly, universities develop or acquire new pedagogic as well as organizational and managerial technologies – from advanced simulators and lab-systems to Learning Management Systems, data-warehousing and Enterprise Performance Monitoring systems. Massive open online courses from international elite universities are one of the fastest growing 'edtech' phenomena in higher education sector. Columbia and Stanford universities and more than sixty other elite universities in seventeen countries are presently serving over 3 million online students globally via the California based company Coursera (<http://www.crunchbase.com/company/coursera>, accessed 29 April 2013). How may the benefits of new technologies be reaped without increasing the institution's vulnerability and operational risk exposures? How can the universities avoid making their back offices overly complex?

Today, it seems that university governance is an experimental field for organizational strategies, and for shifting ruling elites, continuously testing out new models, tools, apps and partners. This is connected to the boundaries of university innovation capability, and raises the question of whether we still continue to experience an era of sectorial and institutional distrust? Is balanced autonomy reachable at all?

The massification of higher education has drawn attention to the shifting student role in different European higher education systems. Witte (2011: 181–182) writes that it is vital to extend governance frameworks to include and explicate the role of students:

> ...the student role in higher education oscillates between [...] marginal voices in an academic oligarchy or a state bureaucracy, an interest group in a representative democracy and consumers of a market enterprise.

Although there is no general or main trend identified across Europe, students seem to be assigned several of these roles in a complementary, rather than in an opposing manner. Students are legitimate players in all governance systems, but with different weightings. Rodgers et al. (2011: 258) argue that UK students are not to be seen as customers in a market or players in a democratic system, but as 'principal stakeholders' voicing their interests towards other external and internal stakeholders and governance players.

Larsen et al. (2009) point to four basic dilemmas relating to university governance reform over the last two or three decades. Firstly, the tension between representative democracy and organizational effectiveness has to be addressed. Democratic practice may slow down the decision processes and subsequently impact on institutional need for prompt measures and instrumental order. Secondly, a dual management structure may collide with the idea of practising integrated management and leadership. Thirdly, since universities are there to serve the larger community, how should their institutional executive and governing bodies reflect this? Should universities demonstrate their autonomy by having internal representatives only, or should they include external stakeholders, and which party should have the majority? And fourthly, how should the balance between centralization and decentralization in more autonomous universities be practised? This concerns the redistribution of authority in the multi-level governance models followed by many countries.

Favero and Bray (2010: 477) point to a series of topics over which faculty and administrators disagree. Mainly such disagreement evolves over what type of shared governance is practised, how much influence faculty has and whether trust levels are adequate. They conclude that the faculty-administrator relationship is both fragile and complex, and that this apprehension is a normative condition across most contexts. The prevailing tension 'is at base related to issues of authority, motivation and job satisfaction, scarce resources, and cultural values' (ibid.: 522).

Jones (2011: 122), in his literature review on faculty involvement in institutional governance, states that there must be sufficiently high levels of trust and communication for any type of effective shared governance. Diverse opinions exist on whether faculty viewed shared governance as an important part of institutional identity, but most faculty think that academic areas (e.g. curriculum, teaching standards) are issues where they have the greatest authority in institutional governance, and that faculty participation in decision making at varying levels and arenas significantly impacts on the institutional performance.

Larsen et al. (2009: 14) advise a more in-depth understanding of 'the growing gap between management intentions and academic realities, and advocate dealing with the lack of trust between managers and academics….' The source of this mistrust is connected to the move from vertical to horizontal forms of governance. Contracts, targets, benchmarks and indicators have replaced steering models based on regulations and laws, resulting in a tighter (political) control of the academics in universities (ibid.: 15). This business model trend is not necessarily the best measure to install shared governance balancing the constituencies on an equal footing.

## *Is There Such a Thing as 'Good Governance'?*

The long term objective of most organizations is to survive. In order to endure, the institutional apparatus has to be robust and must practise 'good governance'. At the institutional level good governance will require transparency and accountability, foster participation and representativeness, promote fairness and equity, accomplish effective and efficient allocation of resources, peacefully resolve conflict, meet obligations to future generations and be future-oriented. This kind of best practice is obviously packed with good intentions, but is it achievable and is the concept useful in our context?

Sheng (2013: 1) offers a list of good governance characteristics, encompassing the following features:

> It is participatory, consensus oriented, accountable, transparent, responsive, effective and efficient, equitable and inclusive and follows the rule of law...[It] is also responsive to the present and future needs of society.

These characteristics may be depicted as in Figure 2.3 below. Related to universities and other tertiary education providers, the characteristics seem fairly relevant. Good governance requires legal frameworks that are enforced impartially and are perceived as legitimate. Participation – either direct or representative, through legitimate channels as opposed to top-down command – is vital to guarantee universities as democratic institutions. Consensus orientation deals with the mediation of different interests and stakeholders such that decisions made and measures implemented are in the best interests of all parties. Accountability addresses the social contract of universities: who will be affected by the decisions made and in what ways do the decisions comply with the interests of the institutional stakeholders? Transparency means that decisions and measures follow common rules and standards, and that they are fully open and accessible to the internal and external stakeholders. Information should be relevant and sufficient, as well as understandable. Responsiveness means that the universities should attempt to attend to requests from all stakeholders within an acceptable timeframe. Equity and inclusiveness are important for universities, particularly in an era of mass education. Equal access and joint partnership in universities will legitimize the institutions as tools of a democratic knowledge society. Lastly, effectiveness and efficiency are core elements in present (and future) university governance. Resources must be spent in a sustainable manner and results must be achieved according to the needs of society. All these themes are discussed at length by Kekäle in Chapter 4 and by Klumpp in Chapter 11.

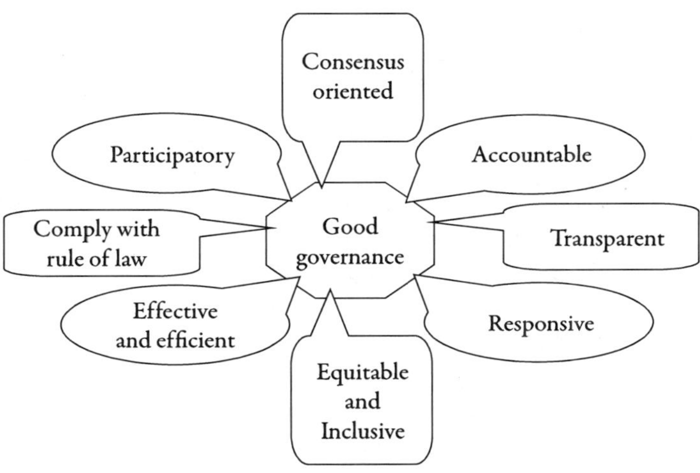


Figure 2.3 Characteristics of Good Governance
Source: Sheng, 2013.

Sheng modifies these characteristics by saying that they are ideals which are difficult to achieve in their totality. Gisselquist (2012) for her part argues that good governance is no more than a management fad, included in the vernacular of present institutional actors. The concept lacks clarity, she claims. In our context of the European universities, good governance includes a lot of presumptive good measures, but they are not necessarily connected to a common theory or even a generic model. Good governance scores low on conceptual validity, and therefore it may not be the best guidance for a reorientation of university structuring and decision processes. Despite the criticism against good governance as a useful and relevant theoretical concept, our question relates to what kind of governance practice leads to resilience.

## Adaptive Institutions?

### *Resilience and Anticipation as Governance*

Our book focuses on the theoretical and empirical concepts of robustness and governance. So we are in a way explaining university structures, policies and processes in both a 'context of discovery' (by using new ideas) and in a 'context of justification' (by introducing new empirical evidence). As institutions, universities are not seen as rational machines, but rather as arenas in which complex organizational processes occur. Cohen et al.'s (1972) classical study of decision making in universities as an anarchistic garbage can process, underlines this conception of unpredictability and complexity, rigorously tested and presented by Selmer-Anderssen in Chapter 6.

So far in history there have been few if any competitors to the universities when it comes to producing and disseminating academic knowledge. Despite one thousand years of history, the future may still bring challenging functional alternatives to universities as core nodes of knowledge production. This of course is a well-known scenario for most universities, and they strive to be more robust in order to be the surviving institutional species of the future society. Robustness is a key phrase in this connection: it requires both resilience and anticipative capacity. Robust organizations have an open mind towards the use of past practice; they simultaneously both believe and doubt their past experience. It is the pitting of an acquired organizational competence or skill against unprogrammed incidences or situations.

Taken together anticipation and resilience impact on the institutional mindfulness which in turn affects the capability to discover and manage unexpected events. Weick et al. (1999: 89–90) draw on the work of Langer (1989, 1997) who sees mindfulness as a process of drawing 'novel distinctions', so that the organization can keep itself situated in and updated on the present. Being aware of the current surrounding environment and the concurrent internal repertoire of actions and measures helps the organization to induce 'capability mindfulness'. Otherwise, relying on routinized distinctions and categories, may lead to mindless behaviour. Subsequently established rules and routines govern the actions regardless of the circumstances, overlooking early warnings and weak signals from the environment. However, collective mindfulness is not only about how scarce attention is displayed in the organization, but also about the quality of this attention.

Anticipation also describes the process of becoming aware of previously unanticipated events, often connected with unwanted incidents. It entails both the act of predicting by reasoning about the future and expecting something as on the basis of a norm. Anticipation is enhanced by three processes of mindfulness (Weick and Sutcliffe, 2001: 54):

i. preoccupation with failures rather than successes
ii. reluctance to simplify interpretations
iii. sensitivity to operations

Resilience is the process of being careful, paying attention to errors that have already occurred and correcting them before they worsen or cause more serious harm. It is enhanced by two additional processes of mindfulness (Weick and Sutcliffe, 2001: 67–78):

iv. commitment to resilience
v. deference to expertise

Universities devoted to resilience also demonstrate comfort with improvisation. Such organizations move decision making rapidly to those with the necessary expertise; they are flexible and attentive (Weick, 1998).

Concerning anticipation, Wildavsky (1991: 77) states that:

> Anticipation is a mode of control by a central mind; efforts are made to predict and prevent potential dangers before damage is done, while…[r]esilience is the capacity to cope with unanticipated dangers after they have become manifest, learning to bounce back.

With such an explanatory hinterland, anticipations are concentrating on how to avoid hypothesized, future harms, while resilience is about troubles that already have happened, learning from history. Anticipation is not deemed a robust strategy when uncertainty, ambiguity and volatility increases, but it works well when known threats and challenges are expected to return. Resilience works better with increasing uncertainty and risk, since it per se encompasses the capability to cope with what is not known in advance. In turbulent times, such as experienced by European universities presently, probably the most robust strategies may be to combine both resilience and anticipation with predominance of resilience. Wildavsky (1991: 122) contrasted the strategies based on resilience and anticipation as depicted in Figure 2.4 below.

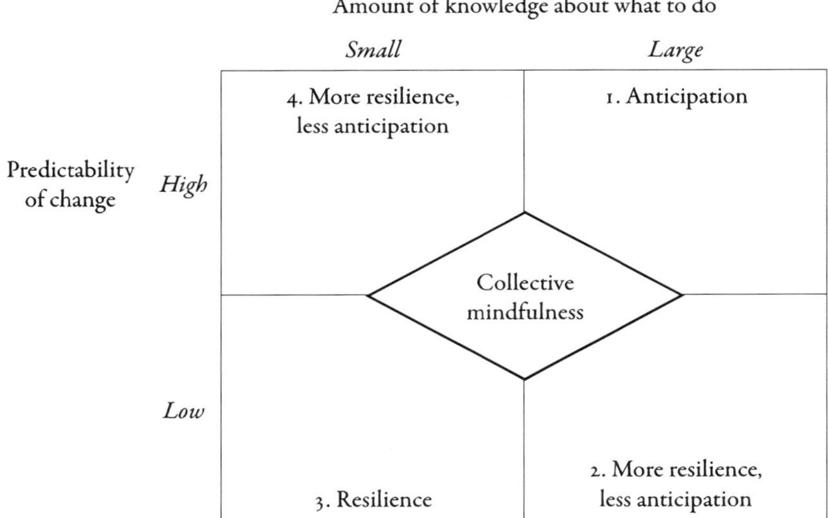


Figure 2.4 Resilience, Anticipation and Mindfulness
Based on: Wildavsky 1991; Weick and Sutcliffe 2001.

Wildavsky (1991: 123) claims that only when there is sufficient knowledge about what will come and what to do is anticipation a safe strategic choice (quadrant 1). Opposite, where both the direction of change and the knowledge of measures are unpredictable, resilience is the proper strategy (quadrant 3). Unpredictable change combined with (relatively) effective and robust preventive measures calls for a mixed strategy (quadrant 2). However, in this case we would rather like to be anticipative since we know a lot about what to do, but the direction of change is not very predictable. Opposite, when we know pretty much what is coming, but relatively little about how to cope with it, we opt for a mixed strategy as well (quadrant 4). In both boxes 2 and 4 we rely more on resilience than on anticipation, since we either may miscalculate the direction of change or misdirect the array of measures. The choice of strategy depends on the internal as well as the external circumstances. Arguably, all four options have to be taken into consideration for European universities when choosing a future pathway.

Weick and Sutcliffe (2001: 10, 42–44) argue that anticipation and resilience constitute the 'collective mindfulness' which in turn affects the capability of the system to discover and manage unexpected events. The five processes (mentioned above) enhancing anticipation and resilience determine the reliability of the system and they enable people to 'manage juxtapositions of events they have never seen before' (Weick et al., 1999: 88–91, 117). Arguably, the concept of collective mindfulness (depicted as the centre rhomb in Figure 4 above) promises a lot; learning from history, listening to contemporary assessments and anticipating the unexpected future. Foresighting future resilience implies both hindsighting past data and analysing current patterns, still being able to envisage other outcomes than those indicated by past and present operations. In short, university resilience calls for flexible strategies and mindful reading of signals from both environment and the organization itself. In the next section we will further discuss this assertion and its relevance to the European universities.

### *Collective Mindfulness as University Best Practice?*

We may apply the five cognitive processes conducive to collective mindfulness presented previously when discussing the universities' search for increased robustness in this section:

Initially, excellent universities understand that long periods of success may breed complacency, so they look for drifts, weaknesses and errors in their ongoing performance. They develop effective systems aimed at monitoring and reporting their daily operations, and in particular at discovering deviations from established standards. Significant discontinuities in a university's environment do not emerge without warning. Ansoff (1975) described such warnings as weak signals, indicating that an early detection and interpretation of those signals could allow the organization to react strategically to surprises ahead of time. Even minor deviations are seen as signals and pre-warnings of how operations might go wrong, so they are 'preoccupied with failures rather than successes'. Early warning signals may often be ambiguous, and although it is not always easy in advance to distinguish weak signals from noise or ephemeral events, mindfulness involves interpretive work directed at weak signals (Weick et al., 1999: 90). The point is to investigate and make sense of the signals rather than a priori assume normalcy (Gidley, 2012). In the field of foresight management this connotation of weak signals originating from Ansoff has been brought into a broad spectre of applications (Hopolainen and Toivonen, 2012). Rossel (2010) argues that sensing weak signals and understanding early warnings help an organization to reveal paradigmatic weaknesses, hegemonic perspectives and various forms of institutional blindness. Mediocre organizations tend to respond to weak signals with a weak response, not so with mindful organizations; 'Mindfulness preserves the capability to see the significant meaning of weak signals and to give strong responses to weak signals' (Weick and Sutcliffe, 2001: 3–4).

Next, a complex world contains an overflow of data confronting universities. What could be discarded as irrelevant? What simplifications may be undertaken without risking throwing away information necessary to avoid surprises, structural changes and unwanted reorientations? Weick and Sutcliffe (2001: 94) claim that simplifications increase the likelihood of eventual surprise. Excellent organizations take steps to create more complete and graded intelligence in relation to the present situation. They encourage their staff to become more alert and employ people whose job is to explore and describe complexity. In many European universities we may observe these 'new professionals' executing assignments vital for the long term challenges of the institutions. However, during times of cost cutting and financial slump, these in-house experts and analysts may also be seen as superfluous. Presumably, universities need in-house capacity to monitor, collect and analyse weak signals from the changing environment. Such capacity may be distributed, or organized into particular staff units; the main point is that such institutional slack is conducive to institutional mindfulness.

Then, the front line operators of the universities, mostly faculty and teachers, need to maintain situational awareness. They need to be sensitive both to the need of external stakeholders, and to the preferences of the students. In times of massified education there is a danger of production pressure and overload (Weick et al., 1999: 97). In times of increased educational efficiency, 'silo' thinking may win through, where faculty and staff operate within restricted spheres of influence, both in educational and administrative fields, having no thought or sense of responsibility for the broader picture. Likewise, university managers must be sensitive to the experience of their 'knowledge production workers' and encourage them to report on their experiences and observations, avoiding a university management culture that Stinchcombe (1990) characterized as 'leaders who don't know what their workers are doing'. A culture of open and non-repressive reporting (Reason, 1997: 195) will counteract a system that does not have adequate information to remain effective. Reporting systems must be backed by an organizational capacity to learn and act upon the information from the front line. All this is summed up in a sort of collective sensemaking (Weick et al., 2005), a theme which is more extensively explained and demonstrated by Selmer-Anderssen in Chapter 6, Degn in Chapter 7 and by Whitchurch and Gordon in Chapter 8.

Also, mindful universities must be committed to resilience. They must not be paralysed or unable to act when the circumstances require it, whether the impulses of change come abruptly or more creepingly. Weick et al. (1999:

100, quoting Wildavsky, 1991) make a distinction between anticipation and resilience. The former refers to prediction and prevention of potential threats before harm is done, i.e. it refers to a capacity building in the present sense. The latter refers to the 'capacity to cope with unanticipated dangers after they have become manifest, learning to bounce back', i.e. to some capability which may be released in some conditional future. Thus, resilience is not simply the capability to absorb change and still persist. In our university context a resilient institution must also be able 'to utilize the change that is absorbed'. Resilience enhances the capability to harvest from the change induced by the environment. Giving formal support to improvisation (Weick, 1998) in order to recombine measures and actions already in its repertoire may result in novel combinations (Weick et al., 1999: 101). Likewise, resilience implies an ambivalent attitude towards past practices, both believing and doubting their past experience. Shocks, errors and failures do not cripple a mindful institution; such events will most probably occur and put stress on the institution. However, the university must be steadfast in its resilience by learning from errors and deviations.

The final cognitive driver of collective mindfulness deals with deference to expertise. This should be an easy match for knowledge organizations such as universities. However, some significant decisions or actions of universities are carried out at short notice, at a high tempo and not always based on solid and relevant evidence: e.g. fee changes in UK, as described by Pritchard in Chapter 5. In such situations, and despite the orderly hierarchy of a university, decisions migrate to the actors with the greatest expertise. The institution gains flexibility by enacting garbage can-like structures (Cohen et al., 1972; March and Olsen, 1986). The important decision maker may not be situated at the top of the pyramid; with a garbage can like structure; 'people loosen the filters on who gains access to what with the result that hierarchical rank is subordinated to expertise and experience' (Weick et al., 1999: 103). In a mindful university, 'structure is a variable and the activity of structuring is a constant' (ibid.: 104), i.e. routines and organizational designs are not as absolute and stable as depicted in the formal organizational chart. Rather, problems are allowed to migrate, and this 'allows a wider variety of people to make sense of novel cues and determine whether they signify a problem or a transient event' (ibid.: 104).

Taking all five cognitive processes together, the first three constituting institutional anticipation and the last two building institutional resilience, it seems that a university being collectively mindful primarily has to be a learning institution. The first four characteristics all point in that direction: how do good learning processes enhance the perceptibility of intra- and extramural signals and how do the institutions gather benefits from the changes made? The fifth characteristic (i.e. deference to expertise) deals with the 'underspecification of structures' (Weick et al., 1999: 102). It focuses on the locus and form of decision making, or on what we in previous sections have argued is the core of university governance.

Not surprisingly, adaptive universities have to learn to change and to match their management models accordingly (Weick and Sutcliffe, 2007). Hernes, in Chapter 14, states that universities that manage to profit from a changing contextual setting could be called 'super-resilient organizations'. In fact, they themselves have contributed to this stimulating environment by developing knowledge and innovation.

## Pulling the Strands Together

### *A Need for Anticipatory Governance?*

A major characteristic of human beings is their capability to anticipate and foresee both their own development and that of their environment. This ability is embedded in the social interaction role behaviour which is per se both reciprocal and anticipatory. Arguably, institutions and organizations often lack this capability of developing the requisite anticipatory aptitude, even if their internal actors are competent in this respect. Thus, anticipatory governance, both as a government-based and an institutionally-based form of anticipation connects to the quest for university resilience. It aims at reducing risks and threats, enhancing capacity and power to respond to events even before they become manifest and repulsive.

The socio-political context of universities is becoming more complex, and change is imposed more rapidly on the institutions than before. To deal with acceleration and extent of changes, institutions must become more sensitive to early warnings and weak signals about long term trends and alternative university futures. Likewise, increasing complexity implies that the university governance systems evolve through adaptive learning. Ideally, anticipatory governance aims at reducing threats before risks emerge, rather than trying to make systems more resilient after the troubles have materialized. Universities need to complement the backward-looking governance model embedded in sector regulations with a forward-looking approach. This is a theme addressed by Karlsen in Chapter 13 applying a Future Workshop to produce images and forerunners of future university adaptation. University decision makers must accept that the past experience is helpful but deficient for generating dynamic policies and robust institutional governance.

We may argue that models and tools for imagining possible, probable and preferred futures should be developed and incorporated in the governance practice of universities. Fuerth (2009: 20) argues that anticipatory governance would be designed to 'employ foresight in the creation and execution of plans of action'. This will give strength to institutions which are able to sense and carry out changes ahead of major events, 'the better to blunt threats and harvest opportunities'. Arguably, Fuerth claims, anticipatory governance would be a system of systems, involving instruments for conducting foresight studies, for integrating foresights and policy processes, for gauging performance and managing institutional knowledge, and also for including an open-minded institutional culture. Obviously, such requirements are not easy to fulfil in universities characterized by systemic mistrust between principal stakeholders and actors (Larsen et al., 2009; Favero and Bray, 2010). Future universities will have to re-establish a governance triangle where the principal actors are residing on an equal or otherwise legitimized footing. This requires trust, confidence and transparency in the intramural interaction pattern.

## *A Model for Institutional Adaptation*

As stated, universities have a thousand years of history. The crucial question now is, are they fit for and do they expect a thousand years' future? What will be the core aspects connected to their long term survival? Is it up to the institutions themselves to decide how they should be structured and governed, or is it more likely that they have to adapt quicker and more humbly to their changing societal environment? What will be the most sustainable and viable university models and what forms of governance will best fit into the different university structures?

In this chapter we have discussed various perspectives on university structure, governance and adaptations. In Figure 2.5 below what we in this book deem the principal factors affecting the universities' future are summarized.

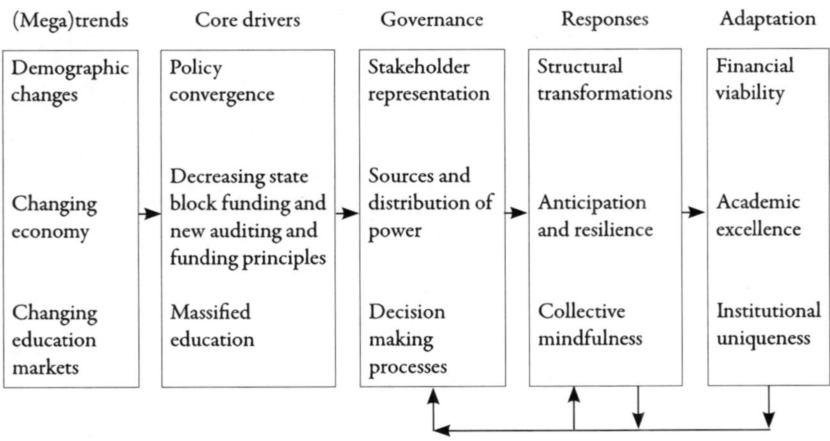


Figure 2.5 A Conceptual Model of Future University Adaptation

The logical structure of this model resembles what Stinchcombe (1968: 106) calls a functional-historicist structure. A genesis of megatrends and core drivers initiates a system of governance, which in turn impacts on the institutional responses resulting in distinctive adaptive patterns. The interrelating triangle of governance-responses-adaptation is recursive. The adaptive outcome influences both the former responses and governance, and likewise the responses will impact on the initial governance architecture. Through future lapses the core drivers will stop impacting upon the triangle; what matters is the recursive loop experienced by the next generations. However this is not, a priori, a stable system because there are likely to be disturbances emerging from external tensions impacting on the adaptations, e.g. new forms of regulation. There could be drastic change in study propensity, new teaching technologies, etc.

With regard to the total functional form of historicist explanations, the end point of genesis is assumed to terminate prior drivers. A functional alternative of university life emerges and starts to reinforce itself, as stated in the following argument by Stinchcombe (1968: 105):

> …[W]hich of a set of functional alternatives is found in a particular society is generally determined by historical events. But once a functional alternative becomes established, it tends to eliminate the causes of the other alternatives and thus to regenerate itself.

The trends and core drivers of the model are such as have been discussed previously in Chapters 4 and 5, although this list may be extended. Prominent governance issues are connected to the 'stakeholder invasion', to the decision processes, and also to the various sources and distribution of power. Power influences who gets what, when, and how. These themes are covered in Chapters 6, 8 and 9.

Major responses are perceived to be structural shifts from lower to higher academic status (cf. academic drift in Chapter 10), or from one ideal type to another as depicted in Table 1. In addition, institutional strengthening by capacity building to cope with change takes place in the recursive processes of anticipation, resilience and collective mindfulness, as in Chapter 7. Finally, adaptations are principally focused on financial viability (bottom line), academic excellence (top ranking) and institutional uniqueness (identity), amply illustrated in Chapters 3, 11, 12, 13 and 14.

As such, this model represents the conceptual scaffolding of our book, hopefully describing how the parts, nuts and bolts are assembled and linked together in order to understand the resilient university models and processes that are emerging throughout Europe.

## References

Ansoff, H.I. (1975). 'Managing Strategic Surprise by Response to Weak Signals', *California Management Review*, 18 (2), 21–33.

Christopher, J. (2012). 'Governance Paradigms of Public Universities: an International Comparative Study', *Tertiary Education and Management*, 18 (4), 335–351.

Clark, B.R. (1983). *The Higher Education System*. Berkeley: University of California Press.

Cohen, M.D., March, J.G., and Olsen, J.P. (1972). 'A Garbage Can Model of Organizational Choice', *Administrative Science Quarterly*, 17 (1), 1–23.

Crellin, M.A. (2010). The Future of Shared Governance. *Directions for Higher Education*, No. 151, Fall 2010:71–81. Available from: <Wiley Online Library (wileyonlinelibrary.com). DOI:10.1002/he.402> accessed 24 January 2013.

Favero, M. del, and Bray, N.J. (2010). 'Herding Cats and Big Dogs: Tensions in the Faculty-Administrator Relationship'. In J.C. Smart (ed.) *Higher Education: Handbook of Theory and Research* 25, pp. 477–541. Springer Science-Business Media B.V.

Fishman, J. (2010). 'Growth in Administrators Outstrips Growth in Faculty Members'. *The Ticker*, 17 August. <http://chronicle.com/blogs/ticker/growth-in-administrators-outstrips-growth-in-faculty-members/26283> accessed 1 March 2013.

Gidley, J.M. (2012). 'Evolution of Education: From Weak Signals to Rich Imaginaries of Educational Futures', *Futures: the Journal of policy, planning and futures studies*, 44 (1), 46–54.

Ginsberg, B. (2011). *The Fall of the Faculty: The Rise of the All-Administrative University and Why It Matters*. Oxford: Oxford University Press.

Gisselquist. R. M (2012). 'What Does Good Governance Mean?' *UNU-WIDER Angle newsletter*, January 2012. <http://www.wider.unu.edu/publications/newsletter/articles-2012/en_GB/01-2012-Gisselquist/> accessed 24 January 2013.

Greenwood, R., and Hinings. C.R. (1996). 'Understanding Radical Organizational Change: Bringing Together the Old and the New Institutionalism', *Academy of Management Review*, 21 (4), 1022–1054.

Gulati, R. (2007). *Managing Network Resources. Alliances, Affiliations and Other Relational Assets*. Oxford: Oxford University Press.

Guldbrandsen, M., and Slipersæter, S. (2007). 'The Third Mission and the Entrepreneurial University Model', In A. Bonaccorsi, and C. Daraio (eds), *Universities and Strategic Knowledge Creation: Specialization and Performance in Europe*, Chapter 4. Cheltenham: Edward Edgar.

Hamel, G., and Välikangas, L. (2003). 'The Quest for Resilience', *Harvard Business Review*, September, 52–63.

Hollnagel, E., Woods, D.D., and Leveson, N. (2006). *Resilience Engineering. Concepts and Precepts*. Aldershot: Ashgate.

Hopolainen, M., and Toivonen, M (2012). 'Weak Signals. Ansoff Today', *Futures*, 44 (3), 198–205.

Jones, W.A. (2011). 'Faculty Involvement in Institutional Governance: A Literature Review', *The Journal of the Professoriate*, 6 (1):117–135.

Koenig, F., and Mellewigt, T. (2006). 'The Uncertainty-Governance Choice Puzzle Revisited: Theoretical Perspectives on Alliance Governance Decisions'. In A. Ariño, and J.J. Reuer (eds), *Strategic Alliances. Governance and Contracts*. Palgrave MacMillan.

Lachs, J. (2011). 'Shared Governance Is a Myth', *The Chronicle of Higher Education*, 6 February. <http://chronicle.com/article/Shared-Governance-Is-a-Myth/126245/> accessed 25 September 2011.

Langer, E.J. (1989). Minding Matters: The Consequences of Mindlessness-Mindfulness. In L. Berkowitz (ed.), *Advances in Experimental Social Psychology*, Vol. 22: 137–173. San Diego: Academic Press.

Langer, E.J. (1997). *The Power of Mindful Learning*. Reading, MA: Addison-Wesley.

Larsen. I.M. (2003). 'Departmental Leadership in Norwegian Universities: In A. Amaral, L.V. Meek, and I.M. Larsen (eds), *Between Two Models of Governance, The Higher Education Managerial Revolution?* pp. 71–88. Dordrecht: Kluwer Academic Publishers.

Larsen, I.M., Maassen, P., and Stensaker, B. (2009). 'Four Basic Dilemmas in University Governance Reform', *Higher Education Management and Policy*, 21 (3), 1–18.

March, J.G., and Olsen, J.P. (1986). Garbage Can Models of Decision making in Organizations. In J.G. March, and R. Weissinger-Baylon (eds), *Ambiguity and Command* pp. 11–35. Marshfield, MA: Pitman.

Minksova, L., and Pabian, P. (2011). 'Approaching Students in Higher Education Governance', *Tertiary Education and Management*, 17 (3), 183–189.

Mintzberg, H., Lampel, J., Quinn, J.B., and Ghoshal, S. (2003). *The Strategy Process*. Harlow: Pearson Education.

Nadler, D.A., and Tushman, M.L. (1989). 'Organizational Frame Bending: Principles for Managing Reorientation', *Academy of Management Executive*, 3 (3), 194.

Nadler, D.A. and Tushman, M.L. (1990). 'Beyond the Charismatic Leader: Leadership and Organizational Change', *California Management Review*, 32 (2), 77–97.

Olsen, J.P. (2005). *The Institutional Dynamics of the (European) University*. Oslo: ARENA – Centre for European Studies, Working Paper, No. 15, March 2005. <http://www.arena.uio-no> accessed 23 January 2013.

Olson, G. (2009). Exactly what is 'Shared Governance'? *The Chronicle of Higher Education*, July 23, 2009:1–4. <http://chronicle.com/article/Exactly-What-Is-Shared/47065/> accessed 25 September 2011.

Poli, R. (2010). 'The Many Aspects of Anticipation', *Foresight*, 12 (2):7–17.

Power, M. (1999). *The Audit Society. Rituals of Verification.* Oxford: Oxford University Press.

Reason, J.(1997). *Managing the Risk of Organizational Accidents.* Aldershot: Ashgate Publishing Limited.

Rodgers, T., Freeman, R., Williams, J., and Kane, D. (2011). 'Students and the Governance of Higher Education: A UK Perspective', *Tertiary Education and Management*, 17 (3), 247–260. Special Issue: Students in Higher Education Governance.

Rossel, P. (2010). 'Making Anticipatory Systems More Robust', *Foresight*, 12 (3), 73–86.

Shaw, M.A. (2012). 'Pursuing Things that Work in European Higher Education Governance', *Comparative and International Higher Education*, 4 (1), 14–18.

Sheng, Y.K. (2013). What is Good Governance? *United Nations Economic and Social Commission for Asia and the Pacific.* <http://www.unescap.org/pdd/prs/Project Activities/Ongoing/gg/governance.asp/> accessed 29 January 2013.

Skolnik, M.L. (1998). 'Higher Education in the 21st Century', *Futures*, 30 (7), 635–650.

Smith, C.V. (2009). 'The Decline of Shared Governance in Higher Education: A Historical Perspective', *KCKCC e-Journal*, Oct 2009. <http://www.kckcc.edu/ejournal/archives/october2009/article/theDeclineOfSharedGove../> accessed 25 January 2013.

Stinchcombe, A.L. (1968). *Constructing Social Theories.* New York: Harcourt, Brace and World.

Stinchcombe, A.L. (1990). 'Leaders Who Do Not Know What Their Workers Are Doing'. In A.L. Stinchcombe, and C. Heimer, *Information and Organizations*, pp. 312–340. Berkeley: University of California Press.

Tierney, W. G, and Lechuga, V.M. (2004). Restructuring Shared Governance in Higher Education. *New Directions for Teaching and Learning*, No. 127. San Francisco: Jossey-Bass.

Välikangas, L. (2010). *The Resilient Organization. How Adaptive Cultures Thrive Even When Strategy Fails.* New York: McGraw-Hill.

Välikangas, L., and Romme, A.G.L. (2012). 'Building Resilience Capabilities at "Big Brown Box, Inc."', *Strategy and Leadership*, 40 (4), 43–45.

Weick, K.E. (1998). 'Improvisation as a Mindset for Organizational Analysis', *Organization Science*, 9 (5), 543–555.

Weick, K.E., Sutcliffe K.M., and Obstfeld, D. (1999). 'Organizing for High Reliability: Processes of Collective Mindfulness', *Research in Organizational Behavior*, 21, 81–123.

Weick, K.E., Sutcliffe, K., and Obstfeld, D. (2005). 'Organizing and the Process of Sensemaking', *Organization Science*, 16 (4), 409–421.
Weick, K.E., and Sutcliffe, K.M. (2001). *Managing the Unexpected: Assuring High Performance in an Age of Complexity.* San Francisco: Jossey Bass.
Weick, K.E., and Sutcliffe, K.M. (2007). *Managing the Unexpected. Resilient Performance in an Age of Uncertainty.* 2nd edition. San Francisco: Jossey Bass.
Westrum, R. (2008). 'Resilience and Restlessness'. In E. Hollnagel et al. (eds), pp. 1–2.
Wildavsky, A. (1991). *Searching for Safety.* New Brunswick: Transaction Books.
Witte, J. (2011). 'Foreword'. *Tertiary Education and Management*, 17 (3), 181–182. Special Issue: Students in Higher Education Governance.
Woods, D.D. (2009). 'Escaping Failures of Foresight'. *Safety Sciences*, 47, 498–501.

ELLEN HAZELKORN

# 3 Higher Education's Future: A New Global Order?

## The Policy Challenge

> One thing seems to be sure: it is unlikely that the effects of the crisis will disappear soon. (van Damme, 2009)

> Once the financial crisis is over (assumed to be several years) there still remains the need to make choices about how a university should function in a changing world. (Caldwell, 2009)

As higher education sits on the cusp of an historic transformation, many of us muse about what it might look like in the future. Over the last decades, access to higher education has expanded from being a privilege of birth or talent or both (the elite phase, according to Trow, 1974) to becoming a right for those with certain qualifications (the mass phase) and eventually an obligation for the vast majority of society and occupations (universal). However, the adjustment pressures of the global economic crisis are putting great pressure on higher education (HE) to demonstrate increased relevance to individuals and society and constitute better value-for-money. The continuing shift to the knowledge-based economy, with the rising demand for and costs of higher education, are occurring at the same time that many governments face serious financial strain – with knock-on effects on/for higher education budgets. Many of these challenges were manifest decades ago, but the confluence of factors associated with the *new economic reality* has intensified their impact. These developments reflect profound changes being brought about by the intensification of globalization, and an investment and resources 'arms race' for world-classness.

While each country and university faces particular and often unique challenges, there are common factors which affect most countries around the world today – issues which have become more acute since 2008. What are the implications of these developments for the overall shape and resilience of our higher education and research systems? To what extent is the current global economic crisis leading to temporary adjustments or to long term changes? As costs and demand rise, will it be possible to sustain mass public higher education at the level we have previously experienced or anticipated, or will there be a profound paradigm shift as governments look at alternative models, such as concentrating funding in only some HEIs, restricting the number of students or relying on for-profit institutions? What are the implications of these different policy choices for access, sustainability and quality? What are the implications for governance and management of higher education, for students and the academy – and for society?

In section one, the chapter presents an overview of three key policy challenges facing policymakers and higher education institutions (HEIs) today. It draws heavily upon political economy, situating the discussion about policy choices within a dynamic inter-relationship between globalization, the political environment and actions of national institutions – in this case higher education. As Marginson (2006: 1; also Hazelkorn, 2011: 10–22) explains, higher education operates as part of a

> complex combination of (1) global flows and networks of words and ideas, knowledge, finance, and inter-institution dealings; with (2) national higher education systems shaped by history, law, policy and funding; and (3) individual institutions operating at the same time locally, nationally and globally.

While individual nations and institutions may pursue their own path, 'they no longer have full command over their destinies' (Marginson and van der Wende, 2007: 13); they are part of a wider geo-political struggle in which 'governments need to invigorate their national innovation systems in the context of a global knowledge economy' (Robertson, 1998: 227). This is especially true in the aftermath of the 2008 global financial crisis, as policymakers and institutional leaders struggle to implement the optimum solution 'under circumstances directly encountered, given and transmitted' from myriad factors (to paraphrase Marx, 1963).

In part two, Ireland is presented as a case study. While there are shared global commonalities, from a neo-institutionalist perspective, national settings and policy choices matter (DiMaggio and Powell, 1992; Musselin, 2011: 463–465). Different countries confronted by roughly similar circumstances often make very different decisions. Ireland is a country struggling to reposition itself as an attractive venue for mobile capital and labour in response to the global economic crisis and accelerating competition; it faces particular challenges sustaining its publicly-funded mass higher education and university-based research system; it needs to ensure that graduates can succeed in the labour market, fuel and sustain personal, social and economic development, and underpin civil society. In contrast to other countries, Ireland has chosen to preserve its social-democratic values, emphasizing the importance of the overall 'system' rather than promoting individual institutional performance (Quinn, 2012).

The third and final section looks at policy trade-offs. The focus is on Europe but not exclusively so. The issues are familiar to all of us, with evidence of 'isomorphism processes play[ing] a driving role' across the higher education sector around the world (Musselin, 2011: 454). Because 'social and economic policy is to a great extent regulated by the conditionalities' of the global economy (Torres and Schugurensky, 2002: 431), the choices adopted by nations and institutions may be constrained – but they do matter. Agency is important: 'global systems of activity and regulation, [operate simultaneously and] alongside national policies and administration and local political relationships…' (Marginson and Rhoades, 2002: 305), albeit often pulling in divergent directions. Given the role played by (higher) education in modern society, how these issues are resolved can have profound implications for the wider ecosystem. The paper looks at these interconnections.

## Context and Contradictions

The European Higher Education Area (EHEA) and the European Research Area (ERA) were launched at a time of great optimism – euphemistically called the 'golden era' of higher education and research. The Lisbon Agenda (Lisbon European Council, 2000) claimed that by 2010 the EU would be 'the most competitive and dynamic knowledge-based economy in the world capable of sustainable economic growth with more and better jobs and greater social cohesion'. A decade later, the global financial crisis of 2008 had led to the tough reality of an increasingly long (re)adjustment period as countries, in different ways, struggled to survive and grow.

> Europe is no longer setting the pace in the global race for knowledge and talent, while emerging economies are rapidly increasing their investment in higher education… too few European higher education institutions are recognised as world class in the current, research oriented global university rankings…And there has been no real improvement over the past years. (European Commission, 2011a)

Not only has the crisis led to high levels of public and private debt and high unemployment, but many of our 'sacred cows', such as the European social model, social solidarity, democratic institutions, egalitarianism, etc., are being challenged. European higher education faces threats to its long-term sustainability (Sassen, 2011).

This section will take a helicopter view of three key policy challenges: 1) the balance between ensuring sustainable higher education systems at the same time that public funding is decreasing and competitiveness increasing; 2) balancing requirements to widen participation and pursue equity while also attracting talent and pursuing excellence; and 3) meeting competitive demands to strengthen knowledge and innovation while maintaining over-all national capacity for a sustainable knowledge society.

### *Building and Maintaining Global Competitiveness*

Competition between nations for a greater share of the global marketplace highlights why governments increasingly regard investment in higher education and R&D as vital for providing the knowledge base essential for economic growth, and now recovery. According to Kelly et al. (2009), the wider impact of higher education on society and the economy exceeds that of many other sectors: 'the multiplier effect of investment/expenditure by the higher education sector works out to be around 1.35' – that is for every £1m spent on higher education, £1.35m is generated by universities (Varghese, 2010: 11). The correlation between economic and research performance is particularly strong in developing countries (Inglesi-Lotz and Pouris, 2012). As a result, higher education is not simply an 'engine of development in the new world economy' (Castells, 1994: 14) but a beacon to attract capital, businesses and talent. For emerging societies, the ability to retain talent is also critical (Kapur and McHale, 2005; Wildavsky, 2010).

However, even before the current crisis, many nations faced major difficulties trying to reach EU/ OECD average spend for higher education/research. Contrasting the steepest decline in growth in 60 years across OECD countries (OECD, 2009), growth in developing countries and economies in transition has been particularly robust in both absolute and relative terms, and is likely to continue to 'stoke the engine of the world economy, over the coming years' (UN, 2011: 6). China is expected to contribute 40 per cent of world economic growth in 2013 compared with 0 per cent for Europe. OECD data show China and South Africa spending much more on R&D as a percent of GDP over the last 10 years; South Korea's trajectory starting ten years ago is also very impressive, and it is now spending more than anyone else on R&D as a percentage of GDP with the exception of Israel and Finland (OECD, 2012a: 14). This reflects

> a deliberate national strategy to become important educational hubs in their area of influence. This is the case in China, Singapore, Malaysia, South Korea and the Gulf countries, all aiming at becoming world class educational and research centers, and challenging the primacy of the USA and Europe. (Knobel, 2011: 2)

These changes reflect real differences in overall performance which shows Europe struggling to translate its strong showing in research and publications into new products and services (European Commission, 2011b), which in turn affects its positioning within the world order.

In the aftermath of the global financial crisis, competition between all nations for a greater share of mobile investment capital and talent has intensified across most sectors, raising the profile of knowledge-intense industries – including higher education. This has brought about a strong emphasis on technology-driven innovation (European Commission, 2009: 26–27); notably, the arts, humanities and social sciences are absent from this model. Rather the spotlight is on research which can demonstrate relevance and deliver (near-term) impact and benefit – in other words, jobs. As economic activities have become more global, some economies have relied increasingly on fewer sectors (OECD, 2011), with Canada being the only G7 country, since the 1970s, to experience periodic bursts of diversification. Accordingly, the EU is focusing on smart specialization – identifying key priorities for knowledge-based development, including building on national/regional strengths, competitive advantages and potential for excellence (European Commission, 2012: 9).

The concept of the 'knowledge economy' is the main policy framework across Europe, and around the world. It is accompanied by a focus on scientific and technological intensity underpinned by a shift in research management and organization, from individuals to teams, from single to multiple and collaborating institutions, and from a national to an international scope – changing the dynamic of research and research practice. Emphasis on the conversion of knowledge into new products and services, through licensing intellectual property rights and creating high-performance start-up companies has transformed knowledge from something which is primarily curiosity-driven to a use-inspired marketable commodity, often with exaggerated expectations and claims of return-on-investment. This has put pressure on researchers and research activity, and on higher education as the central actor. As government and institutions struggle for survival and dominance, there is evidence of a growing tension between seeing higher education as a source of human capital to one which sees higher education as being foremost an arm of industrial or economic policy.

These changes are further reflected in the way many governments have established/ renamed ministries to bring higher education and research together with skills, science, innovation, business, etc.

Global rankings have tracked these shifts in competitive strengths and weaknesses of nations linked to the talent-catching and knowledge-producing capacity of higher education. This has had a revolutionizing effect on perceptions of the 'world order'. While established universities in the US and Europe have continued to be the primary 'winners', the prioritization now being given to investment in higher education and research in emerging societies is beginning to produce shifts in the 'world order' and international division of knowledge. The pervasiveness of focusing on the top 100, however, obscures the changing geography of academic activity, and the transition from a

> bipolar [world] in which science and technology (S&T) were dominated by the Triad made up of the European Union, Japan and the USA…to a multipolar world, with an increasing number of public and private research hubs spreading across North and South. (UNESCO, 2010: xvii)

These developments explain why global rankings have assumed such significance, at a geo-political level, in recent years. It also explains the on-going tension between the EU's major policy agendas – the *Lisbon Agenda* and *Europe 2020* – and the status and reputation of European universities in the rankings. It highlights the dual challenge of improving research quality and productivity, and 'revitaliz[ing] the EU's poorly funded institutions of higher education' (UNESCO, 2010: 19; Hazelkorn and Ryan, 2013).

How can governments balance the need to target resources and expertise in knowledge creation while ensuring the over-all national capacity for sustainable knowledge society?

## *Meeting the Demand for Higher Education*

As societies evolve from natural resource-based primary production, such as mining and agriculture, to more sophisticated, skill- and technology-intensive activities, the educational system has become more or less obligatory for a wide range of occupations and social classes. To underpin the transition from a people-processing institution to a knowledge-producing enterprise (Gumport, 2000), significant public investment in and expansion of higher education and research systems has been sustained by an implicit 'social contract'. This has relied upon higher education's contribution to the overall 'public good' outweighing 'private good' (Calhoun, 2006). The OECD has repeatedly confirmed this strong correlation between educational attainment and social and economic advantages for individuals and society, depicting it as a virtuous circle (Gurria, 2010).

> Even though investing in education has many benefits, one area that has not been focused on enough is tax revenues. At a moment when countries are making huge efforts to consolidate their fiscal positions, education stands out as a generator of greater tax revenues. Let me give you a compelling figure: On average, a man with a university degree will generate $119,000 more in income taxes and social contributions over his working life than someone with a high-school degree only. Even after taking the cost of university education into account, the net public return from an investment in tertiary education is $86 000 for a male, in generated income taxes and social contributions over his working life. Enhancing tertiary education attainment can therefore help governments increase their fiscal revenues, making it easier to boost their social spending, in areas like, for example...education.

Similar arguments have been made about investment in university-based research; science – especially the bio-sciences and key enabling technologies – is privileged as long as there are (demonstrated) expectations of impact and benefit.

Ironically, increasing appreciation of the broad societal and economic benefits of universal higher education and university-based research are occurring at the same time that many countries face demographic pressures, thus threatening national strategies based upon growing knowledge-intensive industries. The difficulty has arisen for a combination of reasons, including greying of the population, the retirement of professionals, postponement of childbirth and the end of the 'baby boomer' bubble – leading to a decline in the number of students, especially those choosing science and technology subjects. In the US, the pool of high-school students is anticipated to fall by 10 per cent over the next decade, and colleges and universities risk being closed down or merging with competitor institutions (Marcus, 2008). The German government predicts that even with 200,000 immigrants a year, Germany's population will shrink from today's 82.5 to 75 million by 2050 (Hazelkorn, 2009).

However, this pattern is not uniform around the world. While the population of developed countries will remain largely unchanged, the world population is still projected to reach 9.3 billion by 2050, an increase of 2.3 billion over 2011 – equivalent to the combined populations of China and India. Most of this growth will be in developing countries (UN, 2011: 1). These growth patterns are responsible for a surging demand for higher education; according to UNESCO, there are almost 160 million students enrolled worldwide in higher education today compared with only 30 million in 1970 (UNESCO, 2009: 9). The overall global demand for places in higher education will peak at 263 million in 2025; India's demand will rise from 9.6 million to 61 million while China's demand will rise from 8 million to 45 million (Böhm et al., 2002; Brandenburg et al., 2008). To meet this escalating demand, at least one sizeable new university will need to open every week over the next decades.

Despite some claims about over-education, 'the demand for individuals who possess a broader knowledge base, more specialised skills, advanced analytical capacities, and complex communications skills continues to rise' (OECD, 2012b: 26). Investment in research-related education is vital, especially for regions and countries which specialize in innovation and are close to the world technological frontier (Aghion and Howitt, 2006), because 'in the new economy where knowledge is the source of wealth creation, human capital becomes as important as financial capital' (BIAC, 2008). By 2020, approximately 31.5 per cent of all jobs will require high qualifications, and 50 per cent medium qualifications. The demand for low qualifications will fall from a third in 1996 to around 18.5 per cent (Hart, 2010). While there is the possibility of oversupply in some areas, there is considerable evidence of an increasing requirement for, and even shortages of, people with adequate levels of qualification in many areas (CEDEFOP, 2008).

The historic decline in growth across OECD countries has exposed fundamental weaknesses in the underpinning funding model and public expectations of higher education. As the costs of higher education rise, many countries have pursued austerity measures; this is widening the gap between state revenues and the cost of provision. Arguments favouring cost-sharing have sought to shift the costs of higher education from the state to the individual at a time when household income is under stress. The gap between rate of change in tuition-fees and household income is most pronounced in the US, but there are similarities elsewhere; tuition-fees are highest in the US, followed by Korea and the UK (McCoy et al., 2009). Global competition has continually pushed up the investment 'arms race' on the basis that if Country A spends €x, then Country B must spend €x + y, and so on. This is putting a phenomenal squeeze on funding and affordability. The EU itself has struggled to preserve its celebrated R&D programme, *Horizon 2020*, in the face of mounting criticism from member states, many of whom are unable to meet the Lisbon 3 per cent GDP target (Ahlstrom, 2013).

Given increasing demands for higher education and research to fuel social and economic prosperity, how can the long term sustainability of European higher education be preserved, and what is the likely model in the future?

## *Assuring Quality and Excellence*

As the importance of higher education for the economy becomes more demonstrable, quality has become a critical differentiator in the world market – a key determinant of reputation and status. This has occurred in tandem with an erosion of previously unswerving public support for public institutions – whether health, social services or education. This has been particularly pronounced in the UK with the rise of neo-liberalism since the 1980s, but the experience is manifest elsewhere, and is heightened because of high levels of personal debt. In return, governments and their publics are looking for verifiable and measurable evidence of value-for-money and return-on-investment, and greater evidence of impact and benefit. How higher education is governed and managed has itself become a major policy issue. At the same time, there are heightened 'concerns about quality, particularly the quality of graduates and research outputs', especially in publicly-funded systems (Harman, 2011: 36). Students, as consumers, are questioning the value of their study programme relative to the tuition fee or institution's status and reputation, and tax-payers want more evidence of the contribution to society as a whole.

In a global higher education marketplace, cross-national comparisons are inevitable, leaving no room for self-promotion (Hazelkorn, 2012). At a time of growing demands for higher education by society and students of all ages and rising costs, there is an emphasis on student learning outcomes and evidence that student performance measures up. The arrival of global rankings has acted as a wake-up call for higher education, challenging self-perceptions of greatness for nations, institutions and individual academics. Despite their limitations (Hazelkorn, 2011; Rauhvargers, 2011), rankings have succeeded in exposing a higher education information deficit. Traditionally higher education has relied on peer review, and other internalized procedures of quality assurance or enhancement. From an outsider's perspective, these reports are written in opaque academic language, making it difficult to compare institutional performance, especially internationally. By placing consideration of quality, performance and productivity within a wider comparative and international framework, rankings have taken the debate outside the traditional bailiwick of higher education and placed it firmly onto the public and policy agenda. Today, there is increasing evidence of government regulation or involvement with quality assurance procedures; Australia has created the Tertiary Education Quality and Standards Agency (TEQSA) as a 'regulator' and there are signs of greater US federal government involvement in a system which has traditionally operated according to its own accreditation processes (Kelderman, 2013; Massaro, 2013). With the involvement of the EU via *U-Multirank* and OECD via *Assessment of Higher Education Learning Outcomes* (AHELO) projects, quality assurance has moved to the supra-national level confirming that higher education has effectively lost its role as the primary guardian of quality (Harman, 2011: 51; Dill and Beerkens, 2010: 313–315).

Today, global rankings have become the simple (and simplistic) tool of choice for a wide range of stakeholders on the presumption (as yet unproven) that they provide a good measure of quality. Many of the indicators simply reveal the growing wealth gap between well-endowed selective research universities and public, mass recruiting teaching HEIs without having anything noteworthy to say about teaching quality or the quality of the student experience (Hazelkorn, 2012; Archibald and Feldmann, 2006). The overemphasis on particular indicators, despite modifications, has narrowed our understanding of the intellectual footprint of higher education across teaching, research and engagement. Nonetheless, they have been transformative, and led to a sea-change across higher education.

What is meant by quality, and is there a (better) way to assess and compare it?

## Using Ireland as an Example

How does the above discussion help us better to understand how the different issues play out in a particular country, and the resulting policy tensions?

Ireland is a small, open economy. Between 1990 and 2008, it underwent an historic transformation from a country dependent on agriculture and traditional manufacturing to one increasingly based on hi-tech and internationally traded services, as the benefits of the knowledge economy began to dominate policy discourse across Europe (Bangemann, 1994). Higher education, long regarded 'as a source of skilled technical labour', began to be seen as essential for economic growth (Harpur, 2010: 77). The *National Development Plan* (NDP, 2007: 17) pledged to enhance enterprise development, and 'improve economic performance, competitiveness...generate new enterprise "winners" from the indigenous sector [and] attract high added value foreign direct investment'. This placed education and university-based research at the centre of policy making in a dramatic new way, and following the pattern in other countries, formed an alliance between government and higher education to 'redefine[e] and reshap[e] the knowledge base of Irish society' (Lindsay, 1996: 2).

During these years, the economy grew dramatically and tax revenue surged, enabling the government to expand expenditure on services and national infrastructure projects. These were good years for higher education, pushing it high up the policy agenda. The core budget increased, and over €3 billion was invested in higher education research and infrastructure. Participation rates rose, partially fuelled by the abolition of tuition fees in 1995, from 44 per cent to almost 60 per cent today. In 2005, Ireland spent only 1.1 per cent GDP (public and private) on higher education, below the OECD of 1.5 per cent GDP, although by 2009 expenditure had risen to meet the OECD average of 1.6 per cent (OECD, 2012c: 244; HEA, 2011: 22) before the crisis kicked in.

By 2009 all had changed. GDP declined by over 11 per cent in 2009 on the back of a smaller but significant decline in 2008 and has barely returned to positive growth since (Trading Economics, 2013). The global financial crisis exposed underlying weaknesses in the structure of an economy overly dependent on housing and construction (IMF, 2009), and funding for public services including higher education. The government adopted a deflationary strategy aimed at increasing Ireland's competitiveness (Hazelkorn, 2011). In 2010, Ireland entered an IMF/EU/ECB bail-out programme. The strategy is to rebuild the economy based on export-led growth with a strong emphasis on building-up human capital and research in science and technology in order to attract foreign direct investment (FDI). Thus, success is dependent upon meeting labour market projections for a minimum 48 per cent of the labour force having qualifications at BA, MA, PhD level, 45 per cent at secondary level and 7 per cent at primary (Forfás, nd). While it is difficult to precisely align supply and demand, any reduction in the level of provision or changes in demographic trends caused by emigration, for example, could lead to graduate shortages at a time when there is a growing demand for graduate labour within high-tech sectors of the economy (McGuinness et al., 2012: 8).

Exchequer funding accounts for 85 per cent of public higher education funding compared with an OECD average of 73 per cent. Expenditure per student is 15.5 per cent below the top OECD quartile if research funding is not included, or 28 per cent below including research funding (HEA, 2010: 111). Rising demand for graduates coincides with an overall 34 per cent reduction in core funding for higher education between 2008 and 2015 and growing student demand for places. This demand reflects overall demographic growth, with the number of potential undergraduate entrants expected to grow from '41,000 in 2010/2011 to 44,000 in 2019/20 (7 per cent) and to just over 51,000 by 2029/2030' (McGuinness et al., 2012: 7); this will bring the total undergraduate and postgraduate students from a current level of 180,000 to almost 300,000 by 2030. Assuming the number of students continues along the lines expected and continuing high levels of emigration, Ireland will have just about the required number of people to meet labour market demand until 2030 (McGuinness et al., 2012: 61–72). However, budget and student numbers are going in opposite directions, and resources per student are declining more precipitously than headline cuts suggest. The government has sought to preserve R&D funding; after an initial reduction of almost 30 per cent between 2009 and 2010, funding was increased albeit this varies across funding agencies and programmes.

The government's policy response to the economic crisis has been influenced and signalled through several major reports and policy initiatives briefly described below:

- *Building Ireland's Smart Economy* (2008) aimed to position Ireland as a knowledge-intensive economy with a 'thriving enterprise sector, high-quality employment, secure energy supplies, an attractive environment, and first-class infrastructure'. It strongly endorsed heavy investment in R&D. Reform and restructuring of higher education was also a central feature (GoI, 2008: 3).
- *Special Group on Public Service Numbers and Expenditure Programmes* (2009) examined expenditure across all government departments, proposing €10.2 million savings from higher education. It questioned spending on research and the emphasis on training PhDs, and proposed amalgamating all research funding into a single agency. It also criticized academic/non-academic contracts (DoF, 2009).
- *Innovation Taskforce* (2010) proposed that Ireland should focus on being a 'clever copycat' rather than developing its own R&D capacity; in other words, Ireland should do the 'D' in R&D (Innovation Task Force, 2010: 15).

- *National Strategy for Higher Education to 2030* (RSG, 2011) recommended rationalization and merger between the 39 institutions to create efficiencies and increase mission diversity, proposing that HEIs should be subjected to greater oversight through a strategic dialogue process and institutional contract. It also suggested a graduate tax or an income contingent loan system as an alternative to no-tuition policy in order to inject needed funds into the system.
- *Towards a Future Higher Education Landscape* (HEA, 2012) set guiding principles and objectives for a 'co-ordinated system of higher education' with an emphasis on mission distinctiveness. Given the financial and competitive pressures, no single institution is expected to cover all disciplines or research fields. The future system will be characterized by differentiation based on qualifications level, discipline specialization, programme orientation, regional engagement, student profile, mode of provision, and research intensity and specialization.
- *Research Prioritisation Exercise* (RPE) (Forfás, 2011) identified fourteen priority areas plus six platform sciences and technology for targeted funding.
- *Quality and Qualifications Ireland* (2012) created a single Quality Assurance authority and regulator for all further education (FE) and HE (public and for-profit sector) institutions (see QQI).

While there are differences in emphasis, together these reports and actions represent a significant move towards greater government steering of a co-ordinated higher education and research system in recognition of its strategic importance. The intention is to increase accountability to deliver outputs in line with national (economic) priorities, in terms of curriculum and graduates, and new products and services. It also reflects the continuing shift from traditional 'primacy of the humanities and classical studies' towards science and technology (Walsh, 2011: 366). The change is also signalled by the reassignment of research to the Department of Jobs, Enterprise and Innovation, and renaming of the Department of Education and Skills (previously education and science); while there is a junior minister for research and innovation linking the two departments, the latter department and the Higher Education Authority (HEA) have effectively lost control of university-based research. A new inter-governmental committee will co-ordinate and steer research funding, and a single research council replaces the former arts and humanities, and science and technology councils. The HEA has been given responsibility to drive policy and system change, shaping the overall higher education landscape and institutional direction, ensuring institutional missions are sufficiently differentiated and performance monitored and funded accordingly. Through a series of inter-related processes, the number of HEIs (some of which have fewer than 1,000 students each) will fall over the next decade from thirty-nine to less than twenty. Similar actions are being taken with respect to FE.

Notably, greater emphasis is being placed on the performance of the system as-a-whole rather than focusing on individual institutions, by ensuring strategic alignment around areas of defined relevance and quality and agreed targets (HEA, 2012). This includes recognizing the importance of teaching and research, and insisting that all HEIs engage in both. Accountability and transparency will be driven through better data collection, and the use of output and performance metrics. Quality assurance is increasingly government-driven rather than institution-led. Inevitably given limitations on the state's capacity to fund mass public higher education at a time of accelerating global competitiveness, greater cost-sharing and reliance on the for-profit sector may provide relief.

In keeping with the strategy of rebuilding the economy, research is being reoriented towards defined priorities. The RPE marks the end of laissez-faire which sought to build a broad base of expertise in favour of strong endorsement for a 'more top-down, targeted approach' with an emphasis on research which links directly to societal and economic needs. Emphasis in the (immediate) future will be on research relevance with a focus on short-term job creation and innovation which is likely to have implications for research and institutional structures, educational programmes and academic careers. This represents a significant shift from higher education as human capital development underpinning civil society to being an arm of economic policy. Some of these developments will positively encourage quality specialization rather than sheer comprehensiveness, but they could equally affect the breadth and balance across disciplinary provision.

Sustainability is the biggest challenge. Rising demand and declining budgets have raised fundamental questions about the threshold for quality. State funding per student has decreased almost 20 per cent since 2007 to €8,000; each undergraduate student pays a 'contribution' due to increase to €3,000 by 2015. There is a student grant system but no loan programme. All postgraduates pay a tuition fee. Comparative data show Ireland at between 19 per cent and 29 per cent lower per student funding than England (HEA, 2011: 5). Typical output data, such as graduates, employability, progression, research activity, student and employer satisfaction etc. remain high, but the staff-student ratio is rising, and the position and number of HEIs in the global rankings have fallen. Various options are under consideration, including a higher contribution from families who can afford to pay, variegated fees for different programmes, allowing institutions to set a market-based fee, restricting student numbers nationally or per HEI, and expanding the role of private providers – but all carry policy and political risks.

## Reconfiguring Mass Higher Education: Policy Trade-Offs

Ireland faces particular difficulties given the severity of the economic crisis and the prolonged recession, but it is not the only country to experience difficulties as a result of the global economic crisis. Nor is it the only country whose higher education system has been rocked by structural change aligned with or precipitated by public financial cut-backs. According to the European University Association which has been monitoring the situation in Europe, major reductions in public funding to higher education have occurred over the years 2008–2012, in the Czech Republic, Greece, Hungary, Iceland, Italy, Latvia, Lithuania, Netherlands, Portugal and Spain. In contrast, Belgium, Finland, Denmark, Norway, Sweden, Austria, France, Germany, Switzerland, Poland and Slovakia have experienced a stable or positive funding environment (Pruvot, 2012).

Higher education has always been competitive, but the confluence of factors associated with globalization has created a new sense of urgency as it becomes increasingly evident that no government can/will be able to afford to fund all the higher education that its citizens demand or society requires. As a result, many governments are promoting major system restructuring underpinned by increased steering. Financial constraints on the state, arising from the on-going global economic crisis, have called the 'public character of higher education…into question' (Musselin, 2011: 455) leading to a paradigm shift in the way in which publicly-funded mass higher education has heretofore been valued and resourced in many (developed) countries. Policymakers and institutional leaders are left pondering a series of fundamental issues: How do we educate a larger proportion of our population to a higher level while resources are reducing/reduced and at a time of increasing competition? How should national funds for higher education and research be strategically oriented to ensure knowledge based growth and competitiveness into the future? And what are the trade-offs between public policy and private good, and between institutional ambition and system coherence?

This section briefly identifies some policy trade-offs in the context of the external drivers discussed in section one and reflecting the Irish case study. Policy trade-offs involve balancing different options or policy goals (Jongbloed, 2004), which become especially acute 'because different stakeholders interpret evidence differently: stakeholders may assign different weights to policy goals and may even define the same goals differently' (Mah, 2008: 192). Another way to consider choices is by devising different scenarios which consider different policy or strategic options at a time of uncertainty; the key point, however, is that 'addressing these choices is not a simple task. While there is a great deal of information available, and it should be consulted, there are also many uncertainties' (Caldwell, 2009).

### *Building a World-Class University*

Today, the world-class research university has become the panacea for ensuring success in the global economy and world science.

> Many countries are building centres of excellence to create the optimum conditions for increasing research quality and impact...Worldwide, the 50 universities with the highest impact – measured by normalised citations to academic publications across all disciplines – are concentrated in a handful of countries... (OECD 2011: 15)

'Being' or 'becoming' a world-class university now drives many national and institutional strategies around the world. There are many national versions (Salmi, 2009; Altbach and Salmi, 2011: 1). Across Europe, there has been a noticeable move away from egalitarianism principles and a rising tension between concepts of elite and mass education (Gidley, 2012: 1022–1023). However, given that the cost of a single world-class university is estimated at approximately $2bn annually (Usher, 2006; Sadlak and Liu, 2007), this strategy requires targeted funding for a select number of universities over many years.

Drawing on the characteristics of the top 20, 50 or 100 universities, Mohrman et al. (2008: 21) describe the emerging global (university) model (EGM) alternatively referred to as the 'Harvard here model' (Moodie, 2009) or the 'Neo-liberal model' (Hazelkorn, 2011). The defining characteristics are: i) mission transcending boundaries of nation-state; ii) increasing intensification of knowledge production; iii) changes in academic roles, productivity and performance systems; iv) diversified funding beyond government support and student contributions; v) state facilitation of partnership between HE and private sector; vi) worldwide recruitment; vii) increasingly complex organizational model with semiautonomous centres and institutes; and viii) global collaboration via networked nodes.

Even for well-endowed nations, policy decisions and resource allocation can be a zero-sum game, leading to policy strains. Dubbed the 'Sheriff of Nottingham' model, to succeed it requires governments to divert limited resources to a few institutions or to effectively 'rob...from the poor to pay the rich' (Currie, 2009a: 1198; Currie, 2009b). Pursuance of this strategy represents a significant volte-face for many (European) countries which have previously promoted an egalitarian approach whereby each HEI within the system was comparable and students would have a similar educational experience. To some extent, this approach reflected less mobile societies, where students usually attended their proximate university; with the advent of new technologies and greater mobility, the underlining assumptions have come under scrutiny.

*Concentrating Excellence*

Because higher education and university-based research play such a fundamental role in creating competitive advantage, it is inevitable that more attention is focused on their capacity and capability for global advantage. Over the past decade, the European Union has slowly, quietly but systematically, restructured European higher education and research, linking the strategy for 'smart growth' with substantial reform via *Europe 2020* (Hazelkorn and Ryan, 2013). Statements applaud the diversity of European higher education but as concerns about global competition have risen, the EU has been less concerned with diversity and more with excellence:

> ...higher education institutions too often seek to compete in too many areas, while comparatively few have the capacity to excel cross the board. As a consequence, too few European higher education institutions are recognised as world class in the current, research-oriented global university rankings... (European Commission, 2011a: 2)

The Framework Programme has switched from encouraging the growth of research to consolidating and concentrating research in centres of excellence. Under both *FP7* and *Horizon 2020*, 15 per cent and 50 per cent, respectively of the research budget is for the European Research Council which is putting funding directly into the hands of 'excellent' researchers and not institutions. The strategy is already helping to consolidate 50 per cent of funding in just fifty universities (Myklebust, 2012; Maassen and Stensaker, 2011).

Can concentration deliver the proposed results and/or will concentrating resources in a few institutions or regions lead to undermining of capacity across all society? By putting substantial funds into research, the EU is effectively highlighting and incentivizing research – as distinct from teaching and learning – and condoning likely knock-on concentration within the sector but also across the EU itself. This type of restructuring was initially thought desirable in order to create 'Silicon somewheres' (Florida, 2002) but has now been shown to have many disadvantages, and may not be either feasible or desirable and could undermine national economic capacity (Evidence Ltd, 2003: 28–31; Lambert Review, 2003; Adams and Smith, 2004; Adams and Gurney, 2010).

To meet the challenges of increasing participation and funding excellence in an era of fiscal consolidation and global competition, many governments are choosing to hierarchically differentiate between types of institutions serving different needs and populations. An alternative model would emphasize horizontal differentiation linked to field specialization, with different institutions as proximate knowledge producers aligned to their expertise and regional/national capacity. Such a model would draw upon the lessons learned from successful global cities and mega-regions, and proposed in another EU strategy for 'regions of knowledge' and 'smart specialization' (Hazelkorn, 2011: 198–199).

## *Increasing Selectivity*

As nations and institutions engage in a reputation race, there is increasing focus on the recruitment of talent – domestic and international high achievers. Because many countries face demographic pressures, access to talent has become a major challenge for national strategies based on growing knowledge-intensive industries. In turn, students can add to the prestige of an institution in addition to bringing revenue; according to Brewer et al. (2002: 60) a prestige-seeking institution often 'place[s] more value on a student's potential contribution to prestige than it does on that student's direct contribution to revenues'. Concomitant with the decline in the traditional student market relative to non-traditional student groups and the intensification of competition for high-achieving and internationally mobile students, student selectivity has become a critical ingredient of the reputation race (Lucido and Thacker, 2011). This has helped push up the status premium of elite universities, their hosting nations and graduates from those institutions.

Simplistic connections are being drawn between excellence and exclusiveness. Some governments and HE leaders worry their universities may not be sufficiently elite or they have too many students thereby threatening their status:

> ...following expansion and democratisation of higher education,...our ability to maximise the talents of the intellectually gifted have diminished...(sic). (Murphy, 2011)

Institutions with lower entry scores are seen as reducing appeal to high achieving students. Tuition fees play a similar role: 'lowering one's tuition relative to one's competitors...[is] perceived as signalling lower quality' (Bowman and Bastedo, 2009: 434). There is a strong shift from offering scholarships to supporting students in 'need' to encouraging 'merit'. These behaviours are amplified by the weightings, assigned by rankings and other performance measurements, to outputs and outcomes which correlate strongly with elite high-achieving students (Hazelkorn, 2011, chapter 4). Thus, high prestige and globally ranked universities are a magnet for high-achieving students, and influence student choice in explicit and implicit ways (Simões and Soares, 2010: 385).

The link between selectivity and excellence is driving national and institutional decision making. There are plenty of examples: the UK is encouraging the recruitment of students achieving AAB or equivalent at A-Level, and Liberal Arts colleges are being created within mass/publicly-funded universities in order to build prestige. Knowing that people with higher levels of education are more likely to migrate (Eurobarometer, 2006), governments around the world are introducing new policies and targeting high skilled immigration – especially in science and technology – to attract 'the most talented migrants who have the most to contribute economically' (Rüdiger, 2008: 5), for example, immigration policy in both Denmark and the Netherlands now favours people with qualifications from top-ranked universities. Financial rating agencies, such as Moody's or Standards and Poor's, also study application outcomes:

> If an institution is not growing and improving selectivity, that would probably be more of a concern than it would have been a decade ago... (Hoover, 2010)

Thus, the objective is to recruit 'students who will be "assets" in terms of maintaining and enhancing...[a university's] position in the rankings' (Clarke, 2007: 38).

### *Escalating System Stratification*

Policies which favour flagship or world-class universities can lead to distortions within the broader system and society, by increasing stratification between elite universities and mass institutions and systems, thereby exposing a widening gap in 'world-classness'. For example, by choosing to concentrate top talent in Seoul National University, there are arguments that Korea has incentivized young people to cram for university entrance examinations and ignore good regional universities, with the (unintentional effect) of contributing to an imbalance in economic growth by depriving regional universities of the best brains (Koreabang, 2012). As more universities 'define themselves as "selective" in an effort to boost their position and prestige...fewer and fewer offer the kind of admissions process that provides real opportunities for poorer students' (Douthat, 2005). The question is not whether opportunities for high-achieving students should be 'eclipsed' to serve 'the needs of an increasingly diverse student population' (Bastedo and Gumport, 2003: 355), but rather the extent to which the push for world-class excellence is, wittingly or unwittingly, driving behaviour and reinforcing social stratification by institutional mission or rank.

Table 3.1 below provides an overview of some emergent and distinctive features which differentiate between elite universities and mass institutions, albeit this is context-dependent. For example, in developed countries, such as the US, elite/selective universities are usually (not-for-profit) private institutions, whereas in developing countries (such as Eastern Europe or Asia) these institutions tend to be public. The converse is true for mass institutions which are often public in the US and hence beholden to a declining public purse whereas in developing countries they are usually (for-profit) private institutions; this means that academically and socio-economically disadvantaged students can end up as the ones reliant on tuition-bearing institutions (OECD 2013: 107–117). High-achieving elite students are more likely to be traditional 18–22 year olds living on or attending a campus-based institution with all the attributes and connections that kind of environment brings; in contrast, worker-learner students are likely to commute and attend part-time (Ehrenberg, 2004; Clarke, 2007; Hossler et al., 1989). MOOCS, hailed by some as a way to bring elite education to the masses, may exaggerate socio-economic stratification as students attending elite universities ably supplement their programme of study while other students depend upon them – their lecturers being the tutor of someone else's material (Weigel, 2013; Xu and Jaggars, 2013). There are implications for academic work; the 'use of technology and people in non-faculty positions (like student assistants) to reduce costs and increase learning in remedial and introductory-level classes will likely occur much more rapidly' at mass institutions in contrast to elite research universities which will 'have access to the resources necessary to maintain full-time tenured and tenure track faculty' (Ehrenberg, 2012: 212–213; Choudaha, 2012). Admittedly, these are rough generalizations, but they suggest a virtuous circle for elite universities and the Matthew effect for the rest. The issue is the degree of increasing stratification within the system; in other words, not simply 'access to what' but 'who gets what'.

Table 3.1 Increasing Stratification

| *Elite Research Universities* | *Mass Teaching HEIs* |
| --- | --- |
| • *Developed countries*: elite/selective HEIs are private cf. in *developing countries*: elite/selective HEIs are public.<br>• On-line/MOOCs used to extend market/global reach putting pressure on non-elite institutions, or provide high-level additional learning value.<br>• Traditional, full-time high-SES and high achieving students.<br>• Campus with credentials and prestige capable of boosting one's status relative to others.<br>• Full-time, tenure-track faculty likely to continue and increase. | • *Developed countries*: mass recruiting HEIs are public HEIs cf. in *developing countries* mass recruiting HEIs are price-sensitive for-profit.<br>• Technology used in for-profits to reduce costs and increase learning in remedial and introductory-level classes putting pressure on non-elite/mid-tier institutions.<br>• Part-time, mature worker-learner student of lower/middle income background.<br>• Metropolitan/commuter or distance learning environments.<br>• Increasing reliance on non-tenured, adjunct/ part-time faculty – often with multiple employments. |

## *Measuring Quality, Value and Relevance*

As globalization accelerates and market principles intrude further, there is a growing necessity to regulate the marketplace. There is greater government steering but this raises questions about the appropriate balance between autonomy and accountability. Focus on value-for-money and return-on-(public) investment has coincided with concern about performance and productivity and competitiveness; there is a heightened realization of the role higher education plays within society and as an economic driver. Inexorably this has led to greater government involvement either directly in the process or in the assessment of outcomes for policy and decision making, but there is also acceptance, perhaps reluctantly within the academy, that measuring and comparing academic performance and productivity is unavoidable.

Quality is usually defined by its outputs, but there is also increasing interest in the impact and relevance of higher education. Different stakeholders value different aspects; e.g. students appraise their credentials vis-à-vis the labour market and lifestyle opportunities, employers consider the capability of graduates, governments want to see skilled human capital and knowledge translated into new products and services. But there is no definitive agreed definition of quality because context is critical; differences between publicly-funded and for-profit or well-endowed not-for-profit private institutions can be considerable Likewise, socio-economic background and national circumstances are key determinants. Because rankings have become a basic litmus test of excellence and reputation in a globalized world, attention has now focused on the link between competiveness, participation, quality and funding.

Higher education has always been competitive, but 'rankings make perceptions of prestige and quality explicit' (Freid, 2005: 17, 89). This has heightened reliance on measures of quantification to measure quality, and frenetic debate about the virtue (or not) of specific indicators. Over time, the current rankings may be overtaken by social networking and online open-source tools, such as TripAdvisor, which will put information directly into the hands of students, employers, peers and the general public, by-passing rankings but also higher education institutions (Boffey,

2011). This includes the growing number of government and other sites with basic institutional data enabling comparison. The question remains, however, as to whether we are measuring what is meaningful or what is easy, to paraphrase Einstein (Hazelkorn, 2013).

The same policy tensions are evident in how university-based research is assessed. Once research is seen to have value and impact beyond the academy, there are implications for the organization and management of research at the national and institutional level, what kind of research is funded, how it is measured and by whom. This is leading to some significant policy rebalancing between concepts of research as vital for human capital development versus its contribution to economic development; between emphasizing researcher curiosity versus aligning research to national priorities; between providing resources for excellence wherever it exists versus targeting resources to strengthen capability or build scale; and between encouraging new and emerging fields of inquiry and/or higher education institutions versus prioritizing existing research strengths through strategies of centres of excellence. *Horizon 2020*, for example, speaks of 'bridg[ing] the gap between research and the market' through the development of 'technological breakthroughs' and translation 'into viable products with real commercial potential'.

Governments and research agencies and institutions have relied on bibliometric indicators which favour a traditional academic model of measuring research at a time when there has been a noticeable shift away from measuring inputs and outputs to evaluating benefit and relevance; from relying solely on peer accountability instruments such as bibliometrics and citations to assessing a wider range of outputs and outcomes through social and public accountability. Traditional methods also undermine the arts, humanities and social sciences which output their research to a wider range of research outlets (European Commission, 2010), and the contribution of research to 'third mission'/regional engagement or civic and social responsibility. End-user or stakeholder esteem is also ignored. There is growing support by many governments and research agencies to embrace a broader range of indicators and methodologies, not just for research assessment but also for academic recruitment and performance, but the more complex the process, the more time-consuming, costly and potentially bureaucratic it can be. Herein lays the difficulty.

## A New Global Order?

During the 1980s, President Ronald Reagan promulgated a strategy for economic growth based on cutting the top tax bracket from 70 per cent to 50 per cent and then to 28 per cent. 'Trickle down' economics or 'Reaganomics' argued that putting more money in the hands of the elite would create more jobs and lessen inequality. International evidence, however, shows the results were the opposite of the ones predicted: while there was some benefit eventually for those who are relatively poor, the distribution of income and wealth has remained unequal. In fact, the huge budget deficits facing many countries today are arguably a result of the low taxation policies favoured by this strategy. Is there a lesson for us today?

The twentieth century was marked by rapid expansion and massification of higher education across most developed countries; this century is marked by globalization. Today, higher education is a core part of a wider geo-political struggle placing it at the centre of policy making. The severity and prolonged nature of the economic crisis, coupled with the acceleration of global competition, has called into question many public and policy beliefs, amongst which are support for publicly-funded mass higher education, widening and unlimited access and participation, curiosity-inspired (basic or fundamental) research and institutional autonomy. The resulting policy trade-offs are exposing major contradictions:

- Pursuing a resource-intensive 'world class university' strategy at a time when public budgets and affordability are declining, and demand for higher education is rising;
- Concentrating excellence in a handful of universities at the same time as requiring enhanced regional capacity and capability;
- Highlighting the importance of research rather than teaching at the same time as evidence supports the need for greater transversal/critical skills gained through enhanced integration between teaching and research;

- Widening inequality through reputational differentiation and socio-economic stratification at the same time as promoting widening access and participation, and the virtues of an inclusive knowledge society;
- Rewarding traditional academic outputs (via rankings or similar processes) at the same time as valuing the contribution of all disciplines and endorsing the importance of social and economic impact, and civic and social responsibility.

The resilience of the system is being severely tested. The changes being implemented represent a transformative paradigm shift in higher education. At a time when higher education is in growing demand by students and society to aid development and recovery, the 'world-class university' is increasingly unfettered by the nation state. But, as it becomes more focused on its global position and less dependent on state funding, recruiting students internationally, is the research university being transformed into a private self-serving entity less committed to its nation/region? Is the global economic crisis being used to justify pursuance of elite agendas because of the wonderful things that 'world class universities' supposedly do for the rest of us? Has the public's interest become confused with private interest?

## References

Adams, J., and Gurney, K. (2010). *Funding Selectivity, Concentration and Excellence – how Good is the UK's Research?* Oxford: Higher Education Policy Institute. <http://www.hepi.ac.uk/455-1793/Funding-selectivity,-concentration-and-excellence---how-good-is-the-UK's-research.html> accessed 27 February 2013.

Adams, J., and Smith, D. (2004). *Research and the Regions: an Overview of the Distribution of Research in UK Regions, Regional Research Capacity and Links between Strategic Research Partners.* London: Evidence Ltd.

Aghion, P., and Howitt, P. (2006). 'Joseph Schumpeter Lecture: Appropriate Growth Policy: a Unifying Framework', *Journal of the European Economic Association*, 4 (2–3), 269–314.

Ahlstrom, D. (17.2.2013). 'EU Research Budget "faces 12 per cent cut"', *The Irish Times*. <http://www.irishtimes.com/news/eu-research-budget-faces-12-cut-1.1253357> accessed 17 May 2013.

Altbach, P., and Salmi, J. (2011). 'Introduction'. In P. Altbach and J. Salmi (eds), *The Road to Academic Excellence: the Making of World-Class Research Universities*, pp. 1–9. Washington, D.C.: The World Bank.

Archibald, R.B., and Feldman, D.H. (2006). *The Anatomy of College Tuition*. <http://www.acenet.edu/news-room/Pages/The-Anatomy-of-College-Tuition.aspx> accessed 27 February 2013.

Bangemann, M. (1994). *Report on Europe and the Global Information Society: Recommendations of the High-level Group on the Information Society to the Corfu European Council*. Bulletin of the European Union, 2 (94). <http://www.cyber-rights.org/documents/bangemann.htm> accessed 18 May 2013.

Bastedo, M.N., and Gumport, P.J. (2003). 'Access to What? Mission Differentiation and Academic Stratification in U.S. Public Higher Education', *Higher Education*, 46 (3), 341–359.

BIAC (2008). 'Comments on the OECD Project on Trade, Innovation and Growth', Paris. <http://biac.org/members/trade/docs/08-01_Innovation.pdf> accessed 18 May 2013.

Boffey, D. (2011). 'Which? Magazine to Test Value of Degrees', *The Guardian*, 22 October.

Böhm, A., Davis, D., Meares, D., and Pearce, D. (2002). *Global Student Mobility 2025*. IDP Education Australia. <http://www.aiec.idp.com/pdf/Bohm_2025media_p.pdf> accessed 27 February, 2013.

Bowman, N.A., and Bastedo, M.N. (2009). 'Getting on the Front Page: Organisational Reputation, Status Signals and the Impact of *U.S. News and World Report* on Student Decisions', *Research in Higher Education*, 50 (5), 415–436.

Brandenburg, U., Carr, D., Donauer, S., and Berthold, C. (2008). *Analysing the Future Market – Target Countries for German HEIs*, Working paper No. 107. Gütersloh: CHE Centre for Higher Education Development.

Brewer, D.J., Gates, S.M., and Goldman, C.A. (2002). *In Pursuit of Prestige: Strategy and Competition in U.S. Higher Education*. Somerset, N.J.: Transaction Publishers.

Burrage (ed.) (2010), *Martin Trow: Twentieth-Century Higher Education: From Elite to Mass to Universal*, pp. 556–610. Baltimore: Johns Hopkins University Press.

Caldwell, Roger L. (2009). 'Two Scenarios for the University of Arizona in 2025'. <http://cals.arizona.edu/dean/planning/rlc-ua-scenarios-jan09.pdf> accessed 27 February, 2013.

Calhoun, C. (2006). 'The University and the Public Good', *Thesis Eleven*, 84 (1), 7–43. London: SAGE. <http://the.sagepub.com/content/84/1/7.abstract> accessed 27 February 2013.

Castells, M. (1994). 'The University System: Engine of Development in the New World Economy'. In J. Salmi, J., and A. Vespoor (eds), *Revitalizing Higher Education*, pp. 14–40. Oxford: Pergamon.

CEDEFOP (2008). *Skill Needs in Europe Focus on 2020*. Luxembourg: Office for Official Publications of the European Communities. <http://www.cedefop.europa.eu/EN/Files/5191_en.pdf> accessed 27 February 2013.

Choudaha, R. (2012). 'The Rise of "Glocal" Students and Transnational Education', *The Guardian*, 21 June.

Clarke, M. (2007). 'The Impact of Higher Education Rankings on Student Access, Choice, and Opportunity', *College and University Ranking Systems – Global Perspectives American Challenges*, Washington, DC: Institute of Higher Education Policy.

Currie, D. (2009a). 'Funding on "Sherriff of Nottingham" Model Would Cut Productivity', Correspondence, *Nature*, 461 (1198), 29 October. <http://www.nature.com/nature/journal/v461/n7268/full/4611198b.html> accessed 27 February 2013.

Currie, D. (2009b). 'The Wrong Way to Fund University Research', *University Affairs*, 7 December. <http://www.universityaffairs.ca/the-wrong-way-to-fund-university-research.aspx> accessed on 27 February 2013.

Dill, D., and Beerkens, M. (2010). 'Reflections and conclusions'. In D. Dill and M. Beerkens (eds), *Public Policy for Academic Quality. Analyses of Innovative Policy Instruments*, pp. 313–335. Dordrecht: Springer.

DiMaggio, P.J., and Powell, W. (1991). 'Introduction'. In Powell, W. and DiMaggio, P.J. (eds), *The New Institutionalism in Organization Analysis*, pp. 1–38. Chicago: University of Chicago Press.

DoF – Department of Finance (2009). *Special Group on Public Service Numbers and Expenditure Programmes*, Dublin: Government of Ireland. *<www.finance.gov.ie/viewdoc.asp?DocID=5861>* accessed 18 February 2011.

Douthat, R. (2005). 'Does Meritocracy Work?', *The Atlantic Monthly*, November. <https://facultystaff.richmond.edu/~Bmayes/Pdf/Meritocracy_Bestclass$Buy_AM.Pdf> accessed 27 February 2013.

Ehrenberg, R. (2012). 'American Higher Education in Transition', *Journal of Economic Perspectives*, 26 (1), 193–216.

Eurobarometer (2006). *Europeans and Mobility: First Results of an EU-wide Survey on Geographic and Labour Market Mobility*. <http://ec.europa.eu/employment_social/workersmobility_2006/uploaded_files/documents/FIRST per cent20RESULTS_Web per cent20version_06.02.06.pdf> accessed 27 February 2013.

European Commission (2009). *Europe's Regional Research Systems: Current Trends and Structures*. <http://ec.europa.eu/invest-in-research/pdf/download_en/kf2008.pdf> accessed 27 February 2013.

European Commission (2010). *Assessing Europe's University Based Research*, Expert Group on the Assessment of University-based Research. Brussels. <http://ec.europa.eu/research/science-society/document_library/pdf_06/assessing-europe-university-based-research_en.pdf> accessed 4 April 2010.

European Commission (2011a). 'Supporting Growth and Jobs – an Agenda for the Modernisation of Europe's Higher Education System', *COM* 567(2). <http://ec.europa.eu/education/higher-education/doc/com0911_en.pdf> accessed on 27 February 2013.

European Commission (2011b). *Innovation Union Competitive Report*. http://ec.europa.eu/research/innovation-union/index_en.cfm?section=competitiveness-report&year=2011> accessed 27 February 2013.

European Commission (2012). *Guide to Research and Innovation Strategies for Smart Specialisation (RIS 3)*. <http://s3platform.jrc.ec.europa.eu/en/c/document_library/get_file?uuid=e50397e3-f2b1-4086-8608-7b86e69e8553&groupId=10157> accessed 27 February 2013.

Evidence Ltd. (2003). *Funding Research Diversity*. London: Universities UK.

Florida, R. (2002). *The Rise of the Creative Class: and How It's Transforming Work, Leisure, Community and Everyday Life*. New York: Basic Books.

Forfás (2011). *Report of the Research Prioritisation Steering Group*. Dublin: Forfás and Department of Jobs, Enterprise and Innovation.

Forfás (nd). *Sharing Our Future: Ireland 2025*. Dublin: Forfás. <http://www.forfas.ie/media/forfas090713_sharing_our_future.pdf> accessed 28 February 2013.

Freid, L. (2005). *Reputation and Prestige in American Research Universities: An Exploration of the History of Rankings and the Increasing Importance of Student Selectivity in Perceptions of Quality in Higher Education*. Dissertation in Higher Education Management. University of Pennsylvania.

Gidley, J.M. (2012). 'Re-imagining the Role and Function of Higher Education for Alternative Futures through Embracing Global Knowledge Futures'. In P. Scott, A. Curaj, L. Vlăsceanu, and L Wilson (eds). *European Higher Education at the Crossroads: between the Bologna Process and National Reforms*, part 2, pp. 1019–1038. Dordrecht: Springer.

GoI (Government of Ireland). (2008). *Building Ireland's Smart Economy: A Framework for Sustainable Economic Renewal*, Executive Summary, <*www.taoiseach.gov.ie/eng/Building_Ireland's_Smart_Economy/Building_Ireland's_Smart_Economy_-_Executive_Summary.pdf*> accessed 15 May 2010.

Gumport, P.J. (2000). 'Learning Academic Labor'. In R. Kalleberg, F. Engelstad, G. Brochmann, A. Leira and L. Mjøset (eds), *Comparative Perspectives on Universities*, pp. 1–23. Stanford, Connecticut: JAI Press.

Gurria, A. (2010). 'Investing in the Future', remarks at the launch of the 2010 edition of *Education at a Glance*. <http://www.oecd.org/document/42/0,3746,en_21571361_44315115_45942378_1_1_1_1,00.html> accessed 27 February 2013.

Harman, G. (2011). 'Competitors of Rankings: New Directions in Quality Assurance and Accountability'. In Shin, J.C., Toutkoushian, R.K., and Teichler, U. (eds), *University Rankings: Theoretical Basis, Methodology and Impacts on Global Higher Education*, pp. 35–54. Dordrecht: Springer.

Harpur, J. (2010). *Innovation, Profit and the Common Good in Higher Education. The New Alchemy*. London: Palgrave Macmillan.

Hart Research Associates (2010). *Raising the Bar. Employers' Views on College Learning in the Wake of the Economic Downturn A Survey Among Employers Conducted on Behalf of the Association of American Colleges and Universities*. <http://www.aacu.org/leap/documents/2009_EmployerSurvey.pdf> accessed 27 February 2013.

Hazelkorn, E. (2009). 'Rankings and the Global "Battle for Talent"'. In R. Bhandari and S. Laughlin (eds), *Higher Education on the Move: New Developments in Global Mobility*, pp. 79–94. New York: Institute of International Education.

Hazelkorn, E. (2011). *Rankings and the Reshaping of Higher Education: The Battle for World Class Excellence*. Basingstoke: Palgrave Macmillan.

Hazelkorn, E. (2012). 'European "Transparency Instruments": Driving the Modernisation of European Higher Education'. In P. Scott, A. Curaj, L. Vlăsceanu and L. Wilson (eds), *European Higher Education at the Crossroads: between the Bologna Process and national reforms*, Volume 1, pp. 339–360. Dordrecht: Springer.

Hazelkorn, E. (2012). *Towards a Future Higher Education Landscape*. Dublin: Higher Education Authority. <http://www.hea.ie/files/TowardsaFutureHigherEducationLandscape.pdf> accessed 18 May 2013.

Hazelkorn, E. (2013). 'Has Higher Education Lost Control over Quality?' *Chronicle of Higher Education*, May 23 2013. <http://chronicle.com/blogs/worldwise/has-higher-education-lost-control-over-quality/32321> accessed 25 July 2013.

Hazelkorn, E., and Massaro, V. (2011). 'A Tale of Two Strategies for Higher Education and Economic Recovery: Ireland and Australia', *Higher Education Management and Policy*, 23 (2), 1–24.

Hazelkorn, E., and Ryan, M. (2013). 'The Impact of University Rankings on Higher Education Policy in Europe: a Challenge to Perceived Wisdom and a Stimulus for Change'. In P. Zgaga, U. Teichler and J. Brennan (eds), *The Globalization Challenge for European Higher Education: Convergence and Diversity, Centres and Peripheries*, pp. 79–100. Bern: Peter Lang.

HEA (2011). *Sustainability Study: Aligning Participation, Quality and Funding in Irish Higher Education*. Report to the Minister for Education and Skills from the Executive of the HEA. Dublin: Higher Education Authority. <http://www.hea.ie/files/files/file/News/SustainabilityReport.pdf> accessed 27 February 2013.

Hoover, E. (2010). 'Application Inflation', *Chronicle of Higher Education*, 5 November. <http://chronicle.com/article/Application-Inflation/125277/?sid=at&utm_source> accessed 27 February 2013.

Horizon 2020. <http://ec.europa.eu/research/horizon2020/index_en.cfm?pg=h2020> accessed 19 May 2013.

Hossler, D.J., Braxton, J., Coopersmith, G. (1989). 'Understanding Student College Choice'. In J.C. Smart (ed.), *Higher Education: Handbook of Theory and Research*, 5, pp. 234–248. New York: Agathon Press.

IMF (2009). *Country Report No. 09/195*, June. <http://www.imf.org/EXTERNAL/PUBS/FT/SCR/2009/CR09195.PDF> accessed 27 February 2013.

Inglesi-Lotz, R., and Pouris, A. (2012). 'The Influence of Scientific Research Output of Academics on Economic Growth in South Africa: an Autoregressive Distributed Lag (ARDL) Application', *Scientometrics*. 95 (1), 129–139.

Innovation Taskforce (2010). *Innovation Ireland. Report of the Innovation Taskforce.* Dublin: Government of Ireland. <*www.taoiseach.gov.ie/eng/Innovation_Taskforce/Report_of_the_Innovation_Taskforce.pdf*> accessed 13 June 2010.

Jongbloed, B. (2004). 'Funding Higher Education: Options, Trade-offs and Dilemmas', *Fulbright Brainstorms 2004 – New Trends in Higher Education.* University of Twente, Netherlands: Center for Higher Education Policy Studies (CHEPS). <http://doc.utwente.nl/56075/1/engpap04fundinghe.pdf> accessed 27 February 2013.

Kapur, D., and McHale, J. (2005). *Give Us Your Best and Brightest: The Global Hunt for Talent and Its Impact on the Developing World, Center for Global Development.* Washington DC: Center for Global Development.

Kelderman, E. (2013). 'Obama's Accreditation Proposals Surprise Higher-Education Leaders', *Chronicle of Higher Education*, 13 February. <http://chronicle.com/article/Obamas-Accreditation/137311/?cid=at&utm_source=at&utm_medium=en> accessed 27 February 2013.

Kelly, U., McLellon, D., and McNicoll, L. (2009). *The Impact of the Universities on the UK Economy. Fourth Report*. London: Universities UK.

Knobel, M. (2011). 'Internationalizing Brazil's Universities: Creating Coherent National Policies Must be a Priority', *Research & Occasional Paper Series.* Berkeley: University of California. http://cshe.berkeley.edu/publications/publications.php?id=386 accessed 25 July 2013.

Koreabang (2012). 'Political Party Proposes to Abolish Top Korean University'. July 12. <http://www.koreabang.com/2012/stories/political-party-proposes-to-abolish-top-korean-university.html > accessed 27 February 2013.

Lambert Review (2003). *Lambert Review of Business-University Collaboration.* London: HMSO. <http://www.hm-treasury.gov.uk/d/lambert_review_final_450.pdf> accessed 27 February 2013.

Lindsey, C.N (1996). 'Statement by HEA': *A Comparative International Assessment of the Organisation, Management and Funding of University Research in Ireland.* Report of the CIRCA Group Europe for the Higher Education Authority. Dublin: HEA.

Lisbon European Council (2000). 'Presidency Conclusions'. <http://www.europarl.europa.eu/summits/lis1_en.htm> accessed 27 February 2013.

Lucido, J., and Thacker, L. (2011). *The Case for Change in College Admissions.* <http://www.usc.edu/programs/cerpp/docs/CERPP_ConferenceReport_FINALforprint.pdf> accessed 27 February 2013.

Maassen, P., and Stensaker, B.(2011). 'The Knowledge Triangle, European Higher Education Policy Logics and Policy Implications', *Higher Education*, 61 (6), 757–769.

Mah, C.L. (2008). 'What's Public? What's Private? Policy Trade-offs and the Debate over Mandatory Annual Influenza Vaccination for Health Care Workers', *Canadian Journal of Public Health*, May–June 2008, 192–194.

Marcus, J. (2008). 'The State of the Union', *Times Higher Education*, 3 July.

Marginson, S. (2006). 'Dynamics of National and Global Competition in Higher Education', *Higher Education*, 52 (1), 1–39.

Marginson, S., and Rhoades, G. (2002). 'Beyond National states, Markets, and Systems of Higher Education: a Glonacal Agency Heuristic'. *Higher Education*, 43 (3), 281–309.

Marginson, S., and van der Wende, M. (2007). *Globalisation and Higher Education*. OECD Education Working Papers 8. Paris: OECD.

Marx, K. (1963) *The Eighteenth Brumaire of Louis Bonaparte* (1852). New York: International Publishers.

Massaro, V. (2013). 'TEQSA and the Holy Grail of Outcomes-based Quality Assessment' in S. Marginson (ed.), *Tertiary Education Policy in Australia*, Centre for Study of Higher Education, University of Melbourne. pp 49–58. <http://www.cshe.unimelb.edu.au/research/policy_dev/docs/Tert_Edu_Policy_Aus.pdf> accessed 25 July 2013.

McCoy, S., Calvert, E., Smyth, E., and Darmody, M. (2009). *Study on the Costs of Participation in Higher Education.* Dublin: HEA. <http://www.hea.ie/files/files/file/Costs_Participation_HE.pdf> accessed 27 February 2013.

McGuinness, S., Bergin, A., Kelly, E., McCoy, S., Smyth, E. and Timoney, K. (2012). *A Study of Future Demand for Higher Education in Ireland. Pre-publication Version. Report to the Higher Education Authority: 15th November, 2012.* <https://share.hea.ie/Extranet/landscape-submissions/a-study-of-future-demand-for-higher-education-in-ireland/view> accessed 11 March 2013.

Mohrman, K., Ma, W., and Baker, D. (2008 'The Research University in Transition: The Emerging Global Model', *Higher Education Policy*, 21 (1), 5–27.

Moodie, G. (2009). Private Correspondence with author, 7 June.

Murphy, M. (2011). 'Government Must Stop Micromanaging Universities', Address to Cork Chamber of Commerce. <http://www.ucc.ie/en/news/fullstory-144045-en.html> accessed 27 February 2013.

Musselin, C. (2011). 'Convergences and Divergences in Steering Higher Education Systems'. In R. King, S. Marginson, and R. Naidoo, R. (eds). *Handbook on Globalization and Higher Education*, pp. 454–468. Cheltenham: Edward Elgar.

Myklebust, J.P. (2012). 'ERC defends Concentration of Grants in Top Research Universities', *University World News*, 11 March 2012, p. 212. <http://www.universityworldnews.com/article.php?story=20120308181711918> accessed 28 February 2013.

NDP (2007). *National Development Plan 2007–2013*. Dublin: Stationary Office. <http://www2.ul.ie/pdf/932500843.pdf> accessed 27 February 2013.

OECD (2009). *Education at a Glance*. Paris: OECD. <http://www.oecd-ilibrary.org/education/education-at-a-glance_19991487> accessed 27 February 2013.

OECD (2011). *OECD Science, Technology and Industry Scoreboard 2011*. Paris: OECD. <http://www.oecd-ilibrary.org/docserver/download/9211041ec004.pdf?expires=1368968018&id=id&accname=guest&checksum=634984 24A802A64C0604CE092439665C> accessed 19 May 2013.

OECD (2012a). *Main Science and Technology Indicators: Volume 2012/1*. Paris: OECD. <http://www.oecd.org/sti/sci-tech/keyFigures_20112_1_EN.pdf> accessed 17 May 2013.

OECD (2012b). *Science and Technology Indicators*. Paris: OECD. <http://www.oecd.org/document/26/0,3746,en_2649_34451_1901082_1_1_1_1,00.html> accessed 27 February 2013.

OECD (2012c). *Education at a Glance*. Paris: OECD. <http://www.oecd.org/edu/EAG per cent202012_e-book_EN_200912.pdf> accessed 17 May 2013.

OECD (2013). *Higher Education in Regional and City Development*. Paris: OECD. <http://www.oecd-ilibrary.org/education/higher-education-in-regional-and-city-development_22183140> accessed 18 February 2013.

Pruvot, E.B. (2012). 'The Impact of the Economic Crisis on Higher Education in Europe', *Presentation to EUA Funding Forum*, 11–12 June, Salzburg. <http://www.eua.be/Libraries/Funding_Forum/EconMonitoringPresentation.sflb.ashx> accessed 27 February 2013.

QQI – Quality and Qualifications Ireland. <http://www.qqi.ie/Pages/default.aspx> accessed 19 May 2013.

Quinn, R., Minister for Education and Skills (2012). Parliamentary Questions <http://debates.oireachtas.ie/dail/2012/04/26/00082.asp> accessed 25 July 2013.

Rauhvargers, A. (2011). *Global University Rankings and their Impact*, Brussels: European University Association. <http://www.eua.be/pubs/Global_University_Rankings_and_Their_Impact.pdf> accessed 18 February 2013.

Robertson, D. (1998). 'The Emerging Political Economy of Higher Education', *Studies in Higher Education*, 23 (2) 221–228.

RSG – Report of Strategy Group (2011). *National Strategy for Higher Education to 2030 – Report of the Strategy Group*. Dublin: Department of Education and Skills.

Rüdiger, K. (2008). *Towards a Global Labour Market? Globalisation and the Knowledge Economy*. London: The Work Foundation. <http://www.workfoundation.com/assets/docs/publications/30_globalisation.pdf> accessed 27 February 2013.

Sadlak, J., and N.C. Liu (eds). (2007). *The World-Class University and Ranking: Aiming Beyond Status*. Bucharest: Cluj University Press.

Salmi, J. (2009). *The Challenge of Establishing World Class Universities. Directions in Human Development.* Washington D.C.: The World Bank.

Sassen, S. (2011). 'A Savage Sorting of Winners and Losers, and Beyond'. In C. Calhoun and G. Derluguian (eds), *Aftermath. A New Global Economic Order?* pp. 21–39. New York and London: New York University Press.

Simões, C, and Soares, A.M. (2010). 'Applying to Higher Education: Information Sources and Choice Factors', *Studies in Higher Education*, 35 (4), 371–389.

TEQSA – Tertiary Education Quality and Standards Agency. <http://www.teqsa.gov.au/> accessed 27 February 2013.

Torres, C.A. and Schugurensky, D. (2002). 'The Political Economy of Higher Education in the Era of Neoliberal Globalization: Latin America in Comparative Perspective'. *Higher Education*, 43 (4), 429–455.

Trading Economics (2013). 'Irish GDP Growth'. <http://www.tradingeconomics.com/ireland/gdp-growth> accessed 27 February 2013.

Trow, M. (1974). 'Problems of the Transition from Elite to Mass Higher Education', reprinted in M. Burrage (ed.), *Martin Trow: Twentieth-Century Higher Education: From Elite to Mass to Universal*, pp. 556–610. Baltimore: Johns Hopkins University Press.

UNESCO (2009). *Global Education Digest 2009*. <http://www.uis.unesco.org/Library/Documents/ged09-en.pdf> accessed 27 February 2013.

UNESCO (2010). *UNESCO Science Report 2010*. <http://unesdoc.unesco.org/images/0018/001899/189958e.pdf> accessed 27 February 2013.

UNESCO (2011). *Global Investments in R&D*. <http://www.uis.unesco.org/FactSheets/Documents/fs15_2011-investments-en.pdf> accessed 27 February 2013.

United Nations (2011). *World Economic Situation and Prospects 2012 Global Economic Outlook* <http://www.un.org/en/development/desa/policy/wesp/wesp_current/2012wesp_prerel.pdf> accessed 11 February 2013.

Usher, A. (2006). 'Can Our Schools Become World-Class?', *The Globe and Mail*, 30 October. <http://www.theglobeandmail.com/servlet/story/RTGAM.20061030.URCworldclassp28/BNStory/univreport06/home> accessed 11 October 2009.

van Damme, D. (2009). 'What have we learned? What to do now? What to do next?'. <www.oecd.org/edu/imhe/43325400.ppt> accessed 18 May 2013.

Varghese, N.V. (2010). *Running to Stand Still. Higher Education in a Period of Global Crisis.* Paris: UNESCO. <http://www.iiep.unesco.org/information-services/publications/abstracts/2010/running-to-stand-still.html> accessed 27 February 2013.

Walsh, J. (2011). 'A Quiet Revolution: International Influence, Domestic Elites and the Transformation of Higher Technical Education in Ireland 1959–1972'. *Irish Educational Studies*, 30 (3), 365–381.

Weigel, M. (2013). 'MOOCs and Online Learning: Research roundup', *Journalists Resource*. <http://journalistsresource.org/studies/society/education/moocs-online-learning-research-roundup#> accessed 19 May 2013.

Wildavsky, B. (2010). *The Great Brain Race. How Global Universities are Reshaping the World.* New Jersey: Princeton University Press.

Xu, D. and Jaggars, S.S. (2013). *Adaptability to Online Learning: Differences Across Types of Students and Academic Subject Areas, CCRC Working Paper No. 54.* New York: New York Community College Research Center, Teachers College, Columbia University.

JOUNI KEKÄLE

# 4 Megatrends Affecting Resilient Universities in Europe

## On the Changing Operational Environment of Higher Education

It can be claimed that the operational environment for universities in Europe is fundamentally changing. In this chapter, I shall provide statistics on some key trends affecting the financial base of society and publicly funded higher education. We shall consider especially potential student intake and enrolment; societal and student expectations of higher education; and the new possibilities these changes bring with them. The examples to be used are taken from the situation in the European higher education sector in 2012/2013.

First there are major changes in demography: the proportion of young age groups entering the age of university enrolment is diminishing while the older age groups are set to increase and will constitute a larger part of the age pyramid in relative terms. Secondly, the EU is going through an economic crisis which is by no means over yet. It is likely that private and corporate investments remain to be targeted on the growing markets of the world where capital appreciation and economic profits are likely to be higher than elsewhere, and that public budgets and university *basic funding* (which is allocated through national funding mechanisms, and not targeted on specific areas beforehand) will diminish or stagnate in Europe due to recession and increased public debt for years to come. Thirdly, there are growing educational markets in China and the so-called Third World, whereas in the old Europe the demand for education will not necessarily increase in a similar manner – unless of course more effort is made to find growing market segments. Fourthly, the new educational technology – eLearning, web-teaching – appears to challenge and add to traditional forms of instruction. And finally, it appears that the expectations of higher education by new student populations and society at large are changing in a post-modern western culture which is characterized by hastiness and shortened time-spans in decision making, business and politics.

Why are these trends fundamental to higher education institutions in Europe? Roughly 70 per cent of funding for universities in the European Union (EU) comes from the government which clearly remains the main source of income (de Dominicis et al., 2011). Fundamental changes – such as the Euro crisis – that alter society's ability to fund higher education are bound to affect the sector. By late 2011, most EU member states had announced budget cuts in higher education (HE), while France and Germany had decided to invest in HE and the Nordic countries remained – at the system level at least – relatively unaffected (Hoareau, 2011). Also rising public expenses due to changing demographics affected the public economy's capacity to fund educational systems.

The ability to attract students is vital for higher education institutions, as education basically exists because of the students. Decreasing student populations increase competition for talented students and exert pressure for structural reforms in higher education in many countries. The majority of countries in Europe use funding allocation formulas in which student enrolment and degrees are a major component – even *the* major component – which fundamentally affects the income of higher education institutions (HEIs) (Jongbloed, 2010). This also applies to income streams through tuition fees. The students are increasingly 'paying customers'; therefore their changing expectations and cultures are a driver for change in ever increasing institutional competition for students and funding. Developments in the economy and in student populations also foster a shift of emphasis towards growing education markets in the developing countries, and stress the importance of new teaching technologies that enable distance learning.

The time horizon for the megatrends to be discussed will be decades. The trends generally push in the same direction: to increase efficiency, short term relevance and quality; and to seek new customers and sources of income. Such trends are connected to fundamental structural phenomena and cannot be altered simply by changing rhetoric– although the way we speak and construct our daily social realities can have an impact on the economy. It can even be maintained that the era of 'distribution politics' – during which higher education and other public services enjoyed ever increasing public funding –has in most European countries changed for the foreseeable future into an era of tight government budgets and increasing accountability. Certainly the pressure for change is there and the trends to be discussed underline this. We are facing severe structural problems: excessively high public debts and a weak competitive edge in many European industries. The growing economies and markets have shifted to developing countries, whereas in the mature economies expenses and sovereign debts are rising and income streams are weakening.

Frank and Gabler (2006) claim that the university is definitionally an organization committed to mapping reality. The apparently increasing superficialization, overflow of information and commercialism all add to the challenges to higher education institutions, which once built their operations around long term, if not eternal, truths and slow accumulation of knowledge. Today, universities are expected to innovate and to produce tangible results in terms of fostering economic growth, student employment, business opportunities and solutions to ecological problems. Simple and quick solutions are often expected, but universities tend to provide complex, long term answers. As Clark (1998) notes, there is a widening asymmetry between societal demands and institutional capacity to respond. Many scholars feel that the very nature of academic work is changing.

By megatrend is meant major change in social, economic, political, environmental or technological conditions that develop gradually but whose influence, once established, may last for decades. Megatrends tend to be international in nature and have a broad influence on several areas of life, including higher education (Möller, 2012; Naisbitt, 1982). In this chapter I shall discuss some 'megatrends' which are bound to make an impact on the HE sector. As noted, these have to do especially with population changes, new technology, declining economy and the changing youth cultures. Other megatrends can also be identified such as for example climate change, increasing potential for conflict, cyber attacks, regional instability and the changing world order (by 2050 China will enjoy greater purchasing power parity than the US power).[1] While these trends are bound to affect society, their impact especially on HEI working conditions can be difficult to predict and indirect in nature, unlike the trends to be discussed here which, when combined, can directly challenge the existing order of things. In part the trends are emergent: for example, it appears that we are generally moving towards diminishing student populations which appear to be a counterbalancing trend to the previous massification of higher education.

The megatrends to be discussed are connected to the current development of the global market economy and welfare state. It appears that the funding of the public sector and allocation of *basic funding* in the higher education sector are facing a new critical period. In the 1990s output/performance-related criteria played an important role in the funding mechanisms for higher education institutions in some European countries (Denmark, Poland, Netherlands, Germany, Sweden and the UK), and there are currently almost twenty countries in the EU where elements of output and performance are driving the HE institutions' budgets (Jongbloed, 2010).

In what follows we shall scrutinize the abovementioned megatrends in more detail and after that discuss how to find ways forward. During the discussion it will become clear that although some general European level drivers of change can be identified on the basis of reliable data, the impact may be country-specific. Norway is an example of a country which has greater freedom to resist many of these changes if politicians so decide, due to its increasing young population, its own currency and oil incomes. However, fierce global competition in business and in labour markets maintain the pressure for quality, innovation and relevance everywhere.

1 See <http://www.businessinsider.com/megatrends-the-6-gamechangers-that-will-change-the-world-in-the-next-decades-2012-12?op=1>.

## Demographic Changes

### *Diminishing Student Generations*

Demographic changes in the group entering the university age (eighteen to twenty-five years old) from the year 2010 to 2025 will significantly affect higher education in many European countries. The age cohorts approaching university enrolment are foreseen to diminish in most European countries (see Modernisation of Higher Education in Europe, *Funding and the Social Dimension*, 2011: 34).

These countries include Spain, Greece and Italy, and especially many post-Soviet countries such as Bulgaria, Czech Republic, Estonia, Latvia, Poland, Romania and Slovakia. Only a few countries such as Denmark, the Netherlands, Sweden, Norway and the UK seem to escape this trend.

After the era of massification of higher education there seem to be new changes on their way. The large post-war generation is retiring and the number of people reaching university enrolment age is considerably smaller than the university systems' educational capacity. Because of this, for example the Finnish Ministry of Education has decided by 2020 to reduce significantly the number of higher education institutions. It is always possible to receive students from other countries (UN 2001). However, as far as total population goes, UN and OECD scenarios would seem to indicate that while the EU net immigration has been 1.5–2 million per year since 2003 (which would be enough to keep the EU population constant), there has been a drop of 6 per cent in net immigration in 2011, and youth is escaping especially from the countries which are suffering most from economic crisis. Spain is the only European country to exhibit a continuous decrease in participation rates in higher education throughout the first decade of the new millennium (EHEA, 2012).

At present the overall picture of HE student immigration from outside the European Higher Education Area (EHEA) seems to be that the following four countries – the United Kingdom, France, Russia and Germany – attract 76 per cent of all students (ibid.). Only four countries, namely

Cyprus, the United Kingdom, France and Ireland, have more than 5 per cent of their own students enrolling for tertiary education outside the EHEA: 'These countries thus seem to be the most attractive countries for students coming from outside the EHEA. At the other end of the spectrum, 16 countries have less than 1 per cent of students enrolling for tertiary education outside the EHEA. The weighted average of all countries is 2.25 %' (EHEA, 2012: 154). As this clearly is not enough, in order to promote international student mobility to European HE, a target that 20 per cent of graduated students should be from abroad has been set within the EU.

All these figures in the Bologna Process Follow-up Report (EHEA, 2012) are related only to degree mobility, and statistical information on credit mobility still has to be taken into consideration when assessing progress towards the 20 per cent benchmark. Estimations based on the Erasmus programme would point to a 7 per cent rate by 2020 (EHEA, 2012: 173). Changes in the student population depend on many factors, but demography is not necessarily the only factor determining the demand for higher education. In Canada, for example, it is rather the demand for a highly skilled and educated labour force that has been a principal driver in the growth of university participation rates: 'To respond to the anticipated economic, social and labour market demands resulting from the demographic shift, universities will need to both expand access to higher education for untapped segments of the population and international students, and increase the quality of education students receive' (Trends in Higher Education, 2011: 5). Similarly in the EU, Commissioner Vassiliou (2011) notes that at the same time as young age groups are diminishing, changing European labour markets increasingly require more graduates: 'Demands are increasing, public funding is diminishing, and indeed the data shows that these trends were underway even before the impact of the global financial and economic crisis'. Vassiliou (2012) elsewhere points out that stimulation of mobility, improvement of quality, broadening of participation and benefiting the economy are crucial steps forward for European higher education.

It appears that the potentially diminishing level of public funding to be discussed in the next two sections may affect higher education in many countries more than the diminishing student populations. For example in

England, according to one estimation (Coleman and Bekhradnia, 2011), the changing social mix of the population, a growing middle class, together with greater fertility among the more affluent social groups will lead to greater demand for higher education than there would otherwise be – even if the total population declines. However, due to tight finances, the British government announced a cut of 10,000 entrant places in 2012 and the number of PhD students funded will also drop almost 20 per cent by 2014 in Britain. Coleman and Bekhradnia (2011) note that with the current policy there may be nearly as many as 100,000 disappointed applicants in 2020, but somewhat cynically they conclude that the most likely response of the government will be to seek ways of enabling additional student numbers without any increase in total cost of the education itself.

### *An Ageing European Population*

Another trend affecting public economy is ageing of the population. The diminishing funding base (increasing public health care costs and decreasing tax revenues) is likely to have consequences for higher education. Yet at the same time new age groups will have free time and may be willing to study on the basis of lifelong learning which may increase demand for higher education. According to the Finnish Ministry of Education Development Plan 2007–2012 (MoE, 2007), demographic change will be a significant challenge in developing the education system during the forthcoming years. At the same time, the number of retired people will continue to increase so that the number of sixty-five-year-olds will be 1.56 times higher in 2020 than in 2007. Since 2005, there have been more people leaving labour markets than joining them.

In a somewhat similar vein, the European Commission has performed a forecasting analysis of development for the twenty-seven EU countries between 2010 and 2060. Their finding is broadly: increase for the population as a whole; rise in the age and fall in the numbers of workers; and rise in the 'grey' population:

> According to the convergence scenario of EUROPOP2010, the EU-27's population is projected to increase to 525 million by 2035, peaking at 526 million around 2040, and thereafter gradually declining to 517 million by 2060. During the same period, the median age of the EU-27's population is projected to rise to 47.6 years. The population of working age is expected to decline steadily, while older persons will likely account for an increasing share of the total population – those aged 65 years or over will account for 29.5% of the EU-27s population by 2060 (17.4% in 2010). (Eurostat, 2011)

If tax incomes, productivity, or the total number of working years among the population are decreasing, the development is likely to destabilize the financial base of society, to put strain on public finances, and to reduce tax revenues. The increased expenditure in pensions and health care seems inevitable as well. This, in turn, is bound to affect all institutions dependent on public funding, including universities.

### *The Changing Economy: The Euro Crisis and its Impact on the HE Sector*

Europe is facing demographic changes in parallel with the global financial and subsequent Euro crisis. These two forces interfere with and affect the funding base of the public sector as a whole, which is likely to affect higher education as a publicly funded operation. The global financial crisis kicked off when the housing bubble in the USA burst in 2007, affecting Europe as well. Causes of the Euro crisis vary by country. In several of them, private debts arising from a property bubble were transferred to sovereign debt as a result of banking system bailouts and government responses to slowing economies. Many banks were considered too big to fail – the consequences for the general public and economy would have been severe. In Greece, unsustainable public sector wage and pension commitments and lack of tax revenues drove the debt increase.

All in all, excessively loose loans and spending, and lack of liability and regulation can be seen as some of the factors causing the financial crisis. Sinn (2010) argues that investment bankers basically gambled with the general public's money, lost almost everything, and left the debt with the government. The world financial system nearly collapsed. Since banks were only liable for a fraction of the capital they were holding, an environment was created which rationalized risk-taking strategies by privatizing profits and socializing losses. In May 2012 the total costs for taxpayers accruing from the Euro crisis were estimated to be 225 billion Euros (Eving, 2012: 1), but the extended crisis and bailout strategies such as the European Stability Mechanism and the conditional promises by the European Central Bank to buy bonds from aftermarkets without limits (if the country in question agrees to obey the conditions agreed upon and to meet the savings required) are bound to raise the public costs further.

In October 2012 German Finance Minister Wolfgang Schäuble proclaimed that whilst most crisis-hit Euro zone countries had made progress on economic reforms, Greece had not. Greece was suffering from burden of public savings and severe recession for the sixth consecutive year (Ebeling, 2012). The Euro zone as a whole has not recovered from the 2008 blow; only Germany has been able to foster economic growth above the year 2008 level. The EU has agreed that public debts should be no more than 60 per cent of the GDP per each country. The average, however, was around 90 in early 2013. At the time of writing new EU-level support and funding packages were needed for countries in crisis. The structural problems remain severe: too high debts; high unemployment rates (around 26 per cent in Greece and in Spain in December 2012); and an industrial structure which does not provide enough income and jobs so that the countries in crisis will be able to solve their financial problems on their own.

What does the Euro crisis mean to the European university sector? The European University Association (EUA, 2011) estimated a year ago that European higher education systems have been affected by the crisis very differently according to their respective national economies. Some countries, such as Norway and France where the young age cohorts are not expected to diminish (ibid., section 2), had benefited from stimulus packages provided by their governments at the beginning of the crisis. Furthermore, there were areas where the university sector had foreseen the impact of the crisis as early as the beginning of 2009 while others were affected only later; a few isolated cases have experienced little direct impact so far: 'The economic crisis has left few higher education systems unaffected. While institutions in most countries still report being faced with uncertainty and expect further – and possibly deeper – cuts to come in the forthcoming months and years, in some countries, such as the United Kingdom, cuts are likely to have a significant restructuring effect on higher education' (EUA, 2011). Another more recent report concludes: 'While all higher education institutions are funded primarily from public sources in some countries, there are a larger proportion of private institutions in others. In addition, levels of public expenditure also vary within the EHEA; the result of the crisis has been an overall decline in public higher education expenditure' (EHEA, 2012).

Altbach et al. (2009) have forecasted that research universities are likely to see significant constraints on their budgets as governments will be unable to provide the resources needed for their continued improvement. In many cases, the priority will be to allocate funds to ensure that access to the higher education system is not dramatically cut. This is in line with the political aims of the European Commission as voiced by Commissioner Vassiliou (2011, 2012, section 2): providing skilled labor force is the first priority, tightly connected to the relevance, innovation and application needed to foster economic growth in the diminishing European economies. European governments are faced with conflicting priorities such as increasing access on the one hand and maintaining the quality of the higher education system on the other with less money (EUA, 2011). As the costs and wages per student tend to rise, governments in the western world seem to become globally unable to maintain their share of the rising costs of higher education, which have been in many countries, especially in England and Northern America, assigned to families or students in the form of tuition fees (Johnstone, 2009).

Another more thematic transformation seems to be going on. The recent EU budget proposal (if it is approved) forecasts *an increase* in research and innovation budgets under Horizon 2020 – at the same time as the total budget for EU would be diminishing. However, the increased funds would be targeted only to specific, top-level and highly relevant areas of research and innovative industry. The universities need to apply and compete for this funding. There are no direct consequences for basic funding as such, but the tight national HE-budgets are likely to remain. It is also possible that this funding is a part of a political steering mechanism, which – accompanied by the tight or diminishing national basic funding for universities – steers the HE sector towards increasing short term relevance in research.

Running from 2014 to 2020, the Horizon 2020 with the additional funds will be targeted at:

- Top-level research in Europe, including an increase in European Research Council (ERC) (€24,598 million).[2]
- Strengthening industrial leadership in innovation. 'This includes major investment in key technologies, greater access to capital and support for SMEs' (€17,938 million).
- Additional funds 'to help address major concerns shared by all Europeans such as climate change, developing sustainable transport and mobility, making renewable energy more affordable, ensuring food safety and security, or coping with the challenge of an ageing population' (€31,748 million).

## The Changing Educational Markets and How to Reach Them

The global education sector is the second-largest area of industry after healthcare (EIE, 2011). While the population in western countries is highly educated, the educational index remains fairly low in many developing countries (see for example <http://en.wikipedia.org/wiki/Education_Index>). In Europe and in the western world, the threat of funding cuts has driven some universities, for example those in in Scotland and England, to seek new income streams by opening or strengthening activities in existing campuses abroad, as part of a strategy to attract more international graduates (European University Association, 2011); eLearning is another solution in reaching new educational markets. The eLearning sector appears

2 See <http://ec.europa.eu/research/horizon2020/index_en.cfm?pg=h2020>.

to growing especially in Asia, Eastern Europe, Africa and Latin America where the growth rate is estimated to be around 16 per cent between 2011 and 2016. In North America and Western Europe the growth rate is estimated to remain around 4–6 per cent (<http://www.ambientinsight.com/Reports/eLearning.aspx>).

Worldwide, the e-education market is a segment with high growth potential. In 2007–2008, the US constituted 60 per cent of the global market and Europe accounted for 15 per cent. The higher education sector has grown from 101 million students in 2000 to 153 million students in 2007 (EIE, 2011). Bates (2010) notes that the demand for online learning exists and is likely to grow, while at the same time campus-based enrolments are likely to decline over the next few years, due to demographics. The two most popular online Master's subjects have been business and education (Bates, 2010). In addition, as already noted, there are untapped segments of the population, which are interested in access to higher education. Finally it can be noted that the funding of education – whatever form and media we might want to choose – remains the crucial issue. Economists often define demand as desire + ability to pay + will to pay. Without a mechanism to fund education the institutions cannot pay salaries and rents needed for the operation.

## Changes in Student and Youth Culture

It is often held that students demand from their studies sound preparation for the labour market. In a secularized world living in short term quartile economy there seems to be a growing need for 'skills' which can be applied in labour markets, as opposed to broad socialization to western civilization. As a result, the orientation has tended to shift closer to participation in vocational training, as opposed to independent classical university studies. O'Neill (2007) maintains that students nowadays tend to see themselves as customers who view their grades not as reflections of their comparative performances but instead as commodities. These trends can be found in

Finnish student culture. Aittola's (1995) interviews with 204 Finnish university students demonstrate that the study years at the university are no longer a classically academic life stage. Instead students divide life between study and part-time employment. The student culture has lost its independence and vitality, and students' life-worlds have become fragmented, more egocentric and sports-oriented than in previous generations.

Changing labour markets, demography and the Euro crisis have forced the European Community to react. The EU Youth Strategy (2012) focuses primarily on non-formal learning as a complementary tool, aiming at acquiring the cross-cutting skills that are, according to the strategy, much appreciated in the labour market. The European Commission also presented a strategy for the modernization of Europe's higher education systems in 2011, and prepared an initiative on rethinking skills to support policy development on skills and competences. The Commission proposed a draft Council recommendation on the recognition and validation of non-formal and informal learning in 2012, and was also working on tools to make it easier to record the skills acquired through non-formal learning (EU Youth Strategy, 2012).

The number of candidates opting to study social sciences at English universities in 2011 dropped dramatically by 20 per cent compared with the previous academic year (Gardner, 2011). This can be explained on the basis of high fees (now up to £9,000 a year) and changed expectations among youth and society. A broad Finnish survey (EVA, 2010) demonstrates that attitudes towards work have changed: young people study as a means of getting work and earning money – which can then be used to do things that really interest them. Work is not a value in itself, as it used to be for the older generations. Students' expectations have changed, and increased the diversity of student cultures. The general trends discussed above would seem indicate that universities will have to compete harder in order to attract students, to retain them, and to provide them with teaching and programmes that they find relevant from the perspective of their 'life project'. The demonstration of quality in this respect may become even more crucial than it is today. Universities may face higher expectations on coaching, non-authoritarian leadership, the use of social media and 'eduintainment' mixing education and entertainment (Vesterinen and Suutarinen, 2011).

## Summary of the Trends and their Potential Consequences to Universities

Universities can be seen as open systems in which an institution receives students and funding from society and produces research, education and degrees in return. An open system can survive only through the kind of exchange which provides it with the resources it needs. Funding is especially vital: student enrolment and degree production are typically connected to funding. Based on the author's elaboration, the discussion of the megatrends and their impact on universities can be summarized in Table 4.1 as follows:

Table 4.1 Summary of the Megatrends' Estimated Influence on Higher Education Institutions and Potential Institutional Responses

| *Megatrends* | *Influence on Higher Education Institutions* | *Potential Institutional Responses* |
|---|---|---|
| Diminishing Student Generations | – Potentially decreasing enrolments<br>– Potentially diminishing income streams and/ or increasing costs per student<br>– Increasing competition for students<br>– Potential changes in system level, structural development | – Search for new educational markets<br>– New sources of financing<br>– Increasing tuition fees<br>– Downsizing |
| Ageing Europe | – Potentially diminishing public funding<br>– Potentially new markets for adult education | – Search for new educational markets, also in adult education<br>– New sources of financing<br>– Downsizing |

| | | |
|---|---|---|
| Economy: Euro Crisis, Recession | – Potentially diminishing public basic funding | – New sources of financing<br>– Concentration on strongest areas<br>– Downsizing<br>– Increase relevance from the funders' point of view |
| The Changing Educational Markets | – Fosters the use eLearning and advanced educational technology<br>– Opens new possibilities and educational markets | – The use of eLearning technology<br>– International marketing and recruitment |
| Changes in Student and Youth Culture | – Potentially more demands and requirements on relevance and employability | – Enhancement of quality and relevance in education |

The megatrends which are summarized in this table have implications for – or effects on – both structural and process aspects of university governance. However, they leave rather open-ended questions about what HEIs can do to adapt to or benefit from these drivers. This depends, among other things, on local institutional and cultural features and upon the strategic choices that the university in question is willing to make. The next section will address some of the options which are available to European universities.

## What the Universities Need to Do

If public basic funding and/or the traditional supply for students are diminishing, universities as publicly funded open organizations face the pressure either to downsize their operations or to find additional or complementary sources of funding and paying students.

Although the pressure for change is coming from different sources, there is a strong tendency within universities to try to avoid or ignore such pressures. Barnett (2011) maintains that the fullest expression of the university's possibilities lies in a reclamation of the universal aspirations that lay in earlier ideas of the university, not in the entrepreneurial models; Hautamäki and Ståhle (2012) argue that universities must not be forced to follow market logic nor short term economic calculations. My own line of argumentation intends to be realistic and descriptive, not political: universities, like any modern organization, need money for salaries and facilities in order to operate and to survive. In national basic funding models, funding is connected to students, degrees and enrolment in many ways. The pressure for better social relevance, accountability and managerial governance has become a universal trend in HE (e.g. Nokkala, 2011). The market logic is already present.

During the former era of distribution politics – when public resources were ever increasing and the traditional roles and expectations of universities were strong – the scope for politics, discourse and rhetoric remained broad. Although political decisions are still involved, there are major concrete and structural forces described in this chapter that act as drivers for change. As noted, increasing sovereign debts severely limit the scope of public expenditures in many national economies, for example. Many universities would still without a doubt like to continue to pursue their long term tasks hoping that the trends and changes discussed here will not affect them. This might be a potential scenario if the political systems choose to find savings elsewhere, or would risk their economy and continue to increase sovereign debts further, and would strongly believe in the power of education and research free of financial pressures of accountability.

In early 2013, it appears that political decision makers may well be hesitant or unable to carry out many unpopular structural changes, which also tend to be harmful for economic growth in the short term. There appear to be more speeches about slowing down the seemingly inevitable changes, but the structural pressures described in this chapter have not, by any means, disappeared. There are also differences by country in the underlying conditions. As noted, Norway, for example, appears not to suffer from diminishing age groups, or from the direct financial consequences of the Euro crisis (due to being outside the EU and because of the oil income the country enjoys). However, avoiding the structural pressures over an extended period of time seems a highly unlikely scenario for most European countries and their higher education sectors. Universities no doubt have a highly varying capacity to react and act on the basis of the pressures in external environment. The outcomes will depend on leadership and internal culture within the universities. The larger and more traditional the university is, the greater the cultural change needed is likely to be – but even here this depends highly on previous culture and leadership patterns (Kekäle, 2001). By and large the trends discussed would seem to give a coherent message for most European countries: the public basic funding is likely to diminish and more funding is likely to be targeted to politically and socially relevant areas; student populations are decreasing, and there appears to be a demand for more relevance in terms of economic outcomes, labour market expectations and changing, perhaps more pragmatic, student needs. As a result, European knowledge policy stresses efficiency, quality, competitiveness and relevance to the society and economy.

Research universities may have to live on past and current merits, but they are also asked to provide the society with convincing and realizable promises for the future. At the same time, demonstrating short term applications or relevance tends to be problematic, as it can take several decades to produce sound applications after the original findings or ideas. In some disciplinary areas such promises may be easier to make than in others: in the field of nanotechnology in Finland, for example, the number of companies utilizing these technologies has risen from 40 in 2005 to over 200 in 2010 (Savolainen, 2010). Of course, there are other types of social relevance too, like the overall feeling of students and stakeholders that education deals with important and timely issues, and helps us to improve our societies and to understand the matters under scrutiny. The problem seems to be that it is difficult to justify new (economically unproductive) expenses for the public purse. Welfare states cannot operate on debt in the long run, but need steady income streams and jobs. Universities are expected to help in this project.

In all areas pure basic research is needed in order to produce applied research (Becher, 1987). Striking the right balance is up to each university. In order to keep its position in the changing situation, a university must:

- identify and foster its strengths
- abandon the idea that every branch of knowledge should be covered
- find ways to attract students and funding
- find new customers and segments of markets
- be able to communicate its mission and relevance in an efficient way
- balance its cost structure with its funding
- co-operate with the society and industry
- be able to organize work and lead change with the existing resources
- be resilient in order to survive

As noted, with the current trends it becomes logically clear that the competition for motivated students and resources will increase. A university has to attract students in order to secure funding; the students should find their studies meaningful and relevant; the research carried out ought to have some sort of social relevance and employability; the students need to take their degrees and get employed. Such chains of social relevance should be visible and without missing links. This means that the universities will need to reconsider their Master's programmes in terms of content, orientation and teaching methods. In the future students may assess this knowledge content more and more from the following point of view: 'Is this information relevant for me, given the things that I want to do in my life?' At the same time the universities will need to find students who remain motivated enough to invest the time and energy needed in order to reach the cutting edge of research. It seems likely that the accountability won't go away – but it becomes more of a function of internal management in universities. The allocation of scarce public resources will be increasingly affected by the qualitative and quantitative outcomes of a university, department, faculty or programme. One of the best ways of saving money is to make the use of buildings and lecture halls more efficient (Schwartz, 2012).

## A Note on Counter-Megatrends and the Potential Opportunities They Can Provide

Developments in society are not necessarily linear, and there may be counteracting trends. During the previous discussion we have identified some of them: for example the fact that as student populations are diminishing in many countries, the demand for high quality education, innovation and relevant research is *undiminished*, and untapped segments of the population and international students are seeking education. In addition, unemployed people often seek to upgrade their degrees or to study in order to get new certification altogether. As a whole, the labour markets expect higher qualifications which are likely to increase the demand for higher education (Hazelkorn, 2012). Large retired cohorts have free time and may be willing to study in terms of lifelong learning and are therefore an increasing potential group of customers for higher education. International students can be accessed via eLearning facilities, immigration, or by establishing campuses abroad. Two major operators in the field, Monash from Australia and Warwick from the UK, have formed a strategic alliance in order to compete better internationally. If basic public funding is under threat, there are alternative sources of income which can compensate: e.g. new EU funds in certain areas. Such development has been going on for some time: the OECD (2012: 50) has found that the share of private funding for tertiary education institutions has increased between 2000 and 2009 in eighteen out of twenty-five OECD countries. The share has increased by 5 percentage points on average, and by more than 12 percentage points in the Slovak Republic and the United Kingdom.

## Concluding Words

The European University Association (2011) notes that public funding is not only diminishing, but its allocation is increasingly connected with, or accompanied by, growing accountability requirements. This has given funding bodies and public authorities increased steering power over universities, but this can have counterproductive effects in that it can significantly limit universities' autonomy and their capacity to manage their own funds freely. This, in turn, can hinder the universities' capacity to overcome the crisis in a successful way, as institutional and financial autonomy has been a prerequisite to overcoming crises.

The demands on accountability and quality are well grounded in the current situation, but at the same time excessively time-consuming quality assessment and monitoring systems – typical reactions to the pressure – easily become counterproductive. Monitoring the bureaucratic procedures within universities will not penetrate the most crucial issue: the quality of teaching and research. If a university intends to increase quality in these issues, it should perhaps try to establish a quality culture in which the basic operations are viewed and reflected by the academics in terms of their relevance to the different stakeholders: Is my teaching and research comprehensible to the students? Does it provide timely and relevant information in terms of academic quality? Does it foster labour market skills and employability while also being of high academic quality? Is the research carried out relevant to stakeholders, and if not, can this be improved without sacrificing academic values? Academic work must also be relevant and interesting for the scholar him- or herself. Intensive and demanding intellectual work cannot otherwise be carried out successfully. Cultural change may be affected by all these stakeholders, but the academics will ultimately have the key influence on the outcomes.

The bank crisis discussed above would indicate that the society and economic systems are far from complete and that history is not over (Fukuyama, 1992). It is somewhat amazing that critical social scientists and economists have not done more work to reveal the conditions which have made possible such enormous transfer of public funds to cover the colossal mistakes made by investment bankers and private sector operators endorsed by politicians. The common metaphor of the 'unproductive' public sector and the 'productive' private sector should be re-evaluated and deconstructed.

Clark (1998; 2004: 175) maintains that there must be things that the university will *not* do regardless of the money offered; and conversely, in basic research there must be 'useless' things that *are* done – for example, teaching classics or philosophy – because the institution is committed to cultivating cultural heritage as well as to economic progress. This all has to do with the profile and the mission of an institution. There is no single best way to organize or to orientate operations towards the future. However, the spirit of self-reliance and invention – and the ability to initiate cooperation – remain a crucial feature for a forward-looking university to provide the relevant academic knowledge of which it is still the best generator. The keys to our future are still in our hands, although the times are changing.

## References

Aittola, T. (1995). 'Origins of the New Student Type: Changes in a Finnish University in the 1980s', *Young* 3 (3), 54–67.

Altbach, P.G., Reisberg, L., and Rumbley, L.E. (2009). *Trends in Global Higher Education: Tracking an Academic Revolution.* A Report Prepared for the UNESCO 2009 World Conference on Higher Education. Paris: UNESCO.

Barnett, R. (2011). *Being a University.* New York: Taylor and Francis.

Bates, T. (2010). 'The Online Higher Education Market in the USA'. <http://www.tonybates.ca/2010/02/08/the-online-higher-education-market-in-the-usa/> accessed 6 October 2012.

Becher, T. (1989). *Academic Tribes and Territories.* Buckingham: SHRE and Open University Press.

Clark, B.R. (1998). *Creating Entrepreneurial Universities: Organizational Pathways of Transformation.* Paris: International Association of University Press.

Clark, B.R. (2004). *Sustaining Change in Universities. Continuities in Case Studies and Concepts.* Maidenhead, Berkshire and New York: SHRE and Open University Press.

Coleman, R., and Bekhradnia, B. (2011). *Higher Education Supply and Demand to 2020.* <hepi.ac.uk/publications. www.hepi.ac.uk/files/2010 demand report master. pdf> accessed 5 May 2013.

de Dominicis, L., Pérez, S.P., and Fernández-Zubieta, A (2011). 'European University Funding and Financial Autonomy. A Study on the Degree of Diversification of University Budget and the Share of Competitive Funding', *JRC Scientific and Technical Reports.* EUR 24761 EN – 2011.<http://erawatch.jrc.ec.europa.eu/erawatch/export/sites/default/galleries/generic_files/JRC6 3682.pdf.> accessed 6 October 2012.

Ebeling, P. (2012). 'Eurocrisis: Greece to Collapse in November'. *International Business Times*, 10 July, p. 1. <http://www.ibtimes.com/eurocrisis-greece-collapse-november-842479> accessed 6 October 2012.

EHEA – The European Higher Education Area (2012). *Bologna Process Implementation Report.* Education, Audiovisual and Culture Executive Agency (EACEA P9 Eurydice). Brussels: European Commission.

EIE – Education Industry in Europe (2011). 'A Comprehensive Analysis of Education Industry Growth'. Bharat Book Bureau. <http://www.bharatbook.com/market-research-reports/Education-Industry-in-Europe.html> accessed 6 October 2012.

EUA – European University Association (2011). 'Impact of the Economic Crisis on European Higher Education'. <http://www.eua.be/eua-work-and-policy-area/governance-autonomy-and-funding/public-funding-observatory.aspx> accessed 6 October 2012.

European Commission (2011). 'Population Structure and Ageing'. Eurostat. Data from October 2011. <http://epp.eurostat.ec.europa.eu/statistics_explained/index.php/Population_structure_and_ageing> accessed 6 October 2012.

EU Youth Strategy (2012). 'Joint Report of the Council and the Commission on the Implementation of the Renewed Framework for European Cooperation in the Youth Field (EU Youth Strategy 2010–2018)'. Brussels, 10.9.2012 COM (2012). <http://ec.europa.eu/youth/policy/eu-youth-strategy_en.htm> accessed 5 May 2013.

EVA (2010). *EVA Attitude and Value Survey 2010: Cultural Revolution in Work Life.* Helsinki: EVA.

Eving, J. (2012). 'Economix. The Euro Zone Crisis: A Primer'. *New York Times*, 22 May. <http://economix.blogs.nytimes.com/2012/05/22/the-euro-zone-crisis-a-primer/> accessed 6 October 2012.

Frank, D.J. and Gabler, J. (2006). *Reconstructing the University. Worldwide Shifts in Academia in the Twentieth Century.* Stanford: Stanford University Press.

Fukuyama, F. (1992). *The End of History and the Last Man.* New York: Free Press.

Gardner, R. (2011). 'Social Science Shunned as Fees Change Student Culture. The Number of Candidates Opting to Study Social Sciences Has Slumped by 20 Per Cent'. *The Independent,* 21 October. <http://www.independent.co.uk/news/education/education-news/social-science-shunned-as-fees-change-student-culture-6279891.html > accessed 6 October 2012.

Hautamäki, A., and Ståhle, P. (2012). *Ristiriitainen tiedepolitiikkamme.* Helsinki: Gaudeamus.

Hazelkorn, E. (2012). *Higher Education's Future: a New Global Order?* A Keynote Lecture delivered to the European Association for Institutional Research. University of Stavanger.

Hoareau, C. (2011). EUROPE: 'What Role for the EU in an Era of Austerity?' *University World News,* 25 September, p. 1. <http://www.universityworldnews.com> accessed 6 October 2012.

Johnstone, D. B (2009). 'Worldwide Trends in Financing Higher Education'. In J. Knight (ed.), *Financing Access and Equity in Higher Education. Global Perspectives on Higher Education,* pp. 1–19. Rotterdam: Sense Publishers.

Jongbloed, B. (2010). *Funding Higher Education: A View Across the Europe.* Center for Higher Education Studies, Twente: The University of Twente.

Kekäle, J. (2001). *Academic Leadership.* New York: Nova Science Publishers.

Modernisation of Higher Education in Europe (2011). *Funding and the Social Dimension.* Education, Audiovisual and Culture Executive Agency (EACEA 9 Eurydice). Brussels: European Commission.

Möller, K-L. (2012). 'A Critical Review of the Megatrends and Their Implications for Procurement'. A Master's Thesis. University of Twente, School of Management and Governance. <http://essay.utwente.nl/61742/1/MSc_KJ_M%C3%B6ller.pdf> accessed 6 October 2012.

Naisbitt, J. (1982). *Megatrends. Ten New Directions Transforming our Lives.* New York: Warner.

Nokkala, T. (2011). 'Organisational Autonomy for Flexible Universities – A European Comparison'. In S. Bergan, E. Egron-Polak, J. Kohler, L. Purser, and A. Spyropoulou (eds), *Leadership and Governance in Higher Education. Handbook for Decision-makers and Administrators, A 4–1,* pp. 1–20. Berlin: Raabe.

OECD (2012). *Education at Glance 2012.* Paris: OECD Publishing. <http://www.oecd.org/edu/eag2012.htm> accessed 6 November 2012.

O'Neill, C. (2007). 'The Impact of Commercialism on the Classroom'. In C. Gilde (ed.), *Higher Education. Open for Business,* pp. 41–55. New York: Lexington.

Savolainen, K. (2010). 'Turvalliset nanoteknologiat olisivat kilpailuvaltti'. Pääkirjoitus. [Safe nanotechnologies would bring us competitive edge.] *Helsingin Sanomat*, 18 July, p. 1.

Schwartz, S. (2012). 'V-Cs, Get Set to Do the Maths (and Prepare the Begging Bowl)'. *Times Higher Education*, 20 December, p. 30.

Sinn, H.-W. (2010). *Casino Capitalism: How the Financial Crisis Came About and What Needs to be Done Now.* New York: Oxford University Press.

Trends in Higher Education (2011). *Volume 1 – Enrolment.* Ottawa: The Association of Universities and Colleges in Canada.

Vassiliou, A. (2011). 'Foreword'. In Modernisation of Higher Education in Europe (2011), *Funding and the Social Dimension*, pp. 3–4. Education, Audiovisual and Culture Executive Agency (EACEA 9 Eurydice). Brussels: European Commission.

Vassiliou, A. (2012). 'Foreword'. In *The European Higher Education Area in 2012: Bologna Process Implementation Report*, pp. 3–4. Education, Audiovisual and Culture Executive Agency (EACEA 9 Eurydice). Brussels: European Commission.

Vesterinen, P-L., and Suutarinen, M. (2011). *Y-Sukupolvi työelämässä.* JTO. Turku: Hansaprint.

UN (2001). 'Replacement Migration: Is It A Solution to Declining and Aging Populations?' United Nations Publications, Ser A/206. <http://www.un.org/esa/population/publications/migration/migration.htm> accessed 6 November 2012.

ROSALIND M.O. PRITCHARD

# 5 Higher Education in a Competitive World: The New British Regime

The concept of resilience has been applied to systems as diverse as engineering, nuclear power, healthcare, disaster management, commercial fishing and civil aviation, and it is now being extended to social and educational processes. It is true that a gap exists between industrial practice and social science, but as two putative 'translators' of resilience (Le Coze and Dupré, 2008) remark: 'The migration of concepts and models from one world to the other is uncontrollable' (ibid.: 25).

We shall begin by following Wreathall's (2006: 275) definition of resilience: '[It] is the ability of an organisation (system) to keep, or recover quickly to, a stable state, allowing it to continue operations during and after a major mishap or in the presence of continuous significant stresses'. This is the common sense view of resilience; but the concept involves more than just the ability to recover from accidents in difficult circumstances: it must be proactive rather than retroactive or reactive. Westrum (2006: 59), whilst granting that resilience is 'the ability to recover from something bad once it has happened', extends the idea beyond recovery to 'The ability to *prevent* something bad from happening'; 'Or the ability to prevent something bad from becoming *worse*' (italics added).

Resilience requires vigilance in the detection of danger: continuous monitoring of system performance and 'a constant state of unease' (Hollnagel and Woods, 2006: 355–356). Safety is a central feature of resilience and one of its goals is the achievement of 'zero trauma' (Hamel and Välikangas, 2003: 54): 'no calamitous surprises, no convulsive reorganisations, no colossal write-offs, and no indiscriminate, across-the-board layoffs' (ibid.). Unexpected shocks can and indeed should be anticipated if management is paying close attention. Accidents represent breakdowns in the processes that produce resilience and it is difficult to balance the competing demands for safety with pressures for efficiency and the attainment of production targets (as required in market-oriented systems) (Woods, 2006: 315). Prescriptive management may help to protect against institutional disaster, but excessive attention to prescription, particularly when connected with reprimands, can result in 'organisational sclerosis' (Nathanael and Marmaras, 2008: 114); and conversely the 'inherent anarchy of practice' can be conducive to organizational safety – or even rescue – by providing 'a mechanism of rapid adaptation' (ibid.: 117). Pavard et al. too (2008: 133) emphasize the potential value of response diversity in a fast-moving environment; it can help to produce non-deterministic, creative processes to cope with crisis situations.

In fact, the relationship between the system and the environment *is crucial* to the concept of resilience, and Nemeth (2008: 4) points out that 'Much of what we see in inquiries about resilience is actually inquiry into where the boundary between the system and the environment should be'. It involves the ability to interpret 'faint signals' (Westrum, 2006: 60–61) and to work out how close the institutional 'vessel' is to the iceberg that may sink it. It is true that 'We are constrained to look at the future in the light of the past' (Woods and Hollnagel, 2006:2) but the present is never the same as the past, and decisions usually have to be made on the basis of insufficient information; hence, the avoidance of misfortune may require inspired guesswork and maverick judgement – both rather mercurial qualities.

It can be difficult to ensure 'zero trauma' when a higher education system is exposed to neoliberalism. In the United Kingdom, higher education institutions (HEIs) previously constructed their identity round the discovery and pursuit of knowledge; but in recent decades they have had to come to terms with situations in which it often seems that only money matters. They have had to do more with less, and have needed to react with resourcefulness, intelligence and resilience. Not all institutions can be winners in high stake contests. In a world of scarce resources, not all can even survive let alone prosper. To do both requires resilience and a robust response to challenge from the socio-political environment. According to Hamel and Välikangas (2006: 60), the most essential thing that life teaches us about resilience is that 'variety matters' because it is the most powerful way of insuring against the unexpected. In the higher education sector, 'variety' implies *competition* and *diversification* both of institutional range and of subject spread.

Competition is at the heart of academic capitalism, and for it to exist, there must be choice. Not all HEIs can be the same, and not all should offer the same courses. Collins Dictionary defines 'competition' as 'a contest in which a winner is selected between two or more entrants' and defines 'competitive' as being 'sufficiently low in price or high in quality to be successful against commercial rivals'. Governments want higher education to be efficient and effective: the first of these implies optimal deployment of (sometimes minimal) resources in order to attain the desired goals, whereas the second means achieving good performance (which involves 'being thorough'). Resilience theorists refer to the obvious tension between the two concepts as 'ETTO', the efficiency thoroughness trade off (Hollnagel and Woods, 2006: 355). If the drive for efficiency is so ruthless as to result in wholesale resource deprivation, it may be impossible to guarantee effectiveness: indeed, entire institutions may fail or be jeopardized; departments and subjects may shut down, and staff may become redundant.

The purpose of the present chapter is to analyse challenges to the good functioning of the British HE system, viewing it through the lens of resilience theory. It will be organized into sections on efficiency and effectiveness, and the final discussion will consist of an analysis in terms of resilience. In what way is the British government seeking to promote competition in higher education? What effect is this having on its institutions, staff and students? How are the various stakeholders attempting to prove their resilience? To what extent should stakeholders, including government, have been able to anticipate and prepare for a profoundly challenging scenario? The chapter deals with a period of transition during which developments have been constantly changing and long-term outcomes are uncertain.[1]

1 The scenario is fast-moving and changes from week to week. It can be challenging in the circumstances just to know what is going on. To a greater extent than would

## The Efficiency Dimension: A New Competitive Game

The most basic achievement in terms of resilience is the ability to survive which in HE requires institutions to recruit and retain enough students for continuing viability. It almost goes without saying that in a market situation, they will be in competition with each other to do so. Famously, Margaret Thatcher proclaimed to the British House of Commons in 1988 'There is no way in which one can buck the market', but it is paradoxical that in order to promote a market based on competition, a significant amount of state regulation seems necessary. This is all the more so as the predominant goal of the British government in recent decades has been a drive for efficiency in terms of cost-cutting (both generally and for HE in particular). Shattock (2011), in a speech to the Warwick University Festival of Social Sciences, identifies two major eras when political policy was, above all, to cut public expenditure: 1979–1980, when the Thatcher government assumed office, and more recently from 2010 onwards when the Coalition of Conservatives and Liberal Democrats periods took power. They inherited a deficit that was the largest in peace time history. The state was then borrowing one pound for every four it spent: £43 billion went on debt interest which was more than the country was spending on schools in England (Her Majesty's Treasury, 2010). It aimed to put higher education on a sustainable footing, and in so doing changed the basis of university funding. This gave rise to developments described by an Oxford historian, Howard Hotson, as 'the most radical experiment ever conducted on a major university system in the modern world'.[2]

---

perhaps be usual, the present chapter will use references from the Press to outline what is *happening* in British HE. It aims to place that information within an interpretative framework, and to ground policy discussion upon those events.

2 Howard Hotson (University of Oxford), Lecture 'Do British Universities Need "Radical Reform"?' delivered at the Chadwick Lecture Theatre, University College London, 11 January 2012.

## *Fees and Student Numbers*

The new fees regime relates to 'efficiency' because it is an attempt to do the same or more work with fewer public resources (see HM Treasury, 2010). Government policy involved raising fees to make them among the most expensive in Europe, and refusing to allocate any state funding for the Arts, Humanities and the Social Sciences, though the Science, Technology, Engineering and Mathematics (STEM) subjects were still to receive such finance (being in the government's judgement more economically useful). Variable tuition fees of up to £3,000 per year had been introduced in 2004, and in 2010, the report of an independent Panel on HE funding and student finance in England, chaired by Lord Browne of Madingley, recommended a large increase in student fees.[3] Its main purpose was to reduce the public funding of the HE system by seeking higher monetary contributions from students after graduation, and removing the blanket subsidy for all. Browne did not recommend an upper limit for fees, because he believed that there was 'no robust way' to identify what it should be, and thought that a cap would 'distort charging by institutions'.

Serious problems, however, arose in relation to the charging of fees in English universities. The government went against Lord Browne's advice and set an upper limit of £9,000 for the 2012–2013 academic session, expecting that only a limited number of universities would charge that figure, and that they might compete with each other for cheapness. But the majority of HEIs announced their intention to charge the maximum, so the government then issued a White Paper in 2011 in which it made English universities compete against each other for students through a 'core and margin' system.[4] About a quarter of all places, ca. 85,000, were to be open to full competition. There was to be 'unconstrained recruit-

3 'Securing a Sustainable Future for Higher Education: an Independent Review of Higher Education Funding and Student Finance' (2010), <http:// www.independent.gov.uk/browne-report/> accessed 27 April 2013.

4 'Students at the Heart of the System', Cm 8122 <https://www.gov.uk/government/uploads/system/uploads/attachment_data/file/32409/11-944-higher-education-students-at-heart-of-system.pdf> accessed 27 April 2013.

ment' of roughly 65,000 high achieving students scoring the equivalent of AAB or better at A-Level.[5] The number of funded places available to English universities and colleges was the 'core'. They needed to fill these places and would lose income if they under-recruited, but could also be penalized for over-recruiting. The room for error was very small, and the penalties for over-recruitment were set at £3,800 per student in 2012–2013, though subsequently an error tolerance of 3 per cent for overall admissions was introduced. In addition, a flexible 'margin' of about 20,000 places was created to reward universities and colleges which combined good quality with value for money and whose average tuition charge (after waivers) was at or below £7,500 per year. In other words, places were reallocated to cheaper institutions. It was intended that employers and charities offering sponsorship for individual places would not count against an institution's student number control. Subsequently, the margin was reduced to 5,000 places redistributed to high quality, good value universities or colleges for 2013 entry. Applicants with ABB+ or equivalent were not to count towards the core for 2013 entry, and the core was intended to encompass 66 per cent of people in English higher education for 2013–2014 entry (UCAS, 2013b).

The new policy was more than an attempt to save money. It was also intended to stratify HEIs and continue the marketization of the sector. It caused immediate anger and dismay on the part of students who were the 'consumers' supposedly at the heart of the system. In November 2010 they took to the streets to protest against the proposed fee increases: they broke into the Conservative Party headquarters and in Regent Street, London, they attacked a car carrying Prince Charles and his wife, the Duchess of Cornwall.

5 The UCAS Tariff A-Levels are scored out of a maximum of 30 points: A=10; B=8; C=6; D=4; E=2.

## *Impact of the Fees Regime*

It is germane to this chapter to ask what the effects of the fees 'hike' have been. This will be discussed in terms of student recruitment, access, gender, subject choice, relations between HE and further education, and impact on institutions. Although the intention is to increase competition, often the opposite happens.

### STUDENT RECRUITMENT

Empirical analysis reveals a pattern of regionally mixed outcomes in relation to applications and acceptances.

The Sutton Trust (2012) performed an independent examination of the statistical trends in applications for 2012–2013, taking account of the fee variance in the different areas of the UK. In Wales and Northern Ireland, fee levels were lower than those in England, and in Scotland, there was no undergraduate fee for Scottish students studying at home, though Scottish universities did charge students from south of the Border.[6] There was an overall decline of 8.8 per cent in England compared with a decline of only 0.7 per cent in the other areas of the UK. The Trust concludes that 'the relative decline in English applications raises concerns about the impact of increased fees'.

The Universities and Colleges Admissions Service (UCAS) End of Cycle report for the 2012 year (UCAS, 2013a) indicates that UK and EU acceptances fell by 53,200 (-11 per cent) compared to acceptances into the 2011–2012 entry. In 2011, fewer than one student in ten chose to defer entry to HE for a year. This was a drop of over 40 per cent, probably in the knowledge that fees were going to rise in 2012. Figures for the UK 2012 entry (ibid.) indicate significant decreases but also some increases as follows:

6 Note that arrangements in other parts of the UK diverge from those in England. Scottish-domiciled undergraduates studying in Scotland currently do not have to pay fees, whereas those in Wales and Northern Ireland paid £3,465 for 2012–2013.

England: 345,600, -51,100 (-13 per cent);
Northern Ireland: 9,800, +300 (+3 per cent);
Scotland: 38,600, +600 (+2 per cent);
Wales: 22,300, -3,000 (-12 per cent).

There has been a significant decline in part-time entrants at both undergraduate and postgraduate levels: since 2010–2011, part-time undergraduate entrants have fallen by 40 per cent while those on postgraduate programmes have fallen by 27 per cent (HEFCE, 2013a). These part-time students include larger numbers from non-traditional backgrounds, and thus their status is particularly likely to have implications for equality and diversity.

## ACCESS

A serious concern was that the high fees would deter students from poorer backgrounds, but this fear has proved unjustified. In fact, entry rates for disadvantaged eighteen-year-olds increased in 2012 in all countries of the UK, reaching new highs in England, Wales and Northern Ireland. UCAS (2012: 6) states: 'This continues a trend of relatively strong proportional increases that have seen disadvantaged 18 year olds being 40 to 60 per cent more likely to enter higher education in 2012 than they were in 2004. In 2012, the entry rate for pupils from English state schools who received free school meals increased to a new high for the period. The entry rate for those who do not receive free school meals *decreased* (author's italics). Both rates are close to levels suggested by extrapolations of their trend over recent cycles'.

In the view of the Sutton Trust (2012: 10): 'This is encouraging in that any potential impact from higher tuition fees does not appear to be having a disproportionate impact on those from less advantaged neighbourhoods'. UCAS (2012: 7) reports that 'the entry rate of disadvantaged 18 year olds into "higher tariff institutions" [i.e. those that demand the highest entry qualifications] has increased in all four countries of the UK; and in England in 2012, a higher proportion of the 18 year old population in disadvantaged areas entered higher tariff institutions than in any other cycle'. However, according to a survey by university marketing advertisers, OpinionPanel, disadvantaged groups were more likely to seek universities with lower fees and/or financial support packages, and to apply to institutions close to their family home (Baker, 2012: 11); and it remains true that access has not widened much at the most selective third of institutions despite OFFA's significant efforts.

The threat of low access for the disadvantaged has been mitigated by government schemes such as 'Aimhigher' and the Office for Fair Access (OFFA). 'Aimhigher' cost about £500 million and was terminated on 31 July 2011; it worked with schools to promote aspiration to HE among disadvantaged young people, and has now been replaced by a National Scholarship Programme. OFFA was established in October 2004 under the Higher Education Act of 2004 and is sponsored by the Department for Business, Innovation and Skills (BIS). Its remit is to safeguard and promote fair access to higher education, e.g. by approving and monitoring 'access agreements'. Its scope was broadened in February 2011 to include retention and student success measures. According to OFFA's Annual Report (2011: 18), take-up of bursaries among students from the lowest income group improved from around 80 per cent in 2006–2007 to 90 per cent in 2007–2008 and to 96 per cent in 2008–2009, with 96 per cent of HEIs reporting a take-up rate of 9 per cent or more. Under the new fees regime, progression to university among disadvantaged students has dropped *less* than among those from richer backgrounds, and the *largest* decline is among those from more advantaged backgrounds.

Many such 'advantaged' students probably took the opportunity to go to university before 2012 when the large fee rise was first applied. Their participation is already high and may have reached saturation point. Some middle-class families are encouraging their children to apply for universities outside the UK, which they expect will give them a distinctive edge in the job market. Ireland is a popular destination for study (Collinson, 2012), as is the United States, especially the Ivy League Colleges where generous bursaries are often available. Some people attend continental HEIs such as the University of Maastricht where half of the undergraduate courses are taught entirely in English. Fees at this well-regarded institution are just £1,500 a year. UK students can qualify for a non-repayable grant from the Dutch government worth £228 per month and a tuition fee loan, if they work part-time while studying (Henry, 2011a).

The recruitment figures for study abroad are relatively modest for the moment, but indicate that in terms of budget competition, these advantaged students and their families do not necessarily want to produce a 'share of their wallet' for high British fees. The parents undoubtedly have the self-confidence, resilience and inter-cultural competence to enable them to send their children abroad for higher education. This movement is a concomitant of globalization, and is happening in other countries too, but the down side is that a national 'brain drain' is being encouraged by the high fees regime.

## GENDER

In terms of gender, there are indications that female participation is holding up much better than male participation. The Universities and Colleges Admissions Service (UCAS, 2012: 8) has shown that men are substantially under-represented: 'Amongst UK 18 year olds, women were a third more likely to enter higher education in 2012 than men. In 2012, the entry rate fell for both men and women but the decrease for men was four times greater than for women. Men are more likely to be accepted than women, though the difference reduced in 2012. Women remain more likely to enter higher education than men are to apply'. The Chief Executive of UCAS, Mary Curnock, has expressed grave concern about this trend.

## SUBJECT CHOICE

Competition requires variety in terms of institutional and disciplinary spread. However, in the climate of financial stringency, choice is shrinking and subject profiles are not necessarily as the government would wish to see them. The University and College Union has published a report (UCU, 2012a) revealing that between 2006 and 2012, the number of full-time degree courses provided in the UK fell by 27 per cent. The reduction in undergraduate courses was sharpest in England (-31 per cent) and Northern Ireland (-24 per cent), but is much lower in Wales (-11 per cent) and Scotland (-3 per cent). There are areas of the country (e.g., the Western Midlands) where students cannot find access to the courses that they want to study, especially as rising costs compel many to study closer to home. Benneworth (2011) also makes the point that pressure for two-year degrees is growing because they are cheaper and get graduates onto the job market sooner; but they put distance between the continental Bologna Process in which most countries are trying to shorten their degree programmes, and the British pattern in which already short courses are set to become even *shorter*.

The government wishes to promote certain subjects that help to make the country economically prosperous. Modern languages are one example, but a report prepared for the British Academy (Tinsley, 2013) indicates that their position within HE is precarious. There is strong evidence that the UK is suffering from a growing deficit in foreign language skills at a time when globally the demand for them is expanding. Linguists accounted for just 3 per cent of undergraduates in the academic year 2010–2011, of whom just over a sixth represents EU or international students (para. 24). UCAS acceptances (August 2012) for European language courses are down 10 per cent and those for non-European language courses have dropped over 14 per cent (para. 25). At university, languages constitute the most gender-marked of all subject groupings with just 33 per cent of language students being male (para. 33). Tinsley concludes that: 'Within higher education, early evidence appears to show that the increasing fees for English students and English universities [are]...having an adverse effect on admissions to four-year language degrees, the Erasmus programme and Year Abroad schemes. Students seem to be deciding that the extra year spent learning a language abroad is simply too costly'.

Above all, the government values and wishes to promote STEM subjects for which it is difficult to recruit. Ramsden (2012, paras 35–36), in a survey of institutional diversity, finds that between 2004 and 2009 there was a clear decline in science and technology subjects, though a significant increase did take place in creative and performing arts, media studies and politics. He concludes that this development *matches demand as evidenced by applicant choice* (italics added). Giving students subjects that they want as consumers may be resulting in behaviour that is the opposite of what the government wants. Over the decade from 2001–2002 to 2010–2011 undergraduate numbers in STEM subjects only increased by 2 per cent, but recently from 2008–2009 to 2010–2011 there has been a surge of 8 per cent, so things may be changing.[7]

Currently, there is fluctuation in applications for STEM subjects. According to the Higher Education Funding Council for England (HEFCE, 2013a), there was a 2 per cent dip in accepted applicants for 2012, but a 7 per cent rise in applications for 2013. Importantly, the House of Lords (2012) produced a special report on STEM subjects in which it deplores the lack of reliable data on the supply and demand of stem subjects, and the fact that the definition of STEM subjects is so loose that it often includes courses with little scientific content. They complain that the recent policy reforms of higher education [i.e. the fees regime] and of immigration [of international students] give rise to concern about the outcome. In fact they anticipate a 'triple whammy' effect due to higher fees, lack of student finance and a decline in the number of overseas students choosing to study in the UK (many of whom do STEM subjects).

## FURTHER EDUCATION

Higher education has been provided outside the universities and colleges for more than sixty years, and government policy has been to support and expand HE within the Further Education sector, focussing on short-cycle, sub-bachelor, vocational programmes (HEFCE, 2006; Parry, 2009a). However, the Further Education Institutions (FEIs) are in a vulnerable position since they have 'no signature qualification owned by or reserved for their own sector, or the security of their own funding ahead of a severe economic downturn' with the result that they tend to be 'unstable, fragile and marginal settings for higher-level work' (ibid.: 340). Parry (2009b: 172) notes the tendency of FEIs and HEIs 'to compete as well as collaborate in reaching new audiences to be served by more flexible forms of higher education'. However, these FEIs are crucial to widening access, and currently

7 Data on demand and supply in higher education subjects. London: HEFCE, <http://www.hefce.ac.uk/data/year/2012/dataondemandandsupplyinhighereducationsubjects/> accessed 27 April 2013.

include more than 170,000 students in over 250 FEIs in England which accounts for about 7.7 per cent of all HE places (Matthews, 2012a: 16). This is a smaller proportion of the whole than when Parry published in 2009: he then estimated the FE share of HE as about one in nine or one in ten, and gave the overall number as 180,000 (Parry, 2009a: 326).

The government wants to move students from more expensive to cheaper courses, hence the FEIs – which charge low fees – ought to find it easy to bid for places. Colleges that are not directly funded by the Higher Education Council for England get their students from universities, which have 'kindly lent these institutions the numbers to run courses on their behalf' (Davies, 2011). But in order to protect themselves in difficult financial circumstances, some universities reduced or withdrew the places that they had allocated for the use of partner colleges, reasoning that if they expanded provision through the FE colleges, it was at their own expense. Concern for their image makes them less inclined to 'lend' places to FE: '[U]niversities are now more conscious of their brands, many of them will wonder whether allowing students to earn their degrees in outside colleges dilutes the value of their awards' (Matthews, 2012a: 17). They may even become reluctant to validate FE programmes, though there are new arrangements to circumvent the need for a university partner by using other validators (Matthews, 2012b: 17). This distancing of FE and HE is an understandable, even predictable, reaction to competition, but is irritating to the government. The Business Secretary, Vince Cable, at a meeting of the Association of Colleges in November 2011 condemned it as 'simply unacceptable' anti-competitive behaviour; though the head of the Council of Validating Universities, James Winter, claimed that plans had 'absolutely not' been thought through (ibid.).

According to HEFCE (2013a: paras 98–100) FEIs are filling their own places first before filling places that are franchised from a university. The number of full-time undergraduates who were taught at an FEI as part of a franchise arrangement fell by more than 4,000 (almost 15 per cent) between 2011 and 2012–2013. But places funded directly through HEFCE increased by 7,500 (26 per cent). Part-time recruitment to undergraduate courses funded by HEFCE fell by 19 per cent – a trend which has been identified as long-term. Both sectors have moved to act in their own interests, and

FE is being helped by HEFCE which has decided on direct funding of an additional nineteen FE colleges in 2013–2014 on the basis of their response to a recent invitation to bid for full-time undergraduate places. This will have the effect of making them more independent of the universities and will give them greater negotiating power.

## ALTERNATIVE PROVIDERS OF HIGHER EDUCATION

It is a Coalition policy goal to encourage competition between publicly funded and non-publicly funded institutions. The government has adopted a number of measures in an attempt to create a level playing field; but some of these are perceived by more traditional institutions as unfair forms of positive discrimination. The criteria for being able to call an establishment a 'university' in England have recently been softened from what they had been in 2004. From 11 June 2012 onwards, 1,000 full time equivalent students are required of whom 750 must be registered on degree courses (including Foundation Degrees). Until this change, the number was 4,000.[8] Recently, ten new institutions have been granted the university title, including some that are monotechnics in terms of their subject spread (Morgan, 2012b: 6–7). The College of Law has become the University of Law, and will be the UK's first 'for profit' HEI: it has been bought by Montagu Private Equity and has ceased to be a charity (as mainstream HEIs are).

Financial support through the Student Loans Company has been made available to students at private HEIs. Thus, certain undergraduates studying a higher education course run by a private provider can now access public loans of £6,000 a year to finance their degree. Though the proportion of such students accessing loans is currently small, the availability of loans to private HEIs spreads resources more thinly, and may well make it more difficult for students at publicly-funded HEIs to access the finance they need.

8 Department for Business Innovation and Skills (11 December 2012) Recognised UK Degrees. <https://www.gov.uk/recognised-uk-degrees> accessed 27 April 2013.

The government has moved to establish student number controls on intakes for designated courses (HEFCE, 2013b). Currently there are 150 alternative HE providers offering one or more HE courses for which students can obtain financial support from the Student Loans Company. This is a 70 per cent increase since 2006–2007 (HEFCE, 2013a: paras 102–104). The government has been accused of a 'rush' to approve private degree courses: figures showed that the number of courses approved in 2011–2012 rose by 77 per cent from 228 in 2010–2011 to a total of 403 in 2011–2012 (Richardson, 2012).

These developments to promote alternative providers are felt by some in the publicly-funded sector to be inequitable. As a UniversitiesUK Research Report states: 'Private providers pose a threat where they openly compete with UK publicly-funded universities' (Fielden et al., 2010: para. 19). The UCU is opposed to the privatization of tertiary education, seeing bitter irony in the juxtaposition between public cuts and private expansion supported by the tax payer. They fear the possibility of 'leveraging public funding to support private profit [to shareholders] while aggressively marketing a poor product to vulnerable non-traditional and lower income students' (UCU, 2010a: 1). The UCU (ibid.: 7) states: 'We are concerned that the companies want the restrictions on university status to be relaxed and to be able to tap into public funding to subsidize their profits without having to put in place any of the academic safeguards that UCU considers to be necessary to preserve the quality of higher education'.

Experience in other countries with 'for profit' HEIs does indicate that risk is involved. In Chile, which has the most privatized HE system in the world, graduates are saddled with huge debts that may represent up to 20 per cent to 30 per cent of their income; as a result mass protests, strikes and occupations have taken place (Gibney, 2012). The Harkin Report in the United States (2012) shows that those who studied at such institutions accounted for 47 per cent of all federal loan defaults, and of those who enrolled at 'for profits' in 2008–2009, 54 per cent had left without a degree by mid-2010. Frances (2012) writes powerfully about the unfortunate consequences of over-reliance on the for-profit sector. She demonstrates that many people are forced to pay *more* for *less* higher education: indeed by 2012, the volume of student debt loan in the US exceeded the volume of credit card debt in the entire nation. She warns: 'Other countries...should be extremely careful in contemplating emulation of the US education policies which encourage the expansion of the for-profit higher education institution' (ibid.: 19). In the UK too, there is evidence that students do not feel that they are receiving a better education since the new fees regime from September 2012 onwards. In fact, 'there is a sharp increase in the proportion of students who feel that they are not receiving good value for money' (Bekhradnia, 2013).

For the present, HEFCE has accepted different regulatory models for alternative providers compared with the public sector, and admit that this will result in 'different levels of assurance and accountability'.[9] They also admit concern that alternative providers are not required to hold access agreements with the Office for Fair Access, with the result that there is no formal mechanism for promoting and monitoring fair access to alternative providers. At present, protection for students in the private sector is inferior to that in the public sector, and there is no requirement for institutions to publish robust information. Subscription to the Office of the Independent Adjudicator is only voluntary. Middlehurst and Fielden (2011) recommend the introduction of a British Private Higher Education Act bringing together all the elements of a regulatory framework for non-publicly funded HE. A Higher Education Bill received its first reading in the House of Lords on 17 May 2012, but it was limited in scope, and plans for such an HE Act have now been shelved.

## EFFECTS OF THE NEW REGIME UPON INSTITUTIONS

Many institutions are finding it difficult to deal with the new fees regime, especially as they are penalized for over- or under-cutting their intake targets. Public funding is decreasing, and needs to be compensated by

9 BIS consultation on 'Applying Student Number Controls to Alternative Providers with Designated Courses' (2013) and HEFCE (2013) Response to BIS Consultation on 'Applying Student Number Controls to Alternative Providers with Designated Courses'. <http://www.hefce.ac.uk/news/newsarchive/2013/ name,76383,en.html> accessed 13 April 2013.

adequate recruitment in order to bring in fee income. Eleven HEIs and fourteen FEIs *exceeded* their limit whereas about 9 per cent *failed to attain* their planned numbers (HEFCE, 2013a: para. 87); 35 per cent of the margin places remained unfilled (ibid.: para. 93). Of the twenty English members of the elite 'Russell Group', the intake at ten has declined.[10] Highly regarded universities such as Imperial College London, Birmingham, Sheffield, Liverpool and Southampton all lost numbers, whilst other members of the Group such as Bristol, University College London, Cardiff, King's College London and the London School of Economics have gained. Different institutions 'gamed' the new system in different ways, some offering money to attract students (Henry, 2011b). Some losses may be compensated in subsequent years. Some less research-intensive institutions (e.g. Greenwich) accepted a fall in recruitment (assumed to be temporary) as a deliberate strategic choice: they set high entry requirements in order to build a reputation for quality, whilst Bristol used the new regime as an opportunity for expansion. Some universities have offered money to students with high grades in order to attract them to their institutions, and some have stipulated very high grades because this appears prestigious and may inspire confidence in the HEI. Hazelkorn (Chapter 3 in the present volume) points out that prestige-seeking HEIs often place more value on a student's potential contribution to prestige than they do on his or her direct contribution to revenue. HEFCE (2013a: paras 92–93) can see no particular pattern relating either to the size of the institution or the size of its margin, but promises to 'take seriously' concerns about the fairness of the implementation of the high grades policy. Total income is now forecast to rise by 2.8 per cent in 2012–2013, rather than by 4.1 per cent as predicted earlier. Future projections are dependent upon student numbers not declining significantly, and even small changes in income can have a material impact on financial positions (ibid.: paras 115–117). There is more competition from foreign countries for non-EU students, and it will be vital to make efficiency savings.

10 The Russell Group represents twenty-four leading UK research intensive universities, all of them pre-1992. It was during this year that the former polytechnics were upgraded to university status and the binary divide was abolished.

It is the post-1992 HEIs that are the most challenged. In the 'Million Plus Group', acceptances fell by 12 per cent and those of the 'University Alliance' by 9 per cent.[11] Numerical fluctuations can pose a considerable challenge, as a case study of London Metropolitan University (LMU) demonstrates. It provides an interesting example of attempts to achieve resilience in the face of difficulties, some of which predated the new fees regime and were of its own making. The Higher Education Funding Council for England had imposed a punishment for discrepancies in student data as a result of which LMU has to repay £34 million to HEFCE over the period of 2010–2013 (2010–2011 £4m; 2011–2012 £10m; 2012–2013 £10m; 2013–2014 £10m (LMU Strategic Plan, 2010)). For the 2011–2012 academic session, it over-recruited about 1,550 students arising from a veritable 'tsunami' of applicants (the Vice Chancellor's words) (Morgan, 2012a: 6). This news was followed by publication of plans for over 200 staff redundancies, though the VC claimed that there was no connection between the fine and the job losses. The University also cut its undergraduate programme provision by 70 per cent to focus on high demand areas (*THE*, 2012). As a result, some students had to transfer to different courses before the end of their degree. It divested itself of 'The Women's Library' in Whitechapel which contains the oldest and most extensive collection of women's history in Europe (Campbell, 2012). These measures were obvious attempts to establish resilience within a threatening environment.

In August 2012, the UK Border Agency (UKBA) revoked LMU's licence to 'sponsor' students from outside the European Union for visas to study in the UK.[12] The UKBA's case was that the attendance of London Met's students was not being properly monitored, and that their English qualifications were sometimes suspect or inadequate. An underlying reason was that, in order to fulfil an election promise, the government wanted to reduce migration figures within the UK from hundreds of thousands to

11 The Million Plus group currently includes twenty-two universities, incorporating post-1992 HEIs and university colleges. The University Alliance also consists overwhelmingly of post-1992 HEIs, and was formed in 2006.

12 The ban was lifted on 9 April 2013.

about 100,000 by 2015. The revocation meant that LMU was temporarily removed from the register of licensed sponsors, and that international students from outside the European Union were no longer allowed to study there. Just at the point where they were making plans to travel to the UK in order to begin their courses, they were advised not to travel. Those already studying within LMU institution were also affected, even though some were within sight of degree completion. They were given 60 days to find study places elsewhere or face deportation. Fewer than half of the International students eligible to stay on at LMU opted to do so, and more than 55 per cent of students found a place elsewhere, though often with higher fees. Needless to say, the loss of these students damaged LMU's budget and reputation. In 2012, it suffered a fall in acceptances of 43 per cent from 2011–2012 which is a serious and risky situation.

The effects of the London Met visa scandal had repercussions for the system on a wider front. The UKBA applied its actions to other institutions too though with less dramatic effect. The impression arose that the UK was unwelcoming to international students, and the number of students from India fell by almost 24 per cent overall, whilst the number of students from Pakistan fell by 19 per cent (Taylor, 2013). Conlon et al. (2011) estimated that in 2008–2009 tuition fees alone amounted to £2442.3 million, and education exports overall were worth £14.1 billion to the British economy, set to rise to approximately £21.5 billion in 2020 and £26.6 billion in 2025 (both in 2008–2009 prices). Hazelkorn (2011: 8) has noted the need for good alignment between higher education and immigration policies. This has not been present recently in British HE, and the government's stance on student visas is, therefore, undermining a very valuable market. The UKBA was split in in 2012, and scrapped altogether in 2013. It was castigated by the Home Secretary for its closed, secretive and defensive culture. However, at time of writing, there were no plans to treat students as a separate category: a step which could and should have been taken.

## The Effectiveness Dimension

Effectiveness is part of the ETTO concept associated with resilience (efficiency and thoroughness trade off). If the number of the UK's top universities is divided by its population, the British have one of the world's best performing HE sectors. It had thirty-two universities in the Top 200 of the Times Higher Education World University Rankings in 2012–2013, coming second after the United States, and excelling in terms of value for money.[13] However, the UK only spends 0.6 per cent of its GDP on higher education – a percentage that is one of the lowest in all the OECD countries, and may threaten its quality position. A report of the '1994 Group', 'Mapping Research Excellence' explores the links between research excellence and funding policy.[14] It argues that although the rankings look good at present, funding is a cause for concern, particularly at a time when the country is relying on research and innovation to help drive economic success. In fact, growth is relatively slow, and this is attributed to the UK having one of the lowest proportional rises in research and development investment in the world, while other countries, including the USA and China, are significantly increasing research investment. But effectiveness in the UK has been achieved at high cost. Two aspects of university functioning that will be dealt with below are administrative load and personal adjustment within the work place.

13 <http://www.timeshighereducation.co.uk/news/the-world-university-rankings-2012–13/421400.article> accessed 30 July 2013.

14 The 1994 Group is a coalition of smaller research-intensive universities founded in 1994 to defend their interests following the creation of the Russell Group earlier that year. 'Mapping Research Excellence', <http://www.1994group.ac.uk/documents/public/MappingResearchExcellence%20hi-res.pdf> accessed 27 April 2013.

### *Administrative Load*

In resilience theory, accidents – whether physical or institutional – have been conceptualized in various different ways, one of which is the quaintly named 'Swiss Cheese Model' (Hollnagel, 2006: 11). In this model, accidents are visualized as the result of weakened barriers and defences represented as holes in a slice of 'cheese'. They are construed as failures of components, rather than failures of the overall system as such. The British government has pressured its HEIs to become more 'efficient' by reducing their dependence upon state funding, but also insists on their 'effectiveness' by introducing heavy requirements for accountability (e.g. through the Quality Assurance Agency (QAA)). Reduced reliance on state funding does not by any means result in increased freedom from state control. One very obvious risk to reputation and recruitment is the danger of performing poorly in quality assessments. The audit culture, and the climate of mistrust that it engenders, have resulted in a hypertrophy of administration. According to the Transparency Approach to Costing survey of 2009–2010 (TRAC, 2011) which analyses the use of academics' time, administration and management account for nearly 32 per cent of the overall time budget at almost all institutions. Almost one third of what is available is therefore spent upon secondary supporting functions rather than upon core functions of teaching and research. This, no doubt, is intended to help preserve the system from disaster by anticipating unexpected shocks; and of course, it also aims at 'optimization' of functioning (within limited resources).

However Hamel and Välikangas (2003) argue that it is more important to make a future than to defend the past: which is what optimization strategies are intended to do. The future cannot be secured if what is being optimized is suffering from what they call progressive 'strategy decay'. Välikangas (2010) warns of 'success traps' which may arise when an organization becomes over-confident and continues the same actions until they are no longer appropriate to changed market realities. Heavy management pressures can disempower employees by creating a culture in which everyone is called upon merely to execute the goals set by those at the top of the hierarchy (ibid.: 179). The result may be a less adaptive and less creative organization that confines itself to existing claims rather than driving towards new ones. The investment of so much energy in administration, audit and quality management may be conducive to safety in the short to medium term, but counter-productive in the long term.

### *Personal Adjustment in the Workplace*

People are one of the most important resources within an institution. When their time is dissipated in wasteful activities, or when their powers are sapped by unhappiness, inefficiency results. Within a climate of scarce resources, unpleasantness may lurk below the surface. Resilience theorist Westrum (2006: 60) puts forward the notion of 'latent pathogens' which are largely invisible at first glance but which exercise a destructive effect from within. They develop and are exacerbated by financial stringency (Komatsubara, 2008). Examples of such pathogens within universities are the personal antagonisms and the formal grievances that people take against one another. In the search for justice or vengeance, a grievance may go all the way to the University Visitor or the Office of the Independent Adjudicator. Even after the grievance has been heard and supposedly settled, colleagues are often unwilling to work together; this can disrupt the cohesion of a course programme, and make the department difficult to manage. A former head of department known to the present author was so upset by the inter-personal aggression and conflict between his staff members that when he finished his term of office, he was clinically diagnosed with post-traumatic stress disorder. Outwardly he *seemed* a tough masculine person who was the epitome of resilience; he *thought* that he had come through his ordeal unscathed, but all the quarrelling had taken a heavy toll upon his health.[15]

Lack of resources, heavy administrative burdens and internecine conflict have led to increased stress within British higher education institutions. Systemic tensions, sometimes impacting upon personal health, are implied by the fact that several Vice Chancellors have resigned before

15 Personal communication to author.

completing their terms of office: Patrick McGhee of the University of East London, Simon Lee of Leeds Metropolitan University, Stephen Hill of Royal Holloway, University of London, Malcolm Gillies of City University and Bill Macmillan of the University of East Anglia (Hodges, 2009). A national survey conducted by the University and College Union (UCU, 2012b) indicated that workload stress levels for UCU members had intensified in the last four years, and were considerably worse in academia than for the British working population as a whole. The resounding conclusion was that academics were one of the most stressed professional groups nationally. In institutions where stress was at its highest – with some exceptions, these were mostly the *less* prestigious HEIs – it was felt that the working environment exacerbated stress and impacted negatively on the well-being of staff. Overall, there was a general sense of unease and uncertainty, with a claim that many respondents lacked information about current change processes or were worried about job security.

One university report included some survey responses as follows:[16]

- 'I don't think there is a good understanding of mental health issues and how that can affect work. [I'm] afraid to discuss this issue in case [I'm] deemed not "capable."'
- 'On a personal level, I am not sleeping, I feel sick every time I open my email and dread any/every meeting as the behaviour of management filters through to those below who believe such open bullying behaviour to be acceptable'.

Many people within this HEI (particularly those within the probationary period) were afraid to bring up issues such as harassment or bullying; they felt that managers could be unsupportive, particularly to those with family/ caring responsibilities, and that the lack of security emanates from government policy rather than the university.

16 Stress Survey conducted in a pre-1992 University. For ethical reasons, its identity has been withheld in the present chapter so as not to embarrass a particular institution.

## The Pursuit of Resilience in British Universities

We have noted above that competition and diversification are crucial for the attainment of resilience, and also that the pursuit of efficiency is a central feature of a marketized system. It is time to take an overview of the developments outlined above.

### *Challenges of Government Policy*

Government action has posed enormous challenges to the British higher education sector to the point where the ability of some institutions to survive let alone thrive is coming into question. HEFCE (2013a: paras 115 and 117) remarks soberly that 'no institutions are likely to face insolvency in the short term', but some will 'face difficulty if they experience repeated falls in student recruitment' and there are 'increased uncertainties relating to student recruitment'. Policy has been characterized by many lurches: in fact, Shattock (2012: 250) argues that policy making in higher education has been mostly reactive rather than proactive, and accuses the government of 'disjointed incrementalism'. A UCU report (2010b) anticipated that more than one in three (49 out of 130) English institutions will face serious consequences as a result of the new funding regime. All of these are post-1992 HEIs. The Chair of UCAS, Professor Steve Smith, in a speech to a British Council conference in Tokyo, has spoken openly of the 'risk of market failure for institutions'.[17]

It will be recalled that the ability to anticipate unfavourable reactions is a feature of resilience, and it is possible to use past experience for this purpose. The government discarded Browne's recommendation not to place an upper limit on fees, and stipulated that HEIs must not exceed fees of £9,000. When it turned out that most wanted to charge the maximum

17 *University World News* (22 May 2013). 'Academics Warn of Market Failure'. <http://www.universityworldnews.com/article.php?story=20130125144312840> accessed 22 May 2013.

amount (which meant more money for their institutions), the authorities had to take remedial action. Yet they should have been able to foresee that most HEIs would wish to charge the higher fee. They could have learned lessons from the behaviour of the HEIs over twenty years ago that institutions do not always cooperate when asked to sell their wares cheap. In 1990, universities were asked to bid for students with the promise that those charging relatively *low* prices would be rewarded by being allowed to recruit higher numbers. The strategy did not work, however, because the Universities Funding Council received very few bids at floor prices (Pritchard, 1994). The same thing happened in 2006 when top up fees were introduced and nearly all HEIs decided to go for the maximum allowable fee. The government's lack of 'foresight through hindsight' constituted a form of policy incoherence which had to be redressed by the draconian corrective of the 2011 White Paper.

In many ways, the new regime militates *against* diversity though competitiveness *requires* diversity. The HE sector is permeated by a tension between forces for homogenization and forces for diversification which Ramsden (2012) argues were already quite strong before the new fees regime. The fact that tuition fees currently cluster around the same level means that their power to stratify institutions is limited; the Sutton Trust has noted this. Moreover, the effect of financial pressure has been to reduce variety in terms of academic programmes (e.g. in London Metropolitan). The decrease in subject offering makes it more difficult for institutions to achieve a distinctive profile, therefore more difficult to be competitive. Subject profile is one way of achieving 'horizontal' differentiation in Teichler's terms (2002), but James Ladyman, commenting for the British University and College Union (2012a: 23) states: 'I am really concerned that under the new funding environment universities will look at concentrating their resources on courses which they believe will deliver the highest financial return. The loss of the block grant has taken away an important measure of financial security that allowed institutions to plan for the future. Provision shouldn't be decided on the basis of short-term popularity contests but when you introduce a market that is what happens'. It is difficult to reconcile sweeping programme rationalization with choice or with diversity of profile; fewer subjects normally mean larger classes which may be inimical to high quality teaching.

The system also demonstrates a curious tension between under-steering and over-steering. Shattock (2011) complains that OFFA has no power to impose any limit on fees and that the QAA has no means to regulate standards, so he wonders how the government can steer the system. Policy, he says, has been 'episodic and inconsistent, generated by a range of forces and events, economic, political and social, more often external to higher education than driven from within' (Shattock, 2012: 243). It emanates from a wide range of governmental or quasi-governmental bodies, and poses serious challenges to HE. HEFCE is now supposed to regulate without the statutory powers that would underpin its new role. It will have few powers over HEIs that do not receive teaching grants (e.g. for the Arts, Humanities and Social Sciences).

Yet in some ways, (over-)steering is resulting in a rigged market that is unfriendly to the publicly-funded universities. The treatment of private HEIs is widely felt to be an unfair form of positive discrimination, and to have developed from back to front. Instead of a legal basis being provided at the beginning, they have been not just *allowed*, but *encouraged* to develop in the absence of such legislation and in the absence of consistent quality control. Despite some negative experience in other countries (the 'for profits' in the USA), tax payers' money is being made available to them via the availability of student loans. Institutional and course approvals have been expedited. The Further Education Institutions too are being facilitated by the authorities. More places are being made available directly to them so that they will be less dependent upon universities and will be able to beat them on price. This will make HE cheaper, but may reduce the quality of the student experience especially for students suited to research-led teaching. Meanwhile, the Border Agency's actions over visas run counter to the need for the HE system to recruit international students in a climate of financial stringency. This recruitment strategy qualifies as a 'harm absorber' (Wreathall, 2006: 281), and the fact that government policy makes it difficult to implement reduces HEIs' resilience.

The new arrangements have not resulted in the denial of HE access to students from poorer backgrounds. However, the way in which this issue has been managed is anti-competitive. In a perfect market, it is assumed that the 'traded' outputs are homogeneous, without economies of scale;

that there is a smooth pattern of demand without peaks and a smooth pattern of supply where the quantity of output is easily adjusted (Bannock and Rees, 2000: 326). The existence of rational consumers is also assumed though these conditions are rarely, if ever, present in education.

One phenomenon that skews the perfect market is the social dimension. This is inherent in the concept of the *quasi-market* which can be defined as 'a public sector institutional structure that is designed to reap the supposed efficiency gains of free markets without losing the equity benefits of traditional systems of public administration and financing'.[18] In higher education, this equity usually relates to the income and social background of those who access the 'product'. The potential social damage of the fees rise has been mitigated by schemes like 'Aimhigher' and OFFA, and by the universities using their own resources to widen access. In order to implement the fees regime, it has been necessary to introduce strong forms of social engineering in a 'managed' market. Such management has not, however, extended to gender, though this has been seriously proposed in order to rescue boys from the under-achievement which was already an established trend even before the introduction of the fees regime which exacerbated it. As Filippakou et al. (2012: 331) point out, it is institutional behaviour and market forces, as opposed to central state planning, that are most important in shaping university development especially in England. In the efficiency-effectiveness trade off, the former is ruthlessly pursued, distancing the British scenario from the 'academic peace' that some other countries, e.g. Finland, seek for their own institutions (Opetusministeriö, 2007).

## *Tensions and Paradoxes*

Peter Scott (2012), writing in *The Guardian*, proclaims the following: '[A]ll the evidence is that Whitehall initiatives produce limited effects, at any rate in the long term. A free-market government surely should appreciate this

18 Quasi-markets: <http://en.wikipedia.org/wiki/Quasi-market/> accessed 16 February 2012.

most of all'. For a system so dedicated to market forces, there is strong, but sometimes clumsy and ruthless state interventionism in the UK HE system. Yet the effects are often paradoxical and the intervention does not always give the desired results. It is little wonder then that in the present chapter, we have observed so many policy contradictions often with unforeseen, counter-productive, collateral effects. In the circumstances, institutions have such great need of resilience that one can well ask what motivational syndrome sustains them.

A resilience theorist (Välikangas, 2010) has a worthwhile insight in this regard. Times are hard, and cuts seem ubiquitous, but not everything turns around money: in fact she believes that we ought not to accept the predominance of extrinsic rewards over intrinsic motivation. She argues that in doing so, we give up some independence of belief and purpose (and potentially also our integrity), making our work lose its personal relevance and reducing our joy in creativity.

> When you do something for the love of it, it elevates your being and frees your spirit. At our best, or at our most human, we are all like...increasingly dedicated idealists who work towards a cause, skilfully harnessing global networks for change. (ibid.: 157–158)

Perhaps this is the driving force behind the resilience that many British universities have so far demonstrated, though not all of them will be able to do so in the future.

## References

Baker, S. (2012). 'Fee Increase Outweighed by "Return on Investment"', *Times Higher Education*, 16 February, p. 11.

Bannock, R., and Rees, E. (1992). *The Penguin Dictionary of Economics.* London: Penguin.

Bekhradnia, B. (2013). *The Academic Experience of Students in English Universities, 2013 Report*. Oxford: Higher Education Policy Institute, Report Summary 61.

Benneworth, P. (2012). 'Cathedrals in the Desert', *Times Higher Education*. Supplement in the *THE* World University Rankings 2011–2012, p. 50.

Campbell, B. (2012). 'A Room of One's Own. Why the Women's Library Should not be Made History', *The Guardian*, 1 May. <http://www.guardian.co.uk/commentisfree/2012/may/01/womens-library-history> accessed 12 May 2013.

Collinson, P. (2012). 'Save £25,000 at University and Join the Tuition Refugees', *The Guardian*, 17 August. <http://www.guardian.co.uk/money/2012/aug/17/save-25000-university-tuition-fee-refugees> accessed 12 May 2013.

Conlon, G, Litchfield, A., and Sadlier, G. (2011). *Estimating the Value to the UK of Education Exports.* London: Department of Business, Innovation and Skills.

Davies, P. (2011). 'An Impoverished Relation', *Times Higher Education*, 8 December, p. 28.

Fielden, J., with Middlehurst, R., Woodfield, S., and Olcott, D. (2010). 'The Growth of Private and For-Profit Providers'. Universities UK. <http://www.universitiesuk.ac.uk/Publications/ Documents/ Private Providersmar10. pdf > accessed 7 January 2013.

Filippakou, O., Salter, B., and Tapper, T. (2012). 'The Changing Structure of British Higher Education: How Diverse is it?' *Tertiary Education and Management*, 18 (4), 321–333.

Frances, C. (2012). *Shattering the Social Contract: Over-reliance on For-profit Higher Education Institutions*. Paper delivered to the European Association for Institutional Research. University of Stavanger.

Gibney, E. (2012). 'The Mañana Project', *Times Higher Education*, 30 August, pp. 36–39.

Hamel, G., and Välikangas, L. (2003). 'The Quest for Resilience', *Harvard Business Review*, September, 52–63.

Harkin, T. (2012). 'For Profit Higher Education: the Failure to Safeguard the Federal Investment and Ensure Student Success'. Prepared by the Committee on Health, Education, Labor, and Pensions, United States Senate. <http://www.help.senate.gov/imo/media/for_profit_report/Contents.pdf > accessed 14 January 2013.

Hazelkorn, E. (2011). *Rankings and the Reshaping of Higher Education: the Battle for World Class Excellence*. Basingstoke and New York: Palgrave Macmillan.

HEFCE – Higher Education Funding Council for England (2006). *Higher Education in Further Education Colleges. Consultation on HEFCE Policy*. Bristol: HEFCE.

HEFCE – Higher Education Funding Council for England (2013a). *Higher Education in England: Impact of the 2012 Reforms, March 2013*. Bristol: HEFCE.

HEFCE – Higher Education Funding Council for England (2013b). *Recurrent Grant and Student Number Controls for 2013/14, March 2013/05*. Bristol: HEFCE.

Henry, J. (2011a). 'Study Cheaper Degrees Abroad, Parents tell Children', *The Telegraph* online, 20 November, <http://www.telegraph.co.uk/education/universityeducation/8901375/ Universities-to-pay-cash-incentives-to-attract-students.html/> accessed 18 February 2012.

Henry, J. (2011b). 'Universities to Pay Cash Incentives to Attract Students', *The Telegraph* online, 20 November, <http://www.telegraph.co.uk/education/universityeducation/8901375/ Universities-to-pay-cash-incentives-to-attract-students.html/> accessed 18 February 2012.

Her Majesty's Treasury (2010). *Spending Review, Cm 7942*. London: Her Majesty's Stationery Office.

Hodges, L. (2009). 'Trouble at the Top: Malcolm Gillies' departure from City University has Revealed an Intense Relationship between Governors and Vice-Chancellors', *The Independent*, 13 August, <http://www.independent.co.uk/news/education/higher/trouble-at-the-top-malcolm-gillies-departure-from-city-university-has-revealed-an-intense-relationship-between-governors-and-vicechancellors-1771004.html> accessed 12 May 2013.

Hollnagel, E. (2006). 'Resilience – the Challenge of the Unstable. In E. Hollnagel et al. (eds), *Resilience Engineering: Concepts and Precepts*, pp. 9–17.

Hollnagel, E., and Woods, D.D. (2006). 'Epilogue: Resilience Engineering Precepts'. In E. Hollnagel et al. (eds), *Resilience Engineering: Concepts and Precepts*, pp. 347–358.

Hollnagel, E., Woods, D.D., and Leveson, N. (2006). *Resilience Engineering: Concepts and Precepts*. Aldershot, Hampshire UK and Burlington, USA: Ashgate.

Hollnagel, E., Nemeth, C.P., and Dekker, S. (2008). *Resilience Engineering Perspectives: Remaining Sensitive to the Possibility of Failure*. Volume 1 of Ashgate Studies in Resilience Engineering. Aldershot, Hampshire UK and Burlington, USA: Ashgate.

House of Lords Science and Technology Committee (2012). *Higher Education in Science, Technology, Engineering and Mathematics (STEM) Subjects*. London: Houses of Parliament.

Komatsubara, A. (2008). 'When Resilience Does not Work'. In E. Hollnagel et al. (eds), *Resilience Engineering: Concepts and Precepts*, pp. 79–90.

Le Coze, J.-C., and Dupré, M. (2008). 'The Need for "Translators" and for New Models of Safety'. In E. Hollnagel et al. (eds), *Resilience Engineering: Concepts and Precepts*, pp. 11–28.

LMU – London Metropolitan University (2010). *Strategic Plan: Transforming Lives, Meeting Needs, Building Careers* 2010–2013. London: LMU.

Matthews, D. (2012a). 'Core and Margin Plan Tests the Limits of Collegial Behaviour', *Times Higher Education*, 16 February, pp. 16–17.

Matthews, D. (2012b). 'Exam Board's Open Marriage Set to Offer Colleges Greater Independence', *Times Higher Education*, 29 November, p. 17.

Middlehurst, R., and Fielden, J. (2011). *Private Providers in UK Higher Education: some Policy Options.* Oxford: Higher Education Policy Institute, Report Summary 53.

Morgan, J. (2012a). 'The Cap has Burst – Expect a Flood of Fines', *Times Higher Education*, 16 February, p. 6.

Morgan, J. (2012b). 'No Risk Posed by 10 Little Newbies', *Times Higher Education*, 29 November, p. 7.

Nathanael, D., and Marmaras, N. (2008). 'Work Practices and Prescription: A Key Issue for Organisational Resilience'. In E. Hollnagel et al. (eds), pp. 101–118.

Nemeth, C.P. (2008). 'Resilience Engineering: the Birth of a Notion'. In E. Hollnagel et al. (eds), *Resilience Engineering: Concepts and Precepts*, pp. 4–10.

OFFA – Office for Fair Access (July 2011). *Annual Report and Accounts 2010–2011*. London: Her Majesty's Stationery Office.

Opetusministeriö (2007). 'Teknillisen korkeakoulun, Helsingin kauppakorkeakoulun ja Taideteollisen korkeakoulun yhdistyminen uudeksi yliopistoksi'. Opetusministeriön työryhmämuistioita ja selvityksiä. <http://www.minedu.fi/export/sites/default/ OPM/Julkaisut/2007/liitteet/tr16.pdf?lang=fi> accessed 12 May 2013.

Parry, G. (2009a). 'Higher Education, Further Education and the English Experiment', *Higher Education Quarterly*, 63 (4), 322–342.

Parry, G. (2009b). 'Student Demand and Institutional Diversification: the Case of England', *Journal of Adult and Continuing Education*, 15 (2), 170–186.

Pavard, B., Dugdale, J., Bellamine-Ben-Saoud, N., Darcy, S., and Samelbier, P. (2008). 'Underlying Concepts in Robustness and Resilience and their Use in Designing Socio-technical Systems'. In E. Hollnagel et al. (eds), *Resilience Engineering: Concepts and Precepts*, pp. 127–142.

Pritchard, R.M.O. (1994). 'Government Power in British Higher Education'. In Pritchard, R.M.O. (2011), *Neoliberal Developments in Higher Education: the United Kingdom and Germany*, pp. 127–148. Bern and Oxford: Peter Lang.

Ramsden, B. (2012). *Institutional Diversity in UK Higher Education*. Oxford: Higher Education Policy Institute, Report Summary 55.

Richardson, H. (2012). 'Ministers "Rush to Approve Private Degree Courses"', *BBC News*, 12 July, <http://www.bbc.co.uk/news/education-18812103/> accessed 12 January 2013.

Scott, P. (2012). 'Higher Education Needs Real Reform, not a Return to the Past', *The Guardian*, 2 January, <http://www.guardian.co.uk/education/2012/jan/02/higher-education-reforms-failure/> accessed 21 February 2012.

Shattock, M. (2011). 'Comparing Cuts in Public Expenditure: the Implications for Higher Education. Keynote Address to the University of Warwick Festival of Social Sciences, May 2011'. <http://www2.warwick.ac.uk/knowledge/themes/07/shattock/> accessed 6 January 2013.

Shattock, M. (2012). *Making Policy in British Higher Education 1945–2011*. Maidenhead, Berkshire and New York: McGraw Hill.

Sutton Trust (2012). 'Analysis of UCAS Applications for 2012/13 Admissions. Independent Commission on Fees, August 2012'. <http://www.suttontrust.com/public/documents/icof-report-ucas-analysis-final.pdf> accessed 6 January 2013.

Taylor, M. (2013). 'Fall in Students from India and Pakistan as Immigration Rules Bite', *The Guardian*, 11 January <http://www.guardian.co.uk/education/2013/jan/11/fall-students-india-pakistan-immigration> accessed 12 May 2013.

Teichler, U. (2002). 'Diversification of Higher Education and the Profile of the Individual Institution', *Higher Education Management and Policy*, 14 (3), 177–188.

*THE – Times Higher Education* (2012). 'World University Rankings', 5 January.

Thompson, J., and Bekhradnia, B. (2010). *The Government's Proposals for Higher Education Funding and Student Finance: an Analyis.* Oxford: Higher Education Policy Institute.

Tinsley, T. (2013). *Languages: the State of the Nation – Demand and Supply of Language Skills in the UK.* London: British Academy.

TRAC (Transparent Approach to Costing) (2011). *Review of Research Cost Relativities Based on the TRAC Methodology. Report by J M Consulting to the UK Higher Education Funding Bodies October 2011.* Bristol: HEFCE.

UCAS – Universities and Colleges Admissions Service (2012). *End of Cycle Report. Publication Reference 12348.* Cheltenham: UCAS.

UCAS – Universities and Colleges Admissions Service (2013a). *End of Cycle Assessment of UCAS Acceptances by Intended Entry Year, Country of Institution and Qualifications Held. UCAS Analysis and Research, 18 January 2013.* Cheltenham: UCAS.

UCAS – Universities and Colleges Admissions Service (2013b). *Student Number Controls: Scenarios and Questions. Last updated on 17.12.2012.* Cheltenham: UCAS.

UCU – University and College Union (2010a). *Subprime Education? A Report on the Growth of Private Providers and the Crisis of UK Higher Education.* London: UCU.

UCU – University and College Union (2010b). *Universities at Risk.* London: UCU.

UCU – University and College Union (2012a). *Choice Cuts: How Choice has Declined in Higher Education. UK Course Provision 2006–2012.* London: UCU.

UCU – University and College Union (2012b). *National Occupational Stress Survey.* London: UCU. <http://www.ucu.org.uk/index.cfm?articleid=5799#demands/> accessed 11 January 2013.

Välikangas, L. (2010). *The Resilient Organisation: How Adaptive Cultures Thrive Even When Strategy Fails.* New York: McGraw Hill.

Westrum, R. (2006). 'A Typology of Resilience Situations'. In E. Hollnagel et al. (eds), *Resilience Engineering: Concepts and Precepts*, pp. 55–65.

White Paper (2011). *Higher Education: Students at the Heart of the System Cm 8122.* London: Department for Business, Innovation and Skills.

Woods, D.D., and Hollnagel, E. (2006). 'Prologue: Resilience Engineering Concepts'. In E. Hollnagel et al. (eds), *Resilience Engineering: Concepts and Precepts*, pp. 2–8.

Woods, D.D. (2006). 'How to Design a Safety Organisation: Test Case for Resilience Engineering'. In E. Hollnagel et al. (eds), *Resilience Engineering: Concepts and Precepts*, pp. 315–325.

Woods, D.D., and Cook, R.I. (2006). 'Incidents – Markers of Resilience or Brittleness?' In E. Hollnagel et al. (eds) *Resilience Engineering: Concepts and Precepts*, pp. 69–76.

Wreathall, J. (2006). 'Properties of Resilient Organizations: An Initial View'. In E. Hollnagel et al. (eds), *Resilience Engineering: Concepts and Precepts*, pp. 275–285.

STIG A. SELMER-ANDERSSEN

# 6 Robustness in Organized Anarchies: Efficient Composting in the Organizational Garbage Cans?

## A Classical Model Challenged by the Present Environment

Any form of contemplation, from the most leisurely to the deepest, requires use of numerous models. Organizational models are intended to provide general guidance and suggestions about how one might proceed when working. In this chapter, one of the most famed of all such constructs, the Garbage Can Model of decision making, will be explored in the context of multi authority organizations. Its robustness is assessed by examining how it relates to resilience and how it produces decisions under varying circumstances, especially with regard to organizational resilience in universities and other organizations with similar characteristics.

Today, universities find themselves residing in complex, turbulent exogenous environments (de Zilva, 2010). While it can be argued that the fundamental organizational form of the universities is unchanged, it is still the case that 'the actual organizational patterns of university governance have changed over the past few decades away from the classical notion of the university as a republic of scholars towards the idea of the university as a stakeholder organization' (Bleiklie and Kogan, 2007: 477), and it is between those two broad sets of university governance conventions that 'organizational and decision-making structures within universities are justified' (ibid.). This chapter proposes that a remake of the Garbage Can Model that includes multiple authorities may be useful in today's higher education institutions, as it makes more visible not only the internal processes but also the interplay between the complex and turbulent exogenous environment and the fundamental internal organizational form, aiding the institutions to improve their resilience.

## *Decision Making in Organizations*

In a landmark book on public policy making, Kingdon (1995) posits that the large puzzle is really about 'What makes people [...] attend, at any given time, to some subjects and not to others?' Judged by its reception when 'A Garbage Can Model of Organizational Choice' by Cohen, March and Olsen was published in 1972, the ideas it presented towards addressing such problems were ideas whose time had truly come.[1] And judging by the number of citations since its publication, those ideas are still in vogue (Lomi and Harrison, 2012). Encompassing how decision makers attended to problems and choice opportunities in organizations, the Garbage Can Model pitted itself against a very familiar organizational model in which decision makers address the problems of the organization, proceed by identifying a number of solutions, and decide upon the most attractive solution, based on the available facts.

Cohen, March and Olsen (1972) (henceforth referred to as CMO) presented a somewhat different perspective:

> Although organizations can often be viewed conveniently as vehicles for solving well-defined problems or structures within which conflict is resolved through bargaining, they also provide sets of procedures through which participants arrive at an interpretation of what they are doing and what they have done while in the process of doing it. From this point of view, an organization is a collection of choices looking for problems, issues and feelings looking for decision situations in which they might be aired, solutions looking for issues to which they might be answers, and decision makers looking for work. (CMO: 2)

1 Throughout this text, the abbreviation 'CMO' will refer to this seminal article by Cohen, March and Olsen.

The Garbage Can Model (henceforth referred to as GCM) is a highly simplified presentation of choice opportunities that arise in most organizations, depicting them as a series of occasions involving one or more problems, a number of decision makers, and possibly some solutions. Choices are then made or not made. When made, they may or may not solve problems.

## *Organized Anarchies*

Classical 'problem solving' models of decision making assume the existence of some common organizational goals, as well as agreed-upon objectives and practices among the decision makers, and a fixed participation structure for the different decisions. In contrast, the GCM applies to scenarios 'where attention is a scarce resource that, when devoted to one thing, cannot be devoted to another; where there are multiple decision arenas that 'compete' for problems, solutions and decision maker time; and where problems and solutions arrive at times exogenously determined and are linked partly by their simultaneous arrivals' (Cohen et al., 2012: 22). The term *organized anarchy* denotes the particular organizational form where such features are prevalent. These features are commonly observable in universities. The GCM explores how decision making might occur within this organizational form.

This particular form is recognized through three distinct general properties. Firstly, preferences are problematic (as when differing goals and objectives are pursued within the same organization). Secondly, the technologies are unclear (as when similar processes are upheld by different means and tools, or understood differently in the different parts of the organization). Thirdly, the participation is inconsistent (as when the individuals' engagement and participation in decision making situations and processes varies over time). These characteristics apply to any organization, at least in part and at least some of the time: 'A theory of organized anarchy will describe a portion of almost any organization's activities, but will not describe all of them' (CMO: 1). Neither the problem solving model nor the GCM will be able to fully represent all relevant aspects of all organizational situations, and Box's (1979) conclusion that although all models are wrong, some might be useful does apply here as well. To be understandable and usable, models will have to leave most things out. While much more precise models of organizational decision making have been attempted using '[n]on-linear fuzzy-rough dependent-chance model and fuzzy-rough simulation based parallel tabu search' or similar models (Xu and Zhou, 2011: 358–364), many will find such models difficult to grasp. A central question, then, must be whether a model like the GCM will still be useful (Miller and Page, 2007).

## *The Garbage Can Model*

In the GCM, choice opportunities are defined as 'occasions when an organization is expected to produce behaviour that can be called a decision' (CMO: 3). The model focuses attention on how four specific streams interrelate and develop over time: a stream of *problems* arriving into the decision arenas, a stream of *energy* from the decision makers, a flow of *solutions*, and a stream of *choice opportunities* arising. The problems being handled in the choice opportunities will require application of some level of energy for them to be solved. As choice opportunities arise, they will be available for eligible problems and eligible decision makers to access. Cohen, March and Olsen (1972: 3) note that '[a]lthough not completely independent of each other, each of the streams can be viewed as independent and exogenous to the system'. These four streams are modelled through six core components: how problems enter into the decision making processes (*problem access structure*), how the decision making itself is structured (*decision structure*), the amount of energy each participant has available to spend on decision making (*energy distribution*), how much energy is needed to reach a decision (*net energy load*), as well as the arrival time for the different problems and for the different decision making occasions. These elements are described at a more detailed level in this chapter's Technical Appendix, but a brief summary of three of the elements is necessary for the development of the multi authority version of the GCM.

The *decision structures* determine the relation between each of the decision makers and each of the choices. The model envisions three different decision structures. In the *unsegmented* variety, any decision maker may participate in any active choice opportunity. In the *hierarchical* structure, the most important decision makers may participate in any of the choices, while participation becomes gradually more limited as the decision makers' importance decreases. In the *specialized* decision structure, decision makers have access to only one of the choices, and each choice can be made by only one of the decision makers.

Problems require *energy* to be resolved. In the GCM this energy is provided by the participants, such that '[t]he distribution of energy among decision makers reflects possible variations in the amount of time spent on organizational problems by different decision makers' (CMO: 7). Three different *energy distributions* are considered. In the first, important people have less energy to spend in the choice opportunities to 'reflect variations in the combination of outside demands and motivation to participate within the organization' (CMO: 7). In the second distribution, all participants have an equal amount of energy to spend. In the third distribution, the most important people can contribute the most energy to the choice situations.

In the model decisions are made whenever the effective energy available in the decision situations is sufficient to overcome the energy requirements of the problems that are active in the same situations. The energy requirement depends upon the *net energy load* scenario of the organization, and is defined as 'the difference between the total energy required to solve all problems and the total effective energy available to the organization over all time periods' (CMO: 5). The GCM uses three levels of organizational load: *light*, *moderate* (where the energy requirement is doubled) and *heavy* (where the energy requirement is tripled). The requirements are set up in such a way that the system contains enough energy to solve all the problems under any load condition.

## *A Flexible and Well-Ordered Process Model*

The CMO article presented the GCM as a conceptual as well as a computational model. Although originally thought to be particularly applicable to universities, the GCM and the organizational form of organized anarchies has been explored and analysed in many different environments (see

Leventhal, 2012; Cohen et al., 2012), and no other computational model has been remodelled as much as the GCM (Carley, 1995: 7) over a range of contexts and scenarios (see Inamizu, 2006, 2009; Fioretti and Lomi, 2010; Knudsen et al., 2012).

Within the model, the streams of problems, decision makers and solutions interact in quite complex ways. It has been noted that this leads to results that may be perceived as complicated and sometimes confusing (Inamizu, 2009: 7). In the literature this has often been interpreted as a consequence of random changes in the decision making process being modelled, and, since decisions in the model are dependent on timing, as a consequence of random decision styles (see Scott, 1998: 299; Hatch 1997: 278; Daft 2004: 467; Brunsson 2007: 14). But as Cohen, March and Olsen (1972) point out repeatedly, the GCM is very simple in its construction, especially when held up against the phenomenon of organizational decision making. Detailed process analysis has shown that the GCM processes proceed in a highly structured fashion – 'an orderly decision-making process in disorderly organization structures' as Inamizu (2009) puts it. Rather than being a result of randomness, the complexity arises out of the model's sensitivity to situations and situational differences.

### *Attention*

Cohen, March and Olsen (1972) point to how attention is one of the two major phenomena that must be investigated to understand organized anarchies: 'This entails the question of how occasional members become active and how attention is directed toward, or away from, a decision. It is important to understand the attention patterns within an organization, since not everyone is attending to everything all of the time' (CMO: 2). In the GCM the decision makers' attention is modelled through the decision structure and the energy distribution scheme through regulating what choice opportunities the decision makers could attend to, and what attention should be given to problems attached to the different choice opportunities. March and Olsen (1976: 40) do at a later stage suggest how the aspect of attention could be singled out and treated as an independent element. With reference to Stinchcombe's (1974) study of attention budgets, they devise an attention structure identical to the mechanisms used for the access and decision structures of the GCM, suggesting that attention may be implemented using three pure types of attention structures modelled as 'unsegmented', 'specialized' and 'hierarchical' attention (March and Olsen, 1976: 40).

Other aspects have been suggested as well. Ocasio (2012: 305–306) points to fads and fashions in problems and to event sequences as two factors that affect temporal coupling of attention to problems and solutions across choice opportunities, observing that 'for March and Olsen (1976), attention structures are rarely constraining – they provide an upper limit on what can be attended to, not a full determination of what is attended to' (ibid.: 308). Some have seen it as a potential problem of the original GCM that the decision makers' attention, including how history, identity and institutional meanings might be included in the steering of that attention, is not included as a separately identifiable variable. Heimer and Stinchcombe (1999: 26) note that 'One great difficulty of the original paper, shared by the computer program by which it was first investigated, is that all the streams related to decisions are endogenous to the organizations and have no causal history inside the organization that gives any exogenous quality to their causal impact on decisions'. While the GCM includes a quantitative causality between what happened in the previous choice opportunity and what will happen in the next (through the forwarding of decisional energy applied in the previous choice opportunity), Heimer and Stinchcombe (ibid.) underscore that there will be a qualitative causality as well, and that this history component often turns out to be a crucial factor in garbage can processes. Such a qualitative causality is not catered for by the original GCM, as there is only one type of energy included in the GCM design.

Some of the choice opportunities will be to set the agenda for what items the organization should attend to, thus framing the attention of the participants in the future. For these choice opportunities, Kingdon's Multiple Streams theory could apply (Kingdon, 1995), necessitating a way of representing Kingdon's three streams of problems, policy and politics. To accommodate for this perspective, the garbage can model could be expanded (beyond the inclusion of multiple authorities proposed in this text) to include a problem dimension, a policy dimension and a politics dimension. Such a scheme would also be suitable for handling the attention aspects outlined by March and Olsen, Heimer and Stinchcombe, Ocasio, or other aspects of attention felt to be sufficiently important to justify inclusion as an independent aspect. It would, however, be a stretch somewhat beyond the scope and space for this chapter, and is not pursued further here. Nonetheless, the multi authority version of the GCM proposed here does discriminate between energies from the different powers, thus implementing a qualitative causality to a certain degree. In the multi authority GCM, decision making 'depends partly on who says it is important, that is, on the history of the item' (Heimer and Stinchcombe, 1999: 30).

## A Multi Authority Garbage Can Model

In the original GCM article, several decision structures are modelled, *but only one at a time*. The authors note that 'actual decision structures will require a more complicated array. Most organizations have a mix of rules for defining the legitimacy of participation in decisions. The three pure cases are, however, familiar applications of such rules and can be used to understand some consequences of decision structure for decision processes' (CMO: 7). In line with this, the conceptual as well as the computational Garbage Can Model was limited to a single authority (in the form of the decision making energy needed to reach a decision). Based on the increasing attention to (and number of organizational models for) multi authority systems (Välikangas, 2010), it would be useful to explore how such 'more complicated arrays' portraying *more than one authority simultaneously present* in the choice opportunities would affect GCM results.

Decision making and governance cannot be separated from authority. Most well-known organizational forms and models assume organizations that operate under a single authority scheme, but during the last twenty years, several multi-authority systems for organization and governance have been developed and used. In Europe: one prominent example would be the CONVERGE SA and its systems architecture evaluation methodology (Jesty et al., 1999).[2] Another example would be the Open Method of Coordination (OMC) launched by the Lisbon European Council in 2000, to help Europe 'become the world's most competitive knowledge-based economy before the year 2010' (European Council, 2000; Gornitzka, 2006, 2007). The OMC is referred to as a 'third way' in European governance, an alternative to intergovernmental negotiations and the Classical Community Model for coordination between multiple authorities. It is considered less rigid and more open than the CCM, and more ambitious and better structured than intergovernmental negotiations (Humburg, 2008: 6; Dehousse, 2002: 4). Across Europe, a general tendency has been noted towards having 'policy instruments to "steer" higher education by remote control' (Neave, 1988: 12). 'Steering from a distance'-models of coordinating multi authority institutions are prevalent in Europe, although with variations in pace between the different countries (Huisman, 2009).

In expanding the Garbage Can Model to be able to model today's multi authority organizations it must be assumed that each authority could itself be organized according to any of the decision structures of the original model, and that more than one of them may be present in the choice opportunities at any one time. The necessary remodelling must include each stakeholder group to supply decision making energy that is quantitatively and qualitatively independent of the decision making energy of the others. Quantitative independence requires that each has its own *energy distribution*, and qualitative independence requires that each has its own *decision structure*. A multi authority version of the GCM would also have to comply with the three specific behavioural assumptions of the original model; the energy additivity assumption, the energy allocation assumption and the problem allocation assumption.

2 The methodology was originally developed under the EU's 4th research programme to evaluate multi authority transportation systems in large European cities.

The three pure types of decision structures implemented in the GCM were an *unsegmented* decision structure, a *hierarchical* decision structure and a *specialized* decision structure. Any authority might be present through any of the three decision structures in the multi authority model. One of the implications will be that the number of possible scenarios will increase as the number of authorities is increased. For one authority, the number of unique combinations of decision structures is three, as in the original model. For two authorities, the number of unique combinations of decision structures among the two will be six, for three authorities it will be ten.[3]

The energy distributions of the original model are kept unchanged. But as it must be assumed that each authority might have any of the energy distributions, this will have a similar effect on the numbers of possible scenarios. For two authorities, the number of unique combinations of energy distributions among the powers will be six, for three it will be ten (rather than three in the single authority model).

As this chapter's Technical Appendix contains descriptions at a somewhat more detailed level on *how* the GCM was remodelled to cater for multiple authorities to participate in the decision making, the remainder of the main text will focus on the *results* and *implications* of the multi authority model. For the remainder of this text, the multi authority version of the GCM will be referred to as MAGCM.

## *A Three Authority Garbage Can Model*

The MAGCM does not distinguish between de jure and de facto powers, and the perspective of today's universities as an organization of internal and external stakeholders suggests the inclusion of a number of stakeholders in the model. Students will be such a group, often having de facto and in many cases de jure power in decision processes. In particular garbage can processes the press, unions, the local community or local business life could all possess de facto power. The results presented in this chapter use three

3 For n authorities, the number of unique combinations is $(n+1)(n+2)/2$.

authorities. This is a number often encountered in literature (see e.g. chapter 2 of this book), both in the context of de jure and of de facto authorities. For the universities in Norway, the Auditor General identifies two de jure authorities within each institution (one academic and one administrative) in addition to the third (but external) de jure authority being the Ministry of Education and Science (Office of the Auditor General, 2004: A.1.8–9).

With the number of authorities being three, the MAGCM will have the following characteristics compared to the original GCM:

- The energy distributions of the original model are kept unchanged, but implementing them independently for each authority results in ten unique combinations of energy distributions in the three authority model.
- The decision structures of the original model are kept unchanged, but implemented independently for each of the authorities. While the number of unique combinations was three in the original (single authority) model, it will be ten in the three authority model, as shown in Table 6.1.

Table 6.1 Decision Structures in Single and Triple Authority Garbage Can Models

| | Triple authority decision structures |
|---|---|
| | D0: UUU |
| | D1: HHH |
| Single authority decision structures | D2: SSS |
| | D3: UUH |
| D0: U (Unsegmented) | D4: UUS |
| | D5: UHH |
| D1: H (Hierarchical) | D6: UHS |
| | D7: USS |
| D2: S (Specialized) | D9: HHS |
| | D9: HSS |

The original GCM resulted in 324 unique organizational scenarios. The three authority setup, having ten rather than three energy distributions and ten rather than three decision structures, encompasses 3,600 unique organizational scenarios.

## Implications of the Multi Authority Garbage Can Model

Cohen, March and Olsen (1972) point to a number of central results that can be assembled from the computational model. They give three of these special attention: those of *problem activity*, *decision maker activity* and *decision difficulty*. Each of those could be calculated in a number of ways, but for the discussions below the results are calculated as described for the original model: *Problem activity* is seen as the total number of periods that a problem is active and attached to some choice, summed over all periods, and reflecting 'the degree of conflict within the organization or the degree of articulation of problems' (CMO: 8). The *decision maker activity* encompasses decision maker energy expenditure, movement and persistence. Due to the way decisions are made in garbage cans, the *decision difficulty* is different from the level of problem activity, and the total number of times that any decision maker shifts from one choice to another was found to reflect the criteria quite well.

A central feature of the GCM is how decisions are made. Three different decision styles are identified in organizational garbage can processes: by *resolution*, by *oversight*, or by *flight*. Decision by resolution is the familiar case of choices actually resolving problems. Decision by oversight relates to choices being made (with a minimum of energy being spent), but without any problems attached to the choice opportunity. Decision by flight denotes choices being made because some problems leave the choice opportunity. The energy available to the choice opportunity then overcomes the energy requirement for the problems that remain. CMO points to the percentage of decisions that solves problems as a fourth central result for the GCM.

As the multi authority model is qualitatively different from the single authority model, results should be analysed and compared to the implications of the single authority model identified by CMO. Eight major properties of garbage can processes were explicitly treated by CMO and will thus require comparison regarding the results obtained by the MAGCM.

1. *It was noted that resolution of problems as a style for making decisions was not the most common style, except under certain conditions.* This feature is retained in the MAGCM, although it resolves problems slightly better than the single authority model. Details are shown in Tables 6.2 and 6.3.[4]

Table 6.2 Proportion of Choices that Resolve Problems by Load and Single Authority Decision Structure

| | Single authority decision structure | | | |
|---|---|---|---|---|
| Load | All | D0 (U) | D1 (H) | D2 (S) |
| Light | 50% | 80% | 49% | 22% |
| Moderate | 36% | 63% | 35% | 12% |
| Heavy | 27% | 56% | 22% | 4% |
| All | 38% | 66% | 35% | 13% |

A striking feature of Table 6.2 is the difference between the three decision structures: in unsegmented decision structures, most to nearly all decisions solve problems, but in specialized decision structures, few to almost none of the decisions solve problems. While basically retained in the MAGCM (Table 6.3), the results present a more balanced picture.

4 Tables 6.2 and 6.3 are similar to Table 1 in the original CMO article, but Tables 6.2 and 6.3 tabulate problem solving per *decision structure* rather than per *access structure* (as it was originally done) because access structure is not related to the number of authorities.

Table 6.3 Proportion of Choices that Resolve Problems by Load and Triple Authority Decision Structure

| Triple authority decision structure | Load | | | |
|---|---|---|---|---|
| | Light | Moderate | Heavy | All |
| D0 (UUU) | 79% | 73% | 41% | 64% |
| D1 (HHH) | 52% | 26% | 19% | 32% |
| D2 (SSS) | 34% | 23% | 16% | 24% |
| D3 (UUH) | 77% | 67% | 28% | 57% |
| D4 (UUS) | 55% | 64% | 25% | 48% |
| D5 (UHH) | 59% | 53% | 21% | 44% |
| D6 (UHS) | 47% | 35% | 21% | 34% |
| D7 (USS) | 43% | 32% | 19% | 31% |
| D8 (HHS) | 38% | 27% | 16% | 27% |
| D9 (HSS) | 38% | 25% | 16% | 26% |
| All | 52% | 42% | 22% | 39% |

2. *It was noted that the process was quite thoroughly and quite generally sensitive to variations in load.* The primary implication of the GCM being studied by CMO was how load level affected the outcome. One pressing question regarding the MAGCM would be whether an organized anarchy running garbage can processes involving several stakeholder groups would handle load differently than an organized anarchy running single authority processes. Table 6.4 shows the overall effects of variation in load for single authority and triple authority processes,[5] compared on the four central results identified by Cohen, March and Olsen (1972).

5 The Table 6.4 setup is the same as used for Table 2 in the 1972 article, so the results for the single authority model should be quite similar. The small discrepancies are probably due to the fact that the numbers here are based on the multi authority model

Table 6.4 Effects of Variations in Load on Single and Triple Authority Garbage Can Processes

| | Load | Mean problem activity | Mean decision maker activity | Mean decision difficulty | Proportion of choices by flight or oversight |
|---|---|---|---|---|---|
| Single authority | Light | 110.9 | 60.0 | 19.6 | 48% |
| | Moderate | 184.3 | 66.3 | 38.0 | 60% |
| | Heavy | 220.4 | 71.5 | 50.6 | 65% |
| Triple authority | Light | 84.2 | 65.5 | 13.0 | 47% |
| | Moderate | 187.0 | 87.1 | 39.9 | 56% |
| | Heavy | 231.9 | 77.7 | 43.6 | 74% |

Comparing the two versions of the GCM in Table 6.4, it is evident that *allowing for several authorities does have an impact on the results*. Although some of the results are close, the multi authority results consistently show larger variations, indicating that the multi authority model is even more sensitive to load.

The mechanism of the multi authority model might in itself contribute to the differences noticed. This could be clarified by comparing single authority results with the results gathered from multi authority scenarios with all three authorities being equal (all unsegmented, all hierarchical or all specialized). These results are presented in Table 6.5. They are generally closer to the single authority numbers, indicating that the increase in variation of the triple authority results in Table 6.4 stems primarily from situations where the stakeholder groups do not all have the same decision structure.

---

being used on one authority only, and that the method used to create the numbers for the proportion of choices made by flight or oversight are not explicitly given in the 1972 article.

Table 6.5 Effects of Variations in Load on MAGCM Processes with Three Identical Authorities

| | Load | Mean problem activity | Mean decision maker activity | Mean decision difficulty | Proportion of choices by flight or oversight |
|---|---|---|---|---|---|
| Three identical authorities | Light | 95.9 | 68.9 | 15.2 | 44% |
| | Moderate | 193.2 | 83.3 | 40.0 | 58% |
| | Heavy | 226.0 | 76.3 | 48.2 | 68% |

The results in Table 6.2 would seem supportive to heuristics[6] like 'no matter what decision structure is being used, the proportion of decisions that solve problems will decline as the load on the organization increases'. Again, the MAGCM results of Table 6.3 present a more balanced picture, indicating a need for some caution to be exercised: while most of the decision structures have the same tendency as the single authority model, one of the decision structures does not. For the UUS (Unsegmented-Unsegmented-Specialized) decision structure, Table 3 shows that the proportion of decisions that solve problems actually increases (from 55 per cent to 64 per cent) as the load increases from light to moderate.

3. *The tendency of decision makers and problems to track each other through choices was observed as a typical feature of the original model.* This systematic behavioural tendency of the model shows even more clearly in the triple authority results, thus further countering the myths of GCMs producing random effects.

4. *Important interconnections among three key aspects of the efficiency of the decision process specified were noted, with problem activity, problem latency and decision times identified as those key aspects.* These interconnections show even more clearly in the triple authority model, with problem latency showing even higher variation between high and low problem

6 i.e. rules of thumb, 'principles which reduce the complex tasks of assessing probabilities and predicting values to simpler judgemental operations' (Tversky and Kahneman, 1974: 1124).

activity (but decision time showing marginally lower variation). As problem activity was seen as a rough measure of potential decision conflicts in the organization, it might not be surprising that processes with three authorities will need even higher activity than processes with only one to keep the latency low.

5. *It was noted that the process was frequently sharply interactive, with some phenomena being dependent on the particular combination of structures involved.* The kind of particular, combination-dependent behaviour of the model is a feature that is at least as prominent in the triple authority version.

6. *It was observed that important problems were more likely to be solved than unimportant ones.* The property is retained in the triple authority model, as important problems had a 35 per cent higher resolution rate than unimportant problems, independent of their arrival time. In the MAGCM, the two most important problems had a mean problem latency of less than one third of the mean latency of the two least important problems.

7. *It was noticed that important choices were less likely to resolve problems than unimportant choices.* The same feature applies to the triple authority model, where the number of unimportant choices that solved problems was 16 per cent higher than the number of important choices that solved problems.

8. *It was observed that although a large proportion of the choices were made, the choice failures that did occur were concentrated among the most important and least important choices.* In the triple authority model this effect is quite noticeable, having a mean of 9 per cent choice failures among the three most important choices, 4 per cent choice failures among the middle four choices, and 10 per cent among the three least important choices.

As a general note regarding the major properties outlined above, Cohen, March and Olsen note that the outcomes will depend strongly on the organizational structure, with the same garbage can operation showing different behaviour under different structural designs or loads. This shows up even more pronounced in the triple authority model, through the even wider range of results. Analysis of the results shows this to be a quite general behaviour, of which the results in Table 6.4 are fairly typical: While *Mean Problem Activity* doubles (from 111 to 220) as the load increases from light to heavy in the single authority model, it nearly trebles (from 84 to 232) in the triple authority model.

## Universities and Multi Authority Garbage Cans

Most organizational models presume an organizational form with common goals and established procedures and instruments for decision making, as well as structures regarding who will participate in making the different decisions. In organizations where this is not the case for parts of the organization, we may instead have the organizational form of an organized anarchy, and decision making may happen according to the GCM. Cohen, March and Olsen assert that 'if the implications of the model are applicable anywhere, they are applicable to a university. Although there is great variation among colleges and universities, both between countries and within any country, the model has general relevance to decision making in higher education' (CMO: 11).

One question would be if this is still the case, almost half a century later. In 2003 and 2004, the Office of the Auditor General of Norway investigated the internal management at the universities of Norway, studying whether the university had adequate structures, instruments and procedures for managing and following up the activities at the universities. Their report concluded that 'the universities' internal management systems do not adequately ensure assessment of performance and attainment of targets, and that systems for proper internal control have not been developed to a sufficient extent', noting that 'the greatest weakness was the absence of concrete objectives and performance targets for what is to be achieved in the short term' (Office of the Auditor General, 2004: 7). Without doubt, the universities of Norway were found to operate with *problematic preferences*. The Auditor General further noted that '[a]t the same time the audit showed that in general the administrators were uncertain as to what instruments were at their disposal' (ibid.: 7): the universities of Norway was found to operate with *unclear technology*. Finally, it was found that, with only minor variations in the management systems between the different universities and faculties, 'Informal management via culture, tradition and dialogue was prominent. However, informal management is always highly individual and not well suited to long-term integrated management' (ibid.: 7). The universities of Norway were found to operate with *fluent participation*. In summary, the investigation of the Auditor General uncovered that the universities in Norway had *organized anarchy* not only as a form applying to parts of the organization parts of the time, but as their *fundamental organizational form*. A few years later, McKinsey's study of the University of Oslo (UiO) found that regarding leadership and execution, 'UiO is like an organized anarchy, the only control is set by external boundaries' (McKinsey, 2008: 23). The studies show that organized anarchy is a form of organizational being so robust and at the same time so flexible that it seems to be working even as a fundamental form, and even in the most knowledge-focused institutions in a modern information society.

Identifying a form of organization with those kinds of features could be seen as a reason for celebration. But when reported in the national press, 'organized anarchy' was seen as some kind of disease that the universities 'suffer from' (*Dagens Næringsliv*, 2010), and both McKinsey and the Auditor General consider it a (serious) weakness. However, in the same report McKinsey sums up findings from interviews with academic staff and management at University of Oslo, showing that staff and management give their own organizational structure a score close to the median among the twenty-eight factors scrutinized. The Ministry of Education and Research (as the owner of the universities) comments that the Auditor General's report 'concludes that the internal management systems do not really constitute an integrated process of planning, implementation and control. The Ministry [...] thinks that the report ought to contain a description of how the internal management is actually done'. With the Auditor General's focus thus being more on theoretical than on practical aspects of managing a university, '[t]he Ministry finds that this does not give a complete or correct picture' (Office of the Auditor General, 2004: 10).

When it comes to de jure authorities, many universities will find themselves in the three-authority situation described by the Auditor General: a ministerial authority, complemented by two intramural authorities; one academic and one administrative (ibid.: A8-A9). To be auditable, the ministerial authority will use a strictly hierarchical decision structure and, as the Auditor General clearly pointed out, this will have to be upheld even within the institution to some degree. But as a broad picture, institutions that used to be under detailed central controls have experienced a shift to a larger degree of autonomy, increasing the role of the academic and administrative authority (Bleiklie and Kogan, 2007; Ferlie et al., 2009), including a transfer of *formal* autonomy from the state (Bleiklie and Michelsen, 2009: 61).

In most universities, the two intramural authorities are not well reconciled. Del Favero and Bray (2010: 477) observe 'that the relationship between faculty members and administrators in colleges and universities is often, if not typically, contentious'. Going deeper into how the two groups differ, they find that:

> The relationship between faculty and administrators is also rooted in a well-documented 'cultural clash' emanating from their widely divergent cultures. This is explained by the fact that faculty and administrators are oriented very differently toward their work and in their relationships to their institutions. Simply, faculty are motivated by their individual, scholarly interests, while administrators are commonly motivated by their responsibility to the collective interests of the institution and often by the need to change to face future challenges.
>
> Administrators' work [...] is driven by the collective. They occupy decision-making roles which require that they consider competing interests – all vying for their share of scarce resources. (ibid.: 480)

With the academic authority thus tending towards a specialized structure and the administrative authority tending towards an unsegmented structure, and the ministerial authority operating through a hierarchical structure, the best suited variety of the triple authority MAGCM would be UHS (Unsegmented-Hierarchical-Specialized). This variety ranks below average among the triple authority results regarding ability to resolve problems under different load conditions (see Table 6.4). Its performance on the core features under different load conditions is shown in Table 6.6.

Table 6.6 Effects of Variations in Load for the UHS Variety of Triple Authority MAGCM

| | Load | Mean problem activity | Mean decision maker activity | Mean decision difficulty | Proportion of choices by flight or oversight |
|---|---|---|---|---|---|
| Triple authority UHS | Light | 68.5 | 56.8 | 11.1 | 53% |
| | Moderate | 195.0 | 85.1 | 40.5 | 63% |
| | Heavy | 237.7 | 79.3 | 38.6 | 77% |

The UHS variety of MAGCM has lower than average problem activity under light load, but higher than average problem activity when the load is moderate or heavy. This particular variety has the peculiar feature of decreasing decision difficulty as the load increases from moderate to heavy. In fact, this variety of triple authority has among the lowest decision difficulty of all under heavy loads, with only the UUS variety showing marginally lower decision difficulty under heavy load.

In the MAGCM all three authorities are given equal power. In actual scenarios other distributions may evolve, and the Auditor General's investigation indicated that the influence from the hierarchical decision structure might be somewhat lower. For some activity areas, it was noted that 'The management of these activities did not seem to be closely linked to any established management chain. It can therefore be queried whether the university management has adequate control [...]' (Office of the Auditor General, 2004: 7).

A growing literature posits that the faculty-administration dichotomy is becoming a model too simple to be useful (see Whitchurch, 2008; Whitchurch and Gordon, this volume). Gornitzka and Larsen (2004) find that a 'dominant development pattern in the 1980s and 1990s is the change *within* administrative staff, which could be interpreted as a *professionalization*'. Schneijderberg and Merkator (2013: 53) confirm this, showing how '[t]he growing complexity of universities results in differentiation and professionalization of functions, tasks and roles for which specific knowledge, permanently updated information and competences are needed'; they refer to studies by Klumpp and Teichler identifying a heterogeneous group of new higher education professionals, 'mostly highly qualified, satisfying the growing need of university management for systematic knowledge about the university and releasing academic and administrative staff from a variety of functions and tasks' (ibid.).

These developments have led to the 'creation of a *third space* between professional and academic domains' (Whitchurch, 2008: 378, italics in the original). Schneijderberg and Merkator (2013: 81) find that shifts regarding what could be considered hubs in the HE arena are strongly indicated, seeing changes that should be interpreted as 'a functional rethinking of professional positions in universities instead of a hollowing out of the (traditional) academic culture of the university' and concluding that:

> From discussing the *Academic overlap* and the *Administrative overlap* it became evident that the bipolar analysis has to be extended by adding a third dimension. This third dimension unlocks the static positions of academic and administrative personnel. Accordingly higher education professionals are not considered on an in-between position. In the shifting arenas of work the three groups of academic and administrative personnel and higher education professional do meet. (ibid.: 82, italics in the original)

Schneijderberg and Merkator have developed the *Overlap Model*, identifying three specific categories of personnel; academic personnel, the Higher Education Professional and administrative personnel, as shown in Figure 6.1.

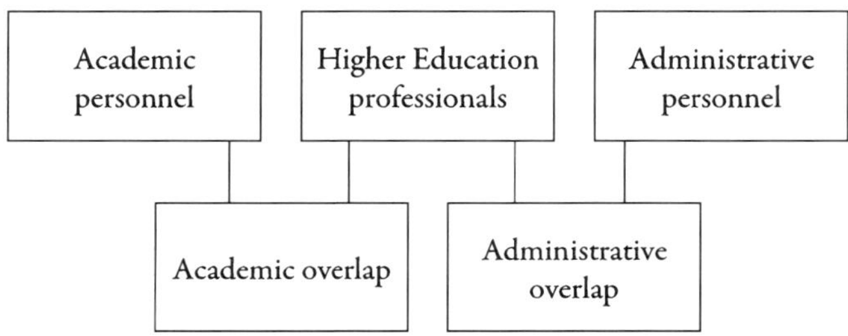


Figure 6.1 The Overlap Model
(after Schneijderberg and Merkator, 2013: 80)

Following Del Favero and Bray's (2010) analysis of the academic and the administrative groups, a triple authority MAGCM version of the Overlap Model would have the academic personnel operating with a specialized decision structure, and the administrative personnel operating with an unsegmented decision structure. Gornitzka and Larsen (2004) and Schneijderberg and Merkator (2013) point to the degree of specialization as a characteristic of the higher education professionals, so the USS (Unsegmented-Specialized-Specialized) variety of the triple authority MAGCM would be the variety that corresponds to the Overlap Model. The performance of this particular variety on how central characteristics vary with load is shown in Table 6.7.

Table 6.7 Effects of Variations in Load for the USS Triple Authority Variety of the MAGCM

| | Load | Mean problem activity | Mean decision maker activity | Mean decision difficulty | Proportion of choices by flight or oversight |
|---|---|---|---|---|---|
| Triple authority USS | Light | 112.7 | 59.8 | 15.8 | 57% |
| | Moderate | 206.1 | 75.1 | 36.8 | 67% |
| | Heavy | 243.8 | 74.6 | 40.1 | 78% |

In Table 6.8, the performance results for the emerging Overlap scenario (USS) of university governance are compared to the results for the classic Control scenario (UHS) (Table 6.8), where the effects of the hierarchical control-and-command authority (sought after, but not found to a satisfactory degree in Norwegian universities by the Auditor General) are much more prevalent.

Table 6.8 Two Specific Triple Authority Varieties of the MAGCM, Means Over All Load Levels

| | Triple authority MAGCM variety | Mean problem activity | Mean decision maker activity | Mean decision difficulty | Proportion of choices by flight or oversight |
|---|---|---|---|---|---|
| 'Control' | UHS | 161.7 | 73.7 | 30.1 | 64% |
| 'Overlap' | USS | 187.6 | 69.8 | 31.0 | 67% |

One interpretation of the differences would be that while both scenarios produce decisions at similar levels with similar difficulty, the UHS variety achieves this by higher decision maker activity and quite a bit less moving the problems around, and the USS variety achieves it with less work by decision makers, but by venting the problems in a much higher number of decision arenas.

### *Governance, Garbage Cans and Resilience*

Weick and Sutcliffe (2007) show how organizations supporting purely hierarchical authorities or authorities that can be embodied in single individuals (as in the specialized decision structure in the GCM) may be at risk when it comes to organizational resilience. They advocate deference to expertise (as opposed to the expert) to promote resilience, stipulating that '[e]xpertise is an assemblage of knowledge, experience, learning and intuitions that is seldom embodied in a single individual', and that '[e]xpertise resides in the heed with which people view their inputs as *contributions* rather than as solitary acts, *represent* the system within which their contributions and those of others interlock to produce outcomes, and *subordinate* their contributions to the well-being of the system, constantly mindful of what that system needs to remain productive and resilient' (Weick and Sutcliffe, 2007: 78, italics in the original). It would follow that only one of the three available decision structures in the single authority GCM would fit the 'expertise'-criteria. While the unsegmented decision structure would be well suited for resilience work, both the hierarchical and the specialized decision structure would make the improvement of resilience a more risky enterprise. However, having more than one authority contribute simultaneously to the choice opportunities, as in the multi authority GCM, this would necessarily include some level of deference by all authorities included. On this aspect, all varieties of the three authority models used for universities would be well suited for resilience work.

The multi authority results create room for exploring further how decision making in multi authority organizations having the organizational form of organized anarchy may relate to the organization's strategic resilience. The common criteria presented by Hamel, Välikangas and Romme (Hamel and Välikangas, 2003; Välikangas, 2010; Välikangas and Romme, 2012a) as well as resilience drivers presented by Weick and Sutcliffe (2007) may be used for this purpose.[7] Embracing both operational and strategic resilience, Välikangas and Romme propose this definition of organizational resilience:

> Organizational resilience: the extent to which people throughout the organization engage in mindful and experimental behaviour, to generate options for the future and as such respond to opportunity as much as adversity. (Välikangas and Romme, 2012a: 32)

The processes of valuing variety, liberating resources and embracing paradox have been identified as three necessary preconditions for building resilience into the organization (Hamel and Välikangas, 2003). Refining these conditions further, Välikangas and Romme (2012a) propose a theoretical framework showing how these conditions interact with organizational performance, organizational resilience and shareholder pressure in publicly owned firms. Figure 6.2 is heavily based on Välikangas and Romme's

7 Much of the literature addresses either operational resilience (adversity-driven, recovery-based, training for and surviving setbacks, how to persist in the face of threat and recovering after a crisis) or strategic resilience (opportunity-driven, renewal-based, change without a crisis, pro-activeness, turning threats into opportunities, engaging in exploration and experimentation) (Välikangas and Romme, 2012a; Välikangas and Romme, 2012b: Hamel and Välikangas, 2003). This text focuses on aspects that are common to both strands.

framework, but adapted to the environment experienced by many universities by exchanging the original's single authority of 'Shareholder pressure' with 'Pressure from the organization's authorities', exchanging 'Generative doubt by CEO' with 'Generative doubt by leadership', and exchanging 'Firm's performance' with 'Organization's performance'.

In Välikangas' and Romme's framework, the precondition of 'liberating resources' identified by Hamel and Välikangas (2003) is contained within the 'resource slack', defined by Välikangas and Romme (2012a: 32) as 'the stock of excess resources that top management perceives to be available for allocating to new ideas or projects'. The precondition of 'valuing variety' and 'embracing paradox' is addressed by 'generative doubt by leadership' (in their original model 'generative doubt by CEO') defined as 'ability of CEO to seek and engage in the experience of not knowing'; and by 'reservoir-for-change mental model' defined as 'managerial values and beliefs that acknowledge (a) the generative role of mindful and experimental behaviour and (b) the strong, but delayed, effect of the latter behaviour on firm performance' (ibid.: 32).

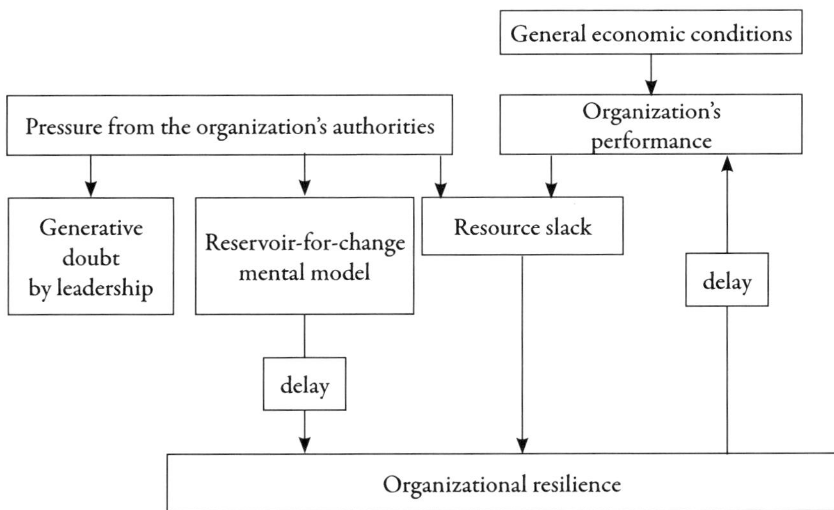


Figure 6.2 Organizational Resilience Theoretical Framework (adapted from Välikangas and Romme, 2012a)

Cohen, March and Olsen (1972) thoroughly elaborate on how resource slack relates to organizations using the organized anarchy form, and specifically how slack relates to four of the basic elements of the GCM, namely those of net energy load, access structure, decision structure and energy distribution. If the assumption holds that the MAGCM relates to slack in the same way as within the single authority GCM, and that slack relates to organizational resilience in multi authority organizations in a way comparable to publicly owned firms, then effects on slack in the different multi authority organizational varieties will affect the capabilities of achieving organizational resilience in these organizational varieties. Some of the effects of changes in slack will apply to the organizational garbage can processes irrespective of the multi authority variety being simulated. One such effect would be how slack affects the access structure of the organization. To sustain the present access structure, slack will have to be increased if the organization values variety more highly by increasing the heterogeneity of its technology and values. If this remains relatively stable in a university while slack is increased, the access structure would be expected to change from hierarchical to specialized, and from specialized to unsegmented. If slack is kept unchanged while the university actively seeks to value variety more highly by increasing the heterogeneity of its technology and values, the opposite effect on access structure would be expected, from unsegmented to specialized, and from specialized to hierarchical (CMO: 12).

But, as Välikangas and Romme (2012a: 7) found, liberating resources through slack in itself does not appear to provide a straightforward explanation of organizational resilience. In addition, Hamel and Välikangas (2003) identified valuing variety and embracing paradox as primary resilience enablers. Välikangas and Romme (2012a) point to how mental models that lack appreciation of mindfulness and experimentation and have a focus on getting quick results will have the opposite effect, lowering the potential for resilience. In identifying the close ties among the expected, the unexpected and mindful organizing, Weick and Sutcliffe (2007) point to how orderliness and predictability are created through the way we exercise mental models and build expectations into organizational roles, routines and strategies. In auditing the universities of Norway against a single-authority hierarchical model, the Office of the Auditor General (2004) found that they all had inadequate management systems and insufficient control. However, the investigation found that the institutions *were* in fact managed, in spite of finding 'that in general the administrators were uncertain as to what [management/managerial] instruments were at their disposal' and that '[t]he management of these activities did not seem to be closely linked to any established management chain'.

The Auditor General, using a single hierarchical audit model, expected to find a relatively small number of well-defined managerial 'instruments', but what they found was that the institutions entertained a near-kaleidoscopic variety of such instruments:

> To the question what instruments the administrators could utilise to discharge their managerial responsibilities, there was a wide variety of responses. There was no systematic understanding of the term 'instruments', and reference was made to everything from planning documents, through budgets, dialogue, meetings, pay negotiations and employee appraisal interviews, to persuasion. Several administrators pointed out that the most important instrument was the understanding of a culture based on discussion, conversation and argument. (ibid.: 18)

These findings fall into the trend identified in studies of professional staff in UK universities, that '[r]ather than drawing their authority solely from established roles and structures, they increasingly build their credibility on a personal basis, via lateral relationships with colleagues inside and outside the university' (Whitchurch, 2008: 394). Features like those reported above, although perceived as highly problematic by the Auditor General, do not seem to be nearly as big a problem for the institutions themselves. The Auditor General reports that most of the administrators (two-thirds) perceive 'their responsibilities and authority as relatively clearly defined, regardless of whether written documents and instructions existed' (ibid.: 18). Managerial situations perceived as containing a number of paradoxical features by the Auditor General, had the same paradoxes easily embraced by the mental models, expectations and actual managing being performed at the universities. The McKinsey study and the investigation by the Auditor General identified organized anarchy as the organizational form in use at the universities in Norway, and pointed to a number of observations indicating the use of mental models and expectations incorporating slack, and the use of many ways of managing and organizing; they also noted how seemingly paradoxical features were developed and entertained in the universities. But although criticized by the McKinsey study and the report of the Auditor General, these are the very features being pointed to as core enablers of organizational resilience (Hamel and Välikangas, 2003; Välikangas and Romme, 2012a; Weick and Sutcliffe, 2007), as well as being fully in line with observations in UK and elsewhere that the universities and their stakeholder groups 'benefit [...] from the involvement of broader constituencies in institutional decision-making' (Whitchurch and Gordon, 2013: 17). One conclusion that can be drawn is that governance embracing the organizational form of organized anarchies does not hinder the development of organizational resilience. Another conclusion is that governance in line with classical command-and-control-oriented organizational models proposed in the McKinsey study and underlying the Auditor General's investigation may well make it more difficult to further develop organizational resilience in universities.

## Conclusion

Organized anarchies were presented as a form characteristic of universities more than forty years ago (CMO), and the extraordinarily simple and useful Garbage Can Model was developed as a tool to come to grips with decision making in organized anarchies. The applicability of the GCM to situations similar to those of the organized anarchy has been confirmed a number of times (see Browning et al., 2006, for an overview), and it has been shown to have application beyond the scope of the single organization (see Peters, 2002). Investigating the universities in Norway, the Office of the Auditor General found evidence of all three general properties separating organized anarchies from other organizational forms. These were found to be present in all universities in Norway (Office of the Auditor General, 2004).

The form of organized anarchies is still found to be the fundamental organizational form of many universities. But although the form is fundamentally unaltered since the 1970s, there have been some dramatic changes in the universities' exogenous environment and in their relations to it. This has been characterized as a movement from 'the university as a republic of scholars towards the idea of the university as a stakeholder organization' (Bleiklie and Kogan, 2007: 477). These exogenous changes have made the question of organizational resilience a pressing issue for institutions in the higher education sector (Hanna, 2003; this present volume passim).

Because the GCM was developed as a single authority model, it was clearly not designed with today's higher education scenario in mind. However, this text proposes how the model can be recreated for the present day situation of several simultaneously active authorities by distributing the decision making power onto these while still keeping them separated.

Using findings from the Auditor General's quite thorough investigation of the management of universities in Norway, it is shown that whilst developing or improving organizational resilience, the organized anarchy form would pose fewer hindrances than a purely hierarchical organizational form. The multi authority GCM is shown to be at least as robust and efficient as the original single authority model. It is shown how a multi authority model may easily be applied to three de jure or de facto authorities, and also how the multi authority model may be applied to emerging university scenarios that include 'the new higher education professionals' as a separate personnel group in addition to the established groups of academic personnel and administrative personnel.

The primary use of organizational models is for representing real organizations, providing general guidance and suggestions about how one might proceed. The GCM, and especially the multi authority GCM, would seem as attractive as ever for that kind of purpose, whether conceptual or computational. This would be even more the case when faced with situations that would be difficult to 'get one's head around' in organizations such as universities manifesting organized anarchy as their primary form for the whole or for parts of the organization. In a higher education landscape that is increasingly privileging resilient institutions (Hanna, 2003), the multi authority Garbage Can Model could be a very useful tool in coming to grips with decision making scenarios in universities, on the strategic as well as the operational level (Morill, 2007).

## References

Bendor, J., Moe, T.M., and Shotts, K.W. (2001). 'Recycling the Garbage Can: an Assessment of the Research Program', *The American Political Science Review*, 95 (1), 169–190.

Bleiklie, I., and Kogan, M. (2007). 'Organization and Governance of Universities', *Higher Education Policy*, 20 (4), 477–493.

Bleiklie, I., and Michelsen, S. (2009). 'The University as Enterprise and Academic Co-determination'. In A. Amaral, I., Bleiklie and C. Musselin (eds), *From Governance to Identity*, pp. 57–78. Dordrecht: Springer.

Box, G.E.P., and Draper, N.R. (1987). *Empirical Model Building and Response Surfaces*. New York: John Wiley and Sons.

Browning, L., Sørnes, J.-O., Sætre, A.S., and Stephens, K. (2006). 'A Garbage Can Model of Information Communication Technology Choice'. In A. Schorr and S. Seltmann (eds), *Changing Media Cultures in Europe and Abroad. Research on New Ways of Handling Information and Entertainment Content*, pp. 417–440. New York: Pabst Science Publishers.

Brunsson, N. (2007). *The Consequences of Decision-Making*. Oxford: Oxford University Press.

Brunsson, N., and Olsen, J.P. (1993). *The Reforming Organization*. London: Routledge.

Carley, K.M. (1995). 'Computational and Mathematical Organization Theory: Perspective and Directions'. *Computational and Mathematical Organization Theory*, 1 (1), 39–56.

Cohen, M.D., March, J.G., and Olsen, J.P. (1972). 'A Garbage Can Model of Organizational Choice', *Administrative Science Quarterly*, 17 (1), 1–23.

Cohen, M.D., March, J.G., and Olsen, J.P. (2012). '"A Garbage Can Model" at Forty: a Solution that still Attracts Problems'. In A. Lomi and J.R. Harrison (eds), *The Garbage Can Model of Organizational Choice: Looking Forward at Forty*, 19–30.

Cohen, M.D., and March, J.G. (1974). *Leadership and Ambiguity*. Berkeley: The Carnegie Commission on Higher Education.

Daft, R.L. (2004). *Organization Theory and Design*. Mason, Ohio: South-Western.

*Dagens Næringsliv* (2010). 'Hudfletter Universitet i Oslo', 9 January, p. 1.

de Zilva, D. (2010). *Academic Units in a Complex, Changing World*. Dordrecht: Springer.

Dehousse, R. (2002). *The Open Method of Coordination: A New Policy Paradigm*. Paper delivered to the First Pan-European Conference on European Union Politics: 'The Politics of European Integration: Academic *Acquis* and Future Challenges'. Bordeaux, 26–28 September.

Del Favero, M., and Bray, N.J. (2010). 'Herding Cats and Big Dogs: Tensions in the Faculty-Administrator Relationship'. In J.C. Smart (ed.), *Higher Education: Handbook of Theory and Research*, Vol. 25, pp. 477–541. Dordrecht: Springer.

European Council (2000). *Presidency Conclusions of the Lisbon European Council 23 and 24 March 2000.* <http://www.europarl.europa.eu/summits/lis1_en.htm> accessed 26 February 2013.

Ferlie, E., Musselin, C., and Andresani, G. (2009). 'The Governance of Higher Education Systems: a Public Management Perspective'. In C. Paradeise, E. Reale, I. Bleiklie and Ferlie, E. (eds), *University Governance – Western European Comparative Perspectives*, pp. 1–19. Dordrecht: Springer.

Fioretti, G., and Lomi, A. (2010). 'Passing the Buck in the Garbage Can Model of Organizational Choice', *Computational and Mathematical Organization Theory*, 16 (2), 113–143.

Giesecke, J. (1994). *Creativity and Innovation in an Organized Anarchy*. University of Nebraska, Lincoln: Faculty Publications, UNL Libraries, Paper 254.

Gornitzka, Å. (2006). *The Open Method of Coordination as Practice – a Watershed in European Education Policy?* Working Paper No. 16, ARENA. University of Oslo.

Gornitzka, Å. (2007). 'Historical Legacies and New Modes of Governance in European Education Policy – the Inception of the Open Method of Coordination'. In J. Enders and F. van Vught (eds), *Towards a Cartography of Higher Education Policy Change*, pp. 165–172. Enschede: CHEPS/ University of Twente Press.

Gornitzka, Å., and Larsen, I.M. (2004). 'Towards Professionalization? Restructuring of Administrative Work Force in Universities', *Higher Education*, 47 (4), 455–471.

Hamel, G., and Välikangas, L. (2003). 'The Quest for Resilience', *Harvard Business Review*, September, 53–62.

Hanna, D.E. (2003). 'Building a Leadership Vision – Eleven Strategic Challenges for Higher Education', *EDUCAUSE Review*, July/August, 25–34.

Hatch, M.J. (1997). *Organization Theory: Modern, Symbolic, and Postmodern Perspectives.* Oxford: Oxford University Press.

Heimer, C.A., and Stinchcombe, A.L. (1999). 'Remodeling the Garbage Can'. In M. Egeberg and P. Lægreid (eds), *Organizing Political Institutions*, pp. 25–57. Oslo: Scandinavian University Press.

Huisman, J. (2009). 'Coming to Terms with Governance in Higher Education'. In J. Huisman (ed.), *International Perspectives on the Governance of Higher Education: Alternative Frameworks for Coordination*, pp. 1–13. London: Routledge.

Humburg, M. (2008). 'The Open Method of Coordination and European Integration. The Example of European Education Policy'. Berliner Arbeitspapier zur Europäischen Integration Nr. 8. Freie Universität Berlin.

Inamizu, N. (2006). *Analysis of Organizational Processes using Multi-Agent Simulator: Reexamination of the Garbage Can Model.* University of Tokyo MMRC Discussion Paper No. 97.

Inamizu, N. (2009). *Inside the Garbage-Can: An Orderly Decision-Making Process in Disorderly Organization Structures.* University of Tokyo MMRC Discussion Paper No. 264.

Jesty, P., Galliet, J.F., Giesen, J., Franco, G., and Ryan, A. (1999). *Converge System Architecture: Architecture Assessment Guidelines.* CORDIS: 4th Framework Research, TAP CONVERGE TR 1101, Work Package SA 3.1.

Kingdon, J.W. (1995). *Agendas, Alternatives, and Public Policies* (2nd edn). New York: Addison-Wesley.

Knudsen, T., Warglien, M., and Yi, S. (2012). 'Garbage Can in the Lab'. In A. Lomi and J.R. Harrison (eds), *The Garbage Can Model of Organizational Choice: Looking Forward at Forty*, 189–227.

Levinthal, D.A. (2012). 'From the Ivy Tower to the C-Suite: Garbage Can Processes and Corporate Strategic Decision Making'. In A. Lomi and J.R. Harrison (eds), *The Garbage Can Model of Organizational Choice: Looking Forward at Forty*, 349–362.

Lomi, A., and Harrison, J.R. (eds) (2012). *The Garbage Can Model of Organizational Choice: Looking Forward at Forty*. Bingley: Emerald.

March, J.G., and Olsen, J.P. (1976). *Ambiguity and Choice in Organizations*. Oslo: Universitetsforlaget.

McKinsey (2008). 'Globalt Ledende Universiteter – Hva kan vi Lære av de Beste?' Presentation given to the Board of the University of Oslo during Meeting of the Board on 17 June 2008.

Miller, J.H., and Page, S.E. (2007). *Complex Adaptive Systems: an Introduction to Computational Models of Social Life.* Princeton: Princeton University Press.

Morrill, R.L. (2007). *Strategic Leadership – Integrating Strategy and Leadership in Colleges and Universities*. Lanham: Rowman and Littlefield.

Neave, G. (1988). 'On the Cultivation of Quality, Efficiency and Enterprise: an Overview of Recent Trends in Higher Education in Western Europe 1986–1988', *European Journal of Education*, 23 (1/2), 7–23.

Ocasio, W. (2012). 'Situated Attention, Loose and Tight Coupling, and the Garbage Can Model'. In A. Lomi and J.R. Harrison (eds), *The Garbage Can Model of Organizational Choice: Looking Forward at Forty*, 293–317.

Office of the Auditor General (2004). *The Office of the Auditor General's Investigation of the Management of the Universities.* Oslo: The Ministry of Education and Research. <http://www.riksrevisjonen.no/en/SiteCollectionDocuments/Dokumentbasen/Engelsk/Document%203/Eng_Doc_3_3_2004_2005.pdf> accessed 1 May 2013.

Peters, B.G. (2002). *Governance: A Garbage Can Perspective. Reihe Politikwissenschaft # 84*.Vienna: Institut für Höhere Studien (HIS).

Schneijderberg, C., and Merkator, N. (2013). 'The New Higher Education Professionals'. In B. Kehm and U. Teichler (eds), *The Academic Profession in Europe: New Tasks and New Challenges*, pp. 53–92. Dordrecht: Springer.

Scott, W.R. (1998). *Organizations: Rational, Natural and Open Systems* (4th edn). Upper Saddle River, N.J.: Prentice-Hall.

Stinchcombe, A.L. (1974). *Creating Efficient Industrial Administration*. New York: Academic Press.

Tversky, A., and Kahneman, D. (1974). 'Judgment under Uncertainty: Heuristics and Biases'. *Science*, 185 (4157), 1124–1131.

Välikangas, L. (2010). *The Resilient Organization. How Adaptive Cultures Thrive Even When Strategy Fails*. New York: McGraw-Hill.

Välikangas, L., and Romme, A.G.L. (2012a). 'Designing for Organizational Resilience'. *Academia.edu*, <http://www.academia.edu/2125405/Designing_for_organizational_resilience> accessed 1 May 2013.

Välikangas, L., and Romme, A.G.L. (2012b). 'Building Resilience Capabilities at "Big Brown Box, Inc"', *Strategy and Leadership*, 40 (4), 43–45.

Weick, K.E., and Sutcliffe, K.M. (2007). *Managing the Unexpected. Resilient Performance in an Age of Uncertainty* (2nd edn). San Fransisco: John Wiley and Sons.

Whitchurch, C. (2008). 'Shifting Identities and Blurring Boundaries: the Emergence of *Third Space* Professionals in UK Higher Education', *Higher Education Quarterly*, 62 (4), 377–396.

Whitchurch, C., and Gordon, G. (2013). 'Reconciling Flexible Staffing Models with Inclusive Governance and Management', *Higher Education Quarterly*, forthcoming, article first published online 8 May 2013, <http://onlinelibrary.wiley.com/doi/10.1111/hequ.12013/abstract> accessed 12 May 2013.

Xu, J., and Zhou, X. (2011). *Fuzzy-Like Multiple Objective Decision Making*. Dordrecht: Springer.

## Technical Appendix: The Garbage Can Model

Although reading the original article by Cohen, March and Olsen (1972) is very highly recommended, this appendix attempts to give a short description of the components of the original Garbage Can Model necessary to establish a basic understanding of the conceptual as well as the computational model.

The Garbage Can Model is concerned with decisional situations called *choice opportunities* modelled over time. The choice opportunities arising will be populated with items from three other streams: a stream of *problems* arriving into the decision arenas, a stream of *energy* from the decision makers, and a flow of *solutions*. The computational model creates simulations that run over a number of *periods*, fixed at twenty in the original model. The number seems to be picked to relate well to the number of *choices*, the number of *decision makers* and the number of *problems* being included. These numbers were set high enough not to miss important information while being low enough to avoid the computations to continue without adding new information. The original model included twenty problems, ten decision makers and ten choice opportunities. Choice opportunities are activated one at a time (one each period) until all choices are active and problems are activated two at a time (two each period) until all problems are active, resulting in all choices and all problems being activated during the first ten periods. With a total of twenty periods this gives equal numbers of periods to work through the fully activated model setup that it takes to activate all components.

The problems are numbered according to difficulty with the most difficult ones having the lowest numbers. Which two problems will be activated each of the ten first periods is defined by a random sequence called 'problem entry times'. Two different random sequences are used for problem entry times in the original model. Similarly, the most important choice opportunities have the lowest numbers, and which one to be activated at each of the ten periods is defined by random sequences called 'choice entry times'. Two different random sequences are used for these as well.

Together with the *net energy load* resting upon the organization, the problem and choice entry sequences describe the different conditions within each organizational variety being simulated. Three load levels are used: *light load*, *moderate load* and *heavy load*.

Two choice entry sequences times two problem entry sequences times three load levels makes up a total of twelve different sets of conditions for each organizational variety to be exposed to.

The organizational variety being simulated is given through three different structures: the *problem access* structure, the *decision structure* of the organization, and *how energy is distributed* among the decision makers. The original GCM includes three varieties of each of these, making up a total of 3x3x3=27 different organizational varieties. Running all 27 varieties through all 12 sets of conditions results in 324 scenarios.

The *decision structures* determine the relation between each decision maker and each of the choices. The model includes three varieties. In the *unsegmented* decision structure ($D_0$), any decision maker may participate in any active choice opportunity. In the *hierarchical* decision structure ($D_1$), low numbered (more important) decision makers may participate in many choices. In the *specialized* decision structure ($D_2$), decision makers have access to only one choice, and each choice can be made by only one decision maker. The relations between decision makers and choices for the three varieties are shown in Figure 6.3.

| | | Choice number | | | | | | | | | |
|---|---|---|---|---|---|---|---|---|---|---|---|
| | | 1 | 2 | 3 | 4 | 5 | 6 | 7 | 8 | 9 | 10 |
| Decision maker number | 1 | 1 | 1 | 1 | 1 | 1 | 1 | 1 | 1 | 1 | 1 |
| | 2 | 1 | 1 | 1 | 1 | 1 | 1 | 1 | 1 | 1 | 1 |
| | 3 | 1 | 1 | 1 | 1 | 1 | 1 | 1 | 1 | 1 | 1 |
| | 4 | 1 | 1 | 1 | 1 | 1 | 1 | 1 | 1 | 1 | 1 |
| | 5 | 1 | 1 | 1 | 1 | 1 | 1 | 1 | 1 | 1 | 1 |
| | 6 | 1 | 1 | 1 | 1 | 1 | 1 | 1 | 1 | 1 | 1 |
| | 7 | 1 | 1 | 1 | 1 | 1 | 1 | 1 | 1 | 1 | 1 |
| | 8 | 1 | 1 | 1 | 1 | 1 | 1 | 1 | 1 | 1 | 1 |
| | 9 | 1 | 1 | 1 | 1 | 1 | 1 | 1 | 1 | 1 | 1 |
| | 10 | 1 | 1 | 1 | 1 | 1 | 1 | 1 | 1 | 1 | 1 |

Decision structure Do: Unsegmented access

| | Choice number | | | | | | | | | |
|---|---|---|---|---|---|---|---|---|---|---|
| Decision maker number | 1 | 2 | 3 | 4 | 5 | 6 | 7 | 8 | 9 | 10 |
| 1 | 1 | 1 | 1 | 1 | 1 | 1 | 1 | 1 | 1 | 1 |
| 2 | 0 | 1 | 1 | 1 | 1 | 1 | 1 | 1 | 1 | 1 |
| 3 | 0 | 0 | 1 | 1 | 1 | 1 | 1 | 1 | 1 | 1 |
| 4 | 0 | 0 | 0 | 1 | 1 | 1 | 1 | 1 | 1 | 1 |
| 5 | 0 | 0 | 0 | 0 | 1 | 1 | 1 | 1 | 1 | 1 |
| 6 | 0 | 0 | 0 | 0 | 0 | 1 | 1 | 1 | 1 | 1 |
| 7 | 0 | 0 | 0 | 0 | 0 | 0 | 1 | 1 | 1 | 1 |
| 8 | 0 | 0 | 0 | 0 | 0 | 0 | 0 | 1 | 1 | 1 |
| 9 | 0 | 0 | 0 | 0 | 0 | 0 | 0 | 0 | 1 | 1 |
| 10 | 0 | 0 | 0 | 0 | 0 | 0 | 0 | 0 | 0 | 1 |

Decision structure D1: Hierarchical access

| | Choice number | | | | | | | | | |
|---|---|---|---|---|---|---|---|---|---|---|
| Decision maker number | 1 | 2 | 3 | 4 | 5 | 6 | 7 | 8 | 9 | 10 |
| 1 | 1 | 0 | 0 | 0 | 0 | 0 | 0 | 0 | 0 | 0 |
| 2 | 0 | 1 | 0 | 0 | 0 | 0 | 0 | 0 | 0 | 0 |
| 3 | 0 | 0 | 1 | 0 | 0 | 0 | 0 | 0 | 0 | 0 |
| 4 | 0 | 0 | 0 | 1 | 0 | 0 | 0 | 0 | 0 | 0 |
| 5 | 0 | 0 | 0 | 0 | 1 | 0 | 0 | 0 | 0 | 0 |
| 6 | 0 | 0 | 0 | 0 | 0 | 1 | 0 | 0 | 0 | 0 |
| 7 | 0 | 0 | 0 | 0 | 0 | 0 | 1 | 0 | 0 | 0 |
| 8 | 0 | 0 | 0 | 0 | 0 | 0 | 0 | 1 | 0 | 0 |
| 9 | 0 | 0 | 0 | 0 | 0 | 0 | 0 | 0 | 1 | 0 |
| 10 | 0 | 0 | 0 | 0 | 0 | 0 | 0 | 0 | 0 | 1 |

Decision structure D2: Specialized access

Figure 6.3 The Three Decision Structures in the Garbage Can Model

The relationship between problems and choices follows a similar scheme, with the problem *access structures* determining the relation between each problem and each of the choices. The model includes three different problem access structures. *Unsegmented* access ($A_0$) gives any active problem access to any active choice. *Hierarchical* access ($A_1$) lets important problems access any active choice, gradually restricting access for gradually less important problems. In the *specialized* access ($A_2$) each problem has access to only one choice and each choice is accessible to only two problems.

The energy needed to solve the problems is provided by the participants and it is distributed among them in different ways in the different organizational situations. Three different energy distributions are modelled, such that '[t]he distribution of energy among decision makers reflects possible variations in the amount of time spent on organizational problems by different decision makers' (CMO: 7). In energy distribution $E_0$, important people have less energy to spend in the choice opportunities, which might 'reflect variations in the combination of outside demands and motivation to participate within the organization' (CMO: 7). In energy distribution $E_1$, all participants have an equal amount of energy to spend, and in energy distribution E2, important people have more energy, a situation opposite that of Eo, as shown in Table 6.9. In each of the three variations, the sum of the decisional energy provided by all decision makers (the maximum amount of energy that can be applied to all problems at any one time) is 5.5.

According to the model, decisions are made whenever the effective energy available in the decision situation is big enough to overcome the energy requirements of the problems that are active in the same situation. The amount of energy needed depends on the *net energy load* situation in the organization, and is defined as 'the difference between the total energy required to solve all problems and the total effective energy available to the organization over all time periods' (CMO: 5). There are three levels of organizational load specified: *light load* (fixed at 1.1 in the original model), *moderate load* (where the energy requirement is doubled to 2.2), and *heavy load* (where the energy requirement is tripled to 3.3). These load numbers are set up in such a way that the system produces a high variation of results as the organizational load changes, but limited by the criterion that the system should contain enough energy to solve all the problems under any load condition when applied optimally.

Table 6.9: Energy Distributions in the Garbage Can Model

| | | Decision maker energy | | |
|---|---|---|---|---|
| | | E0: Important decision makers have less energy | E1: All decision makers have equal energy | E2: Important decision makers have more energy |
| Decision maker number | 1 | 0.1 | 0.55 | 1.0 |
| | 2 | 0.2 | 0.55 | 0.9 |
| | 3 | 0.3 | 0.55 | 0.8 |
| | 4 | 0.4 | 0.55 | 0.7 |
| | 5 | 0.5 | 0.55 | 0.6 |
| | 6 | 0.6 | 0.55 | 0.5 |
| | 7 | 0.7 | 0.55 | 0.4 |
| | 8 | 0.8 | 0.55 | 0.3 |
| | 9 | 0.9 | 0.55 | 0.2 |
| | 10 | 1.0 | 0.55 | 0.1 |

For the Garbage Can Model to support multiple authorities some method of differentiation between the different stakeholder groups participating in the decision making process will be required. The method chosen to implement this feature is to give each of the authorities its own decisional energy with its own energy distribution and its own decision structure, thus achieving the necessary qualitative as well as quantitative separation between the powers participating in the choice opportunities. In this way, each decision maker will have his/her energy from exactly one of the authorities being implemented in the multi authority Garbage Can Model (MAGCM), with each authority having the possibility to be organized according to any of the decision structures of the original model independent of how the distribution of the other authorities is organized, and such that more than one of them may be present in the choice opportunities at any one time. Quantitative independence requires that each authority has its own *energy distribution*, and qualitative independence requires that each has its own *decision structure*.

The MAGCM will also have to comply with the three specific behavioural assumptions of the original model, these being the *energy additivity assumption*, the *energy allocation assumption* and the *problem allocation assumption*. While the third is not affected by the number of authorities, compliance with the first two must be assured. Both assumptions will hold if the energy is seen not as a single scalar value (as in the original model) but as a vector formed by the energies from each of the stakeholder groups. The energy from each authority will then be separate scalar components of the energy vector. Seeing the energies from each of the authorities as the scalar components of an n-dimensional Euclidian vector (for n different authorities) will enable both assumptions to be met if the energy from the individual decision maker is added only to the total energy contribution of the stakeholder group the decision maker belongs to. In the computational model, the resultant energy of all the authorities would then be calculated as the absolute length of the n-dimensional energy vector. As the Pythagorean Theorem applies to such vectors, the absolute length is easily calculated by taking the square root of the sum of the squares of the energy contribution from each of the stakeholder groups being represented.

The computational multi authority GCM model is heavily based on the original Fortran programme, making the minimum of adjustments necessary to allow for multiple authorities to participate in the choice opportunities. The original model's scalar energy variable is replaced with an energy vector as outlined above. Organizations with three authorities thus will be represented by three-dimensional vectors. The original model's energy additivity assumption is adhered to by allowing each participant to contribute energy only to the dimension that corresponds to the authority s/he represents. It is the absolute length of the resultant energy vector that needs to have a higher value than the choice opportunity's energy requirement for a choice to be made. The load factor of the original model is kept unchanged in the computational multi authority model, but raised to the degree corresponding to the number of authorities (as the authorities are assumed to be fully independent of each other).

When the number of authorities is set to three, using the vector energy approach outlined above, the following adjustments must be done to the computational model:

- The energy scalar E of the original model is replaced by an energy vector $V=(E_{a1}, E_{a2}, E_{a3})$ representing the independent energies of the three authorities.
- The three authority load level is defined as *[load level]*([load factor])*$^3$ (with *3* being the number of authorities, and with *load level* and *load factor* being identical to the original model). The original levels of 1.1 (for light load), 2.2 (for medium load) and 3.3 (for heavy load) will be 1.331 (for light load), 2.662 (for medium load) and 3.993 (for heavy load) in the three authority model.
- The energy distributions of the original model are kept unchanged, but implemented independently for each authority resulting in ten unique combinations of energy distributions in the three authority model.
- The decision structures of the original model are kept unchanged, but implemented independently for each authority, giving ten unique decision structure combinations.

In the multi authority model, decision makers are allowed to represent one and only one of the authorities. Keeping as many as possible of the numbers identical to the original model, the number of decision makers is kept at ten also in the three authority model. With the number of authorities being three, one of the authorities has four decision makers representing it, while the other two authorities are represented by three decision makers each.

The original model resulted in 324 unique organizational situations. The three authority model, having ten rather than three energy distributions and ten rather than three decision structures, results in 3,600 unique organizational situations.

LISE DEGN

# 7 Making Sense of Management: A Study of Department Heads' Sensemaking Processes in a Changing Environment

## Introduction

With the growing political attention to and discursive constructions of *the knowledge economy*, the universities are often highlighted in public debate as important providers of technological innovation and of a highly skilled labour force as vital instruments for societies in the ever more competitive global economy. This has, over the past decades, led to many attempts to define once and for all what the university *really* is, how it should be run, and indeed what its purpose is (Habermas, 1987; Nowotny et al., 2001; Gibbons et al., 1994; Etzkowitz and Leydesdorff, 1997). A particular area of debate has been the management issue – how is a university most efficiently managed, and is it possible or even relevant to speak of efficiency when referring to universities?

The renewed interest in the universities as players in the knowledge economy has also brought a wave of higher education reforms in Europe, where most, if not all, European universities have been subject to some type of reform aimed at strengthening institutional management. The reforms have typically contained elements of professionalization and a strengthening of institutional leadership, e.g. via the introduction of governing or supervisory boards with varying amounts of formal power. These boards range from being the highest authority in higher education institutions (Denmark) to being optional, advisory units (The Netherlands). Other general reform trends include increased focus on performance-based funding, increased institutional autonomy and accountability, as well as the implementation of elaborated quality assurance mechanisms (de Boer and File, 2009: 14). This also means that managers at all levels at universities have been thrust into a maelstrom of ideas, most of which question their role and legitimacy.

Naturally these changes have attracted the attention of scholars across Europe – as well as the rest of the world – and a large amount of literature on the governance and management of higher education has emerged over the past decades (e.g. Amaral et al., 2002; Neave and Van Vught, 1991; Maassen, 2006; Ferlie et al., 2008); the changing identities of academics and university managers also attract scholarly attention (e.g. MacFarlane, 2011; Deem, 2006; Henkel, 2000; Whitchurch, 2008). It is the intention of the present study to build on this body of research by contributing a national case study which it is hoped will yield interesting insights into the workings of a national higher education reform process.

Denmark stands out as an interesting case, as the policy initiatives concerning higher education institutions have gone from being relatively moderate in what could been termed the initial wave of higher education reforms in the 1970s and 1980s (Stensaker et al., 2007; Eurydice, 2000), to implementing quite far-reaching governance and management reforms in the 2000s – particularly exemplified by the Danish University Act of 2003. This reform introduced significant breaks with the academic tradition of self-organization and self-management, e.g. by abolishing the collegiate management principle, where Rector, Deans and Department Heads were elected among their peers, substituting it with a more professionalized employment principle, where the board appoints a Rector, who appoints the Deans etc. (Aagaard and Mejlgaard, 2012). As in many other European countries, the reforms were greeted by a powerful defence of the traditional idea of *academic management*, emphasizing values such as democracy, collegiality, freedom etc, mainly stemming from the academic staff at the universities.

In the crossfire between these strong normative beliefs and the demands for change, we find the Department Heads. They operate in the intersection between politics and production and are at the same time, at least in Denmark, faced with the task of handling the balance between roles as managers, and as academic researchers, as they are required to have a distinctive academic career behind them to be considered for the job as Department Head. These *production room* managers are thus responsible for the implementation of change at the department level while at the same time handling their own changing role. They are in other words both *changers* and *changees*, and are required to make sense of the situation both to themselves and to the academic and administrative staff that they lead. And it is exactly this *sensemaking process* which is the focal point of the present chapter.

## Reforms and Ideas as Catalysts of Sensemaking

Sensemaking is a term which has become increasingly mainstream – both in scholarly circles amongst organization theorists and students, but also in everyday life and discourse: how often does one stop and say (or think): 'let me just make sense of what you are telling me'. The reason for this is that there is an increasing feeling of complexity in modern society, and thus an increasing need for complexity reduction at both individual and collective level. In other words there are too many or excessively conflicting inputs to a process which leads to a need for selection and segregation of inputs which are manageable to the individual or the organization.

The basic assumption of this paper is that higher education reforms can be seen as catalysts of sensemaking as they introduce new ideas into an existing, highly institutionalized network of ideas, thus disrupting a situation which has already been assigned meaning. Sensemaking as a theoretical term (cf. Weick, 1995; Weick et al., 2005) describes the process whereby people attempt to create meaning in the disrupted context by extracting specific cues and placing them in an order that is sensible to them: turning circumstances into a situation in which it is possible to act sensibly. The *output* of sensemaking is thereby the creation of action – or indeed a meaningful situation in which action is possible. As Karl E. Weick, one of the founding fathers of sensemaking theory (Weick et al., 2005: 415) puts it: sensemaking is not about finding the true meaning and thus the true course of action, but about the 'continued redrafting of an emerging story so that it becomes more comprehensive, incorporates more of the observed data, and is more resilient in the face of criticism'. Sensemaking can thereby be seen as an antecedent to decision making, as it creates a meaningful story and establishes premises upon which decisions can be made. 'Sensemaking to determine the extent of agreement on preferences and cause-effect relations is a precondition of decision strategies' (Weick, 1995: 112). The sensemaking processes of Department Heads thus do not only satisfy their individual need for meaning, but also pertain to the governance structures of the organization, as they contribute to the construction of 'third order controls', i.e. the premises on which future decisions can be made and the possible directions of future sensemaking processes (Weick, 1995).

The sensemaking process is 'strongly influenced by cognitive frameworks in the form of institutional systems, routines and scripts' (Mills, 2003: 55), but the disturbing element(s) however also play a significant role in the creation of meaning. This highlights the need to look at both new disrupting ideas, like reform impulses, and older institutionalizing ideas, e.g. university culture, but also calls for a framework sensitive to both continuity and change. To this end, we shall introduce a relatively new branch of institutionalism, aptly named ideational institutionalism, and discuss how it – in combination with the sensemaking perspective – offers an explanatory framework which is very suited for studies of change in higher education.

The basic tenet of ideational institutionalism is that ideas matter because they: 'shape how we understand political problems, give definition to our goals and strategies, and are the currency we use to communicate about politics. By giving definition to our values and preferences, ideas provide us with interpretive frameworks that make us see some facts as important and others as less so' (Béland and Cox, 2011: 3). Ideas – understood as normative and causal beliefs – work as impulses that affect and inspire our ongoing sensemaking processes by offering various lenses through which actors can view and construct their preferences and understandings of their environment. Ideas are therefore important to study because they act as both restricting and transformational impulses (or cues in a sensemaking terminology). Consequently ideas about higher education shape the way I view myself as a researcher and as an actor within the academic system: they propose goals and legitimize or favour certain strategies to attain these goals. They make it possible for me to be understood by my peers and indeed allow me to identify who my peers are.

Two distinct dimensions of the ideational framework deserve a bit more attention, as they indicate how the approach distinguishes itself from related approaches, and also how it relates and contributes to the sensemaking perspective.

Firstly, a vital assumption, which shapes the theoretical understanding of the present study, is that ideas and institutions are analytically distinct. Béland and Cox (2011: 9) describe this distinction by proposing that: '... ideas are the foundation of institutions. As ideas give rise to people's actions and as those actions form routines, the results are social institutions'. Ideas are thus embedded in institutions, and the relationship between the two is seen as a dynamic and mutually constitutive one (Campbell, 2004), where they act both as restricting structures and as enabling constructs (Schmidt, 2011). It is exactly this conceptualization that distinguished ideational institutionalism from historical institutionalism, for example, where institutions are viewed as deterministic. This view implies that historical institutionalism struggles to explain change in the absence of exogenous shocks (Campbell, 2010).

Ideas, as opposed to institutions, are thereby seen as dynamic in the sense that they are not stable and delimited entities, but subject to change as they are re-coupled with other ideas in sensemaking processes. This leads to the second assumption, namely that ideas are always part of a larger ideational network. Following Carstensen (2010: 850), it is argued that ideas connect to other ideas, drawing meaning from them and revitalizing them with new meaning, much like words in a sentence. However an idea is not necessarily exclusively connected to one network, but might lend itself to several networks, thus offering several different translations. An example, highly relevant in a higher education policy perspective, is that the idea of autonomy can be connected to several different idea-networks, e.g. a *new public management* network, where autonomy is connected with ideas of efficiency, marketization and competition and thereby becomes a matter of institutional accountability. On the other hand, autonomy can also be connected with ideas of academic freedom, collegiate management and *Bildung*: ideas that form what could be termed the *Republic of Science*-idea network (Polanyi, 1962). Here autonomy becomes a matter of independence from outside interference.

These different translations (Czarniawska-Joerges and Sevón, 2005) are in the present framework seen as sensemaking processes. The concept of sensemaking forms the bridge between ideational institutionalism and the individual actors, as it describes how ideas, for instance about management in higher education, are translated and reshaped by authoring actors who are co-creators of their own environment. Ideational institutionalism has thus far been primarily concerned with broad policy analyses, e.g. Berman's study of Social Democratic movements in Sweden and Germany, highlighting how different ideas lead to different political choices in the two countries, in spite of the common ideological basis (Berman, 2001), and Marc Blyth's analysis of the economic ideas of the twentieth century and how these ideas make institutional change possible (Blyth, 1999).

Sensemaking as a theoretical concept thus lends a helping hand to ideational institutionalism by offering a series of tools with which it is possible to analyse the way organizations and their members handle the actual translation of ideas. The extended definition of the term offered by Weick (2005: 409) is that: 'Viewed as a significant process of organizing, sensemaking unfolds as a sequence in which people concerned with identity in the social context of other actors engage ongoing circumstances from which they extract cues and make plausible sense retrospectively, while enacting more or less order into those ongoing circumstances'. This definition holds the vital characteristics of sensemaking – some of which are mainly descriptive, while others are more applicable in an analysis of sensemaking in organizations.

Firstly, sensemaking is understood as an *ongoing*, *retrospective* and *social* process concerned with *plausibility* rather than accuracy. This means that sensemaking is considered to be a continuous process with no discernible beginning or end. Actors are continuously exposed to the flux of impulses, actions and events, which prompts new sensemaking efforts. That sensemaking is retrospective means that an event is not discovered to be meaningful per se – the meaning is created by looking backwards in time and connecting it with other events. Even though this gives the impression of a strictly cognitive and individual process, a vital characteristic of sensemaking is that it always plays out in a social space. Inspired by social psychology, Weick (1995: 39) reminds us that all sensemaking processes are performed in the imagined or actual presence of others. It is therefore not only the scripts, ideas and mental models of the sensemakers themselves that are taken into account, but also the imagined or experienced scripts, ideas and mental models of others. This also means that the primary goal of sensemaking is not accuracy but plausibility, as it is the most direct route to further action: 'Because "objects" have multiple meanings and significance, it is more crucial to get some interpretation to start with than to postpone action until "the" interpretation surfaces' (Weick, 1995: 57).

Secondly sensemaking is about – and can be analysed by looking at – how actors *construct identities*, *extract cues* and *enact them* back into their environment. A vital component of sensemaking processes is thereby identity construction which entails regarding the sensemaker as 'an ongoing puzzle undergoing continual redefinition, coincident with presenting some self to others and trying to decide which self is appropriate' (Weick, 1995: 20). It is thereby important to look at which self (e.g. academic, manager, strategist, administrator, victim etc.) is used as a frame of reference in the sensemaking process, as this influences which cues are deemed relevant, and extracted from a continuing flux of ideas, events and impulses (Weick et al., 2005). When cues have been extracted, they are enacted back into the world, to make the situation more sensible (Weick et al., 2005: 410).

In this way sensemaking is about *choosing* which cues are to be noticed and dealt with, and thereafter organizing these elements, e.g. by creating categories, and labelling them. Within the present context, Department Heads can create identifiable categories (the good university manager) by extracting cues from the external impulses and ideas (the need for strategic abilities), internal culture (the intangible product of the universities) and their own background (their academic interest in management and organization).

A final comment on the sensemaking framework relates to the distinction between individual and organizational sensemaking processes. The two levels of sensemaking within this framework are seen as inextricably linked, because individual sensemaking is both influenced by and influential on the collective, organizational sense of *self*. The Department Heads of this study interact with employees, other managers, stakeholders etc., in organizational activities, wherein the sense that they are continually making is turned into action, e.g. the formulation of strategic documents, discussions about departmental issues etc. In other words, when the individual sensemaking processes affect management practice, this shapes the organization, both through the actions that ensue, but also through the premises that are adopted (Weick, 1995; Weick et al., 2005).

## *The Study*

The Danish university system was, as mentioned in the introduction, significantly transformed in 2003 by way of a large scale reform of both the institutions themselves, i.e. the organization, management and legal status, and later in 2007 of the entire sector via extensive mergers. The Danish universities went from being institutions of state to being self-owning institutions with independent budget responsibilities and professional governance structures. The biggest changes were the transition from the collegiate management system to an appointed hierarchy of managers, and the replacement of the University Senate with a board consisting mostly of external members (Folketinget, 2003). In 2007 this reform was followed by large scale mergers where universities amalgamated with each other and with governmental research institutions, now forming a university landscape of eight universities, as opposed to the previous twenty-five research institutions.

Of these eight I have chosen to zoom in on two, quite different, representatives. One, Aarhus University, is what might be called a traditional, Mode 1 university which has however recently initiated a very comprehensive transformation process affecting both the organization and its strategic goals. The other, Aalborg University, is a newer establishment, founded in 1974, with the explicit aim of advancing problem- and project-based learning and a very strong focus on interdisciplinarity in research, i.e. more a Mode 2 oriented institution. The present study is based on sixteen semi-structured interviews with current and previous Department Heads from the two selected universities.[1] The Department Heads are distributed among the fields of natural science, social science and the humanities, and were selected with three criteria in mind: department size, experience as a Department Head, and an assessment of the degree of tradition characterizing the discipline of the department in question. The case-universities and the respondents were chosen to obtain a high degree of variation and thus an understanding of how (if at all) different circumstances affect the sensemaking processes.

When looking at sensemaking processes the basic premise that no *real truth* is out there cannot be sufficiently stressed – there is no true construction, and thus no true reading and interpretation of the data. Sense is made through language and the respondents therefore make sense while talking. The interviews themselves are a part of the process which influences the way sense is made, and the topics that I bring into this process also have an effect. As Weick puts it, sensemaking 'like all organizing occurs amidst a stream of *potential* antecedents and consequences' (Weick et al., 2005: 411, emphasis in original).

## Making Sense of Management

The basic assumption was, as mentioned, that a constant flow of ideas of change would be a significant driver for sensemaking processes, which also quickly became apparent – the feeling of a disruption or disturbance is evident in all the interviews. The initial step in any sensemaking process

1 The Danish university sector consists of eight universities with a total of approximately 164 departments.

would then, according to Weick, be the formulation of a problem that guides behaviour and a goal towards which one can work. This 'bracketing' or 'noticing' (Weick et al., 2005) is a way of reducing the complexity of a problem-filled situation.

The study revealed that two very different sensemaking processes were at work, constructing two different narratives about the problems that are relevant to deal with, the relations that are affected by these problems and the actions necessary to solve them:

> ...it is possible that when they looked at the surface of it all, of course there were department councils and academic councils and students and Senates and all these things, and there were fancy Minutes and there were democratic processes, but it just so happens that it wasn't there– at least not always – that the decisions were made. They were made in completely informal fora by those who had seized power...[2]

> ...in the old system, which was a democratic organ, [...] we sat around these tables and voted on everything [...] right to each other's faces. What came before such a vote? [...] There were fierce discussions and alliances and screenings [...] so that when you came to the meeting it was simply a formality. [...] [But] the democratic bodies took a serious blow [already] in '93. And [...] at that time we sat in rooms like this and assured each other that they might have passed a new law, but that was not going to cost us our democratic decision-making structure. And that [the loss of the democratic decision-making structure] was exactly what happened.

These quotes illustrate how the same cue can be assigned completely different values: how the past can be construed as both negative and positive, depending on the sensemaking strategy, naturally affecting how appropriate action and legitimate goals are constructed. In the first quote we see how the democratic processes of the previous university management system are valued negatively: a feint used to cover up the 'actual' decision making processes taking place behind the curtain. The same situation is described in the second quote, only now with a positive valuation, emphasizing the active debate culture of the past.

2 All quotes in this section have been translated by the author.

We thus see the contours of two different strategies underlying the sensemaking processes, both highly influenced by the interpersonal and group relations as well as by new and older ideas.

The first strategy is clearly aimed at retaining as much as possible from the previous situation, which would enable the participants to resume the interrupted activity, i.e. maintain status quo or at least continue on the existing path – one might label this *the preserving strategy* as it revolves around a positive valuation of the past, and the preservation of the arm's length relation between academia and the political system/society. The Department Heads using this strategy tend to construct change as negative and disaffirming by evoking existing ideas of democracy, traditional university culture and academic autonomy. The past is viewed in a positive light which would naturally entail a negative attitude towards change – why fix it, if it is not broken? Here the extracted meaning is one of (unwarranted) lack of trust from the surrounding society, and thus a devaluation of the work that was being done.

> ...It is not that there isn't a legitimate claim from society to gain insight into what we are doing, but it is also a question of: if you want us to perform a task, then rely on us to do so [...] And that's where I don't think the politicians show us the trust that we could wish for. And after all, they give us a lot of money, and you don't do that if you don't trust people to do the job.

The reform and the ensuing professionalization of the management structure in Denmark were heavily influenced by an idea of decision making authority. This was constructed as a necessary item in the management-toolbox in order to enable the managers to make executive decisions and avoid the democratic trap outlined above, where decisions were contingent on a very long and opaque negotiation process. In the *preserving* narrative of sensemaking, the use of this authority however is seen as an admission of failure: if you make decisions against the will of the academic staff, you are a poor manager – you will have lost. One Department Head describes a situation which illustrates this point quite vividly:

> You would be a strange manager to launch something against the wishes of your staff, but in principle you have the ability to do it. But then I doubt that you would have a constructive, positive organisation [...]. I remember that we were designing

> a course (X), and there was debate about which of two very different elements (Y) to use, where the majority said: let's use this one, because that is what's used in the industry, and the ones who were doing the course said: we would like to try this [...]. Then the 'grand old men' of the department said that it certainly would be a little strange if we insist upon something that contradicts the ones who are doing the job. So they [the ones who were running the course] were allowed to run it the way they wanted. It turned out to be wrong, but then again, we have to make things work, we have to move forward in a constructive way.

This quote also tells the story of the relationship with the academic staff, and highlights the value ascribed to this relationship. In many ways it is described as a parent-child relation, where the Department Head claims the role of the supervising and protecting parent, and the academics are the developing prodigies. The role of management is in this way constructed as protecting and safeguarding academic production from external threats (such as reform impulses). These are also to some extent linked to top-level management, whose expectations are construed as more 'raw' and performance-oriented than previously.

The second strategy that emerges from the sensemaking processes studied here might be labelled *the evolving strategy*, and tends to aim more towards change, connecting itself to an ongoing story about the need for change in university. The past is viewed as problematic and thus change is inevitable and possibly even overdue.

> ...Danish universities have to accept that there is a different competitive pressure on almost all dimensions than there was twenty-thirty years ago and we cannot keep doing things the same way.

The expectations that are believed to exist in society are ones of transparency and relevance, which are assigned positive value. The Department Heads who employ this strategy construct the changes in organization and management structure as mainly positive and affirming by connecting it to already existing ideas about the development of higher education: their subject, their department, the academic community in general and often also themselves:

> …there was also in some way a greater […] awareness of the meaning of the collective among the employees […] [and] the idea that […] this is not just a collection of one-man businesses that just happen to be working within the scope of a department, but that we actually have some things in common […], and that we benefit from some common services, […] which demands co-ordination and pooling of resources.

The problem constructed here is that 'the old system' had built-in shortcomings which prevented the organization from functioning properly. It is clear that sensemaking here draws meaning from the new idea of professionalized management, as cues like enhanced decision making authority are constructed as legitimate means towards the goal of good academic production. This tool is thus a positive aid, however naturally contingent upon sensible communication with the employees.

> Being an elected manager is one thing, being an appointed one is another. An elected manager is kind of responsible to the ones that have elected him/her, and will sometimes do something that can be un-conducive to reaching the goals that are set. An elected manager will not lock horns with people as much, an elected manager will not touch upon the sore spots, but an appointed one is obliged to do whatever it takes, including talking to people about their strengths and weaknesses […] to get to where we are going.

The *evolving strategy* in general draws meaning from newer ideas of entrepreneurialism, dynamic capacities and strategy, thus decision making authority becomes a legitimate tool in management. The relationship between manager and academic staff is also articulated as more professionalized and somewhat distanced, as the key objective of management is developing and guiding rather than preserving. The role of management is to make sure that 'we get where we are going' and indeed to *define* where we are going. The study thus shows that there are very different ways of handling change impulses – there are different stories that can be told depending on the valuation and categorization of the cues that are extracted. However the two strategies have one very central thing in common, namely when it comes to defining the concept of management.

The interesting thing is that there is a general tendency to distance oneself from the concept of steering and *hard* management – both sensemaking strategies emphasize that it is a very important characteristic to be a *soft*, empathic leader. A clear distinction is drawn between *management* and *university management*, which also lends legitimacy to the refusal of the concept of external managers. Only one of the Department Heads embraces the idea that managers from other sectors could become managers in the university, and even this is simply viewed as the lesser of several evils:

> ...it would be hard if it wasn't the right person, but they exist too. And isn't it better to try and find such a person, than to take a researcher who doesn't really want to do it, or worse: to take a semi-poor researcher, who is also a semi-poor manager, who then says: 'at least now I have a justification in life'.

A central part of both strategies thus seems to be negative categorization and labelling, i.e. I am not that kind of manager, university is not that kind of organization etc. In other words both strategies produce a category – *a (hard) manager* – against which one defines oneself. This creates a new social category, *the university manager*, and enhances the social bond to the institution. This indicates that the university as an institution is in both strategies seen as the primary reference group, i.e. the group whose perspective provides the most salient frames (Shibutani, 1955), and thereby a very powerful influence on sensemaking processes. The two strategies however differ in the way that this conceptualization is used to facilitate action.

The evolving strategy uses the social identification as a management tool by constructing it as a necessity in order to 'get where we are going', given that it produces legitimacy among the academic staff. In other words, if you are a *hard manager* (i.e. constructed as a private sector-style manager) you will lose the support of the academic staff, and thus not be able to act. This indicates a strategic use of reference group. The preserving strategy also emphasizes the legitimacy reasons for *soft management* but tends to connect it more to the manager's own sense of self and to older ideas of collegial management and classical university thinking, indicating a more *emotional* use of reference group.

### *Consequences for Management Practice?*

The two sensemaking strategies and the narratives they produce are clearly linked to the self-perception of the Department Heads. The way they view themselves, the self that they use as a frame of reference, obviously influences which strategy they employ, and further frames their practice as managers. Even though the borders are fuzzy it is possible to extract three distinct discursive constructions of the role as Department Head from the descriptions – each with a different set of values, tools and legitimate actions ascribed to it, and each stemming from the sensemaking strategies described above.

#### SHIELDERS

This type of Department Head employs *the preserving strategy* and thus perceives external change impulses as disruptive, unwarranted and often unreasonable. This construction offers legitimacy to a continuation of the existing practice to the highest degree possible. These Heads view their role as an absorber of change, thus shielding the 'real' workers from these change impulses. There is a tendency to see the job as an obligation and to identify primarily with the academic staff. The Department Heads adopting this role tend towards decoupling talk from action, e.g. constructing strategies by describing ongoing activities as future strategic priorities.

#### CO-ORDINATORS

The co-ordinator is a somewhat 'schizophrenic' type, as both strategies are applied in the sensemaking process. Most often this type ascribes a positive value to the past, but also speaks positively about many of the ongoing change processes. Co-ordinators tend to articulate a conflict-ridden view on loyalty, as they are trying to balance being loyal to the employer (Dean, Rector, board etc.) versus being loyal to the employees (academic staff). The primary difference between the co-ordinator and the shielder is the action pattern associated with the role. Where the shielder was primarily a passive absorber of change, the co-ordinator assumes a more active mediating and conveying role, attempting to translate change impulses in a preserving direction. The appropriate action pattern for this type of Department Head is one of subtle guidance.

### AGENDA SETTERS

Agenda setter types use *the evolving strategy* in their sensemaking process and thus draw meaning from many of the ideas of change that emerge in the higher education idea network at the moment. The agenda setter describes a mainly positive view on university management, and a clear ambition for the department or academic field. This type of Department Head is one that initiates change of his/her own accord, and thus assumes a much more active role in the development and transformation of ideas and impulses. This type also describes a will to manage and to pursue the job actively.

## Conclusions and Implications

In the Danish case it becomes clear that a (surprisingly) large number of the Department Heads describe themselves as what I have called shielders or co-ordinators: indeed, thirteen of the sixteen respondents can be said to fit these categories. Interestingly, it seems that the way they view themselves as managers is connected to their experience as Department Heads – and not to their organizational affiliation or to their disciplinary background (humanities, social or natural sciences). The more experienced Department Heads tend to use the preserving strategy, and describe themselves in shielder and/or co-ordinator terms, and more recently appointed Department Heads can more often be seen as agenda setters, using the evolving sensemaking strategy.

This indicates that ideas about strategic management, professionalization and entrepreneurialism are having a hard time finding their way into the idea-networks that the Department Heads employ when making sense of their own role, and that old and institutionalized ideas about management and the university – illustrated by the conceptualization of management described above – still have significant impact. It is therefore perhaps not surprising that more experienced Department Heads, who have been 'in the system' longer, tend to adhere more to the highly institutionalized ideas of university governance structures, and may disregard the new ideas about strategic, professionalized university management as irrelevant, while Department Heads who do not have experience with the previous structures have a more difficult time with this.

This is also mirrored in the fact that even though many Department Heads describe joy and excitement when speaking of their job – primarily the agenda setters and the co-ordinators – this is often done with a touch of ambivalence, as if it is not legitimate to connect academia to management. This concern with legitimacy reflects the social aspect of sensemaking, as sense is clearly constructed with an audience in mind. The study indicates that the horizontal and vertical relations are also influential factors in the extraction of cues, and often it is the expectations and images of others that assist the sensemaking. This means that the Department Heads construct certain expectations that they believe others to have, either the expectations of academic and administrative staff or the expectations of Deans, Rectors, society or the political system, and that these expectations guide the sensemaking processes. Another social aspect which has emerged from the study is that the shielder types – and to some extent the co-ordinator types – identify much more with the academic staff than with their own role as leader and therefore experience internal conflict when it comes to loyalty and the use of authority. The agenda setter types emphasize their own expectations as important, which could be seen as a sign that this type of Department Head identifies more with the role as manager, and thus distances him/herself from the previous role as a researcher.

In other words, there are many forces at work when looking at how new impulses affect sensemaking and management practice in universities. In the present study I have attempted to show how the sensemaking processes of Department Heads are influenced by various ideas and institutions that simultaneously restrain and enable new enactments and identity constructions. The Department Heads do struggle with restricting structures, imagined and experienced expectations and institutionalized idea networks, but as the analysis has shown they still find room to manoeuvre, and to construct their own role and space in the organization. This is exemplified by the considerable difference between the shielder-type manager and the agenda setter-type manager.

These findings could also prove interesting when looking at the *organizational identity constructions*, i.e. 'how organizational members perceive and understand "who we are" and/or "what we stand for" as an organization' (Hatch and Schultz, 2000: 15). It is clear that the sensemaking processes of the Department Heads also speak to this institutional-level understanding of what the purpose and values of the university are – and question if the university is even the primary source of identification. Looking at the results of the present study, there are indications that typology could also prove a relevant framework when looking at the construction of organizational identity. As mentioned above, the shielders use academic conceptualizations to make sense of new ideas and disturbances, and there are indications that they feel more closely connected to the academic community than to the specific organization for which they work. This would be well in line with Rosemary Deem's (2004) observation: 'As a number of commentators have noted, in the 1970s (Moodie and Eustace, 1974), in the 1980s (Jarratt, 1985) and more recently (Henkel, 2000), academic loyalty tends to be oriented towards the basic academic unit and subject or discipline, not the interests of the university as a whole', but as the typology shows, it is also only part of the story. The agenda setters, and to some extent the co-ordinators, seem to have a closer bond to the organization as such, but still adhere to what could be termed an institutional identity, namely the *university manager* described above. More in-depth studies of these identification issues are however needed to illuminate these complex workings.

The findings that are summarized above certainly all speak to the resilience of the ideas surrounding higher education institutions – and the impact that this resilience has on the managers attempting to make sense of the changing environment. The manager typology and the common construction of *the university manager* illustrate that the ideas are indeed flexible and broad enough to encompass even somewhat antagonistic constructions of identity, without losing common ground. In other words, they bend and they flex to maintain a meaningful sense of self – even in the face of very challenging and changing environments.

## References

Aagaard, K., and Mejlgaard, N. (eds) (2012). *Dansk forskningspolitik efter årtusindskiftet* (Danish research policy in the new millennium). Aarhus: Aarhus Universitetsforlag.

Amaral, A., Meek, L., and Larsen, I.M. (eds) (2002). *The Higher Education Managerial Revolution?* Dordrecht: Kluwer Academic Publishers.

Béland, D., and Cox, R.H. (2011). *Ideas and Politics in Social Science Research Ideas and Politics*. New York: Cambridge University Press.

Berman, S. (2010). 'Ideology, History, and Politics'. In D. Béland, and R.H. Cox (eds), *Ideas and Politics in Social Science Research*, pp. 105–126. New York: Oxford University Press.

Blyth, M. (1999). *Great Transformation: Economic Ideas and Political Change in the Twentieth Century*. Cambridge: Columbia University.

Campbell, J.L. (2004). *Institutional Change and Globalization*. Princeton: Princeton University Press.

Campbell, J.L. (2010). 'Institutional Reproduction and Change'. In G. Morgan, J.L. Campbell, C. Crouch, O.K. Pedersen, and R. Whitly (eds), *Oxford Handbook of Comparative Institutional Analysis*, pp. 87–115. New York: Oxford University Press.

Carstensen, M.B. (2010). 'The Nature of Ideas, and Why Political Scientists Should Care: Analysing the Danish Jobcentre Reform from an Ideational Perspective', *Political Studies*, 58, 847–865.

Czarniawska-Joerges, B., and Sevón, G. (2005). *Global Ideas: How Ideas, Objects and Practices Travel in a Global Economy*. Frederiksberg: Liber & Copenhagen Business School Press.

Deem, R. (2004). 'The Knowledge Worker, the Manager-Academic and the Contemporary UK University: New and Old Forms of Public Management?', *Financial Accountability & Management*, 20 (2), 107–128.

de Boer, H., and File, J. (2009). *Higher Education Governance Reforms across Europe* (MODERN project). Brussels: ESMU.

Deem, R. (2006). 'Changing Research Perspectives on the Management of Higher Education: Can Research Permeate the Activities of Manager-Academics?', *Higher Education Quarterly*, 60 (3), 203–228.

Etzkowitz, H., and Leydesdorff, L. (1997). *Universities and the Global Knowledge Economy: a Triple Helix of Academy-Industry-Government Relations*. London: Pinter.

Eurydice (2000). *Two Decades of Reform in Higher Education in Europe: 1980 onwards*. European Commission (DG Education and Culture) <http://www.ihep.org/assets/files/gcfp-files/TWODECADESREFORM.pdf> accessed 27 April 2013.

Ferlie, E., Musselin, C., and Andresani, G. (2008). 'The Steering of Higher Education Systems: a Public Management Perspective', *Higher Education*, 56 (3), 325–348.

Folketinget (2003). *Forslag til Lov om universiteter* (Proposal for Law on Universities, The University Act). Copenhagen: The Danish Parliament. <www.retsinformation.dk/Forms/R0710.aspx?id=100418> (in Danish) accessed 27 April 2013.

Gibbons, M., Limoges, C., Nowotny, H., Schwartzman, S., Scott, P., and Trow, M. (1994). *The New Production of Knowledge – the Dynamics of Science And Research in Contemporary Societies*. London: Sage Publications.

Habermas, J. (1987). 'The Idea of the University: Learning Processes', *New German Critique*, 41, Special Issue on the Critiques of the Enlightenment (Spring–Summer, 1987), 3–22.

Hatch, M.J., and Schultz, M. (2000). 'Scaling the Tower of Babel: Relational Differences between Identity, Image, and Culture in Organizations'. In M. Schultz, M., J. Hatch, and M.H. Larsen (eds), *The Expressive Organization: Linking Identity, Reputation, and Corporate Brand*, pp. 13–35. Oxford: Oxford University Press.

Henkel, M. (2000). *Academic Identities and Policy Change in Higher Education*. London: Jessica Kingsley.

Maassen, P. (2006). *The Modernisation of European Higher Education. A Multi Level Analysis*. Paper presented at the Directors General for Higher Education Meeting. Helsinki, 19–20 October 2006.

Macfarlane, B. (2011). 'The Morphing of Academic Practice: Unbundling and the Rise of the Para-Academic', *Higher Education Quarterly*, 65 (1), 59–73.

Mills, J.H. (2003). *Making Sense of Organizational Change*. New York: Routledge.

Neave, G., and Van Vught, F. (eds) (1991). *Prometheus Bound: The Changing Relationships Between Government and Higher Education*. Oxford: Pergamon Press.

Nowotny, H., Scott, P., and Gibbons, M. (2001). *Re-Thinking Science: Knowledge and the Public in an Age of Uncertainty*. Cambridge: Polity Press.

Polanyi, M. (1962). 'The Republic of Science: its Political and Economic Theory', *Minerva*, 1 (1), 54–73.

Schmidt, V.A. (2010). 'Reconciling Ideas and Institutions through Discursive Institutionalism'. In D. Béland, and R.H. Cox (eds), *Ideas and Politics in Social Science Research*, pp. 64–89. New York: Oxford University Press.

Stensaker, B., Enders, J., and de Boer, H. (2007). *The Extent and Impact of Higher Education Governance Reform across Europe, Comparative Analysis and Executive Summary. Final Report to the Directorate-General for Education and Culture of the European Commission*. Enschede: CHEPS.

Tsoukas, H., and Chia, R. (2002). 'Organizational Becoming: Rethinking Organizational Change', *Organization Science*, 13 (5), 567–582.

Weick, K.E. (1995). *Sensemaking in Organizations*. Thousand Oaks: Sage Publications.

Weick, K.E., Sutcliffe, K., and Obstfeld, D. (2005). 'Organizing and the Process of Sensemaking', *Organization Science*, 16 (4), 409–421.

Whitchurch, C. (2008). 'Shifting Identities and Blurring Boundaries: the Emergence of 'Third Space Professionals' in UK Higher Education', *Higher Education Quarterly*, 62 (4), 376–395.

CELIA WHITCHURCH AND GEORGE GORDON

# 8 Universities Adapting to Change: Implications for Roles and Staffing Practices

## Introduction

A number of external drivers have led UK universities to consider how they might become more adaptive and flexible. These include increasingly market-oriented environments and competition between institutions for staff and students, as well as Government policies seeking to address socio-economic agendas (HEFCE – Higher Education Funding Council for England, 2009; 2010a, b; UCEA – Universities and Colleges Employers Association, 2006; UUK – UniversitiesUK, 2007a, 2007b; BIS – Department for Business, Innovation and Skills, 2011). There is also pressure on institutions to consider the benefits of collaboration, as well as mechanisms such as outsourcing and shared services (for instance SFC – Scottish Funding Council, 2007; UUK, 2011; HEFCE, 2012). More recently, the granting of degree awarding powers to vocational and private providers in the UK 'to meet the changing needs of employers, individuals and their communities' (Department for Business, Innovation and Skills, 2011: 10) is likely to intensify market competition, particularly for overseas students.

In England, the introduction of student tuition fees has further focused attention on the quality of the student experience, at a time when student profiles are changing as a result of demand for lifelong and workplace learning initiatives. There is also pressure to ensure that the sector is attractive to talented staff (HEFCE, 2006, 2010a; UCEA, 2008): and there is greater mobility between higher education and other sectors, with individuals from applied disciplines, as well as specialist professionals, being appointed externally in what is now a global labour market (Kim and Locke, 2010; Henard, 2012).

A more segmented higher education sector, increasing diversity within institutions, and variability in what individual institutions can afford to pay, have obliged institutions to find ways of addressing these new challenges, particularly in relation to employment practices:

> Staffing structures and costs will need to be examined in order to respond to these pressures and to meet changing demands from students, employers and other stakeholders...How can the sector become more flexible at a time of change while maximizing the talent and commitment of its people? (HEFCE, 2010a: 3)

A diversifying workforce, resulting from, for instance, the incorporation of professional disciplines into higher education, an increase in part-time and fractional contracts, and roles with both academic and professional components (Gordon and Whitchurch, 2010; Whitchurch, 2013) has, by default, modified aspects of the employment relationship. Outwith what might be seen as a core of staff who have a balanced teaching, research and knowledge exchange portfolio are a significant minority of staff whose experiences, needs and expectations diverge from this norm. For instance, in institutions which themselves do not have a balanced portfolio of teaching and research, and may cater for a local or more vocationally oriented student body, staff may be mature, full-time entrants from the health professions and embark on a doctorate part-time after appointment, alongside other responsibilities. They may also be involved in teaching and applied research in multi-disciplinary teams with external members (Smith and Boyd, 2010). Furthermore, in the UK, only 52 per cent of academic staff continue to undertake both teaching and research, and 17 per cent are described as being in grades 'other than' than professor, senior lecturer and lecturer (HESA – Higher Education Statistics Agency, 2012). Thus, Enders and de Weert describe an increasingly 'T-shaped profession', involving both 'depth of disciplinary knowledge and broader transdisciplinary knowledge and skills', in which 'T-shaped people are equipped with competences and skills which are relevant for employment outside academia, but also for an increasing diversification of job tasks within the academic profession' (Enders and de Weert, 2009: 262).

Based on recent research undertaken for the UK Leadership Foundation for Higher Education (LFHE) (Whitchurch and Gordon, 2013), this chapter illustrates ways in which universities are demonstrating resilience by, for instance, reviewing the implications of contracts that reflect teaching, research and service in different ways, roles that are undergoing redefinition, and changing career paths, motivations and rewards. This reflects contemporary ideas about resilience as being 'the ability to dynamically reinvent business models and strategies as circumstances change' via 'continuous reconstruction' (Hamel and Valikangas, 2003: 53, 55), thereby anticipating and preparing for future conditions. At the same time, however, they tread a careful path in seeking to maintain staff motivation and morale. This is likely to involve recognizing that different staffing models may be required for different activities, functions and departments, and understanding how these might work in practice.

## Method and Case Studies

The study drew on two sets of qualitative interviews:

With sixteen 'expert witnesses' in higher education and other sectors in the UK (10), Hong Kong (4), Ireland (1) and the US (1), who acted as system commentators. These included Vice-Chancellors, Pro-Vice-Chancellors with a human resources remit, Heads of Administration, Directors of Human Resources, representatives of unions, UniversitiesHR (the national body of Directors of Human Resources) and the Committee of University Chairs (CUC). The witnesses were selected initially from discussions with the Leadership Foundation and with professional bodies such as UniversitiesHR, and also via early interviews with the witnesses themselves. Each one brought expertise and experience in specific areas of interest, often from more than one institution, and were able to provide a system-wide view.

With thirty-seven senior and middle management staff in seven institutions, including Vice-Chancellors; Pro-Vice-Chancellors; Heads of Administration; heads of other functions such as human resources, academic services and estates; Deans and Heads of School; academic managers; members of governing bodies and representatives of partner institutions.

The institutions were selected after discussions with the Leadership Foundation and senior commentators in the higher education system about institutions where there was evidence of innovative practice. For this reason the seven institutions were not intended to be representative of the system as a whole, although an even balance was sought between pre- and post-1992 institutions, and also in relation to geographical spread, so as to reflect the impact of history and locale. The institutions included:

- Three pre-1992 institutions, two of which were members of the Russell Group, explained below.
- Three post-1992 institutions, two of which were involved in partnerships, and the third a specialist institution.
- One private institution.

Two of the institutions were in Scotland, three in the south of England and two in the Midlands. The Further and Higher Education Act 1992 removed the binary line between the universities and former polytechnics in the UK, so that convention now distinguishes between those which existed prior to the Act (pre-1992) and those created at any point afterwards (post-1992). After 1992, in the enlarged university sector, institutional groupings emerged based on similarities of profile and ethos. The first of these was the Russell Group of leading research-intensive universities.

## Adapting to Change

The study demonstrated that institutions were using a range of mechanisms that enabled them to adapt as specific needs arose. These were not necessarily part of an overall strategy but introduced greater flexibility where there was an opportunity to do so, sometimes in a segment of the institution rather than across the board. There was a sense that the system, and individual institutions, are now so complex that 'one-size-fits-all' solutions are unlikely to be appropriate, and that institutions are responding according to their circumstances, and a range of variables such as academic profile, student mix, locale and, not least, local relationships with staff and unions. The introduction of more flexible practices has tended to occur, therefore, where circumstances make this possible, leading to the comment that:

> I see in the sector isolated examples of…management teams trying to do things differently. What I don't see is any coherent or co-ordinated approach. (Former Vice-Chancellor, expert witness, post-1992 institution)

The following are examples of ways in which specific arrangements were being adjusted. There was no particular pattern to these in relation to individual institutions, although institutions with a broader spectrum of activity appeared to have more room for manoeuvre:

- The use of annualized contracts whereby individuals' hours could be varied to meet peaks and troughs in demand, for instance in term time, or to provide evening and weekend cover, although they would receive a monthly salary.
- The use of term time-only contracts or contracts that do not cover a full year.
- Benefit packages that offer financial and other types of reward to meet specific needs including for instance, flexitime, off-campus working and trade-offs between pay and leave entitlement.

- The extension of the working week to increase teaching hours, including evenings and weekends, and to make more effective use of the estate.
- A broadening of criteria for promotion to recognize and reward, for instance, achievement in teaching, scholarship, or pedagogical research; introducing a new programme; bringing research to the market; links with professional practice, the community or the business sector; and giving strategic leadership.
- The use of titles that are seen as valued and appropriate, such as Associate Professor or Teaching/Professorial Fellow, to reflect these broader criteria, and new job descriptions for promoted posts such as senior lectureships.
- Flexible career tracks to accommodate, for instance, teaching and research, teaching and scholarship, teaching-only or research-only roles at different points in an individual's career.
- Extraordinary promotion procedures to retain people who are being headhunted by other institutions.
- Offering part-time and casual staff the opportunity to participate in, for instance, staff development and appraisal, peer review and quality assurance processes.
- The development of teams that can teach across a range of programmes in ways that can be adjusted if necessary year on year.
- Discretionary use of workload models to accommodate the balance of activity at departmental as well as at individual levels.
- Playing to individual strengths when determining individual and team workloads.
- The use of new style employment contracts that do not distinguish between academic and non-academic roles, and give professional staff equivalent status in undertaking work with academic components such as tutoring, programme development and institutional research and development.
- Allowing staff to retire gradually by moving them on to part-time contracts, under pension schemes that allow flexible retirement in conjunction with a reduction in hours.

- Consideration of whether teaching and learning methods could be made more efficient, and whether staff might be trained in reading and marking techniques.

Cumulatively such mechanisms enable institutions to make adjustments on an evolutionary basis, although tipping points may occur, such as a new senior management team, staff turnover, or internal restructuring.

There was also evidence of individual institutions flexing their practices at a strategic level in pursuit of their missions and aspirations. For instance, the pre-1992 institution that was not a member of the Russell Group, but wished to maintain its broad academic footprint and research profile, had made institution-wide reductions which included shifting those who were less successful in research towards teaching, whilst trying to accommodate individual strengths. The Vice-Chancellor took the view that it was no longer tenable for all staff to be involved in both teaching and research, and that some individuals in each faculty should be dedicated to one or the other, with appropriate reward structures. There had also been some merging of departments with a view to integrating disciplines more closely to facilitate crossover of teaching.

Some UK universities have also begun to develop selective partnerships with private providers in relation to services such as foundation programmes, study skills and English language training (Fielden, Middlehurst and Woodfield, 2010; Woodfield, Fielden and Middlehurst, 2011; Middlehurst and Fielden, 2011). This enables them to extend their portfolios and diversify their staffing practices. Such partnerships are seen as valuable where the private partner has niche expertise, or can offer links into professional practice, work-based learning and employer engagement. Some private providers have ambitions to allow their staff to undertake research, particularly in relation to practice. Sometimes tutors are also provided by, or transferred from, the partner university. All these factors create, or have the potential to create, issues of comparability in relation to conditions of service. Partnering arrangements also require link persons within the institution to ensure that joint working meets institutional standards and criteria, and can 'shift the internal dynamics (new skills needed in terms of managing and integrating external [staff])' (Sloan, 2011).

*Vignette 1: The Not-For-Profit Company*

Not-for-profit companies owned or partly owned by higher education institutions have been established in the UK and in countries such as Hong Kong to deliver self-funding, adjunct programmes including two-year/associate and foundation degrees, professional and continuing education, executive Master's degrees, higher diplomas and short courses.

Common features include:

- Staff employed on limited term or annualized contracts, who would be unlikely to undertake research.
- Annualized contracts giving continuity of employment and pension rights, with additional staff recruited if necessary on a fixed term basis.
- Employment of individuals who wish to have a portfolio of activity and effectively work as self-employed consultants.
- Reward packages that can be individualized if necessary, including market supplements, to attract appropriate and high quality recruits.

In some cases, individuals may share directly in profits, and such enterprises may be located on a satellite campus, with library and IT facilities purchased from the owner university, and/or space rented on the main campus.

Others have developed employee or partnership models, for instance to foster regional agendas on employability.

*Vignette 2: An Employee Partnership Model*

An employee partnership model for the management of facilities and estates included a range of staff from cleaners to engineers, and was wholly owned as the trading arm of the university. It was hoped that this would offer benefits from both public and private sectors: 'What we were trying to get at in terms of efficiency and standards was our non-pay spend rather than our pay spend...So whilst value for money and cost efficiency [is] part of the mix, they're not the entire story. The other part of the mix is about delivering service levels and Key Performance Indicators that are appropriate to the business…and the changing expectations of our customer base…both internal customers as well as the student body' (Estates and Facilities Manager, post-1992 institution 1). The institution would, at least in the initial stages, be the principal client, but it would be a more contractual relationship than had existed in the past.

Terms and conditions were likely to be varied for future employees so as to enable the partnership to compete for external contracts with providers whose overheads would be lower than those in a higher education institution. The company would also be expected to offer consultancy to other higher education institutions and to develop best practice. At the same time, if staff numbers needed to be increased at pressure points in the year, the possibility remained of bringing in externally contracted staff. The managing director was a voting member, and a member of the senior management team a non-executive member of the partnership board, to ensure that the interests of both the partnership and the university were covered.

At the other end of the spectrum from employee partnership is a consortium model, incorporating a range of institutions who continue to employ their own staff. There might be a variety of contracts across the consortium, and even within partner institutions. Although the majority of staff would see themselves as belonging to component institutions, those employed centrally, as well as the leaders of shared programmes and modules, might identify to a greater extent with the consortium.

*Vignette 3: A Partnership Consortium*

In one instance this model provided opportunities for sharing library and information services and student management systems; for the design and delivery of a networked curriculum by teams spanning different institutions; and also for services such as careers, human resources and staff development.

This collaborative approach involved maintaining a balance between the perceived advantages of belonging to the consortium and the autonomy of partner institutions, including managing the expectations of staff from different types of providers about, for instance, teaching hours, leave entitlements, and the balance of teaching and research or scholarship; establishing parity of esteem and consistent standards for similar activity between institutions; minimizing duplication between central and local provision; and establishing mechanisms for developing longer term strategy.

The success of the consortium model is likely to depend on incremental development, in that it may not be possible to move immediately to the standardization of practice, although mechanisms such as staff surveys may help with convergence across constituent partners. In the initial stages there is likely to be a dependence on existing networks and contacts, although these also can act to protect local interests. There is likely to be pressure for central lead teams, and the introduction of service level agreements with agreed targets and outcomes.

A number of mechanisms more commonly used in the private sector were also being adopted by some publicly-funded institutions, including, for instance:

- Increments based on increased responsibility and/or performance rather than being awarded automatically year-on-year.
- The use of non-pensionable, one-off payments to reward success at individual or team level.
- Development of a job evaluation framework that reflected the institution's mission.

There were some examples of outsourcing, largely in relation to facilities management. None of the case study institutions had outsourced functions such as human resources, finance or student services, though some institutions were looking at the possibility in relation to, for instance, IT services, student email and payroll. Core services such as finance and human resources were generally seen as integral to an institution's mission and operations, and the focus tended to be on making existing models work better. As well as significant set up costs, the feeling among heads of administration was that outsourcing would not deliver substantial savings or other benefits. Perhaps more significantly, others quoted ensuring the quality of the student experience and consistency of provision (for instance in relation to campus services) as militating against outsourcing to external providers, who might not offer a rapid response if problems occurred. There was a sense of doing what was right for the institution, so that the arrangement had local credibility. Again the employment 'equation' came into play:

> If you compare the sector's cost base with the commercial market for these services… we probably pay more than we should, on a commercial basis. But of course one of the things that comes with having your staff directly employed is the loyalty that that engenders…There's a dividing line between getting something that is competitive and appropriately procured, and the loyalty and ability of the staff to be able to do anything that you care to ask them… (Estates and Facilities Manager, post-1992 institution 1)

With respect to shared services, a number of respondents made the point that the sector has longstanding examples at a national level, for instance the Universities and Colleges Admissions Service (UCAS), the Joint Information Systems Committee (JISC), Inter-library loans and the Universities and Colleges Employers Association (UCEA). Another model is exemplified by Jobs.ac.uk which is owned by one institution that sells its services to other institutions. Thus, within the concept of shared services is the potential for a range of models, described by one respondent as 'a continuum from an institution designing services that others can buy, all the way through to a more integrated delivery model with everyone having an equal stake around it' (Head of Administration, pre-1992 institution 2). Perhaps for this kind of reason, others felt that sharing services could only be successful between institutions which had similar profiles, quality standards and business models, bearing in mind that they may also be in competition with each other. Furthermore, sharing was often driven by the needs of students following joint programmes in different institutions for common provision of, for instance, web platforms and library and information services. There remained a sense that potential savings were likely to be outweighed by additional overheads, and in practice this model was more likely to be successful in large conurbations where institutions were co-located.

## Practical Implications of Universities Adapting to Change

There was consensus among respondents in the UK that the National Framework Agreement (JNCHES – Joint Negotiating Committee for Higher Education Staff, 2003) allowed institutions significant flexibility in responding to change. There was also general acknowledgement of the centrality of the psychological contract with staff, as opposed to formal terms and conditions of employment, in supporting institutional goals:

> We're in the service business, as a higher education institution, and in the service business, when we are relying on the human capital of our academics and our professional teams, keeping those troops motivated is critical for offering a good service to the consumer, the consumer being the student and the person funding the student... It's absolutely vital that we have our staff motivated, engaged, aligned with what our vision is. (Chair of Governing Body, post-1992 institution 1)

The relationship between institutions and their staff has been based traditionally on intrinsic motivations with employment packages that include, for instance, annual increments and final salary pensions for the majority of staff, and the psychological contract is underpinned by mutual and reciprocal expectations arising from this equation:

> Superimposed on whatever the legal contract says, you've got this psychological contract, with the softer side of things, the spirit of the contract...you cannot breach that in an organization where you're relying on those people to deliver the service... Now you might have to road test that, but you ideally want to hold on to it... (Chair of Governing Body, post-1992 institution 1)

It is therefore the interpretation of a formal contract of employment, rather than the contract itself, that forms the basis of the psychological contract. This is likely to vary according to custom and practice in individual institutions. Examples include the degree of accountability of staff when they are not in the classroom; whether weekend work would be regarded as overtime, particularly in institutions with traditions of fixed hours; and whether staff should be required to live within a certain radius of the university. The issue of managing expectations on both sides was one that recurred, although there was a nice distinction between being overly prescriptive in those expectations, allowing space for individuals and roles to grow, and providing no guiding frameworks. Whatever arrangements are in place, however, their dependence on facilitative relationships, both formal and informal, is likely to be critical.

### *Management Relationships*

A significant number of respondents spoke of key relationships, for instance with line managers, and between the senior management team and middle managers such as heads of department. A sense of partnership with staff came through the narratives, particularly around developing shared solutions. The psychological impact of change was not to be underestimated, and there was acknowledgement that people could move quickly from a sense of security to feeling vulnerable. Listening, empathetic skills and a willingness to spend time with individuals were seen as vital in introducing any change, particularly for line managers, thus:

> ...leaving time for personal conversations...allowing time for what is really a personal process, rather than just an HR process... (Chair of Governing Body, post-1992 institution 1)

Common initiatives, used to facilitate and develop relationships, included:

- Annual staff reviews for discussion of progress and aspirations.
- Agreed plans for raising performance if expectations had not been met.
- (In the UK) the use of the Investors in People award to develop a culture of feedback and appreciation.
- Employee wellbeing programmes.

Devolved resource allocation and management within institutions has fostered flatter relationships in which heads of department and functional areas of activity have significant day-to-day responsibility for budgets and staff. In some cases, a deliberate attempt had been made to spread this responsibility, for instance, to course leaders:

> [we're] putting the power into the course leaders to make the decisions about how they deliver...what we are saying is that, there's your unit of resource, you've got to manage within that, and then they've got freedom with the course teams to make decisions...we'll drive efficiency through that, not worrying about how many hours everybody's on... (Dean of School 1, post-1992 institution 1)

Thus, at a day-to-day level:

> I would always get my line managers with their team to determine what is the workload, including things like open days, interviews, everything that has to be done, and work with the team to look at how that is going to be managed on a reasonable basis. (Dean of School 2, post-1992 institution 1)

Although some academic staff may see career advantage in taking on management and leadership responsibilities, there was also evidence of a need to build confidence at middle management level, reinforcing the point that managers are often 'ill prepared' (Hall, 2009: 8), and that there may be a lack of understanding about their roles (de Boer, Goedegebuure and Meek, 2010). Thus one second tier manager commented that: 'we are really HR managers as well...because we are responsible for [programme leaders]... one of my [programme leaders'] lecturers is on probation, and there seems to be a lack of understanding of [mutual] responsibilities...' (Academic Manager, post-1992 institution 2). This was particularly the case in institutions that drew heavily on teachers from industry, the creative arts and the professions, where there could also be issues about drawing together the contributions of part-time, hourly paid staff 'into a harmonious whole' (Academic Manager, post-1992 institution 2).

At the same time, increased student numbers and expectations mean that management responsibilities, even at the level of a module or programme, are more onerous, and individual members of staff expect to be offered credit for them, for instance in workload models, career paths and reward structures. However some respondents pointed out that including a realistic component for activities other than classroom teaching, such as leading a module or designing an online programme, could lead to a situation where time for teaching was severely reduced, particularly by those who were reluctant to teach.

There was also some evidence in the UK of different cultures in pre- and post-1992 institutions, with more of a tradition of self-accountability in the former, whereas in the latter '[t]he notion of earning and being accountable and managing your time, your resource, your connections…isn't there…' (former Vice-Chancellor, post-1992 institution). A sense of autonomy in the pre-1992s, particularly around research, contrasts with a stronger tradition of management per se, with full-time rather than rotational academic managers in the post-1992s, although some pre-1992 institutions were also moving to the appointment rather than election of senior managers such as Pro-Vice-Chancellors. Each institution, therefore, is likely to build its own employment proposition in the light of contextual variables.

### *Reward and Retention*

The concept of the employment 'package', which incorporates scope for 'soft' benefits as well as formal contractual requirements and obligations, is gaining currency in higher education. This is sometimes incorporated in an annual statement of, for instance, the monetary value of pay, pension, annual leave, development training and programmes of study. It can also include performance related pay, so that 'even if the confirmed base pay may be lower, the actual full benefits package may be better' (Head of Administration, pre-1992 institution 2). Many institutions, especially those in attractive campus environments, regarded this as part of the employment proposition, as well as social and sports facilities. Such packages can also be used as a negotiating tool when, for instance, institutions establish companies or joint ventures.

Some institutions also use non-pensionable one-off payments linked to individual, team and institutional performance, for instance bonus payments for individuals who reach student recruitment targets, develop a new programme, or bring in research funding, thereby making a direct link between individual and institutional performance. There was also an example of goodwill gesture by one institution, on the occasion of its acquiring degree awarding powers, of a one-off payment to all employees; another gave a bonus plus two extra days of leave to employees in recognition of a successful quality audit.

Despite increasing awareness of the need for recognition of teaching excellence linked to scholarship, it was suggested that there was, nevertheless, still work to be done in developing appropriate criteria for teaching and scholarship that would stimulate high quality programmes. There was also a sense that any reward system was part of the overall employment equation, so that rewards 'are fine, but there have got to be accountabilities...it is the freedoms, the managed and accountable freedoms' (former Vice-Chancellor, post-1992 institution). Individual cases may need to be judged on a one-off basis, without institutional guidelines or direct comparators, and there may be equity issues around, for instance, conditions of service, intellectual property and entitlement to support for conferences, about which ongoing negotiation is likely to be required. This is particularly the case for staff who are not necessarily on academic contracts but who undertake work with an academic component such as tutoring or institutional or curriculum research.

### *Careers and Career Development*

There is increasing recognition that the range of activity with which institutions were involved required greater flexibility in career frameworks and development opportunities, as well as the possibility of crossovers and secondments to other sectors. Thus, 'job families [are being] created to recognise the importance of a mixed economy' (Director of Human Resources, pre-1992 institution 1). Changing approaches to the relationship between teaching and research, and the impact of this on contractual arrangements, are shown in Box 1:

*Box 1: The Teaching/Research Nexus*

There was evidence of the creative use of contracts across the spectrum of teaching and research, teaching and scholarship, teaching-only, and research-only roles. While the private UK institution and post-1992 institutions were seeking to develop research and scholarship to inform teaching, the pre-1992 institutions, which had a more balanced teaching and research profile, had adopted strategies geared to reinforcing the quality of both teaching and research. The view was expressed more than once that the historic trilogy of teaching, research and administration/third mission/knowledge exchange may no longer be tenable, although teaching should be informed by scholarship, and there was no reason why this should not be a prime focus. As one respondent from a pre-1992 institution put it, 'Why allocate time to mediocre research?' Nor could it necessarily be expected that leading researchers would be leading teachers, although it was not simply a question of giving more teaching to less successful researchers, which was unlikely to enhance the student experience. Some might, for instance, become involved in entrepreneurial, partnership or widening participation activity, and/or develop Mode 2 research in these areas. It was also important that a focus on teaching and learning did not lead to a failure in research. With the aim of creating attractive programmes of learning for students that built institutional reputation, one institution was providing exemplars to help staff progress with their teaching. An associated issue was how to devise criteria that rewarded excellence in teaching and scholarship.

There is also evidence of institutions adapting traditional portfolios of teaching, research and third mission, for instance incorporating knowledge exchange activity and pedagogical research, with associated criteria for advancement. The University of Strathclyde, for instance, has developed job level descriptors for different categories of staff (academic professional, knowledge exchange professional, research associate/fellow and teaching associate/fellow) at different stages of a career pathway. The introduction of a knowledge exchange (KE) pathway (KE Assistant, KE Associate, KE Fellow, Senior KE Fellow, Principal KE Fellow) illustrates recognition accorded to this area of activity. A Senior KE Fellow, for instance, would be expected to develop proposals, engage in individual and collaborative projects and implement KE programmes, as well as teaching and supervising research students. In doing this they would establish links with industry and funding bodies, author papers and conference presentations and lead KE teams. In all these pathways, greater responsibility for managing people, involvement in strategic decision making and the establishment of international reputations is expected at more senior levels. There are also signs that people in fields such as knowledge exchange are increasingly marketable, especially if they have an understanding of both academic and business worlds, and that attention to appropriate employment conditions will be key to attracting and retaining their talents.

The development of managers with responsibilities for staff at school and departmental level was generally seen as being in need of reinforcement. They had a key role to play in identifying and providing development for staff with potential, particularly in teaching, as well as in playing to existing strengths. This was increasingly vital in agreeing the balance of individual portfolios with staff, providing motivation at local level, and in making links between individuals, teams and the institution. Such experience might be gained via, for instance, running large research teams and substantial degree programmes. Concerns were also raised about giving younger academic staff the opportunity to develop their careers, such as attending conferences, seminars, social and networking events.

## Challenges

A number of system-wide challenges emerged in relation to the diversification of roles and staffing practices. Tension can arise from the priority accorded to teaching, research and scholarship at institutional, departmental and individual levels, and as research income becomes harder to attract, maintaining a balance may become more difficult. At the same time, there was recognition that teaching should be valued in its own right, with provision for promotion on the basis of teaching linked to scholarship, innovative practice and income generation/reputational impact. There were also issues around dealing with subject areas that are perceived as weak, including whether they should be reinforced, merged into other areas, or withdrawn. Institutions are endeavouring to address these challenges in ways that are optimal for them vis-à-vis their individual missions and profiles.

As institutions become more globalized there has also been an increase in overseas campuses (Fielden, 2011), with different arrangements, for instance, for nationals employed on local terms and conditions; staff recruited from other countries to work on the project or campus; and academic staff from the home country. It is therefore possible to have staff working overseas on home contracts alongside local staff on local contracts. There can be morale issues associated with adjustment to different cultures, and in having ongoing commitment from 'flying faculty'. A joint research project, for instance, may be a significant incentive for individuals to commit to working in an overseas institution.

Comparability issues are likely to arise, irrespective of type of institution or staffing practices, in relation to the use of mechanisms such as performance related pay which might be seen as disadvantaging individuals whose roles are less high profile in terms of contributing directly to institutional objectives. There could also be instances, particularly in devolved structures, of different models being adopted in different Schools in relation to teaching and research profiles and reward structures. This could happen, for instance, where one school was more successful in attracting research funding.

There was also concern, particularly by senior managers, about making the link between individual and institutional performance, and this represented a balancing act between collective considerations and academic autonomy, managed between senior management teams and heads of schools and departments. Typically, central management teams were well connected with changes in government policy and legislation, while local managers were aware of implementation issues, for instance in relation to delays in the approval of posts or of new programmes. Therefore good communication channels, 'that put the human face on the institution' (Director of Human Resources, pre-1992 institution 2), were paramount. Critical success factors in overcoming such challenges were likely to include an investment of time in dialogue with individuals about their contributions, at the same time as taking an institutional overview of comparability issues.

In considering such challenges, institutions are experimenting with approaches that both anticipate and work with changing circumstances, taking a proactive stance rather than simply responding to change after it has occurred, in ways that might be described as 'resilient' (Hollnagel et al., 2006; Hamel and Valikangas, 2003; Valikangas, 2010). These include identifying trends in relation to, for instance, staff and student aspirations, seeking opportunities rather than simply responding to perceived threats, acknowledging uncertainty whilst making the best of new policy environments or market conditions, and recovering their equilibrium after unforeseen perturbations, across Hamel's spectrum of cognitive, strategic, political and ideological challenges (Hamel and Valikangas, 2003: 54). Mechanisms such as pulse surveys help them to do this in environments that have been described as 'supercomplex' (Barnett, 2000). Furthermore, a desire to achieve equity, transparency, and to offer recognition for performance in a diversifying range of activity via collaborative management reflects ideas of resilient organizations as involving top level commitment, a just and learning culture, awareness, preparedness, flexibility and opacity (Wreathall, 2006: 279–280).

Resilience is therefore likely to involve a receptiveness to both immediate, local circumstances and to possible futures. For instance, there was awareness that the introduction of new practices might be perceived differently by different groups of staff. Thus, whilst longstanding staff might see annual review as an additional burden or even intrusion, younger staff might see it as an opportunity to gain feedback and add to their portfolio:

> While [some] see it as a control mechanism, there's lots of young staff said to me, 'I want this because I want to know how I can get promoted. I want to know how well I've done…'. It's instructive in itself, who sees it as negative and who sees it as positive. (Dean of School 1, post-1992 institution 1)

There may also be generational issues, with up-and-coming staff being motivated by a broader range of rewards and incentives, including using technology to work in ways that fit in with lifestyles. It was therefore apparent that the higher education system, and a significant number of institutions, were in a process of transition. As in Barnett's supercomplex environments, such a process may indeed be ongoing, creating conditions of permanent provisionality and uncertainty, in which resilience becomes even more critical.

## Conclusions

The study suggests that, despite significant pressures on universities to respond to both market and government agendas, institutions are preserving stability in their structures and relationships at the same time as being proactive and innovative in adjusting existing arrangements and experimenting with new practices. This might be summarized as cautious adaptation, absorbing requirements for change at the same time as maintaining core purposes and values. One respondent cited examples of 'institutions really working towards trying to get the best of a new marketized world, but also being respectful of the culture, ethos and values of the institution' (former Vice-Chancellor, post-1992 institution). However, strategies for responding to change are only likely to work in practice if they are handled sensitively at local level, in ways that suit the needs of specific disciplines and cohorts of staff. Although some practices continue to evolve, as suggested by Henkel (2000), others, for instance in cases where new partnerships are established, can involve significant re-orientation of roles.

Resilient cultures therefore go beyond what might be achieved by strategic planning models such as the Boston Box, or assessment of strengths, weaknesses, opportunities and threats (SWOT analysis) (see Temple and Whitchurch (1989) for the application of organizational models to higher education). These are likely to depend on diverse approaches for different activities and being open to opportunities and options, as suggested by the classical contingency theorists (Burns and Stalker, 1961; Lawrence and Lorsch, 1969). This approach was further developed by Pettigrew and Whipp (1991) to include an understanding of internal and external environments, a valuing of staff contributions, understandings of the link between overall direction and the activities of individuals, the nomination of key leaders who are able to work with staff in delivering benefits of new initiatives, and establishing a vision for the organization that is coherent and feasible. The study described in this chapter illustrates how institutions address, through their assessment of turbulent environments, consideration of appropriate reward mechanisms, review of strategic options, involvement of middle managers in decision making, and establishment of two way channels of communication, endeavouring to match their approaches to local environments and opportunities, although there is ongoing work to be done in joining up these approaches institutionally and regionally. It remains to be seen whether there is a correlation between success, survival and resilience.

The study also demonstrates how contingency approaches reflect more democratic forms of management and leadership. Such leadership facilitates what Hamel terms the 'paradox' of unity and diversity (Hamel and Valikangas, 2003: 63), a mixed economy of activities that is open to possibilities but continues to generate a sense of commitment from staff, with a higher degree of internal differentiation than might be required in less complex environments (see also Morgan, 2006). Thus both institutions and stakeholders benefit from the involvement of broader constituencies in institutional decision making and knowledge building (Benington, 2011; Feldman and Khademian, 2007; Ferlie, Musselin and Adresani, 2008; Quick and Feldman, 2011). This involves continual attention to 'informational and relational work' (Feldman and Khademian, 2007: 320). In similar public management contexts, Benington refers to ways in which 'policy...is increasingly shared with informal networks of users...with a sharing of risks and rewards...[so that] value is continuously created and co-constructed...' (Benington, 2011: 34, 36, 39, 43). The study suggests, therefore, that institutions are revisiting management and governance practices with the aim of creating capacity to adapt before situations become acute and crisis action is required. In doing so they are bringing together a range of expectations, talents and commitments from a diversifying workforce in complex environments. In turn, local managers, including heads of department, have a key role to play in managing staff, supporting institutional aspirations and developing solutions that are in tune with specific needs.

## References

Barnett, R. (2000). *Realizing the University in an Age of Supercomplexity*. Buckingham: Open University/ SRHE.

Benington, J. (2011). 'From Private Choice to Public Value?' In J. Bennington, and M. Moore (eds), *Public Value: Theory and Practice*, pp. 31–51. Basingstoke: Palgrave Macmillan.

Burns, T., and Stalker, G. (1961). *The Management of Innovation*. London: Tavistock.

de Boer, H., Goedegebuure, L., and Meek, V.L. (2010). 'The Changing Nature of Academic Middle Management: A Framework for Analysis'. In V.L. Meek, L. Goedegebuure, R. Santiago, and Carvalho, T. (eds), *The Changing Dynamics of Higher Education Middle Management*, pp. 229–241. Dordrecht: Springer.

Department for Business, Innovation and Skills (BIS) (2011). *Students at the Heart of the System*. London: HMSO.

Enders, J., and de Weert, E. (2009). 'Towards a T-Shaped Profession: Academic Work and Careers in the Knowledge Society'. In J. Enders, and E. de Weert (eds), *The Changing Face of Academic Life: Analytical and Comparative Perspectives*, pp. 251–272. Basingstoke: Palgrave Macmillan.

Feldman, M., and Khademian, A. (2007). 'The Role of the Public Manager in Inclusion: Creating Communities of Participation', *Governance: An International Journal of Policy, Administration and Institutions*, 20 (2), 305–324.

Ferlie, E., Musselin, C., and Andresani, G. (2008). 'The Steering of Higher Education Systems: a Public Management Perspective', *Higher Education*, 56 (3), 325–348.

Fielden, J. (2011). *Leadership and Management of International Partnerships*. London: Leadership Foundation for Higher Education.

Fielden, J., Middlehurst, R., and Woodfield, S. (2010). *The Growth of Private and For Profit Higher Education Providers in the UK*. London: UniversitiesUK.

Gordon, G., and Whitchurch, C. (eds) (2010). *Academic and Professional Identities in Higher Education: The Challenges of a Diversifying Workforce*. International Studies in Higher Education. New York: Routledge.

Hall, A. (2009). *Getting to Grips with Human Resource Management. Resources for Governors of UK Universities and Higher Education Colleges*. London: Leadership Foundation for Higher Education/Committee of University Chairs.

Hamel, G., and Välikangas, L. (2003). 'The Quest for Resilience', *Harvard Business Review*, September 2003, 52–63.

Henard, F. (2012). *Re-managing the Academic Workforce: Global Challenges and Opportunities*. Conference on Managing the Academic Workforce: Global Challenges and Opportunities. London, UK: 3–4 July 2012.

Henkel, M. (2000). *Academic Identities and Policy Change in Higher Education*. London: Jessica Kingsley.

HEFCE – Higher Education Funding Council for England (2006). *The Higher Education Workforce in England: A Framework for the Future*. Bristol: HEFCE.

HEFCE – Higher Education Funding Council for England (Oakleigh Consulting) (2009). *Evaluation of the Impact of Public Policy and Investments in Human Resource Management in Higher Education since 2001*. Bristol: HEFCE.

HEFCE – Higher Education Funding Council for England (2010a). *The Higher Education Workforce Framework 2010*. Overview Report. Bristol: HEFCE.

HEFCE – Higher Education Funding Council for England (PA Consulting) (2010b). *The Future Workforce for Higher Education*. Overview Report. Bristol: HEFCE.

HEFCE – Higher Education Funding Council for England (2012). *Collaborations, Alliances and Mergers in Higher Education: Consultation on Lessons Learned and Guidance for Institutions*. Bristol: HEFCE.

HESA – Higher Education Statistics Agency (2012). *Resources of Higher Education Institutions 2009/10*. Cheltenham: HESA.

Hollnagel, E., Woods, D., and Leveson, N. (eds) (2006). *Resilience Engineering: Concepts and Precepts*. Aldershot: Ashgate.

JNCHES – Joint Negotiating Committee for Higher Education Staff (2003). *Framework Agreement for Modernisation of Pay Structures*. London: UCEA.

Kim, T., and Locke, W. (2010). *Transnational Academic Mobility and the Academic Profession*. Centre for Higher Education Research and Information (CHERI), Open University: London.

Lawrence, P., and Lorsch, J. (1969). *Developing Organizations: Diagnosis and Action*. Reading, Mass: Addison-Wesley Publishing Company.

Middlehurst, R., and Fielden, J. (2011). *Private Providers in UK Higher Education: some Policy Options*. Oxford: Higher Education Policy Institute (HEPI).

Morgan, G. (2006). *Images of Organization*. Thousand Oaks: Sage.

Pettigrew, A., and Whipp, R. (1991). *Managing Change for Competitive Success.* Oxford: Wiley.

Quick, K., and Feldman, M. (2011) 'Distinguishing Participation and Inclusion', *Journal of Planning Education and Research*, 31 (3), 272–290.

SFC – Scottish Funding Council (York Consulting) (2007). *Review of Shared Services and Collaborative Activities in Scotland's Universities.* Edinburgh: Scottish Funding Council.

Sloan, K. (2011). *Managing Commercial Relationships and Skills Needed to Effectively Deal with the Business Sector.* Presentation to 9th Heads of University Management and Administration Network in Europe (HUMANE). Winter School Alumni Network (WSAN). 30 September 2011.

Smith, C., and Boyd, P. (2010). *Becoming an Academic: The Reconstruction of Identity by Recently Appointed Lecturers in Nursing, Midwifery and the Allied Health Professions.* Conference on Academic Identities in the Twenty First Century. University of Strathclyde 16–18 June 2010.

Temple, P., and Whitchurch, C. (1989). *Strategic Choice: Corporate Strategies for Change in Higher Education.* Manchester: Association of University Administrators (AUA).

UCEA – Universities and Colleges Employers Association (2006). *Recruitment and Retention of Staff in Higher Education 2005.* London: UCEA.

UCEA – Universities and Colleges Employers Association (2008). *Where Are We Now? The Benefits of Working in HE.* London, UCEA.

UUK – UniversitiesUK (2007a). *The Changing Academic Profession.* London: UUK.

UUK – UniversitiesUK (2007b). *Talent Wars.* Policy Briefing. London: UUK.

UUK – UniversitiesUK (2011). *Efficiency and Effectiveness in Higher Education: A Report by the UniversitiesUK Efficiency and Modernisation Task Group.* London: UUK.

Välikangas, L. (2010). *The Resilient Organization: How Adaptive Cultures Thrive Even When Strategy Fails.* New York: McGraw Hill.

Whitchurch, C. (2013). *Reconstructing Identities in Higher Education: The Rise of Third Space Professionals.* New York: Routledge.

Whitchurch, C., and Gordon, G. (2013). *Staffing Models and Institutional Flexibility.* London: Leadership Foundation for Higher Education.

Woodfield, S., Fielden, J., and Middlehurst, R. (2011). 'Working Together: Partnerships between Publicly Funded HEIs and "Private Providers" in the UK', *perspectives: policy and practice in higher education*, 15 (2), 45–52.

Wreathall, J. (2006). 'Properties of Resilient Organizations: An Initial View'. In E. Hollnagel, D. Woods, and Leveson, N. (eds), *Resilience Engineering: Concepts and Precepts*. Aldershot: Ashgate.

MARIA HINFELAAR AND MICHAEL O'CONNELL

# 9 Shall We Dance? Dynamic Collaborations, Alliances and Mergers in the Shifting Irish Higher Education Landscape

## Introduction

Consolidation and collaboration feature strongly among the instruments deployed by individual institutions or policymakers to develop and reform higher education provision. There is a considerable body of international literature examining and defining collaboration, alliances and mergers (CAMs) in higher education. Merger typologies across Australian, UK, Dutch and US systems were presented in seminal work by Goedegebuure (1992), Harman (2003, 2008), Harman and Meek (2002) and Pritchard (1993, 1998). Other research has focused on the long-term human aspects of mergers (Pritchard and Williamson, 2008; Locke, 2007), while strategic and educational dimensions were reviewed by Rowley (1997) and Ursin (2010). The Higher Education Funding Council for England (HEFCE, 2012) proposes guidelines and best practice for CAMs.

Policies and operating environments vary from country to country, leading to different strategic responses from higher education institutions (HEIs). However, that is not to say that CAM phenomena are local. In an age of international rankings and league tables, HEIs operate on a global stage in which the competition, the scope for collaboration and the benchmarks for success are all international. National education policies may also be harmonized with supranational strategies such as *EU Horizons 2020*, which emphasizes the competitiveness of an entire trading block. OECD countries are converging towards a public policy framework for tertiary education 'in which detailed administrative direction is diminished, institutional autonomy widened and accountability mechanisms strengthened', coupled with trends towards enhanced institutional strategic leadership (Santiago et al., 2008: 90, 122). Hamel and Välikangas (2003: 53) describe strategic resilience as 'the ability to dynamically reinvent business models and strategies as circumstances change'.

Such converging trends in steering models for HEIs would be highly relevant in a CAM context and this topic has been little researched. Since the phenomenon is international, there is merit in modelling how and why CAM moves happen along similar recognizable patterns across various jurisdictions, particularly focusing on the institutional leadership responses. This chapter presents a case study showing how Limerick Institute of Technology (LIT) has to date deployed CAMs to be resilient and to enable its development and growth in an era of rapid change in Ireland. Drawing on recent international literature, the authors propose a synthesized analytical framework for CAMs and leadership responses which are then applied to the LIT case. The proposed two-way typology, distinguishing between scenarios where the HEI 'needs to' or 'wishes to' embark on a CAM move, will provide practitioners and researchers internationally with insights into how an institution's leadership can steer through these choppy waters to maintain institutional resilience.

## Context: A New Higher Education Strategy for Ireland

Coate and MacLabhrainn (2009) aptly describe the Irish system as 'unruly' and 'quirky' in nature, due to a patchwork of social, religious, political, cultural and economic interests which have made it difficult to chart any coherent strategic path for the burgeoning publicly funded HEIs. In 2011/12 the publicly funded binary higher education sector in Ireland served around 200,000 full-time and part-time students; it comprised seven universities, fourteen institutes of technology (IOTs), three teacher education colleges and a considerable number of affiliated smaller providers (HEA, 2012b). The system is in a phase of profound change: it is undergoing significant economic contraction while concurrently needing to accommodate rising demographic trends. The national strategy for higher education to 2030 (DES, 2011) sets out objectives to address these challenges, with institutions required to map out their current and future profiles which includes their envisaged CAM partners – a reduction in the number of providers is one of the stated aims, though the proposed optimum configuration was initially left to the institutions themselves. This resulted in a reluctance on the part of the HEIs to overcommit themselves, and two years after the launch of the new strategy the system was no nearer to determining its future reconfiguration. The governance model for HEIs is statutorily prescribed in separate legislation for the IOTs and the universities (Irish Government, 1997/2006), providing for a shared governance model featuring the Governing Body (legal), the President (executive) and the Academic Council (faculty expertise). Governing Body approval is required under its reserved functions in the domains of strategic planning, finance and significant decisions regarding CAMs.

The publication of the strategy was followed by a number of policy documents issued by the Higher Education Authority (HEA) to HEIs. Recommendations include instruments such as strategic dialogue regarding institutional positioning and profiling, funding models, regional clusters, mergers and criteria for the establishment of technological universities. The latter might result from a consolidation process in the IOT sector, subject to re-designation. Following review and dialogue with each HEI on where they proposed to position themselves, a government-approved landscape for the reconfigured higher education system for the next couple of decades would ensue by mid-2013. However, there were inconsistent signals from central government on policy direction, with for example two international reports offering contradictory advice. By early 2013 a more directive policy agenda emerged driven by the Minister himself, urging institutions to take 'a long hard look' at their aspirations that may have been 'predicated on wishful thinking', identifying a serious mismatch between these aspirations and the system change and rationalization actually required (Quinn, 2012: 6–7).

## Recent International Praxis: CAMs in Response to a Competitive Environment

Mergers as well as loosely or highly formalized collaborations of all kinds feature strongly in institutional and system-level responses to the emerging challenges. Goedegebuure (2011) distinguishes between policy-induced (national/ system level/ top down) mergers and incidental (institutional level/ bottom up) CAMs. Two broad motivations for policy-induced mergers exist: 'sorting out the system' and 'raising the bar'. These can be further analysed into objectives achieving economies of scale (cost savings) or scope (synergies). Mature system-level mergers which are about 'raising the bar' and 'becoming world class' in response to the competitive global environment are characterized by high concentration of talent, significant investment (spanning both public and private sources), and favourable governance features which enable institutions to make decisions and manage resources unencumbered by bureaucracy. Non-merger CAM initiatives appear as points on the competition/ collaboration spectrum where relationships between institutions are complex and multi-faceted. Goedegebuure (2011) describes how in the characteristically free-market Australian system, strategic collaborations can stretch to partnering with private firms to deliver both ancillary and core services such as online education.

System restructuring occasionally creates unanticipated outcomes, painting a picture of policy development as 'semi-rational, semi-structured and semi-planned' (ibid: 3). In the Dutch non-university sector for instance, mergers resulted in an unexpectedly small number of large institutions, not related back to the minimum size conditions which were part of the government's original policy. In such an environment, institutional leadership needs to recognize that strategic positioning is adaptive with actions leading to reactions, but with 'actors more likely to sustain than reactors' (ibid: 14).

Tirronen and Nokkala (2009) describe the Finnish HE system's menu of responses to the regional and global competitive environment which commenced in 2006 and included both policy-induced and institutionally-driven models, classifying these into economic and strategic objectives respectively. With the Finnish approach being considerably more directive than the Australian approach, they note the semi-voluntary nature of some strategic actions which are 'steered' by policy. With regard to CAMs, typical system-level rationales were advanced: realignment of public resources, reducing overlaps through creating larger entities, pursuing cost savings and improving quality. Coupled with the expected demographic decline in Finland in the medium term, these measures will result in a fall in the number of universities from twenty to fifteen by 2020. However, the considerations were not merely economically driven: through a targeted top-down plan for 'stratification and differentiation' leading to unique institutional profiles, the government designated a number of institutions that would be elevated to international research universities, whereas other institutions would refocus on their own regions or specializations. For instance, the Aalto University was established from a merger of three institutions in Helsinki, endowed with an investment of €700m enabling it to compete globally.

Institutional cooperation and strengthening of profiles was accompanied with significant reform in governance and leadership in all Finnish universities. These reforms envisage a two-tier system with governing boards and academic senates and a strong professional management core, designed to lead to effective decision making with financial autonomy. It was Clark (1998) who first introduced the concept of a 'strengthened steering core' for the modern university endowing governors, central management groups and academic departments with an ability to be flexible and react to expanding and changing demands; this is now viewed as the norm throughout OECD countries (Santiago et al., 2008: 122).

Shattock (2010: 44) developed the concept of the strengthened steering core further: 'a machinery which combines strategic capability with executive powers but also contains a collegial and representational character…

for the steering core to work there must be mutual trust between the decision makers, an institutional ability to check facts, re-work data, consult internally and present a case'. Given such non-linear and iterative scenarios, generic models mapping different levels and intensity of change management are relevant. A matrix proposed by Nadler and Tushman (1989, 1990) presents incremental versus strategic change as the first dimension; applying this to a CAM context, some HEI collaborations may have a limited incremental effect on just a couple of departments, whereas a merger would fall into the strategic category as it has a profound impact on the HEI's identity. The second dimension distinguishes between reactive changes in response to events or a series of events, versus anticipatory changes which are initiated from an assessment of external events that may occur in turbulent environments. It is argued that organizational reorientations which are both strategic and anticipatory require highly complex leadership approaches which include diffusing leadership throughout the organization – in HEI terms, this would mean fully harnessing its strong steering core.

Moving on to the Irish HE system, it must be noted that this has neither had the free-market environment of the Australian sector nor the strongly directive environment of Finland described above. It is logical, therefore, that CAM moves in Ireland to date are best analysed at the institutional level rather than the system level. Hinfelaar (2012) proposes a framework to analyse drivers for exploration and decision making, distinguishing between push and pull factors for CAMs. Push factors are external, implying certain inevitabilities or even threats driving organizational defence mechanisms and change; pull factors can be internally driven or created by attractive options perceived by institutions, aligned with ambitions for organizational development. Examining the case of one institutional merger, the conclusion is reached that 'even though deliberations may be influenced by a complex, simultaneous interplay of push and pull factors, at least one of these categories should be so overwhelming that it drives the decision to go ahead and merge' (Hinfelaar, 2012: 45).

Table 9.1 A Two-Way Typology of CAM Rationale and Activity

| *CAM activities* | *Objectives* | *Drivers* | *Policies* | *Leadership approaches* |
|---|---|---|---|---|
| *What we need to/ are steered to do* | *Economic*<br><br>Efficiency gains in larger units through mergers or fully shared services. Stratification to select one or two world class institutions, coupled with governance reform for accountability. | *Push factors*<br><br>External pressures or defence mechanisms: imposed rationalization or mergers to ensure viability. | *Policy induced (top down)*<br><br>Sorting out the system: achieving economies of scale or scope. Raising the bar: developing a world-class university system, assisting national competitiveness. | *Reactive and linear*<br><br>Engaging in incremental changes or singular CAMs, responding to external events. |
| *What we might wish to do as institutions* | *Strategic*<br><br>Mergers or partnerships to create strategic clusters of expertise. Differentiation to achieve competitiveness. Governance reform to strengthen autonomy. | *Pull factors*<br><br>Attractive strategic options: expansion or status upgrading through mergers and deep alliances. | *Incidental (bottom-up)*<br><br>Collaborative responses to competitive pressures, aspiring to world class status. Strategic positioning: intra-sector, cross-sector or public-private mergers/ alliances. | *Anticipatory and fluid*<br><br>Strengthened steering core involved in iterative process. Strategic reorientation and change management may involve multi-faceted CAMs. |

A synthesis of this literature review is presented in an analytical framework set out below (Table 9.1, above) which aligns drivers, objectives and policies for CAMs at institution and system level. Responding to a competitive environment, organizations may be steered to engage in singular CAMs which are linked to economic imperatives or top-down changes, either to rationalize the system or to raise the quality bar. On the other hand, CAMs that organizations may wish to enter in 'bottom-up fashion' are usually strategic rather than reactive in nature and are expected to lead to attractive outcomes for stakeholders. Along a spectrum of lesser or greater autonomy for its leadership, the steering core of the resilient HEI will need to engage in more and more complex risk assessments and iterative, anticipatory decision making if the policy environment is less clear or less directive, or indeed more turbulent – requiring capacity for continuous reconstruction as described in Hamel and Välikangas (2003). In such cases the CAM initiative may be a multi-faceted strategic reorientation changing the identity of the organization. It is proposed that this broad two-way typology may be applicable to CAMs across diverse HE systems. In the section to follow, this typology will be explored and illustrated in the context of the highly diverse CAM experiences of Limerick Institute of Technology in Ireland.

## Competitive and Competing CAM Options: The Case of Limerick Institute of Technology

Limerick Institute of Technology (LIT) is a multi-campus higher education institution based in the Mid-West of Ireland with a history dating back to 1852 and an enrolment of around 5,000 full-time and 1,500 part-time learners. It is positioned in the non-university sector of the Irish binary HE system, offering industry-focused programmes primarily for its own region across a wide-ranging portfolio of disciplines (engineering, science, information technology, business, social care, services, art and design). As is typical in the IOT sector, undergraduates comprise the bulk of a diverse student population, many of them on laddered or sub-degree programmes. However, LIT has expanded its applied research capacity in recent years to an annual research income at over €4 million; it has 200 postgraduate students, and has three thriving incubation centres supporting export-focused startup companies which have created almost 400 jobs since 2007.

The theme of LIT's *Vision and Strategy to 2020* is reflective of its profile: 'Active Leadership in Education, Enterprise and Engagement'. Under the shared governance model, this strategic plan was organically developed by the President with participation by the senior executive team, a subcommittee of the Governing Body and a strategy group comprising senior and middle management, general staff and student representatives and Academic Council members. LIT's dynamic strategic positioning began in 2006 with collaboration in a multi-institutional consortium involving partners across the binary divide, then moved on to the integration of a smaller institution into LIT over an eighteen-month period to 2011, and progressed to a proposal in 2012 that LIT merge with two other IOTs leading to eventual designation as the Munster Technological University. Confronted with a shift in emphasis in national policy, this proposal was then paused and a decision taken with effect from 2013 to engage in enhanced and deeper collaboration within the original 2006 consortium as a 'regional cluster'. Each of these CAM moves is described in detail below.

### *Cross-Sector Collaboration: The Shannon Consortium Alliance*

LIT's first serious collaborative venture was undertaken in 2006, when it co-founded the Shannon Consortium with the University of Limerick (UL), Mary Immaculate College of Education (MIC) and the Institute of Technology Tralee (ITT). The consortium's stated aims were to coordinate and develop specific HE innovations in the region, 'thus achieving a greater impact on students and staff than is possible by any individual institution acting alone...with each partner contributing according to its distinctive, yet complementary strengths' (McCutcheon and Moran, 2012). The immediate driver for establishing the Shannon Consortium, however, was the launch of the Strategic Innovation Fund (SIF) by the HEA, representing a major injection of additional funds for successful institutions. A precondition was that proposals had to be collaborative. As the funding envelope for SIF appeared very generous (this was before the collapse of the 'Celtic Tiger' economy in 2008), many of the twenty-one eligible institutions around the country engaged in multiple ad hoc partnerships with complex governance arrangements in an attempt to maximize their share of the funds. The leaders of the four Shannon Consortium partner institutions agreed to take a more strategic approach through an exclusive and integrated proposal across several strands – this was a conscious decision which explicitly accepted the risk of missing out on opportunities with other potential partners. The strategy paid off: where many institutions' bids were only partially successful, the Shannon Consortium achieved an impeccable score and attracted over €22 million in SIF funds over a four-year period.

The main thematic strands for the collaborative projects were supporting access and lifelong learning, teaching and learning support for staff and students, joint graduate research degree training, the development of a national centre of excellence for mathematics and science teaching and a joint procurement network. The projects delivered tangible outcomes, such as a shared foundation programme for non-traditional cohorts through a downtown centre in Limerick, the joint development and rollout of a learning styles diagnostic test for first-year students and a regional teaching excellence award for academic staff. However, activity was curtailed when funding ran out and scaled-down versions of only a few projects remained. The exception was the Shannon Consortium Procurement Network, a framework for joint tendering to procure goods and services. It is spectacularly successful with many other HEIs joining, yielding significant savings, e.g. €2 million cumulatively to LIT alone since its inception.

It is striking that the Shannon Consortium's comprehensive array of projects did not include collaboration in the core area of the institutions: academic programmes. This was no accident; SIF guidelines precluded projects in joint development or delivery of programmes, and a major opportunity to commence streamlining and rationalization of the fragmented Irish HE system was missed by policymakers. Therefore, the type of collaboration which the Shannon Consortium engaged in could be characterized as a loose alliance rather than a deep alliance which did not really change the modus operandi and left the majority of staff and students untouched. The impact of some projects was local rather than collective and prospects of sustainable collaboration in these areas evaporated as soon as funds dried up. Nonetheless, in an independent evaluation of the success of SIF the Shannon Consortium was viewed as a national example of 'a successful collaboration that has become a brand name within its region' (HEA, 2010: 8).

### *Limerick Institute of Technology and Tipperary Institute: A Very Swift Merger*

LIT's trajectory along benign and relatively non-committal forms of collaboration was rudely interrupted in 2009/10, when a range of circumstances led to the incorporation of a smaller college in a neighbouring county. Unlike the ad hoc Shannon Consortium collaboration, this CAM move deeply involved the LIT Governing Body. The Tipperary Institute (TI) had been recommended for closure (or absorption into a larger entity) as part of a government review into public expenditure (McCarthy, 2009), which found that TI had an excessively high cost base and unsustainably low student numbers. A process was agreed that would lead to the dissolution of the TI board and the transfer of undertakings to LIT by September 2011. Ahead of the integration date, a viability plan was proactively implemented by a senior LIT manager as the Acting CEO for TI to begin addressing the cost issues. Within two years, student numbers doubled and this was achieved within existing resources while also reducing the overall cost, thereby saving the Exchequer approximately €3m per annum. The merger was cited as a successful example of public sector reform in the context of the IMF/ EU programme (Irish Government, 2012) – the first rationalization of the configuration of HEIs in Ireland for a couple of decades. The country was battling to regain its competitiveness and resilience, and this was being mirrored in its HE sector.

The incorporation of TI into LIT was a classic example of an unequal merger, where the survival wish of the smaller partner drove it into the arms of the bigger partner, who embraced this strategic opportunity to expand its scope and size – notwithstanding the significant operational issues brought by the merger process. The driver for TI in its decision making process was that it felt threatened with extinction, which was a 'push' factor arising from external pressures; in the case of LIT, the attractive 'pull' factor of enlargement and strengthening its competitive position in the new higher education landscape provided the overriding rationale for undertaking the merger (Hinfelaar, 2012). However, the decision to go ahead was not straightforward and was underpinned by a comprehensive risk analysis and due diligence exercise carried out by the Governing Body of LIT. Obvious key concerns were the potentially negative impact on LIT's financial position, employment security for staff and academic quality reputation through the incorporation of the perceived 'weaker' partner. To mitigate such risks, a number of immovable internal milestones were agreed and sine qua non conditions negotiated with the funding agency. These conditions were drawn up at joint steering group meetings comprising members of the two governing bodies, the LIT President and the Acting CEO of TI who had a dual reporting line since he was on secondment from LIT. The resulting document was submitted to policy-makers on behalf of both institutions and was accepted in full, so that it was possible to implement the merger without any slippage of deadlines. A new Governing Body was appointed with effect from the date of merger, which included several members of both outgoing boards who now had a significant CAM experience under their belts.

### *Conflicting Demands: The 'Regional Cluster' versus the 'Technological University'*

Within the IOT sector, the prospect of achieving technological university (TU) status appeared to be the major positive component of the national higher education strategy. IOTs must amalgamate to achieve TU designation; apart from meeting challenging quality criteria which may appear somewhat contradictory: these include doubling or trebling research postgraduate students as a percentage of overall enrolment while also maintaining cohort sizes of sub-degree students and increasing flexible learning provision. While still in the throes of incorporating TI with the attendant human resources, legal and systems issues, LIT therefore had to prepare the organization for the emerging higher education landscape. Governing Body and the executive management team carried out in-depth analyses of potential benefits and risks associated with several options ranging from full merger with specific institutions to staying autonomous but engaging in collaborations, bearing in mind national policy considerations and possible responses from other HEIs. The outcome was that LIT did not wish to be left behind in a third tier of institutions (i.e. behind the seven traditional universities and any new technological universities in a group of IOT 'stragglers'), as it was felt that would severely weaken the competitive position of the institution and its graduates. The understanding in the sector at the time was that IOTs that did not progress to TU status were in danger of being downgraded to further education colleges. In spite of misgivings about embarking on a large-scale merger process, Governing Body approved a proposal to go down the TU route. Early in 2012 LIT signed a memorandum of understanding with the IOTs in Cork and Tralee to form the Munster Technological University (MTU). Projections for this combined entity were to have 22,500 learners across its pre-existing fourteen campuses spanning a 175-km radius by 2016. It was envisaged that the MTU would make major contributions to the wider region through enhanced critical mass in the provision of higher education programmes and research (LIT, CIT, ITT joint submission to HEA, July 2012).

Clearly, to deliver on such an ambitious proposal there would be a requirement to align the portfolio and content of academic programmes – a highly complex and contentious exercise. Given the distance between partner institutions, it would not be desirable or necessary to close down local provision of entire disciplines, but some sacrifice and specialization would result from the merger (frequently referred to as 'elimination of unnecessary duplication' by policymakers). At the same time, however, all HEIs were required under the national strategy to form 'regional clusters' which would be geographically proximate and cross-sectoral; to engage in a coordinated analysis of programme offerings and 'ensure coherence and comprehensiveness of provision locally and regionally'; and to 'proactively come together to examine the scope for rationalization of programmes and the effectiveness of the regional use of current and capital resources' (HEA, 2012b: 21).

This left LIT, and other IOTs engaged in similar consortia, with the puzzling question of how to implement a micro-level review of programme provision with its neighbouring university partner in a 'regional cluster', and at the same time consolidate programme offerings with its geographically more distant IOT partners in the aspired MTU. Even assuming that a university would be happy to negotiate with an IOT on an equal footing about which programmes would succumb to the cause of 'eliminating unnecessary duplication', it is difficult to see from the IOT's perspective how such a battle could be fought on multiple fronts. Since rationalization of academic programmes may involve co-delivery or staff transfers, industrial relations and cost issues would arise immediately due to significant disparity in academic staff contracts between the university and the IOT sectors. HEFCE (2012: 47) cautions against underestimating the cost of cross-sector CAMs in areas such as harmonizing pay and benefit structures. The Shannon Consortium carried out initial work in mapping its undergraduate programmes during 2011, but this was not progressed. Other elements of effective regional clusters (HEA, 2012b: 24–25) were being pursued: shared services, formalized arrangements with the further education sector and joint approaches to labour market training for the unemployed.

It was evident, however, that Consortium activities were increasingly dominated by pragmatic and economic imperatives, rather than strategic imperatives. Continuing some of the 'loose alliance' activities previously funded by SIF did not require deeper commitment within the academic core of the partner institutions. This not only applied to LIT which had set its long-term strategic sights on technological university designation with other IOT partners. Following in the footsteps of a research alliance forged by Trinity College Dublin and University College Dublin, UL set up a strategic alliance outside the Shannon Consortium with the university in Galway in 2010 to strengthen their research profile, boost new technology and offer high-value electives to final-year students. Clearly, the strategic paths undertaken by both the university and IOT partners within the Shannon Consortium were diverging. This was in spite of exhortations by the HEA that 'mergers may or may not take place but regional clusters *must* develop' (HEA, 2012b: 23), and the clear understanding that the bar for regional clusters would be significantly higher than the 'soft' targets of the former SIF programme.

### *Everything Changed Utterly...Revisiting Strategic Direction*

One year after the agreement was signed by the prospective MTU partners, Irish HE policy development took a new turn which dropped a bombshell on the ambitions and projections drawn up by the individual HEIs in their responses submitted under the strategy implementation programme. A gap analysis document commissioned by the HEA and presented by the Minister stated that that there would be little likelihood, on the basis of the institutional submissions, that 'voluntary collaboration would lead organically to meeting the principles and achieving the objectives of the national strategy' (HEA 2012b: 14). The report also pointed out that the system would not be able to afford the projected steep increase in postgraduate numbers in the IOT sector, though it was acknowledged that this had been inspired by the criteria for TU designation. Reviewing the various proposed CAMs across the full breadth of the HE sectors, many of which came in for scathing criticism either for being too shallow or for being unrealistic, the following comment was made about the MTU:

> The proposed merger seems driven more by a desire for university status than the culmination of strong existing relationships exploiting the natural synergies of the component institutions [LIT, Cork IT and IT Tralee], as already exists within the Shannon Consortium. (ibid.: 25)

System governance and coordination were announced which would 'curtail the ambitions of institutions through compacts that are achievable and capable of being funded', coupled with a funding model that would 'reward larger and more efficient institutions' (ibid.: 28–29). This would address increasingly serious financial and quality issues experienced by some of the smaller colleges including some IOTs, whilst firmly decoupling the consolidation agenda from the status upgrading agenda. As for technological universities, these would only materialize in one or two cases after a considerable and 'arduous' number of years post-merger. Regional cross-binary clusters involving strong, autonomous institutions would be the priority. In a keynote speech, the Minister for Education and Skills reinforced the importance of a strong IOT sector in responding to skills needs as well as research and development needs of the enterprise sector (Quinn, 2012: 3); this was interpreted as a commitment that such activity would not be stripped from IOTs that opted not to look for TU designation. This position was confirmed in the finalized document which recognized a category of stronger, stand-alone IOTs such as LIT, alongside some groupings of IOTs that would merge but that were given no guarantees that their ambitions to be designated as TUs would be successful (HEA, 2013) – even though the invitation to progress to the next planning stage clearly gave them hope.

There appeared to be no political will or resources for the IOT sector to transform itself into a TU sector within a foreseeable timeframe, and there was a real risk that the pathway towards meeting TU criteria might be cut off even if merger processes with distant partners were irreversible. Such a scenario would drain away resources and weaken performance as opposed to creating the aspired efficiency gains and enhanced status. LIT had to reassess its strategic direction. The shift in tone and language of policymakers meant that, suddenly, maintaining and enhancing LIT's profile as a strong and successful institute of technology became attractive again. Utilizing the shared governance mechanism, LIT took a decision to shelve the MTU project and further develop the Shannon Consortium on the basis of autonomy and equal partnership. It was felt this direction provided a better fit with the local and regional remit of LIT, allowing the institution to focus on Limerick instead of being pulled towards Cork. Compared with the decision a year before to develop the MTU memorandum of understanding following a protracted and rigorous analysis of options, the decision to exit from the process was more straightforward. The central steering core of executive managers, staff and student representatives and governing body members drawn from regional industry and community sectors demonstrated speed of response and agility in reversing their earlier decision, once they fully understood the new information. The news was well received by stakeholders and work on progressing regional cluster objectives was resumed.

## Discussion and Conclusion

The LIT case would confirm Lang's (2002) proposition that institutional CAM moves are part of a continuum rather than discrete unrelated actions, although this continuum proved to be hardly predictable and smooth. Therefore, with Goedegebuure (2011: 3), based on our experience we believe that policy development and implementation both at the system and the institutional level are at best 'semi-rational, semi-structured and semi-planned' – this may be due to unexpected changes in the policy environment as well as moves by partner institutions. The loose, incremental collaboration of the Shannon Consortium was purported to become a deeper strategic alliance but deviated from this trajectory for a period of time; the incorporation of Tipperary Institute was unforeseen but took place at breakneck speed; it was subsequently overtaken by signing an agreement to pursue a merger with two other IOTs as the potential future 'Munster Technological University' which would be an amalgamation on an unprecedented scale in the Irish context. LIT then withdrew from this proposal when there was a shift in national policy emphasis which, in LIT's view, made it extremely unlikely that the MTU ambition would become a reality. Such rapid changes in direction may seem surprising, but they can be logically explained in the context of the proposed CAMs' analytical framework and can be seen as an illustration of how to build resilience.

A CAM move may mean different things to different partners. The government-supported merger between LIT and TI was driven by economic considerations for TI in addressing serious deficiencies, as opposed to opportunistic strategic development objectives for LIT. These considerations broadly aligned with push factors for the smaller institution, and pull factors for the larger one. Once the decision was approved by the organization's steering core and the funding agency accepted certain sine qua non conditions, the process moved ahead in linear fashion and became a management project. The response of both organizations, while different because of their circumstances, was primarily a reaction to the external drivers.

LIT's intention to become a potential founding partner of a much larger new organization, the MTU into which it would be subsumed, was overwhelmingly driven by strategic vision and the pull factor of status upgrading in order to become more competitive. This decision also bore the hallmarks of 'incidental' action-reaction dynamic and reorienting change management, as LIT and its partners were determined not to lose ground compared with other IOT consortia that were springing up around the country. However, the rationale for this decision was swept away when national HE policy direction became clearer. The leadership response had to be fluid and anticipatory, with the steering core repeatedly drawn into reassessing strategies and revisiting decisions taken earlier, opting to enhance LIT's performance as a strong, autonomous IOT.

LIT's membership of the Shannon Consortium had become economically driven as it was for the other partners, even though Irish policymakers were promoting 'regional clusters' as a combination of strategic and economic deliverables that would involve closer collaboration and rationalization of academic programmes. The binary Irish HE system and culture has traditionally been too rigid to facilitate collaborative responses that are truly cross-sectoral and that go beyond superficial and incremental arrangements – thereby creating some conflict with stated public policy. Overcoming these obstacles was going to be the major challenge in implementing the decision to prioritize the regional cluster.

Notwithstanding the typical uncertainties and ambiguities in the environment in which HEIs operate, our proposed framework presents a synopsis for understanding the motivating drivers at the institutional level, as well as national system-level policies and objectives for different types of CAMs as they appear to be unfolding in various jurisdictions. They fall into two broad categories, which are aligned with actual multiple CAM moves describing the case of LIT in Ireland (Table 9.2). A further dimension of typical leadership responses is proposed, which range from linear and reactive to fluid and anticipatory, depending on the adaptive capacity required. In their quest for resilience, institutions may engage in CAMs because they need to, are directed to or wish to, and that will shape the depth of the deliberations by the full steering core of the institution and ultimately their engagement with partners.

While the data underpinning our study were unique to LIT's institutional perspective which clearly placed limitations on the research methodology, the findings may be relatable to other HEIs in Ireland and internationally. The integrated CAM typology and framework presented here should be of assistance in strategic positioning to other HEIs and to policymakers, both as practitioners and researchers. Further qualitative studies to test the robustness of the typology are recommended.

Table 9.2 Two-Way CAM Typology Applied to Limerick Institute of Technology

| *CAM activities* | *Objectives* | *Drivers* | *Policies* | *Leadership approaches* |
|---|---|---|---|---|
| *What we need to do/ are steered to do* | *Economic* | *Push factors* | *Policy induced (top down)* | *Reactive and linear* |
| | Shannon Consortium collaboration (cross-sector), responding to competitive funding calls and engaging in shared services. | Faced with viability crisis, TI opting for dissolution and transfer of undertakings to LIT. Funding reforms driving programme rationalization and system diversity. | Government support for incorporation of TI into LIT. Encouraging regional clusters through incentivized strategic funding and Ministerial direction. | Risk management and containment, once specific CAM move was approved by institute's steering core and sine qua non conditions met. |
| *What we might wish to do as institutions* | *Strategic* | *Pull factors* | *Incidental (bottom-up)* | *Anticipatory and fluid* |
| | LIT and two IOT partners proposing to merge as Munster Technological University. Conflicting government policy to form regional clusters and centres of expertise. | LIT expanding size and scope through incorporation of TI. Desire to be upgraded to university status, versus desire to retain autonomy. | LIT responding to technological university consortia elsewhere. Reaction from established universities to potential newcomers. | Iterative reviews of options. Steering core deciding on deeper regional alliance, withdrawing from MTU. Reformulating ambition to set the benchmark as a strong IOT. |

# References


Clark, B.R. (1998). *Creating Entrepreneurial Universities.* Oxford: Elsevier Science.

Coate, K., and MacLabhrainn, I. (2009). 'Irish Higher Education and the Knowledge Economy'. In J. Huisman (ed.), *International Perspectives on the Governance of Higher Education: Alternative Frameworks for Coordination*, pp. 198–216. New York: Routledge Press.

DES – Department of Education and Skills (2011). *National Strategy for Higher Education to 2030, Report of the Strategy Group.* Dublin: Irish Government.

Goedegebuure, L.C.J. (1992). *Mergers in Higher Education: A Comparative Perspective.* Enschede: University of Twente.

Goedegebuure, L.C.J. (2011). 'Mergers and More: The Changing Tertiary Landscape in the 21st Century'. HEIK Working Paper. Oslo: University of Oslo, <http://www.uv.uio.no/english/research/groups/heik/heik-working-paper-series/docs/HEIKwp201201_goedegebuure.pdf> accessed 5 March 2012.

Hamel, G., and Välikangas, L. (2003). 'The Quest for Resilience', *Harvard Business Review*, 81 (9), 52–63.

Harman, G., and Harman, K. (2003). 'Institutional Mergers in Higher Education: Lessons from International Experience', *Tertiary Education and Management*, 9 (1), 29–44.

Harman, G., and Harman, K. (2008). 'Strategic Mergers of Strong Institutions to Enhance Competitive Advantage', *Higher Education Policy*, 21 (1), 99–121.

Harman, K., and Meek, V.L. (2002). 'Introduction to Special Issue: Merger Revisited: International Perspectives on Mergers in Higher Education', *Higher Education*, 44 (1), 1–4.

HEA (2010). *Report of the Strategic Innovation Fund Evaluation.* Dublin: Higher Education Authority.

HEA (2012a). *Institutional Responses to the Landscape Document and Achieving the Objectives of the National Strategy for Higher Education: A Gap Analysis.* Dublin: Higher Education Authority.

HEA (2012b). *Towards a Future Higher Education Landscape.* Dublin: Higher Education Authority.

HEA (2013). *Report to the Minister for Education and Skills on System Reconfiguration, Inter-institutional Collaboration and System Governance in Irish Higher Education.* Dublin: Higher Education Authority.

HEFCE (2012). *Collaborations, Alliances and Mergers in Higher Education – Consultation on Lessons Learned and Guidance for Institutions.* London: Higher Education Funding Council.

Hinfelaar, M. (2012). 'Emerging Higher Education Strategy in Ireland: Amalgamate or Perish', *Higher Education Management and Policy*, 24 (1), 33–48.

Irish Government (1997). *Universities Act (1997).* Dublin.

Irish Government (2006). *Institutes of Technology Act 2006.* Dublin.

Irish Government (2012). *Implementation Body Public Service Agreement 2010–2014, Second Progress Report.* Dublin.

Lang, D.W. (2002). 'A Lexicon of Inter-institutional Cooperation', *Higher Education*, 44 (1), 153–183.

LIT (2011). *Vision and Strategy to 2020.* Limerick: Limerick Institute of Technology.

LIT (2012). *Submission in Response to HEA – Towards a Future Higher Education Landscape*, Limerick: Limerick Institute of Technology.

Locke, W. (2007). 'Higher Education Mergers: Integrating Organisational Cultures and Developing Appropriate Management Styles', *Higher Education Quarterly*, 61 (1), 83–102.

McCarthy, C. (2009). *Report of the Special Group on Public Service Numbers and Expenditure Programmes.* Dublin: Department of Finance.

McCutcheon, P. and Moran, E. (2012). 'The Shannon Consortium – A Model for Regional Inter-institutional Collaboration', *Leadership and Governance in Higher Education*, Supplement (2012), Vol. 02, 72–88.

Nadler, D.A. and Tushman, M.L. (1989). 'Organizational Frame Bending: Principles for Managing Reorientation', *Academy of Management Executive*, 3 (3), 194–204.

Nadler, D.A. and Tushman, M.L. (1990). 'Beyond the Charismatic Leader: Leadership and Organizational Change', *California Management Review*, 32 (2), 77–97.

Pritchard, R.M.O. (1993). 'Mergers and Linkages in British Higher Education', *Higher Education Quarterly*, 47 (2), 79–102.

Pritchard, R.M.O. (1998), 'Institutional Lifecycles in British Higher Education', *Tertiary Education and Management*, 4 (1), 71–80.

Pritchard, R.M.O., and P. Willliamson (2008). 'Long-term Human Outcomes of a "Shotgun" Marriage in Higher Education: Anatomy of a Merger, Two Decades Later', *Higher Education Management and Policy*, 20 (1), 1–23.

Quinn, R. (2012). *Speech by Minister for Education and Skills, Ruairi Quinn TD, on Higher Education Reform, 22 November 2012.* Dublin: Irish Government.

Rowley, G. (1997). 'Mergers in Higher Education: A Strategic Analysis', *Higher Education Quarterly*, 51 (3), 251–263.

Santiago, P., Tremblay, K., Basri, E., and Arnal, E. (eds) (2008). 'Special Features: Governance, Funding, Quality'. In *Tertiary Education for the Knowledge Society*, Vol.1, pp. 67–317. Paris: Organisation for Economic Cooperation and Development.

Shattock, M.L. (2010). *Managing Successful Universities* (2nd edn). Maidenhead: Open University Press.

Tirronen, J., and Nokkala, T. (2009). 'Structural Development of Finnish Universities: Achieving Competence and Academic Excellence', *Higher Education Quarterly*, 63 (3), 219–236.

Ursin, J., Aittola, H., Henderson, C., and Välimaa, C. (2010). 'Is Education Getting Lost in University Mergers?', *Tertiary Education and Management*, 16 (4), 327–340.

PÅL BAKKEN AND INGRID STORM

# 10 Academic Drift and Diversity: Institutional Dynamics in Norwegian Higher Education

## Introduction

The Norwegian higher education sector has gone through significant changes during the last two decades, with a doubling in the number of universities and a sharp increase in the number of postgraduate degree programmes. The higher education sector in Norway has traditionally been organized as a binary system of research oriented universities and university colleges offering vocational education. However, opportunities for change in institutional status have blurred the distinction, and contributed to a process of institutional and academic drift. The main question posed in this paper is whether this process leads to increased homogeneity.

Several governmental reforms in the last decades aimed to increase the higher education institutions' robustness. In addition, many institutions have had – and still have – ambitions to increase their status in the institutional hierarchy. The motives for this status change are many, among them is to increase their competitiveness. The concept of resilience is thus relevant both at a governmental and institutional level. The Norwegian legislation allows the higher education institutions to change institutional status, conditional upon specific criteria. Three Norwegian university colleges have obtained status as universities since 2004, and others have plans and strategies for changing their institutional status. Academic drift is also evident in the establishment of new institutions in the higher education sector. Mergers between Norwegian university colleges, both conducted and planned, can be seen as tools for obtaining university status. Norwegian universities have, with one exception, not been part of any merger in the new millennium.

In this paper, the ongoing processes of academic drift in higher education are analysed, with a particular focus on institutions' efforts to reach a higher formal status and the consequences this has for diversity in the Norwegian higher education landscape. We will later see that institutional drift leads to a more structurally homogeneous sector, because university colleges are changing their formal status and becoming more university-like. On the other hand, we observe a greater diversity *within* the single institution, as more institutions are offering a plurality of study programmes.

The paper analyses the general driving forces behind academic drift and the institutions' own motives for advancement. It also describes the immediate effects these developments have on the institutional landscape and on diversity among the institutions. One could argue that in some respects the increase in the number of postgraduate programmes offered by new universities and university colleges represents a process of homogenization. Despite these developments, the institutional profiles are still quite diverse. The study of Norwegian developments can also be relevant for understanding processes of academic drift internationally.

## Approach

Literature and theories on academic drift, diversity and mergers, as well as documents from Norwegian higher education institutions, are used to analyse the findings and to describe the motives for advancing their institutional status. Some macro-effects of academic drift are described using information from the Database for Statistics on Higher Education in Norway (DBH).[1]

1 The Database for Statistics on Higher Education (DBH) is a data warehouse which holds data on a broad range of topics in the sector of higher education and research in Norway. The DBH is initiated by the Norwegian Ministry of Education and Research and assigned to Norwegian Social Science Data Services (NSD). It functions as an

## The Norwegian Context

There are several ways to organize the education system: these can be categorized into three main models (Kyvik and Stensaker, 2011: 17–19).

1. binary systems, with clear distinctions between the university and non-university sectors
2. unified systems, where (almost) all education is organized at universities
3. stratified or hierarchical systems, with a multitude of different types of institutions with a clear hierarchy

Norway has a so-called binary system with two 'sectors' (university colleges and universities) with the same degree structure, but with different emphases on teaching and research, and with study provisions at various degree levels. In Norway, the two sectors share the same legislation. The distinction between them is unclear, and has varied over time. In most countries with a binary system there is an ongoing academic drift: vocational education is getting more like that of a university, and research has gained importance among staff (Kyvik and Stensaker, 2011: 20). The Norwegian binary system is flexible – unlike many other binary systems – in the sense that the university colleges can offer doctoral education and achieve university status. By the end of 2012 there were altogether seventy-nine higher education institutions in Norway with more than 240,000 students. Seen in relation to its population (5 million) Norway has a relatively high number of higher education institutions.

The Norwegian institutional landscape was for many years characterized by a few universities and a large number of colleges. In 1994, the 'University College Reform' reorganized the college sector, and ninety-eight smaller colleges were transformed into twenty-six larger university colleges. With the exception of that reform, the Norwegian higher education

important steering and decision making tool by providing quantitative parameters for the use of both the Ministry and the educational institutions in the sector.

landscape was remarkably stable until 2003, with few opportunities for advancement in the institutional hierarchy. The first Norwegian university, the University of Oslo, was established in 1811, followed by the establishment of universities in Bergen, Trondheim and as the latest in the twentieth century Tromsø (1972). By the end of the millennium there were only four universities in Norway. From 2004 onwards, four new institutions became universities: Norwegian University of Life Sciences, University of Stavanger, University of Agder and University of Nordland.

In 2003, Norway implemented a comprehensive reform of higher education, known as the 'Quality Reform', behind which there were two main objectives: firstly the national need for quality improvement in higher education and research, and secondly the Bologna Process and Norway's obligations in this respect (Skodvin, 2012: 10). The reform gave the higher education institutions more administrative and academic autonomy from government. It also placed more weight on incentive based elements of the funding system, giving the institutions more funding if they 'produced' more graduates. One effect of this was that the institutions offered more educational programmes in order to attract more students, thus creating a more competitive higher education market. Another important element of the reform was the establishment of the Norwegian Agency for Quality Assurance in Education (NOKUT), and a new system of accreditation. The new system allowed university colleges to apply to NOKUT for university status, subject to specific criteria being met. In addition university colleges were allowed to apply for status as specialized universities which in turn were allowed to apply for status as universities, and non-accredited institutions were allowed to apply for status as accredited HEIs. The increased autonomy meant that the institutions gained the opportunity to act more strategically, and many university colleges started working towards attaining university status. This, together with the economic rewards, the new and more competitive higher education market and the new system of institutional accreditation gave the institutions both incentives and opportunities to obtain university status. Some non-university institutions already had the right to offer PhD degrees, and considered obtaining university status as a way of adjusting the map to the territory.

In 2008, a governmental expert group, the 'Stjernø Commission', submitted its report on the future structure of Norwegian higher education. The Commission's view was that there were too many small institutions with too many small and vulnerable academic environments. To increase stability and robustness, it proposed that the higher education sector should change from many small institutions to between eight and ten large multi-campus universities; the government was to decide on these mergers (NOU, 2008: 3, 77). However, this proposal met opposition, among both politicians and higher education institutions. The government shared the Commission's view on the need for larger units and academic environments, but did not want to impose it. The government wanted more cooperation (and mergers) through *voluntary* processes. From 2010 onwards, the government stimulated cooperation, concentration and division of labour by funding collaborative projects between different institutions. This funding supported merger plans and other forms of institutional partnerships. Currently, the Norwegian higher education sector consists of (number of institutions in 2012 in parentheses):

- Universities (eight)
- Specialized universities (nine)
- State university colleges (twenty)
- Other institutions (about forty private colleges, defence colleges, art academies etc.)

Traditionally, universities offer both undergraduate and postgraduate degree programmes, whereas university colleges are more oriented towards offering vocational education at undergraduate level (and can be compared with *Fachhochschulen* and polytechnics). The Norwegian system is flexible in that university colleges can also offer programmes at Master's and PhD level, and can also apply NOKUT for university status. Specialized universities offer professional education at all levels within a narrow field, for example, one is specializing in Architecture and Design and one in Sports Science. The universities have full self-accreditation rights, meaning that they do not have to apply to NOKUT when establishing a new programme. The university colleges have self-accreditation rights at the bachelor degree level, but have to apply to NOKUT for the accreditation of Master's and PhD degree programmes. The specialized universities have no restrictions in their special discipline area and have the same rights as university colleges in other areas.

In this paper the focus is on one category of institutions: the university colleges and their aspiration to achieve status as a university. However, much of the description and many of the analyses are also valid for other kinds of institutional advancements in the institutional hierarchy. As a prerequisite for university status, university colleges have to establish a certain number of degree courses at Master's and PhD level, which in turn requires the development of large and high quality academic environments. It is quite demanding (both time-wise and financially) for a university college to develop enough degree courses, especially at PhD level. When a university college has obtained the right to provide five degrees at Master's level and four at PhD level, it can apply to NOKUT for university status. If NOKUT approves, the institution has to apply to the Ministry of Education and Research before it can achieve the new status. So far, the Ministry has approved all such applications, following NOKUT's approval.

There are in principle three different strategies which university colleges can follow in order to become universities (e.g. Bleiklie, Ringkjøp and Østergren, 2006: 48):

1. by fulfilling the criteria alone
2. by merger with other university colleges
3. by merger with an existing university

Up until now (2012), three university colleges have followed the first strategy and become universities: in addition Molde University College has been upgraded to a specialized university. Many university colleges are following the second strategy in order to become universities: Oslo University College and Akershus University College have already merged, partly in order to become a university. The former Tromsø University College followed the third strategy, and has merged with the University of Tromsø, and in August 2013 Finnmark University College merged with the University of Tromsø. There will probably be more such mergers, as there are ongoing discussions in at least two university colleges about merging with a university.

## Diversity between the Institutions and within the Single Institutions

The concept of diversity can relate to different levels of the higher education system: the whole system, sectors, institutions, programmes and academic disciplines (Huisman, 1998: 79). In this paper, the focus is on diversity at the system and institutional levels.

Diversity can be seen both as the differences *between* the institutions and the differences *within* the single institutions. Kogan (1997: 49) claims that the homogenization of the sector could result in an internal diversification of each institution, as they have to broaden the scope of what has traditionally been taught in a university. Vaira (2009: 142–144) describes the ongoing process of homogenization of the higher education institutions in Europe as a result of international and national developments, such as the Bologna Process and institutional rankings. Vaira also claims that, due to increased competition for resources and students, higher education institutions are becoming more complex. In addition to non-university institutions trying to emulate universities, universities provide more short courses and vocational education than before, thus becoming more like other institutions in the higher education sector ('vocational drift'). This means that universities and university colleges increasingly compete on the same market and for the same resources. Another type of diversity is described by Huisman (1998: 101), who finds that governmental regulations in the Netherlands have led to increased diversity at the programme level between Dutch universities.

In Norway, like in most countries, diversity is considered desirable and is a political goal (Huisman, 1998: 75). The availability of different institutional profiles and educational provision is thought to increase the students' choices and meet the complex demands from society and business. Norwegian university colleges have traditionally provided vocational education like nursing, engineering and teaching, whereas the universities have provided more academically oriented education. When university colleges obtain university status, these new universities continue to provide vocational education, but at the same time they increase their offering of academic education.

The oldest universities have longer traditions and reputations as research institutions than the new universities. They also have far larger budgets and more research activity. The main bulk of the funding is governmental (from the Ministry of Education and Research). In the sector as a whole, the performance based components of the governmental funding comprise about 30 per cent of the total funding; about 60 per cent is a basic component and about 8 per cent is strategic based research financing.[2] These long-established universities are getting a far larger non-performance based funding than the new universities and the university colleges. According to an evaluation of the financing system ordered by the Ministry (Econ, 2008: 14), the research component of the funding represented 24 per cent of the universities' funding, and 4 per cent of the university colleges' funding. This shows that there were still big differences in the funding and research activity among the institutional categories. The oldest universities constitute the main bulk of the numbers representing the universities, as they are – overall – far larger than the new universities. The new universities can capture increased resources by doing well on the performance based indicators. However, better performance on these indicators, like credit points earned and PhD candidates, will often require more spending on education activities. The funding system can be said to contribute to maintaining the established differences between the different institutions, even when they formally belong to the same category.

2 The basic component of the funding comprises about 60 per cent of the total funding, the performance based education component about 25 per cent and research component about 15 per cent. About 8 per cent of the research component is strategically funded, the rest is performance based. The education component depends on the number of credit points taken and number of students on international exchange programs. The performance based part of the research component depends on scientific publications, PhD candidates and allocations from EU's Framework programmes and Norwegian Research Council.

## Driving Forces behind Academic Drift

Four distinct but interrelated mechanisms of homogenization, outlined in the theoretical literature on organizations, can shed light on the process of academic drift (Skodvin and Stensby, 2010: 7–10). DiMaggio and Powell (1983: 150–153) describe three mechanisms of 'institutional isomorphism'. The first is 'coercive isomorphism', whereby outside pressures such as government sanctions and authority relations ensure that institutions abide by the same laws and regulations. 'Mimetic processes' take place when organizations imitate each other to achieve status, creating cultural trends and norms that are not directly related to economic incentives or sanctions. 'Normative pressures' refer to the process whereby formal university education and professional networks imbue the individuals running the institutions with the same academic norms and values. Finally, a population ecological perspective describes the process of 'competitive isomorphism' where institutions become similar as they compete with one another for the same economic resources on the same terms (Huisman, 1998: 100).

Academic drift can be seen at different levels: in the academic environments, in the study programmes, at the institutional level and at the national level. The academic drift can be influenced by many different actors:

- The academic community itself, with its increasingly formal academic competency. In Norway, the proportion of academic staff in university colleges with a PhD degree has increased from 27 per cent in 1999 to 43 per cent in 2011. This means that it is easier for the institutions to meet the staff requirements for accreditation of Master's and PhD degrees, thus making it easier to be accredited as a university. In addition, the increasingly competent academic environments have an interest in developing study programmes at an increasingly higher degree level, independent of the striving towards university status.
- The leaders and management can also drive this development with their ambitions on behalf of the institutions.

- The students are increasingly likely to study for postgraduate degrees. The proportion of Master's degree students has increased from 22 per cent in 2003 to 27 per cent in 2011, and the number of doctoral students has doubled from 2003 to 2011.
- Employers are more likely than before to hire employees with a Master's degree. In many cases a Bachelor's degree will no longer be sufficient to get a highly skilled job.
- Local politicians and Members of Parliament may want a university in their region.
- The parliament and the government might contribute to these developments by issuing incentives through laws and regulations.

In addition to the above mentioned factors and actors, the use of institutional rankings, which are primarily based on the outcomes of research as a measure of success, may influence the university colleges to copy the highest ranked institutions, namely the large research universities (Vaira, 2009: 144).

## The Institutions' Motives behind their Institutional Drift

When institutions apply to NOKUT for institutional accreditation, there is no requirement in the regulations to state *why* they want new institutional status. However, one can often find the motives behind the wish for a new and higher status in the applications and in the evaluation reports. In this section, data from all the sixteen institutional accreditations in 2003–2011 are included (four were university accreditations, four were specialized university accreditations and eight were university college accreditations). Only the officially expressed arguments in favour of a new institutional status are included in this section, not the informal arguments and not arguments against new institutional status.

Some institutions did not express the reasons behind their application, but it can be gleaned from the application that the primary motive is a general desire to *strengthen the education and research activity*. In other cases the motives are more specific and also more clearly expressed. There is often a combination of reasons behind the desire to achieve a new status, and the impact of the different reasons may differ from institution to institution.

The most frequently used arguments for trying to achieve new and higher status are *of a formalistic type*:

- *Status*. A new and formal place in the hierarchy and the title 'university' is a motive in itself. This motive is connected with several of the other arguments, for instance autonomy and attractiveness.
- *Autonomy*. A change in status means that the institution can provide more new degree programmes and courses without applying to NOKUT in advance.
- *Adjustment of the map to the territory*. Institutions want to achieve the recognition that they think they deserve due to the standard of their education and research.

There are also some arguments about *attractiveness and recruitment*:

- *External funding*. Increase the possibility of receiving external research funding.
- *Recruitment of students and staff*. The title 'university' may make recruitment of students and staff easier.
- *Network and cooperation*. A new and higher status was seen as a means to make the institutions more attractive in cooperation with business, labour market and other higher education institutions in Norway and abroad.

In addition, there were also some arguments referring to *the role of the institution*:

- *National role*. A new and higher status was in some cases seen as a way to strengthen the national role as a supplier of education and research.

- *Regional role.* Enhanced status was in some cases seen as a way to strengthen the regional role as a supplier of education and research.

Most of the specific motives (for instance *status*, *funding*, *recruitment* and *national/regional role*), as well as the primary motive (to strengthen the education and research activity) can be seen as means to increase the institutions' robustness.

All these motives, as well as the main argument many institutions use (that the status will enhance the research and education), can be seen as a result of all the types of isomorphism. *Competitive isomorphism* takes place when the institutions compete for economic resources, students and staff, and see a formal transition to university as a comparative advantage in the recruitment of students and academics. The title 'university' is also considered to make it easier for the institutions to gain access to networks and to establish cooperation with other institutions. The same goes for autonomy: universities can start new provisions at a higher degree level more quickly and easily than university colleges, making the new status a comparative advantage. The greater autonomy that comes with university status can also be seen in the light of the theory of *coercive isomorphism*, due to the governmental regulations of the sector. *Mimetic processes* and *normative pressure* can be considered as underlying factors that explain the academic drift in institutions and thereby their expressed motives. Most of the arguments represent a university-like development of the institutions, hence a drift towards homogenization.

## Mergers as a Tool for Advancement in the Institutional Hierarchy

Mergers are an essential part of the dynamics of many countries. Goedegebuure (2012: 5–6) argues that mergers in Denmark and Finland can be seen as an adaptation to a more open and competitive global arena, with the existence of rankings as a driving force behind the mergers. He also claims that mergers in other countries are examples of positioning in a competitive market (Germany, Estonia, United Kingdom and France). Goedegebuure (2012: 3) distinguishes between policy-induced mergers and incidental mergers.

*Policy-induced mergers* are typically a result of nationally and politically decided reforms, and reflect the need for establishing a larger and stronger sector capable of dealing with more autonomy through more professional institutional management. The Norwegian reforms and other political measures can be seen in this light. The 'University College Reform' in 1994, the Stjernø Commission's suggestions of mergers in 2008, and the recent governmental stimulation and backing of merger processes in Norway (from 2010 on), can be seen in the light of the need for more robust institutions. The government saw the need for larger institutions, in order to create more competitive units and promote quality enhancement in research and education. Like Goedegebuure (2012), the Stjernø Commission also used international competition as an important background for their proposals.

*Incidental mergers* are initiated by individual institutions and have a broader range of backgrounds and motives. Among them are lifting the institution's standing and reputation (status), increasing the diversity of study provision, increasing the efficiency of operation and increasing the research profile. Most of the recent as well as the forthcoming mergers in Norway are incidental. Many of the merger processes among Norwegian university colleges have an explicit aim: namely to achieve university status. The preference for merger in order to achieve a new and higher institutional status is partly due to the fact that it is relatively demanding (both academically and economically) for a single institution to establish enough PhD degrees to become a university on its own. In addition, mergers are in many cases seen as a tool for advancement in the institutional hierarchy. Thus, the motives behind the mergers are in many cases the same as for institutional drift. The wish to become more robust and increase competitive ability can be considered as an underlying cause for merger. The incidental mergers in Norway in the recent years have been between state university colleges and between private colleges, with one exception: the merger between the University of Tromsø and two university colleges.

The largest and most internationally competitive institutions in Norway (University of Oslo, University of Bergen and the Norwegian University of Science and Technology) have not been part of any merger in recent years (since 1995). This indicates that the argument about competition in Norway can best be applied to competition *nationally*, not internationally. The policy-induced and the incidental mergers share some important motives, especially the need to make the institutions more robust and to strengthen education and research activity.

In the light of the theories of isomorphism, the underlying motives for mergers are similar to those for institutional drift. *Competitive isomorphism* is an important process, as mergers often are seen as a tool for better positioning in a competitive market, thus making the institution more resilient. The governmental stimulation and backing of mergers can be seen in the light of *coercive isomorphism*. *Mimetic processes* and *normative pressure* can – as for institutional drift – be considered as underlying factors that explain the use of merger as a tool.

## Institutional Drift and Diversity

Since 2003, the Norwegian higher education institutional landscape has changed.

- The number of universities has doubled, from four to eight.
- The number of specialized universities has increased from six to nine.
- The number of state university colleges has dropped, from twenty-six to twenty.
- The number of private university colleges has increased from twenty-nine in 2003 to thirty-four in 2012.

The numbers in the bullet points indicate a drift towards a higher status in the institutional hierarchy. The number of universities and specialized universities has increased, in both cases because of university colleges' institutional drift. At the same time the number of private university colleges has increased, mainly because new providers of higher education have entered the scene. Academic/institutional drift is an ongoing trend, and further mergers and new universities are expected in the future.

The changes in the institutional landscape can be illustrated by the growing proportion of the total student mass enrolled at universities and the declining number at state university colleges. Figure 10.1 shows the proportion of the total student population at each institutional category and projections for the future. The chosen years are 2003 (when the 'Quality Reform' was implemented), 2012 (the latest figures) and 2020 (the near future).

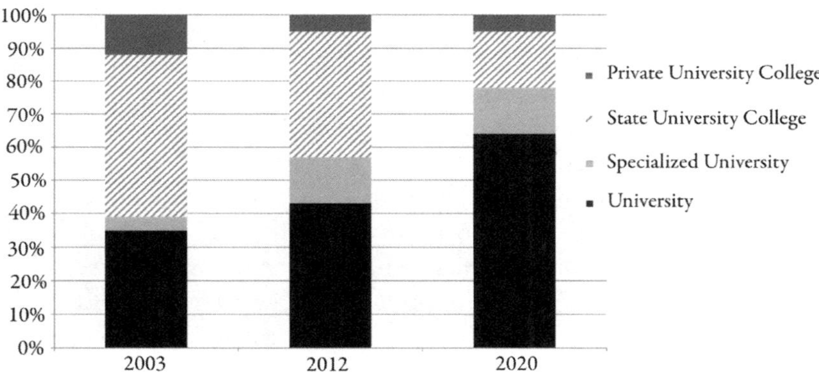


Figure 10.1 Proportion of the Total Student Population in Each Institutional Category Source: Norwegian Social Science Data Services / Database for Statistics on Higher Education in Norway <http://dbh.nsd.uib.no/> accessed 13 March 2013.

In 2003 the universities' share of the student mass was 35 per cent and in 2012 it was 43 per cent. Taking existing institutional plans into account, it will reach approximately 64 per cent in 2020. At the same time the proportion of students at state university colleges will drop from 49 per cent in 2003 to approximately 17 per cent in 2020.[3] However, these numbers

3 The figure for 2020 is based on existing plans and strategies among some of the university colleges:

only reflect the *formal* transformation of university colleges to universities. University colleges have developed Master's and PhD programmes at an increasingly higher rate, in order to obtain university status. In 2003, there were forty-five Master's degree programmes offered by twenty-five university colleges, in 2010 there were 122 offered by twenty-two university colleges (Skodvin and Stensby, 2010: 13). In the same period of time the number of doctoral degree study programmes increased from six to nearly fifty.[4] The more postgraduate courses the university colleges develop, the more they start resembling universities, whether or not they obtain the formal status. As a result, diversity in the sector diminishes.

Despite these developments, the university colleges still have a large proportion of their students enrolled in programmes at bachelor degree level and a small proportion at Master's level. Master's students, as a proportion of the total student mass, constituted 8 per cent at the state university colleges in 2012; the corresponding number at the universities was 45 per cent. This indicates that there is still a significant difference between the institutional categories. The proportion of Master's students at the three university colleges that obtained status as universities increased from 9 per cent in 2003 to 24 per cent in 2012. This shows that institutions that have qualified for a higher level in the institutional hierarchy start resembling the institutions at this higher level, at least on this particular indicator.[5]

On closer inspection, we find that despite the new formal status of many Norwegian higher education institutions, their profiles are still quite diverse. This is evident when examining the Ministry of Education and

---

Oslo and Akershus University College have expressed ambitions to become a university. Buskerud and Vestfold University Colleges have plans to merge and ambitions to become a university. The same is true of Gjøvik, Lillehammer and Hedmark University Colleges. Telemark University College has expressed ambitions for merger with an existing university. Narvik University College has plans to obtain specialized university status. Finnmark University College merged with the University of Tromsø in August 2013.

4 Source: Norwegian Social Science Data Services / Database for Statistics on Higher Education in Norway.

5 Source: Norwegian Social Science Data Services / Database for Statistics on Higher Education in Norway.

Research's so-called 'flower diagrams'.[6] The diagrams show the institutional profiles of Norwegian higher education institutions in five dimensions:

- Institutional Size
- Education
- Research
- Internationalization
- Relations with Society

To examine the diversity in the higher education sector, the profiles of the two newest Norwegian universities (University of Agder and University of Nordland), one typical university college (Østfold University College) and one long-established university (University of Bergen) have been studied. The following comparisons are based on data from 2012.[7] A more thorough analysis of the diversity among Norwegian higher education institutions, with visualizations of the flower diagrams, can be found in Skodvin (2012: 13–28).

We find that the new universities' profiles fall somewhere in between the old universities and the university colleges. This is not very surprising, considering that the new universities are in the process of academic drift away from the typical university college and towards the classical university. The new universities still have quite a clear vocational profile. On the research and international dimension they are still far behind the old universities, but far ahead of the university colleges. This is evident on many of the indicators: the University of Bergen has for example a much larger PhD production than the other institutions. The University of Bergen also has a much higher score than the other institutions on indicators like outgoing and incoming exchange students, the number of courses taught

6 The diagrams show the institutional profiles of Norwegian higher education institutions. They consist of about twenty indicators, grouped in five dimensions (<http://dbh.nsd.uib.no/styringsdata/typologi_rapport.action?request_locale=en>). They are based on and quite similar to the Umap Profile Viewer (<http://www.u-map.eu/>).

7 With the exception of data on the indicator 'publications with international co-authors' where data are from 2011.

in English and publications with international co-authors. These findings are in accordance with Skodvin (2012: 26), who points out that there are striking differences between the new and the old universities, and that the new universities have not become pale copies of the old ones.

## Conclusion

During the last ten years, three Norwegian university colleges have become universities, one has become a specialized university and one has merged with an existing university. There has been an increase in postgraduate degree programmes at the university colleges and at the new universities.

Two large Norwegian university colleges have merged, and taking existing plans into account, there will be more mergers in the future. The institutions' motives behind the mergers are in many cases that it will be easier to obtain new and higher institutional status, thus the mergers are *tools* for institutional drift. The mergers do not necessarily influence diversity in the educational sector as a whole, but the larger the educational unit is, the more it can provide diverse education within a single institution. In addition, a merger between a university and a university college will provide a diversified institution simply by combining two institutions with different profiles and study provisions prior to the merger.

The university colleges' motive for wanting a status change is primarily a general desire to strengthen their education and research activity, which is thought to be easier as a university than as a university college. More specifically, the most used arguments are that status as a university is a benefit in itself; greater autonomy and increased attractiveness (funding, recruitment, networks) are vital too. The theory of competitive isomorphism can shed light on many of these motives: the institutions compete for students and funding, and consider increased status and greater autonomy as competitive advantages. Coercive isomorphism is also a factor, as governmental regulations influence the educational market and make it possible for the university colleges to become universities. Mimetic processes and normative pressure can be considered as underlying factors that explain some of the academic drift and the expressed motives.

The concept of resilience helps to explain the institutions' striving for a higher status, including the will to merge. The competitive situation in which many institutions find themselves is one driver for their will to increase their formal institutional status. Many of the university colleges use merger as a tool for obtaining this new status. In many respects, one can observe a *convergence* in the sector. The new universities have become quite like the old universities in their organizational structure and in their increased emphasis on research and postgraduate study. This trend is likely to continue, due to the on-going processes of academic drift, and many university colleges are getting more university-like in their efforts to achieve university status. In sum, these developments lead to a more structurally homogeneous sector.

However, many differences between the institutions remain. The institutional profiles show that there are still large differences in disciplinary profile, the research dimension and the international dimension between the oldest universities, the new universities and the university colleges. The chief explanations for these differences are the weight of tradition and reputation, and the fact that the oldest universities' budgets are far larger than the ones of the new universities and the university colleges. This distinction between institutions is also found in countries where former polytechnics have been renamed as universities, for example in the United Kingdom (Kyvik and Stensaker, 2011: 18). In addition, we see a greater diversity *within* the institutions, as the same developments that lead to homogeneity in the sector as a whole result in both university colleges and universities offering a plurality of courses and degrees. University colleges and the new universities offer an increasing number of Master's and PhD degrees even as they continue to offer vocationally oriented study programmes.

The Stjernø Commission prescribed that the higher education sector should change from many small institutions to between eight and ten large multi-campus universities. This has not happened yet, but there is a slow trend in that direction. There will most likely be more mergers and thus larger units in the sector. There are many different reasons for this development. The 'Quality Reform' in 2003 reinforced the competitive element of the sector. The existence of rankings and the increasing focus on them, suggests a more competitive situation. The government also wants larger academic communities and institutions. In addition, as Goedegebuure (2012: 14) argues, increased global competition for talent, along with increased student mobility and a 'de-nationalization' of research, compels institutions to a greater extent to act strategically. For some of these institutions, merger will be the answer to the challenges.

Currently, the Norwegian higher education system gives the institutions the opportunity to rise in the institutional hierarchy. However, it is not unlikely that the option for institutional advancement will change in the future. One possibility is that the opportunity for institutional advancement is abolished, so that aspiring university colleges are not given the opportunity to gain university status. This would in effect re-create a more non-flexible binary system. Such a change has already happened in Sweden, where no university colleges have been given university status since 2005 (Benner, Stensaker and Unemar-Öst, 2010: 36). Three of Norway's political parties have passages in their party programmes that indicate a possibility for such a change.[8] Another possibility is that the government decides that all institutions should be allowed to call themselves universities (without the current requirements). A release of the university title will create a unitary system similar to the ones in Spain, Australia and the United Kingdom.

To sum up, the higher education sector is becoming more structurally homogeneous, because university colleges are becoming more university-like, and because some university colleges are changing their formal status. However, many differences in the sector remain, and we can observe an increased diversity within the institutions. The students still have a plurality of options in their study choices. The complex demand for a diversified labour force from society and business seems likely to be met also in the future, as institutional diversity still exists and the diversity within the institutions seems to be increasing.

8 <https://www.hoyre.no/admin/filestore/Filer/Politikkdokumenter/Hyres_landsmte/HLM2013/Stortingsvalgprogramforelopigversjonetterlandsmotet.pdf>, <http://sv.no/Forside/Politikken/Arbeidsprogram/Program-09-13-bokmal> and <http://www.venstre.no/files/sentralt/program2013/stortingsvalgprogram_2.utkast.pdf>.

## References

Benner, M., Stensaker B., and Unemar-Öst, I. (2010). 'Universitets- och Högskolepolitiken. Avsikter och Konsekvenser för de Nya Lärosätena'. Stockholm: KK-stiftelsen.

Bleiklie, I., Ringkjøb, H-E., and Østergren, K. (2006). *Evaluation of the Quality Reform*, Report 9. The Research Council of Norway. <http://www.uib.no/filearchive/delrapport-9-kvalitetsreformen9.pdf> accessed 7 May 2013.

DiMaggio, P.J., and Powell, W.W. (1983). 'The Iron Cage Revisited: Institutional Isomorphism and Collective Rationality in Organizational Fields', *American Sociological Review*, 48 (2), 147–160.

Econ (2008). 'Evaluering av finansieringssystemet for universiteter og høyskoler'. Report No. 133, 2008. <http://www.econ.no/stream_file.asp?iEntityId=4066> accessed 7 May 2013.

Goedegebuure, L. (2012). 'Mergers and More: The Changing Tertiary Education Landscape in the 21st Century'. Higher Education: Institutional Dynamics and Knowledge Cultures (HEIK), Working Paper 2012/01, University of Oslo. <http://www.uv.uio.no/english/research/groups/heik/heik-working-paper-series/docs/HEIKwp201201_goedegebuure.pdf> accessed 7 May 2013.

Huisman, J. (1998). 'Differentiation and Diversity in Higher Education Systems'. In J.C. Smart (ed.), *Higher Education: Handbook of Theory and Research* (Vol. XIII), pp. 75–110. New York: Agathon Press.

Kogan, M. (1997). 'Diversification in Higher Education: Differences and Commonalities', *Minerva*, 35 (1), 47–62.

Kyvik, S., and Stensaker, B. (2011). 'Høgskolen Stord/Haugesund – fusjon, fisjon eller status quo?' The Nordic Institute for Studies in Innovation, Research and Education (NIFU), Report No. 12 2011. <http://www.nifu.no//files/2012/11/NIFUrapport2011-12.pdf> accessed 7 May 2013.

Norges offentlige utredninger. (2008). 'Sett under ett: Ny struktur i høyere utdanning (NOU 2008:3)'. Oslo. Report published by a committee appointed by the Norwegian government. <http://www.regjeringen.no/nb/dep/kd/dok/NOUer/2008/NOU-2008-3.html?id=497182> accessed 7 May 2013.

Skodvin, O-J., and Stensby, B.R. (2010). 'Does Size Matter? The Norwegian HE Landscape in Change'. Paper presented at EAIR Forum, 2010. Valencia. <http://www.nokut.no/Documents/NOKUT/Artikkelbibliotek/Kunnskapsbasen/Foredrag%20og%20artikler/UA%202011/Skodvin_og_Stensby_Does_size_matter.pdf> accessed 7 May 2013.

Skodvin, O-J. (2012). 'How to Measure Institutional Profiles in the Norwegian HE Landscape'. In A. Curaj, P. Scott, L. Vlasceanu, and L. Wilson (eds), *European Higher Education at the Crossroads*, pp. 905–934. Dordrecht: Springer.

Vaira, M. (2009.). 'Towards Unified and Stratified Systems of Higher Education? System Convergence and Organizational Stratified Differentiation in Europe'. In B.M. Kehm and B. Stensaker (eds), *University Rankings, Diversity and the New Landscape of Higher Education*, pp. 135–153. Rotterdam: Sense Publishers.

MATTHIAS KLUMPP

# 11 Higher Education Efficiency: Questions, Methods, Results and Implications

## Introduction

Higher education efficiency has been a long-standing research issue, especially in relation to research productivity (Bottomley and Dunworth, 1974; Barth and Vertinsky 1975; Banker, 1986; Ahn et al., 1988; Cohn et al., 1989; Johnes and Johnes, 1993; Ramsden, 1994; Beasley, 1995; Dundar and Lewis, 1995; Hashimoto and Cohn, 1997; Glass et al., 1998; Stahl et al., 1998). But during the last fifteen years, this narrow, qualitative field of analysis within universities has been broadened in terms of methods and comparative international views as well as implications for the practice of higher education management (Madden et al., 1997; Ng and Li, 2000; Jongbloed and Vossensteyn, 2001; Korhonen et al., 2001; Feng et al., 2004; Johnes, 2006; Kocher et al., 2006; Kao and Hung, 2008; Sarrico, 2010; Zangoueinezhad and Moshabaki, 2011; Klumpp and Zelewski, 2012). Tight budgets impel the public stakeholders as well as university leadership cadres to demand effective instruments for accountability which are often interpreted as performance or productivity measurement instruments.

This chapter gives an overview regarding approaches to efficiency analysis in higher education, including a case study to clarify differences in efficiency measurement methods. It reports on some distinguished international findings and outlines the implications for higher education research and management.

## Efficiency and Resilience

The two concepts of efficiency and resilience both address core questions of the modern university and are deeply intertwined. On the one hand efficiency is necessary for resilience: without the ability to steer efficiently, the basic requirement for resilience is not present: namely, the *ability to recover from external shocks or prevent their impact* upon the university (Westrum, 2008: 59; Wreathall, 2006: 275). This is because without proper resources and their efficient use, no such operations (recovering, preventing) are feasible. Moreover, institutional efficiency or productivity can be understood as a *multiplying factor* in the general resilience capacity of an institution. On the other hand resilience is also needed for efficiency: the ability to recover from or altogether prevent negative influences may clearly increase the long-term productivity of a university institution. This applies even more strongly with increasing competition and changes in the world of higher education in the wake of the two major trends, *internationalization* and *massification*. The concept of international mass higher education puts very high demands on university operations in research and teaching, and requires a high level of resilience to succeed efficiently on a long-term basis. In this case, resilience too can be seen as a *multiplying factor* to an existing efficiency level within any university institution.

Finally, both areas can be seen *independently* as major strategic objectives and pre-requisites for modern universities within an international and highly competitive environment: In order to react swiftly to the complex and rapid changes in higher education environments worldwide, universities have to be *resilient* to a very high degree. And they also have to be very *efficient* in order to live up to expectations from many societal and individual stakeholders regarding their quality outputs, scientific impact and excellence as well as accountability for state and private money put into their operations.

Some authors even see efficiency and resilience on the one hand as antagonistic to security and preparedness on the other hand (e.g. Woods, 2006), but this can be interpreted as a question of the overall *time perspective of efficiency*: in the very *short-term* (i.e. one month or several months). This may be true as safety and preparation measures (resilience investment) may reduce cost-efficiency in an organization. But in a long-term perspective (i.e. several years), appropriate safety and preparation measures will usually 'pay off': they will help prevent disasters and break-downs and therefore increase the long-term efficiency of the organization. As most universities do operate on such a long-term perspective, it is viable to assume that such an antagonistic view may not be adequate for higher education management.

## Efficiency as a Research and HEI Management Question

The efficiency or productivity of university operations has been a long-standing research and management question and is *complex* due to the very special nature of the university as an organizational *type* and due also to the complexity of the university *outputs* themselves. Since the functions of universities in the three areas of research, teaching and 'third mission' (often termed 'transfer', 'outreach', 'community services' (Zomer and Benneworth, 2011: 82) consist of a multitude of output indicators, possible productivity measurements are by definition manifold.

Nevertheless, there are specific expectations regarding the output of universities which can be expressed through equally specific efficiency questions. Those questions are essential for university management as many decisions taken within universities address resource allocation and are therefore directly connected to production settings. Examples of such management questions linked to higher education decisions are depicted in the following Table 11.1.

Table 11.1 Management Questions and Management Decisions Regarding Efficiency

| | Research | Teaching | Third Mission |
|---|---|---|---|
| Management Question (*Example*) | – How efficient are specific research groups and faculties (compared to other groups and faculties)? | – How efficient are specific teaching/ study programmes (compared to other programmes)? | – How efficient are specific university co-operations within the region? |
| Management Decision (*Example*) | – Should specific research groups and faculties receive more funding?<br>– Should specific groups receive more management support? | – Should specific study programmes be supported by PR/ advertising effort?<br>– Should specific programmes be closed? | – Should specific university co-operations be prolonged or ended? |

The *comparative* view regarding several universities has been established by various research contributions, e.g. Cohn et al., 1989; Beasley, 1995; Dundar and Lewis, 1995; Glass et al., 1998; Ng and Li, 2000; Korhonen et al., 2001; Kocher et al., 2006; Kao and Hung, 2008; and Sarrico 2010. In one of the latest *data collection endeavours* supporting a comparative international view the EUMIDA project supported by the European Commission collected, for example, staff, student and graduate data (Bonaccorsi et al., 2010).

## Methods of Performance and Productivity Measurement

Methodologies used in measuring the efficiency of university operations have been manifold – and interestingly have many similarities to ranking endeavours in the output field. Figure 11.1 provides a structuring overview regarding the basic categories (A to D) for performance and productivity measurement. The four depicted categories and their examples according to Figure 11.1 can be outlined in detail as follows:

A. Simple one-dimensional outputs as *performance measurements* with just *one* output indicator are quite often used in higher education management and policies, e.g. for comparing universities (or departments thereof) regarding their number of graduates per year; or universities, faculties and even research groups regarding the number of publications, patent registrations or citations per year. For third mission activities, indicators such as number or turnover of spin-offs or the total number of their employees are used to measure performance on a university or faculty level.
B. Usually most university and even faculty ratings use a number of output indicators combined in relation to the specific objective of the ranking (see for example Van Vught and Ziegele 2012). For a ranking of teaching quality a combination of teacher-student-ratio, student satisfaction, international orientation and expert reputation might be used. For a research ranking a combination of industry income (third party funding), publications, citations and peer reputation might be used. The most commonly used method to calculate the overall score for such combined indicator rankings is weighted scoring systems, allocating each indicator a share out of a total of 100 per cent weighted distribution. All individual scores (with the same span of possible values e.g. from 0 to 100) are multiplied with this weighting and then added up for the total score.
C. Simple *productivity* metrics usually operate with a relation between one output indicator (e.g. number of publications) and one input indicator (e.g. one researcher per one million Euro [currency] budget). Essential for the distinction between performance and productivity measurement (efficiency) is the inclusion of an input indicator, commonly addressed as the 'size question' (as usually performance indicators favour larger institutions or units which more easily reach higher output numbers for example in terms of graduates or publication numbers).

Though the division of output number by input numbers is used most often, theoretically also the division of inputs by outputs is feasible and may sometimes also yield interesting insights: For example the question of what budget has been spent on average to recruit one graduate or achieve one publication or one patent may be interesting in many circumstances too.

D. For the inclusion of multiple input and multiple output indicators a number of methods are available in order to calculate a measurement result; the two most commonly used ones are *stochastic frontier analysis* (SFA) and *data envelopment analysis* (DEA):

i. SFA: The *stochastic frontier analysis* uses a given production function in order to calculate productivity measures from the input and output data (Aigner et al., 1977; Kumbhakar and Lovell, 2000). If such a production function is known this is a very feasible method, as it indicates clearly the improvement potential for all non-efficient units (Jacobs, 2001; Cullinane et al., 2006; for universities see for example: Stevens 2005). But if there is no known production function for all relevant inputs and outputs this is less valuable though assumptions may be made (Coelli, 1995).

ii. DEA: The *data envelopment analysis* was proposed in 1978 and developed further as a non-parametric multi-criteria efficiency measurement method (cf. Charnes et al., 1978; Charnes et al., 1991; Seiford, 1996; Pedraja-Chaparro et al., 199; Cooper et al., 2000; Kleine 2004, Zhu and Cook, 2007; Thannasoulis et al., 2008). It is commonly used in multi-dimensional output industries such as service industries (i.e. health care: Butler and Li, 2005; ecological analysis: Dyckhoff and Allen, 2001) and also *education and higher education* (i.e. McMillan and Datta, 1998; Taylor and Harris, 2004; McMillan and Chan, 2006).

| | One-dimensional Output Measurement | Multi-dimensional Output Measurement |
|---|---|---|
| Simple Output Indicators<br><br>(*Performance* Measurement) | (A) Simple Output Metrics, e.g.<br>• Number of Graduates per University per Year<br>• Number of Reviewed Publications per University per Year<br>• Number of Patents registered per University per Year | (B) Complex (Combined) Output Measurement Systems, e.g.<br>• Ranking Systems as e.g. ARWU, THE WUR or QS Ranking<br>• Performance Based Funding Systems with Several Indicators |
| Input and Output Indicator *Relation*<br><br>(*Productivity* Measurement) | (C) Simple Productivity Metrics, e.g.<br>• Total Teaching Cost per Graduate at one University<br>• Number of Reviewed Publications or Citations in Reviewed Journals per Faculty Head (three Years)<br>• Amount of Third Party/ Industry Income per Faculty Head<br>• Total Number of Registered Patents per 1 Mil. Euro (Currency) University Budget | (D) Complex Productivity Calculations, e.g.<br>• Stochastic Frontier Analysis for Number of Faculty Members and Number of Graduates and Amount of Third Party/Industry Income<br>• Data Envelopment Analysis for University Budget (Input) and Number of Graduates, Number of Publications as well as Number of Patents (Output) |

Figure 11.1 Comparison of Performance and Productivity Measurement Schemes

Existing *criticism* regarding the different fields of measurement usually addresses the following areas: it is acknowledged that *single* output indicators cannot quite depict the complex task of a university, especially since they do not take into account the distinction between the objective areas of research, teaching and third mission, neglecting the *Humboldt Principle* of an assumed or desired unity of these areas within universities as a founding principle. Additionally with just one output measurement the size of the higher education institution is crucial: larger universities have a comparative advantage in this perspective (*Matthew Effect*).

From these typical critical arguments it is obvious that in developing adequate measurement and comparison systems in higher education the tendency should be directed towards systems in Category D with simultaneous multiple input and multiple output measurements. The methodology options in this last field are outlined further in the next section in the form of a comparative case study of university efficiency.

## University Efficiency Case Study

In order to shed more light on the complex question of university efficiency, a sample data set and *data envelopment analysis* method[1] are applied as outlined in Category D. Based on the latest Times Higher Education (THE) World University Ranking 2012/2013 (as of October 2012) a sample of the 84 European universities[2] among the top 200 ranking positions is selected, due to the fact that for these top 200 THE publishes *detailed output scores* in five different areas:[3]

- *Teaching Score* (Weighting: 30.0 per cent); included in this category are five sub-indicators: teaching reputation with 15 per cent weighting, the indicator staff-to-student-ratio with 4.5 per cent weighting, the indicator doctorate-to-bachelor degrees awarded (2.25 per cent),

1 See annex for an extensive outline regarding the DEA methodology as well as detailed data from the case study.

2 Out of the top 200 ranked institutions, 84 are based in Europe. Though for four of them not all five output indicators are published (excluded) and for further six institutions the yearly budget was not published on the respective university homepage (excluded); therefore the final dataset includes 74 European universities, ranked according to the total THE scores in a new ranking from 1 to 74 (alternatively the ranking positions published by THE among the top 200 could be used).

3 Institutional scores are only published for the total values within the five categories, not the 13 sub-indicators.

number of doctorates awarded (6.0 per cent) and the indicator of institutional income per academic staff member with 2.25 per cent weighting.

- *International Outlook* (7.5 per cent); included into this indicator category are the ratio of international to domestic students (2.5 per cent), the ratio of international to domestic staff (2.5 per cent) as well as the share of journal papers within the last five years with an international co-author (2.5 per cent).
- *Industry Income* (2.5 per cent); this represents industry income as an indicator for the volume and value of knowledge transfer to industry as well as innovation support and consultancy (2.5 per cent).
- *Research – Reputation and Publications* (30.0 per cent); included in this indicator category are the reputation for research excellence from the THE reputation survey (16,000 respondents) with 18.0 per cent, the university research income (staff- and purchasing power parities-normalized) 6.0 per cent and research output (journal papers) per staff head.[4]
- *Research – Citations* (30.0 per cent); this indicator group contains one single indicator (worth 30.0 per cent) as all citations for papers of one university provided by Thomson Reuters for the five-year-period 2006 to 2010 (50 million citations to 6 million journal articles).

THE also sustains the important information that these indicators and weightings have not been changed since the last ranking of 2011/2012, which allows for timeline comparisons as opposed to other ranking systems where indicators (at least on the sub-category level) and/ or weightings have been changed sometimes without public notice. The THE ranking is targeting 'research-led universities' and for example excludes universities with less than 200 annual publications (journal papers) from 2006 to 2010 (altogether 1,000) as well as universities without undergraduate teaching (though this is hard to comprehend as a 'research-led university' criterion).

4 These last two indicators (together 12 per cent) are the only ones in relation to size and therefore themselves already represent efficiency indicators.

Data collection takes place within each and every individual university; for the case of missing data points (minor indicators such as industry income) the lower 25th percentile is added as average sample data from all other data. All data are normalized with the Z-score representing a cumulative probability (a score of 98.0 therefore denotes the fact that in 98 per cent of all university cases a university will rank below the specified university). The published indicators can be discussed and criticized for many reasons, among others for example the fact that the weightings applied are very subjective and will never be able to reflect the very special situation of each individual university in a specific higher education system. For example, the potential to gain third party or industry funding may be highly dependent on the location and the overall financial setup of the economy and the research system in a specific country. But for reasons of international and methodological comparison, this dataset may be accepted as the best that is readily available for an analysis of efficiency research applications. Furthermore, THE weightings indicators are used individually with the published scoring values. For analysing efficiency, the *input indicator 'yearly budget'* (2011) is used according to university homepage statistics.[5] All indicator values are shown in Table 11.2.

Within this dataset an *individual* measure (such as 89.7 THE score points on *teaching* for the University of Oxford, compared to i.e. 91.2 for Cambridge) would constitute a *Category A* 'Simple Output Metric' performance measurement as explained above. A complex multi-dimensional measurement such as the *overall* THE score value would define a *Category B* performance analysis: for example the institutional comparison of *total* THE scores across *all five* indicators with 73.1 points for the London School of Economics, 73.0 points for the Ecole Polytechnique Lausanne (CH), 72.4 points for the Karolinska Institute Stockholm (SE) and 70.4 points for the University of Munich (DE).

5 Converted to the Euro currency with the average two year exchange rates published by the European Central Bank.

Table 11.2 Top 10:[6] University Dataset from THE WRU and Budget Data (2011/2012)

| | THE Ranking Position | THE Score | O1: Teaching | O2: International Outlook | O3: Industry Income | O4: Research | O5: Citations | I: Budget 2011 in € |
|---|---|---|---|---|---|---|---|---|
| University of Oxford, UK | 1 | 93.7 | 89.7 | 88.7 | 79.8 | 98.1 | 95.6 | 1093538183.5 |
| University of Cambridge, UK | 2 | 92.6 | 91.2 | 83.6 | 59.1 | 95.6 | 96.2 | 942019644.7 |
| Imperial College London, UK | 3 | 90.6 | 88.0 | 91.4 | 87.5 | 90.9 | 93.0 | 837396247.1 |
| University College London, UK | 4 | 85.5 | 83.5 | 89.0 | 45.1 | 88.8 | 86.8 | 953219016.8 |
| University of Edinburgh, UK | 5 | 76.1 | 68.4 | 78.9 | 43.8 | 71.3 | 90.8 | 773930363.6 |
| London School of Economics, UK | 6 | 73.1 | 70.8 | 87.2 | 42.9 | 80.3 | 66.5 | 277906866.1 |
| École Polytechnique Fédérale Lausanne, CH | 7 | 73.0 | 62.4 | 98.8 | 49.8 | 57.0 | 95.0 | 646111065.7 |
| Karolinska Institute, SE | 8 | 72.4 | 66.3 | 64.5 | 71.4 | 75.7 | 77.3 | 604377426.4 |
| Ludwig-Maximilians-Universität München, DE | 9 | 70.4 | 65.4 | 54.7 | 42.0 | 66.5 | 85.8 | 488600000.0 |
| University of Manchester, UK | 10 | 70.1 | 65.9 | 77.9 | 43.2 | 67.7 | 76.9 | 962018693.4 |

Enlarging this to a real *productivity* perspective, Table 11.3 shows some examples for a *Category C* 'Simple Productivity Measurement' in the relation of one output indicator and one input indicator (budget) each (i.e. 0.235 research points per €1 million budget for the ENS Lyon (FR) or 0.219 points for the University of St Andrews (UK)).

6 The complete dataset is presented in Table 11.5 in the annex.

Table 11.3 Top 10:[7] Simple Productivity Analysis Outcome-Budget-Indicator (Score p. mil. €)

| | THE Score / Budget | Teaching / Budget | International / Budget | Income / Budget | Research / Budget | Citations / Budget | Budget 2011 in € |
|---|---|---|---|---|---|---|---|
| École Normale Supérieure de Lyon, FR | 0.447 | 0.371 | 0.555 | 0.263 | 0.235 | 0.724 | 110000000.0 |
| Royal Holloway, University of London, UK | 0.357 | 0.199 | 0.602 | 0.208 | 0.180 | 0.645 | 153605489.1 |
| University of Sussex, UK | 0.285 | 0.177 | 0.389 | 0.163 | 0.200 | 0.462 | 197160320.6 |
| University of St Andrews, UK | 0.283 | 0.216 | 0.432 | 0.195 | 0.219 | 0.384 | 199550503.0 |
| Birkbeck, University of London, UK | 0.268 | 0.160 | 0.483 | 0.171 | 0.177 | 0.422 | 172426094.6 |
| London School of Economics, UK | 0.263 | 0.255 | 0.314 | 0.154 | 0.289 | 0.239 | 277906866.1 |
| Lancaster University, UK | 0.242 | 0.175 | 0.355 | 0.148 | 0.190 | 0.341 | 214902371.2 |
| University of East Anglia, UK | 0.213 | 0.129 | 0.300 | 0.134 | 0.121 | 0.372 | 229546697.7 |
| Trinity College Dublin, IR | 0.211 | 0.158 | 0.318 | 0.123 | 0.126 | 0.332 | 265745000.0 |
| Durham University, UK | 0.205 | 0.143 | 0.263 | 0.116 | 0.150 | 0.315 | 295978310.0 |

Finally, a *Category D* 'Complex Productivity Measurement' with the example of a data envelopment analysis (DEA) is shown in the subsequent section of this chapter.

## Data Envelopment Analysis Case Study Results

The above stated input (budget) and output (THE scores for teaching, international orientation, industry income, research/publications and research/citations) are calculated in a data envelopment analysis (Banxia

7 The complete dataset is presented in Table 11.6 in the annex.

Frontier Analyst, Output-Maximization, BCC Model) in order to attain a single relative efficiency measure for each of the 74 universities in the dataset. The results are shown in Table 11.4 compared to the THE score and THE ranking position (positions according to THE total score 1 to 74).

Table 11.4 Top 17:[8] Complex Productivity Analysis: Data Envelopment Analysis Results

| University | THE Ranking Position | Efficiency Ranking Position | THE Score | Efficiency Score |
|---|---|---|---|---|
| University of Oxford, UK | 1 | 1 | 93.7 | 100.0 |
| University of Cambridge, UK | 2 | 1 | 92.6 | 100.0 |
| Imperial College London, UK | 3 | 1 | 90.6 | 100.0 |
| London School of Economics, UK | 6 | 1 | 73.1 | 100.0 |
| École Polytechnique Fédérale de Lausanne, CH | 7 | 1 | 73.0 | 100.0 |
| Katholieke Universiteit Leuven, BE | 12 | 1 | 66.1 | 100.0 |
| Wageningen University and Research Center, NL | 16 | 1 | 63.2 | 100.0 |
| Delft University of Technology, NL | 19 | 1 | 61.6 | 100.0 |
| Ghent University, BE | 27 | 1 | 58.4 | 100.0 |
| Eindhoven University of Technology, NL | 36 | 1 | 55.6 | 100.0 |
| Maastricht University, NL | 37 | 1 | 55.5 | 100.0 |
| Royal Holloway, University of London, UK | 39 | 1 | 54.9 | 100.0 |
| KTH Royal Institute of Technology, SE | 50 | 1 | 52.9 | 100.0 |
| Universität Basel, CH | 51 | 1 | 52.8 | 100.0 |
| Albert-Ludwigs-Universität Freiburg, DE | 53 | 1 | 52.3 | 100.0 |
| Technical University of Denmark, DK | 56 | 1 | 51.7 | 100.0 |
| École Normale Supérieure de Lyon, FR | 63 | 1 | 49.2 | 100.0 |

8 The complete dataset is presented in Table 11.7 in the annex.

As can be seen in the table (and as further outlined in Figure 11.2), the efficiency measurement reveals quite *different* ranking and 'success' of individual universities compared to the THE ranking with simple output measures.

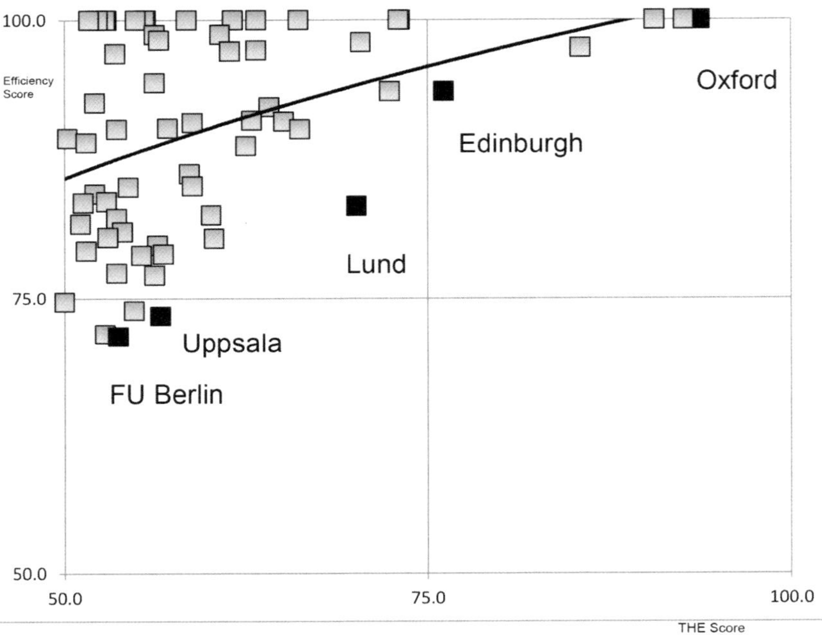


Figure 11.2 Efficiency-THE-Score Matrix

It has to be recognized from the following comparison that overall output (performance view) and the introduced efficiency view are different fields or 'disciplines' for universities:

- On the one hand, there are universities like e.g. Oxford, Leuven or Edinburgh which realize *high* efficiency scores and are ranked *high* within THE ranking at the same time. At the other end, there are also *low* performing universities in the efficiency perspective as well as in THE ranking (e.g. Newcastle, Frankfurt, Reading or Leeds).

- However, there are major exemptions from this '*correlation view*': universities like ENS Lyon, Freiburg, Basel or Maastricht are *very efficient* (100 per cent efficiency leaders) but are found in the *lower* half of the THE ranking – whereas universities like Uppsala, Sheffield, Aarhus or Manchester have high THE ranking scores bur very low efficiency scores.
- Finally, it has to be observed that by general comparative standards, the overall efficiency scores of all 74 universities with the minimum value of 71.5 are very high. This implies that the maximum efficiency improvement potential is 28.5 per cent. As in other datasets these values reach lower levels; it also can be observed that the international top universities seem to have similar efficiency levels (though it can *not* be stated if this level is comparatively low or high – as this DEA measure only reveals relative efficiencies among the analysed universities).

A similar picture is described in Figure 11.3 with the ranking positions regarding the THE ranking and the efficiency measurement instead of total scores. Though the correlation is somewhat lower (0.398 instead of 0.436 for the scores), the overall message remains: there are highly ranked but also very low ranked universities in the output-only THE perspective, which are all very (100 per cent) efficient.

These results are supported by a detailed correlation view between efficiency and size. As also indicated by the negative correlation (Pearson, r = -0.15), in general it is easier for *smaller and medium sized universities* to reach high efficiency levels, though there are major exemptions such as the large universities of Oxford, Cambridge, Leuven or Geneva with a large budget and high efficiency scores at the same time.

This can be explained theoretically by the increasing co-ordination efforts and also exponentially increasing costs with increasing topic specialization in larger institutions – as larger institutions typically have more specialized personnel (for example very small subject areas for individual Chairs and institutes with high specialist personnel costs for professors, researchers and also equipment).

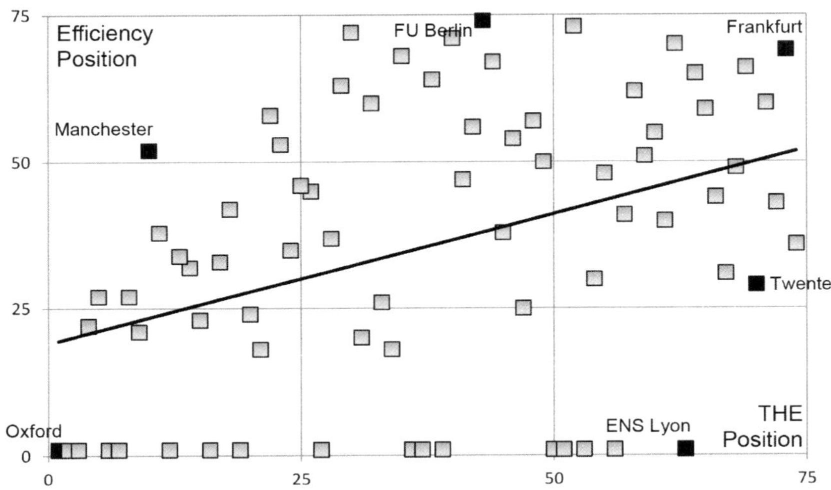


Figure 11.3 Efficiency-THE-Position Matrix

## *Implications*

First of all it has to be emphasized that for management implications and decisions, *further analysis* of all efficiency measurements is needed in order to understand the complex connections regarding productivity in university operations.

One such *exemplary* further insight could be the *relation* between the output scores regarding research (citations) and international orientation from the case study discussed above. With the *correlation factor of 0.20*, it is obvious also from the distribution of institutions that there is a slightly positive correlation which can be used in favor of enhancing overall university productivity: If it may be assumed that the correlation indicates the positive impact[9] of international orientation on citations (which may be very well explained by the fact that an internationally known university

9 Though the exact causal implication of the correlation *cannot* be derived in a statistical sense from this data.

may have higher chances of being cited by researchers), then management decisions enhancing international orientation may also *increase research productivity* by enhancing the citations of university research output.

This constitutes a good example of how further analysis insights can support decisions within the university in order to enhance efficiency. Other detailed analytical approaches may address the interaction of research and teaching as well as other success factors for university operations such as location and regional networks, gender issues, leadership and organizational matters.

From the outlined case study as well as previous research (see Figure 11.4) regarding university efficiency the following implication areas and hypotheses may be derived:

1. The efficiency perspective or dimension for universities is *different* from other views and should be measured, discussed and evaluated *independently* from other questions in higher education. As it is a major question for university success and resilience, it should be *stressed increasingly* in different contexts such as budget allocation, personnel and organizational matters as well as study programme design.
2. *Detailed analysis approaches* are necessary in order to increase the understanding of complex productivity themes within university operations – for example should further research approaches try to establish discipline specific analysis for efficiency – which is today very hard due to limited public access to university budget data, especially below the overall university level.
3. There are strong indications showing a very specific position of university operations – especially in research but also in teaching – regarding the question of economies of scale. Many research results suggest that there are *diseconomies of scale* for larger university institutions, though for smaller institutions there are measurable economies of scale (which can be explained by increased distribution of fixed cost assets, concept work and communications for example). Therefore a theoretically important 'optimal size of university operations' seems to be located in a medium-size field (e.g. for teaching between an overall number of roughly between 10,000 and 30,000 students). Smaller universities usually have less than 10,000 students, large ones more than 30,000.

As the last implication is the most specific and also intriguing observation from this efficiency perspective, a further comparison and analysis regarding this topic of *economies of scale* within universities is presented.

In addition to the results from the above case study addressing European universities, similar research results are known for example for *Australian* universities (Worthington and Higgs, 2011). As shown for the average teaching costs per graduate in Figure 11.4 below, the lowest costs (and therefore the highest overall efficiency regarding teaching) are realized by mid-sized universities like Charles Sturt University, University of Technology Sydney (UTS) or University of Western Sydney (UWS). In terms of number of graduates, smaller universities like Adelaide, University of Western Australia (UWA Perth) or Australian National University (ANU, Canberra) are facing higher costs per completion. The same high level of cost can be found with larger institutions such as Universities of Sydney and Melbourne or Monash University.

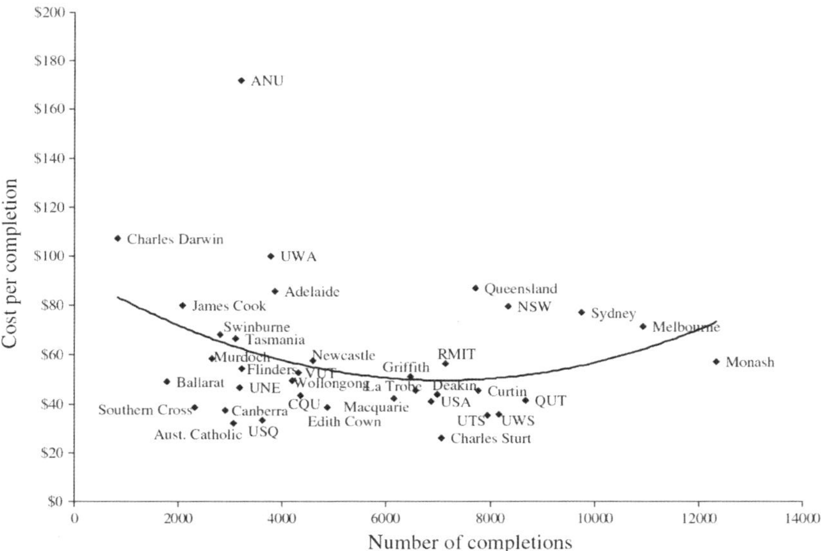


Figure 11.4 Graduate Number-Cost-Relation
Source: Worthington and Higgs, 2011: 389.

This shows that the recorded observations regarding economies of scale for smaller universities and diseconomies of scale for larger institutions may be an international and constant phenomenon, especially in the field of teaching.

## Conclusions

The presented observations are generalized in Figure 11.5, indicating three volume-dependent size areas and their respective economies of scale for teaching and research: (i) For small university institutions and operations with low production volumes, strong economies of scale, especially in teaching, are proclaimed. (ii) For medium-sized universities, only minor economies of scale can be assumed. (iii) For large university institutions with large production volumes diseconomies of scale are observed, especially in research – this can be seen as the 'excess cost' of excellence as especially in the natural sciences there are increasing cost areas due to laboratory and facility expenses, e.g. for such installations as CERN in the physics discipline or others. The performance areas of *third mission* operations within the university can be assumed to have similar economies and diseconomies of scale, positioned *between* the lower specific costs for teaching operations and the higher specific costs for research operations in higher education: On the one side it is assumed that the average operating costs of such third mission activities (e.g. research transfer, regional cooperation, society interaction) are on average higher than in teaching because the time and resource investment in cooperation activities outside the university is usually high (i.e. it takes more time to interact with institutions and persons *outside* the university than with students *inside*). On the other side it can be assumed that the average operational cost of third mission activities is in most cases lower than research operations cost, because it addresses mainly transfer of *existing* research results and the qualification of necessary people to conduct third mission activities is on average lower than in research. These assumptions have to be sustained further, especially for different disciplines – for example it can be assumed that the average cost levels for teaching and research in the *natural sciences* are higher than in the social sciences, but presumably with an average cost development depending on the production volume of university operations in different areas.

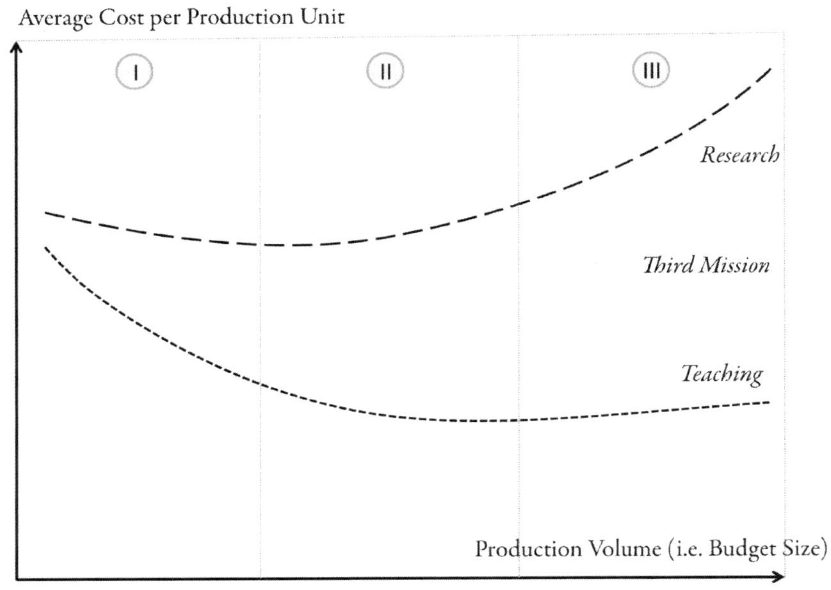


Figure 11.5 Efficiency-Volume-Relation (Assumption)

Finally, it has to be stressed that the unknown and difficult relationship of *efficiency and quality* has to be taken into account too (Dismuke and Sena, 2001). The current 'minimum-level-approach' regarding quality (assuming a minimum standard quality level for all outputs, e.g. the same quality of all PhD graduates or citations) has to be questioned strongly in order to further enhance efficiency measurement concepts.

Further, this can be linked to the ETTO (Efficiency-Thoroughness Trade-off) principle as thoroughness can be seen as proximate to quality in university operations. As Hollnagel outlines for security concepts and concerns, reduced efficiency usually leaves room for thoroughness. An increase in efficiency leads *ceteris paribus* to less room for thoroughness (Hollnagel, 2009; Hollnagel, 2002); therefore increased efficiency in higher education research and teaching may also result in a lower quality level, e.g. by a reduced time for quality control or for counselling students.

This severe concern regarding efficiency and quality as conflicting targets has to be addressed by quality management within universities, in order to avoid such adverse effects as described. This may even lead to a request for public authorities to *increase* resources for higher education.

a. With increased efficiency and accountability requests: as overhead costs increase with increasing accountability regimes, this shall not lead to fewer resources for quality control – therefore resource allocation would have to be raised by increasing third party and competitive funding;
b. If output and institutional size levels are increasing and average cost levels are also increasing, lack of resource backing could lead to diminishing quality levels in university research and teaching; in order to avoid this, resource allocation should plan for increased average cost levels and attribute higher cost shares for larger institutions.

As this obviously contradicts widely-held beliefs, further research is crucially needed about how to steer university operations efficiently as well as linking them to higher education funding and accountability schemes on a systemic policy level.

And it has become quite obvious that *university efficiency* is a major question that has to be addressed in research as well as in higher education university leadership concepts in order to create the modern, resilient and successful institutions that our societies need for their education systems and general well-being.

# References

Ahn, T., Charnes, A., and Cooper, W.W. (1988). 'Some Statistical and DEA Evaluations of Relative Efficiencies of Public and Private Institutions of Higher Learning', *Socio-Economic Planning Sciences*, 22 (6), 259–269.

Aigner, D., Lovell, C.A.K., and Schmidt, P. (1977). 'Formulation and Estimation of Stochastic Frontier Production Function Models', *Journal of Econometrics*, 6 (1), 21–37.

Banker, R.D., Charnes, A., and Cooper, W.W. (1984). 'Some Models for Estimating Technical and Scale Inefficiencies in Data Envelopment Analysis', *Management Science*, 30 (9), 1078–1092.

Banker, R.D., Conrad, R.F., and Strauss, R.P. (1986). 'A Comparative Application of Data Envelopment Analysis and Translog Methods: an Illustrative Study of Hospital Production', *Management Science*, 32 (1), 30–44.

Barth, R.T., and Vertinsky, I. (1975). 'The Effect of Goal Orientation and Information Environment on Research Performance: a Field Study', *Organizational Behavior and Human Performance*, 13 (1), 110–132.

Beasley, J.E. (1995). 'Determining Teaching and Research Efficiencies', *Journal of the Operational Research Society*, 46, 441–452.

Bonaccorsi, A., Brandt, T., De Filippo, D., Lepori, B., Molinari, F., Niederl, A., Schmoch, U., Schubert, T., and Slipersaeter, S. (2010). *Feasibility Study for Creating a European University Data Collection*. Brussels: EU Commission Documents.

Bottomley, A., and Dunworth, J. (1974). 'Rate of Return Analysis and Economies of Scale in Higher Education', *Socio-Economic Planning Sciences*, 8 (5), 273–280.

Butler, T.W., and Li, L. (2005). 'The Utility of Returns to Scale in DEA Programming: an Analysis of Michigan Rural Hospitals', *European Journal of Operations Research*, 161 (2), 469–477.

Charnes, A., Cooper, W., and Rhodes, E. (1978). 'Measuring the Efficiency of Decision Making Units', *European Journal of Operational Research*, 2 (6), 429–444.

Charnes, A., Cooper, W.W., and Thrall, R.M. (1991). 'A Structure for Classifying and Characterizing Efficiency and Inefficiency in Data Envelopment Analysis', *Journal of Productivity Analysis*, 2 (3), 197–237.

Coelli, T. (1995). 'Estimators and Hypothesis Tests for Stochastic Frontier Function: a Monte Carlo Analysis', *Journal of Productivity Analysis*, 6 (3), 247–268.

Cohn, E., Rhine, S.L.W., and Santos, M.C. (1989). 'Institutions of Higher Education as Multi-Product Firms: Economies of Scale and Scope', *Review of Economics and Statistics*, 71 (2), 284–290.

Cooper, W.W., Seiford, L.M., and Tone, K. (2007). *Data Envelopment Analysis – a Comprehensive Text with Models, Applications, References and DEA-Solver Software*. New York: McGraw-Hill.

Cullinanea, K., Wang, T.-F., Song, D.-W., and Ji, P. (2006). 'The Technical Efficiency of Container Ports: Comparing Data Envelopment Analysis and Stochastic Frontier Analysis', *Transportation Research Part A: Policy and Practice*, 40 (4), 354–374.

Dismuke, C., and Sena, V. (2001). 'Is there a Trade-off between Quality and Productivity? The Case of Diagnostic Technologies in Portugal', *Annals of Operations Research*, 107 (1–4), 107–116.

Dundar, H., and Lewis, D.R. (1995). 'Departmental Productivity in American Universities: Economies of Scale and Scope', *Economics of Education Review*, 14 (2), 199–244.

Dyckhoff, H., Allen, K. (2001). 'Measuring Ecological Efficiency with Data Envelopment Analysis (DEA)', *European Journal of Operational Research*, 132 (2), 312–325.

Feng, Y.J., Lu, H., and Bi, K. (2004). 'An AHP/DEA Method for Measurement of the Efficiency of R&D Management Activities in Universities', *International Transactions in Operational Research*, 11 (2), 181–191.

Glass, J.C., McKillop, D.G., and O'Rourke, G. (1998). 'A Cost Indirect Evaluation of Productivity Change in UK Universities', *Journal of Productivity Analysis*, 10 (2), 153–175.

Hashimoto, K., Cohn, E. (1997). 'Economies of Scale and Scope in Japanese Private Universities', *Education Economics*, 5 (2), 107–116.

Hollnagel, E. (2009). *The ETTO Principle – Efficiency-Thoroughness Trade-Off: Why Things that Go Right Sometimes Go Wrong*. Farnham, Burlington: Ashgate.

Hollnagel, E. (2002). 'Dependability of Joint Human-Computer Systems'. In Anderson, S., Felici, M., and Bologna, S. (ed.), *Computer Safety, Reliability and Security*, pp. 4–9, Series Lecture Notes in Computer Science, Vol. 2434. Heidelberg: Springer.

Jacobs, R. (2001). 'Alternative Methods to Examine Hospital Efficiency: Data Envelopment Analysis and Stochastic Frontier Analysis', *Health Care Management Science*, 4 (2), 103–115.

Johnes, G., and Johnes, J. (1993). 'Measuring the Research Performance of UK Economics Departments: An Application of Data Envelopment Analysis', *Oxford Economic Papers*, 45 (2), 332–347.

Johnes, J. (2006). 'Measuring Efficiency: a Comparison of Multilevel Modelling and Data Envelopment Analysis in the Context of Higher Education', *Bulletin of Economic Research*, 58 (2), 75–104.

Jongbloed, B., and Vossensteyn, H. (2001). 'Keeping up Performances: an International Survey of Performance-based Funding in Higher Education', *Journal of Higher Education Policy and Management*, 23 (2), 127–145.

Kao, C., and Hung, H.-T. (2008). 'Efficiency Analysis of University Departments: an Empirical Study', *Omega*, 36 (4), 653–664.

Kleine, A. (2004). 'A General Model Framework for DEA', *Omega*, 32, 17–23.

Klumpp, M., and Zelewski, S. (2012). 'Economies of Scale in Hochschulen – Das Beispiel der Hochschulfusion Duisburg-Essen', *Hochschulmanagement*, 7 (2), 47–52.

Kocher, G.M., Luptacik, M., and Sutter, M. (2006). 'Measuring Productivity of Research in Economics: A Cross-country Study Using DEA', *Socio-Economic Planning Sciences*, 40 (4), 314–332.

Korhonen, P., Tainio, R., and Wallenius, J. (2001). 'Value Efficiency Analysis of Academic Research', *European Journal of Operational Research*, 130 (1), 121–132.

Kumbhakar, S.C., and Lovell, C.A.K. (2000). *Stochastic Frontier Analysis*. Cambridge: Cambridge University Press.

Li, M., Boehm, B., and Osterweil, L.J. (2005). 'Unifying the Software Process Spectrum', International *Software Process Workshop, SPW 2005*, Beijing, May 2005, Revised Selected Papers. Berlin, Heidelberg: Springer.

Madden, G., Savage, S., and Kemp, S. (1997). 'Measuring Public Sector Efficiency: a Study of Economics Departments at Australian Universities', *Education Economics*, 5 (2), 153–168.

Maleki, G., Klumpp, M., and Cuypers, M. (2012). 'Higher Education Productivity and Quality Modelling with Data Envelopment Analysis Methods'. In M. Klumpp (ed.), *The 2012 European Simulation and Modelling Conference Proceedings*, pp. 231–233. Essen: Eurosis/FOM Essen.

McMillan, M.L., and Chan, W.H. (2006). 'University Efficiency: A Comparison and Consolidation of Results from Stochastic and Non-Stochastic Methods', *Education Economics*, 14 (1), 1–30.

McMillan, M.L., and Datta, D. (1998). 'The Relative Efficiencies of Canadian Universities: a DEA Perspective', *Canadian Public Policy*, 24 (4), 485–511.

Ng, Y.C., and Li, S.K. (2000). 'Measuring the Research Performance of Chinese Higher Education Institutions: an Application of Data Envelopment Analysis', *Education Economics*, 8 (2), 139–156.

Pedraja-Chaparro, F., Salinas-Jimenez, J., and Smith, P. (1997). 'On the Role of Weight Restrictions in Data Envelopment Analysis', *Journal of Productivity Analysis*, 8 (2), 215–230.

Ramsden, P. (1994). 'Describing and Explaining Research Productivity', *Higher Education*, 28 (2), 207–226.

Sarrico, C.S. (2010). 'On Performance in Higher Education – Towards Performance Government', *Tertiary Education and Management*, 16 (2), 145–158.

Sarrico, C.S., Teixeira, P., Rosa, M.J., and Cardoso, M.F. (2009). 'Subject Mix and Productivity in Portugese Universities', *European Journal of Operational Research*, 197 (2), 287–295.

Schwarz, J. (2013). *Messung und Steuerung der Kommunikations-Effizienz. Eine theoretische und empirische Analyse durch den Einsatz der Data Envelopment Analysis.* Dissertation Universität Basel, Basel.

Seiford, L.M. (1996). 'Data Envelopment Analysis: the Evolution of the State of the Art (1978–1995)', *The Journal of Productivity Analysis*, 7 (2/3), 99–137.

Stahl, M.J., Leap, S.L., and Wei, Z.Z. (1998). 'Publication in Leading Management Journals as a Measure of Institutional Research Productivity', *Academy of Management Journal*, 31 (3), 707–720.

Stevens, P.A. (2005). 'Stochastic Frontier Analysis of English and Welsh Universities', *Education Economics*, 13 (4), 355–374.

Taylor, B., Harris, G. (2004). 'Relative Efficiency among South African Universities: a Data Envelopment Analysis', *Higher Education*, 47 (1), 73–89.

Thanassoulis, E. (2001). *Introduction to the Theory and Application of Data Envelopment Analysis: a Foundation Text with Integrated Software*. Dordrecht: Springer.

Thannasoulis, E., Portela, M.C.S., and Despic, O. (2008). 'Data Envelopment Analysis: the Mathematical Programming Approach to Efficiency Analysis'. In H.O. Fried, C.A. Knox Lovell, and S.S. Schmidt (eds), *The Measurement of Productive Efficiency and Productivity Growth*, pp. 251–419. Oxford, New York: Oyford University Press.

Van Vught, F.A., and Ziegele, F. (2012). *Multidimensional Rankings – The Design and Development of U-Multirank*. Dordrecht: Springer.

Westrum, R. (2008). 'A Typology of Resilience Situations'. In E. Hollnagel, C.P. Nemeth and S. Dekker (eds), *Resilience Engineering Perspectives: Remaining Sensitive to the Possibility of Failure*, pp. 55–65. Aldershot, Hampshire, Burlington: Ashgate.

Woods, D.D. (2006). 'How to Design a Safety Organisation: Test Case for Resilience Engineering'. In E. Hollnagel, D.D. Woods and N. Leveson (eds), *Resilience Engineering: Concepts and Precepts*, pp. 315–325. Aldershot, Hampshire, Burlington: Ashgate.

Worthington, A.C., and Higgs, H. (2011). 'Economies of Scale and Scope in Australian Higher Education', *Higher Education*, 61 (4), 387–414.

Wreathall, J. (2006). 'Properties of Resilient Organizations: An Initial View'. In E. Hollnagel, D.D. Woods, and N. Leveson (eds), *Resilience Engineering: Concepts and Precepts*, pp. 275–285. Aldershot, Hampshire, Burlington: Ashgate.

Zangoueinezhad, A., and Moshabaki, A. (2011). 'Measuring University Performance Using a Knowledge-Based Balanced Scorecard', *Iran International Journal of Productivity and Performance Management*, 60 (8), 824–843.

Zhu, J. and Cook, W.D. (eds) (2007). *Modeling Data Irregularities and Structural Complexities in Data Envelopment Analysis – A Problem-Solving Handbook*. New York: Springer US.

Zomer, A., and Benneworth, P. (2011). 'The Rise of the University's Third Mission'. In J. Enders, H.F. de Boer, and D.F. Westerheijden (eds), *Reform of Higher Education in Europe*, pp. 81–102. Rotterdam: Sense Publishers.

## Acknowledgement

This chapter presents results connected to the research project HELENA, supported by the German Ministry for Education and Research (BMBF), administered by DLR with the ID No. 01PW11007. The author is grateful for this support.

## Annex

This technical annex presents detailed information regarding the *introduction to the DEA methodology* as well as the data for the calculated *case study* from the chapter.

Data envelopment analysis (DEA) studies different Decision Making Units (DMUs), the definition of which is rather open in order to guarantee flexibility in the term's application. Generally, a Decision Making Unit can be seen as 'the entity responsible for converting inputs into outputs and whose performances are to be evaluated' (Cooper et al., 2007: 22). In order to ensure relative comparisons, different DMUs are evaluated and compared with each other, each DMU showing a specific level of managerial effort and decision making success. The common model for measuring efficiency as simple output per input ratio cannot be used for the data envelopment analysis (DEA); therefore a *non-parametric mathematical programming approach* is used for the evaluation of DMUs' relative efficiency. In contrast to typical statistical approaches which compare a DMU's relative efficiency with an average DMU efficiency level, DEA *compares* each DMU's relative efficiency with only the *best* DMU. An efficiency measurement is implemented by constructing the Production Possibility Set (PPS) on the one hand and by calculating the maximum possible improvement of the output within the PPS on the other hand (Thanassoulis, 2001: 37). For efficiency calculation, it is assumed that there are n DMUs and it is supposed that inputs and outputs comply with the following assumptions (Cooper et al., 2007: 22):

- For each input and output, there are numerical, positive (>0) data to be chosen for all Decision Making Units.
- Selected values (inputs, outputs and the chosen DMUs) should depict the interest of managers towards the relative efficiency evaluations.
- Basically, there is a preference for *smaller* inputs and *larger* outputs, which is why these principles are reflected by the efficiency scores.
- There is a need for congruency of different inputs' and outputs' indicator units.

In general, within DEA two different basic models can be distinguished: The CCR model and the BCC model. The CCR model, named after the authors Charnes, Cooper and Rhodes (1978), is the basis model with constant returns to scale. One of the first model enhancements, the consideration of variable returns to scale, led to the development of the BCC model (named after its authors Banker, Charnes and Cooper in 1984). For both models and their efficiency measurement, the following assumptions are made (Li et al., 2005: 239):

| | |
|---|---|
| n | the number of DMUs to be evaluated |
| $DMU_j$ | the $j^{th}$ DMU |
| m | the number of inputs to each DMU |

| | |
|---|---|
| s | the number of outputs to each DMU |
| $x_{ij}$ | amount of the I[th] input consumed by $DMU_j$ |
| $y_{kj}$ | amount of the k[th] output produced by $DMU_j$ |
| eff | abbreviation for efficiency |
| $v_i$ | the weight assigned to the i[th] input |
| $u_k$ | the weight assigned to the k[th] output. |

One basic characteristic of the CCR model is the multi-output and multi-input reduction to a single (weighted) virtual input/output combination for each Decision Making Unit. For a certain DMU, measuring its efficiency and comparison with other Decision Making Units in the system is enabled. Usually executed by a series of linear programming formulations, the single DMU's performance comparison facilitates a ranking of the different analysed DMUs and scales their relative efficiency from low to high, whereby the last one is 100 per cent efficient. The CCR model contains both, a maximization and a minimization problem. The maximization problem, which is described as a productivity form, is consulted for detecting the relative total efficiency of all DMUs. In contrast to that, the CCR model's minimization problem calculates an edge productivity function, which identifies the relative efficient reference DMU for each inefficient DMU in regard to the envelopment form (encircling all real DMU as technical production frontier). Detecting DMUs' relative technical efficiency requires on the one hand detection of each DMU's technical efficiency and on the other hand the comparison of all DMU's efficiencies. These steps are executed in DEA's simultaneous arithmetic operation (Schwarz, 2013: 87–88), described as follows:

$$eff \;\; \text{DMU}j_0 = \frac{\sum_{k=1}^{s} M_k Y_{kj_0}}{\sum_{i=1}^{m} V_i X_{ij_0}}$$

The calculation of the DMU's efficiency value results from the consideration of the weighted inputs and weighted outputs. By the help of quantified inputs and quantified outputs, DEA generates via a quotient one single efficiency ratio for each DMU. The weighted factors are endogenously determined and allow the pooling of heterogeneous input and output factors with different units of measurement in one efficiency ratio. Hereby, each DMU's weights are considered optimally in order to maximize the efficiency value and determine only the definitely provable inefficiency. The analysis for the maximization problem is attached to each DMU, which means that for n DMUs, quotient programmes need to be solved. On the way to solving the maximization problem, a fractional programming error occurs, which can be overcome by the help of the Charnes-Cooper transformation. This is done via transforming the quotient programme into a linear programming problem. By the help of the following figure, the different scales of CCR and BCC are depicted in the case of a single input and single output.

In Figure 11.6, H illustrates a scale-efficient DMU (on the production function). Inspection of DMU K reveals that point XJ/ XK stands for the input saving technical efficiency, XK/ YL represents the output increasing technical efficiency, XI/ XK stands for the gross scale efficiency (in case of variable scales), XI/ XJ shows the pure scale efficiency with a corrected input and YL/ YM stands for the pure scale efficiency with corrected output. Calculating the DMUs' efficiency, it can be observed that DMU H has the highest level of efficiency. Building the border production function under the assumption of *constant returns to scale* (CCR) therefore complies with a line through the origin. This function with the assumption of *variable returns to scale* (BCC) is built by combining the points J, H and L. As this is the case, the area of production opportunities is limited by the partly linear connection with input and output. Therefore, in the case of variable returns to scale, the DMUs J, H and L are efficient, whereas DMU K is inefficient.

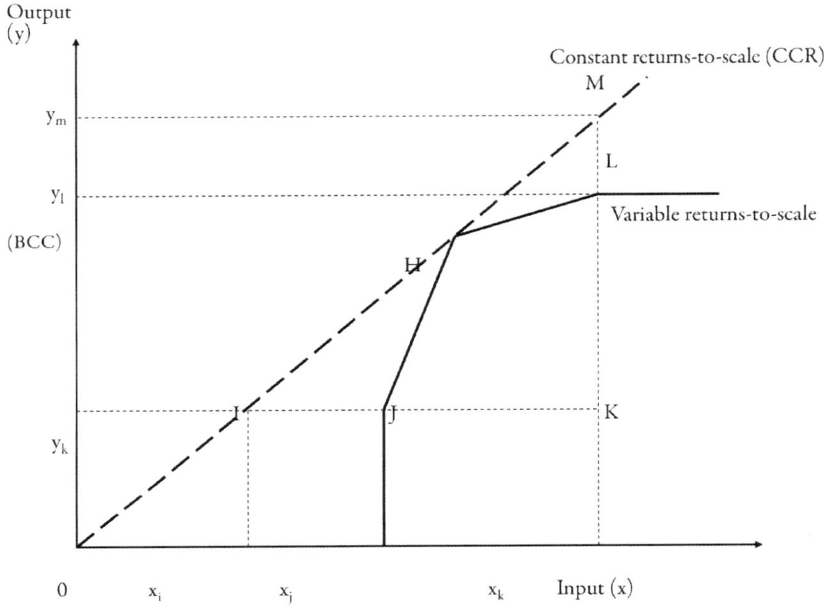


Figure 11.6 DEA Frontier Graph – CCR and BBC Model

It can be noted therefore that in a CCR model usually only one DMU can be efficient (in rare cases two DMUs may lie exactly on the same origin line as depicted), whereas for most settings a more realistic BCC model several DMUs are expected to be efficient. This applies also to university production settings as shown by Maleki, Klumpp and Cuypers (2012).

The analysed and calculated case study data for European Universities is presented in the following tables and figures.

Table 11.5 University Dataset from Times Higher Education World University Ranking and Budget Data (2011/2012)

| | THE Ranking Position | THE Score | O1: Teaching | O2: International Outlook | O3: Industry Income | O4: Research | O5: Citations | I: Budget 2011 in € |
|---|---|---|---|---|---|---|---|---|
| University of Oxford, UK | 1 | 93.7 | 89.7 | 88.7 | 79.8 | 98.1 | 95.6 | 1093538183.5 |
| University of Cambridge, UK | 2 | 92.6 | 91.2 | 83.6 | 59.1 | 95.6 | 96.2 | 942019644.7 |
| Imperial College London, UK | 3 | 90.6 | 88.0 | 91.4 | 87.5 | 90.9 | 93.0 | 837396247.1 |
| University College London, UK | 4 | 85.5 | 83.5 | 89.0 | 45.1 | 88.8 | 86.8 | 953219016.8 |
| University of Edinburgh, UK | 5 | 76.1 | 68.4 | 78.9 | 43.8 | 71.3 | 90.8 | 773930363.6 |
| London School of Economics, UK | 6 | 73.1 | 70.8 | 87.2 | 42.9 | 80.3 | 66.5 | 277906866.1 |
| École Polytechnique Fédérale Lausanne, CH | 7 | 73.0 | 62.4 | 98.8 | 49.8 | 57.0 | 95.0 | 646111065.7 |
| Karolinska Institute, SE | 8 | 72.4 | 66.3 | 64.5 | 71.4 | 75.7 | 77.3 | 604377426.4 |
| Ludwig-Maximilians-Universität München, DE | 9 | 70.4 | 65.4 | 54.7 | 42.0 | 66.5 | 85.8 | 488600000.0 |
| University of Manchester, UK | 10 | 70.1 | 65.9 | 77.9 | 43.2 | 67.7 | 76.9 | 962018693.4 |
| King's College London, UK | 11 | 66.2 | 53.5 | 86.0 | 42.4 | 59.3 | 82.8 | 623243037.6 |
| Katholieke Universiteit Leuven, BE | 12 | 66.1 | 59.7 | 56.6 | 99.7 | 71.0 | 67.2 | 720631780.0 |
| Leiden University, NL | 13 | 65.1 | 54.0 | 54.8 | 46.1 | 67.1 | 78.4 | 514700000.0 |
| Utrecht University, NL | 14 | 64.1 | 48.0 | 47.3 | 82.6 | 64.7 | 82.4 | 767354000.0 |
| Georg-August-Universität Göttingen, DE | 15 | 63.2 | 50.0 | 51.0 | 34.4 | 52.5 | 92.5 | 412101313.0 |
| Wageningen University, NL | 16 | 63.2 | 54.9 | 79.2 | 100.0 | 53.7 | 73.8 | 710000000.0 |
| Erasmus University Rotterdam, NL | 17 | 62.9 | 44.5 | 62.8 | 62.0 | 64.1 | 80.2 | 542000000.0 |
| University of Bristol, UK | 18 | 62.5 | 50.1 | 71.9 | 38.7 | 51.7 | 85.4 | 486122672.2 |
| Delft University of Technology, NL | 19 | 61.6 | 59.9 | 67.7 | 99.9 | 75.1 | 45.1 | 520600000.0 |
| Universität Heidelberg, DE | 20 | 61.4 | 61.4 | 61.3 | 40.7 | 49.0 | 75.5 | 316700000.0 |
| Durham University, UK | 21 | 60.7 | 42.3 | 77.7 | 34.3 | 44.5 | 93.3 | 295978310.0 |

| | | | | | | | | |
|---|---|---|---|---|---|---|---|---|
| Lund University, SE | 22 | 60.3 | 43.6 | 64.4 | 34.2 | 61.3 | 77.1 | 700000000.0 |
| University of Amsterdam, NL | 23 | 60.1 | 45.6 | 57.0 | 49.0 | 61.3 | 75.1 | 600000000.0 |
| University of Groningen, NL | 24 | 58.8 | 43.8 | 49.8 | 85.2 | 61.0 | 71.6 | 576000000.0 |
| University of Zürich, CH | 25 | 58.8 | 50.0 | 84.1 | 38.3 | 41.6 | 80.0 | 1008015048.7 |
| Université Paris-Sud, FR | 26 | 58.6 | 48.0 | 63.9 | 28.4 | 45.9 | 82.9 | 450000000.0 |
| Ghent University, BE | 27 | 58.4 | 46.4 | 49.1 | 95.9 | 56.7 | 71.3 | 410000000.0 |
| University of York, UK | 28 | 57.1 | 41.9 | 71.9 | 38.4 | 43.9 | 83.4 | 303579327.9 |
| Technische Universität München, DE | 29 | 56.8 | 51.2 | 61.5 | 49.7 | 42.4 | 76.5 | 1095000000.0 |
| Uppsala University, SE | 30 | 56.6 | 48.6 | 56.3 | 44.1 | 63.9 | 58.2 | 596410285.3 |
| University of St Andrews, UK | 31 | 56.5 | 43.2 | 86.3 | 38.9 | 43.8 | 76.6 | 199550503.0 |
| University of Helsinki, FI | 32 | 56.4 | 42.8 | 48.3 | 31.1 | 53.0 | 77.7 | 643056099.9 |
| Trinity College Dublin, IR | 33 | 56.2 | 41.9 | 84.5 | 32.8 | 33.5 | 88.1 | 265745000.0 |
| University of Sussex, UK | 34 | 56.2 | 34.9 | 76.7 | 32.1 | 39.5 | 91.1 | 197160320.6 |
| University of Sheffield, UK | 35 | 56.2 | 49.5 | 68.1 | 41.5 | 46.2 | 71.0 | 511332556.4 |
| Eindhoven University of Technology, NL | 36 | 55.6 | 44.1 | 69.8 | 100.0 | 51.8 | 63.8 | 312600000.0 |
| Maastricht University, NL | 37 | 55.5 | 39.7 | 85.2 | 99.1 | 53.2 | 62.5 | 343421000.0 |
| Aarhus University, DK | 38 | 55.3 | 35.7 | 66.4 | 69.7 | 54.6 | 71.6 | 789599000.0 |
| Royal Holloway, University of London, UK | 39 | 54.9 | 30.5 | 92.5 | 31.9 | 27.7 | 99.0 | 153605489.1 |
| University of Nottingham, UK | 40 | 54.8 | 48.1 | 70.1 | 38.3 | 50.8 | 62.8 | 607653340.3 |
| University of Warwick, UK | 41 | 54.4 | 48.9 | 80.9 | 35.3 | 50.5 | 58.8 | 498251956.1 |
| Radboud University Nijmegen, NL | 42 | 54.0 | 35.7 | 53.4 | 41.7 | 54.3 | 73.3 | 500250000.0 |
| Freie Universität Berlin, DE | 43 | 53.7 | 53.1 | 60.9 | 32.8 | 56.5 | 51.5 | 392500000.0 |
| University of Copenhagen, DK | 44 | 53.6 | 42.2 | 73.5 | 39.7 | 40.4 | 74.3 | 1047874149.0 |
| Université de Lausanne, CH | 45 | 53.6 | 33.0 | 82.7 | 45.8 | 44.8 | 76.2 | 333360595.4 |
| University of Southampton, UK | 46 | 53.6 | 37.9 | 77.4 | 41.8 | 38.9 | 79.2 | 519585226.1 |
| University of Geneva, CH | 47 | 53.5 | 36.2 | 95.3 | 32.4 | 42.5 | 73.1 | 604511699.5 |
| University of Glasgow, UK | 48 | 53.0 | 37.3 | 69.7 | 44.1 | 40.2 | 78.1 | 535347349.4 |
| VU University Amsterdam, NL | 49 | 52.9 | 40.5 | 47.1 | 58.5 | 45.1 | 74.2 | 459700000.0 |
| KTH Royal Institute of Technology, SE | 50 | 52.9 | 47.5 | 86.1 | 100.0 | 49.7 | 49.1 | 443481685.7 |
| Universität Basel, CH | 51 | 52.8 | 37.1 | 89.8 | 64.2 | 23.2 | 87.8 | 366100074.4 |

| | | | | | | | | |
|---|---|---|---|---|---|---|---|---|
| University of Leeds, UK | 52 | 52.8 | 41.5 | 66.6 | 41.3 | 48.6 | 65.8 | 575339501.0 |
| Albert-Ludwigs-Universität Freiburg, DE | 53 | 52.3 | 48.3 | 54.9 | 81.1 | 33.0 | 72.4 | 280900000.0 |
| Queen Mary, University of London, UK | 54 | 52.1 | 33.1 | 87.0 | 42.7 | 30.0 | 85.4 | 356743644.0 |
| Lancaster University, UK | 55 | 52.1 | 37.7 | 76.2 | 31.8 | 40.9 | 73.2 | 214902371.2 |
| Technical University of Denmark, DK | 56 | 51.7 | 37.9 | 77.0 | 98.7 | 30.0 | 76.9 | 558000000.0 |
| Karlsruhe Institute of Technology, DE | 57 | 51.5 | 46.3 | 64.5 | 82.9 | 38.9 | 63.4 | 397000000.0 |
| University of Bern, CH | 58 | 51.5 | 43.0 | 77.3 | 42.0 | 36.0 | 69.7 | 603582236.0 |
| University of Exeter, UK | 59 | 51.3 | 33.2 | 74.1 | 37.1 | 38.1 | 78.1 | 292767617.2 |
| RWTH Aachen University, DE | 60 | 51.1 | 45.3 | 53.9 | 63.1 | 32.4 | 73.8 | 605130013.0 |
| University of Vienna, AU | 61 | 50.2 | 44.3 | 86.3 | 29.1 | 46.7 | 52.4 | 509700000.0 |
| Université Catholique de Louvain, BE | 62 | 50.0 | 38.6 | 64.3 | 34.5 | 40.5 | 68.8 | 370000000.0 |
| École Normale Supérieure de Lyon, FR | 63 | 49.2 | 40.8 | 61.0 | 28.9 | 25.9 | 79.6 | 110000000.0 |
| University of Liverpool, UK | 64 | 49.0 | 38.7 | 73.7 | 46.4 | 37.5 | 64.8 | 475658192.0 |
| University of Reading, UK | 65 | 48.8 | 39.3 | 72.4 | 35.2 | 41.1 | 61.3 | 258880538.4 |
| University of East Anglia, UK | 66 | 48.8 | 29.6 | 68.9 | 30.7 | 27.7 | 85.5 | 229546697.7 |
| University of Aberdeen, UK | 67 | 48.8 | 31.9 | 84.1 | 48.9 | 34.3 | 71.5 | 261612005.6 |
| Université Joseph Fourier, Grenoble, FR | 68 | 48.6 | 36.6 | 56.3 | 36.3 | 26.5 | 81.8 | 300000000.0 |
| Newcastle University, UK | 69 | 48.6 | 37.9 | 74.4 | 37.4 | 30.5 | 72.1 | 454491402.5 |
| University of Twente, NL | 70 | 47.9 | 35.8 | 61.5 | 79.7 | 46.4 | 55.6 | 279400000.0 |
| University College Dublin, IR | 71 | 47.9 | 31.1 | 76.5 | 35.3 | 31.8 | 74.9 | 442000000.0 |
| University of Leicester, UK | 72 | 46.7 | 33.0 | 83.7 | 34.9 | 32.5 | 66.5 | 416200918.0 |
| Goethe-Universität Frankfurt, DE | 73 | 46.4 | 33.3 | 57.6 | 41.4 | 29.7 | 73.9 | 489500000.0 |
| Birkbeck, University of London, UK | 74 | 46.2 | 27.6 | 83.2 | 29.4 | 30.5 | 72.8 | 172426094.6 |

Table 11.6 Simple Productivity Analysis: Budget-Outcome-Indicators (Score per 1 mil. €)

| | THE Score / Budget | Teaching / Budget | International / Budget | Income / Budget | Research / Budget | Citations / Budget | Budget 2011 in € |
|---|---|---|---|---|---|---|---|
| École Normale Supérieure de Lyon, FR | 0.447 | 0.371 | 0.555 | 0.263 | 0.235 | 0.724 | 110000000.0 |
| Royal Holloway, University of London, UK | 0.357 | 0.199 | 0.602 | 0.208 | 0.180 | 0.645 | 153605489.1 |
| University of Sussex, UK | 0.285 | 0.177 | 0.389 | 0.163 | 0.200 | 0.462 | 197160320.6 |
| University of St Andrews, UK | 0.283 | 0.216 | 0.432 | 0.195 | 0.219 | 0.384 | 199550503.0 |
| Birkbeck, University of London, UK | 0.268 | 0.160 | 0.483 | 0.171 | 0.177 | 0.422 | 172426094.6 |
| London School of Economics, UK | 0.263 | 0.255 | 0.314 | 0.154 | 0.289 | 0.239 | 277906866.1 |
| Lancaster University, UK | 0.242 | 0.175 | 0.355 | 0.148 | 0.190 | 0.341 | 214902371.2 |
| University of East Anglia, UK | 0.213 | 0.129 | 0.300 | 0.134 | 0.121 | 0.372 | 229546697.7 |
| Trinity College Dublin, IR | 0.211 | 0.158 | 0.318 | 0.123 | 0.126 | 0.332 | 265745000.0 |
| Durham University, UK | 0.205 | 0.143 | 0.263 | 0.116 | 0.150 | 0.315 | 295978310.0 |
| Universität Heidelberg, DE | 0.194 | 0.194 | 0.194 | 0.129 | 0.155 | 0.238 | 316700000.0 |
| University of Reading, UK | 0.189 | 0.152 | 0.280 | 0.136 | 0.159 | 0.237 | 258880538.4 |
| University of York, UK | 0.188 | 0.138 | 0.237 | 0.126 | 0.145 | 0.275 | 303579327.9 |
| University of Aberdeen, UK | 0.187 | 0.122 | 0.321 | 0.187 | 0.131 | 0.273 | 261612005.6 |
| Albert-Ludwigs-Universität Freiburg, DE | 0.186 | 0.172 | 0.195 | 0.289 | 0.117 | 0.258 | 280900000.0 |
| Eindhoven University of Technology, NL | 0.178 | 0.141 | 0.223 | 0.320 | 0.166 | 0.204 | 312600000.0 |
| University of Exeter, UK | 0.175 | 0.113 | 0.253 | 0.127 | 0.130 | 0.267 | 292767617.2 |
| University of Twente, NL | 0.171 | 0.128 | 0.220 | 0.285 | 0.166 | 0.199 | 279400000.0 |
| Université Joseph Fourier, Grenoble, FR | 0.162 | 0.122 | 0.188 | 0.121 | 0.088 | 0.273 | 300000000.0 |
| Maastricht University, NL | 0.162 | 0.116 | 0.248 | 0.289 | 0.155 | 0.182 | 343421000.0 |
| Université de Lausanne, CH | 0.161 | 0.099 | 0.248 | 0.137 | 0.134 | 0.229 | 333360595.4 |

| | | | | | | | |
|---|---|---|---|---|---|---|---|
| Georg-August-Universität Göttingen, DE | 0.153 | 0.121 | 0.124 | 0.083 | 0.127 | 0.224 | 412101313.0 |
| Queen Mary, University of London, UK | 0.146 | 0.093 | 0.244 | 0.120 | 0.084 | 0.239 | 356743644.0 |
| Universität Basel, CH | 0.144 | 0.101 | 0.245 | 0.175 | 0.063 | 0.240 | 366100074.4 |
| Ludwig-Maximilians-Universität München, DE | 0.144 | 0.134 | 0.112 | 0.086 | 0.136 | 0.176 | 488600000.0 |
| Ghent University, BE | 0.142 | 0.113 | 0.120 | 0.234 | 0.138 | 0.174 | 410000000.0 |
| Freie Universität Berlin, DE | 0.137 | 0.135 | 0.155 | 0.084 | 0.144 | 0.131 | 392500000.0 |
| Université Catholique de Louvain, BE | 0.135 | 0.104 | 0.174 | 0.093 | 0.109 | 0.186 | 370000000.0 |
| Université Paris-Sud, FR | 0.130 | 0.107 | 0.142 | 0.063 | 0.102 | 0.184 | 450000000.0 |
| Karlsruhe Institute of Technology, DE | 0.130 | 0.117 | 0.162 | 0.209 | 0.098 | 0.160 | 397000000.0 |
| University of Bristol, UK | 0.129 | 0.103 | 0.148 | 0.080 | 0.106 | 0.176 | 486122672.2 |
| Leiden University, NL | 0.126 | 0.105 | 0.106 | 0.090 | 0.130 | 0.152 | 514700000.0 |
| Karolinska Institute, SE | 0.120 | 0.110 | 0.107 | 0.118 | 0.125 | 0.128 | 604377426.4 |
| KTH Royal Institute of Technology, SE | 0.119 | 0.107 | 0.194 | 0.225 | 0.112 | 0.111 | 443481685.7 |
| Delft University of Technology, NL | 0.118 | 0.115 | 0.130 | 0.192 | 0.144 | 0.087 | 520600000.0 |
| Erasmus University Rotterdam, NL | 0.116 | 0.082 | 0.116 | 0.114 | 0.118 | 0.148 | 542000000.0 |
| VU University Amsterdam, NL | 0.115 | 0.088 | 0.102 | 0.127 | 0.098 | 0.161 | 459700000.0 |
| École Polytechnique Fédérale Lausanne, CH | 0.113 | 0.097 | 0.153 | 0.077 | 0.088 | 0.147 | 646111065.7 |
| University of Leicester, UK | 0.112 | 0.079 | 0.201 | 0.084 | 0.078 | 0.160 | 416200918.0 |
| University of Sheffield, UK | 0.110 | 0.097 | 0.133 | 0.081 | 0.090 | 0.139 | 511332556.4 |
| University of Warwick, UK | 0.109 | 0.098 | 0.162 | 0.071 | 0.101 | 0.118 | 498251956.1 |
| University College Dublin, IR | 0.108 | 0.070 | 0.173 | 0.080 | 0.072 | 0.169 | 442000000.0 |
| Imperial College London, UK | 0.108 | 0.105 | 0.109 | 0.104 | 0.109 | 0.111 | 837396247.1 |
| Radboud University Nijmegen, NL | 0.108 | 0.071 | 0.107 | 0.083 | 0.109 | 0.147 | 500250000.0 |
| Newcastle University, UK | 0.107 | 0.083 | 0.164 | 0.082 | 0.067 | 0.159 | 454491402.5 |
| King's College London, UK | 0.106 | 0.086 | 0.138 | 0.068 | 0.095 | 0.133 | 623243037.6 |
| University of Southampton, UK | 0.103 | 0.073 | 0.149 | 0.080 | 0.075 | 0.152 | 519585226.1 |
| University of Liverpool, UK | 0.103 | 0.081 | 0.155 | 0.098 | 0.079 | 0.136 | 475658192.0 |

| University of Groningen, NL | 0.102 | 0.076 | 0.086 | 0.148 | 0.106 | 0.124 | 576000000.0 |
|---|---|---|---|---|---|---|---|
| University of Amsterdam, NL | 0.100 | 0.076 | 0.095 | 0.082 | 0.102 | 0.125 | 600000000.0 |
| University of Glasgow, UK | 0.099 | 0.070 | 0.130 | 0.082 | 0.075 | 0.146 | 535347349.4 |
| University of Vienna, AU | 0.098 | 0.087 | 0.169 | 0.057 | 0.092 | 0.103 | 509700000.0 |
| University of Edinburgh, UK | 0.098 | 0.088 | 0.102 | 0.057 | 0.092 | 0.117 | 773930363.6 |
| University of Cambridge, UK | 0.098 | 0.097 | 0.089 | 0.063 | 0.101 | 0.102 | 942019644.7 |
| Uppsala University, SE | 0.095 | 0.081 | 0.094 | 0.074 | 0.107 | 0.098 | 596410285.3 |
| Goethe-Universität Frankfurt, DE | 0.095 | 0.068 | 0.118 | 0.085 | 0.061 | 0.151 | 489500000.0 |
| Technical University of Denmark, DK | 0.093 | 0.068 | 0.138 | 0.177 | 0.054 | 0.138 | 558000000.0 |
| University of Leeds, UK | 0.092 | 0.072 | 0.116 | 0.072 | 0.084 | 0.114 | 575339501.0 |
| Katholieke Universiteit Leuven, BE | 0.092 | 0.083 | 0.079 | 0.138 | 0.099 | 0.093 | 720631780.0 |
| University of Nottingham, UK | 0.090 | 0.079 | 0.115 | 0.063 | 0.084 | 0.103 | 607653340.3 |
| University College London, UK | 0.090 | 0.088 | 0.093 | 0.047 | 0.093 | 0.091 | 953219016.8 |
| Wageningen University, NL | 0.089 | 0.077 | 0.112 | 0.141 | 0.076 | 0.104 | 710000000.0 |
| University of Geneva, CH | 0.089 | 0.060 | 0.158 | 0.054 | 0.070 | 0.121 | 604511699.5 |
| University of Helsinki, FI | 0.088 | 0.067 | 0.075 | 0.048 | 0.082 | 0.121 | 643056099.9 |
| Lund University, SE | 0.086 | 0.062 | 0.092 | 0.049 | 0.088 | 0.110 | 700000000.0 |
| University of Oxford, UK | 0.086 | 0.082 | 0.081 | 0.073 | 0.090 | 0.087 | 1093538183.5 |
| University of Bern, CH | 0.085 | 0.071 | 0.128 | 0.070 | 0.060 | 0.115 | 603582236.0 |
| RWTH Aachen University, DE | 0.084 | 0.075 | 0.089 | 0.104 | 0.054 | 0.122 | 605130013.0 |
| Utrecht University, NL | 0.084 | 0.063 | 0.062 | 0.108 | 0.084 | 0.107 | 767354000.0 |
| University of Manchester, UK | 0.073 | 0.069 | 0.081 | 0.045 | 0.070 | 0.080 | 962018693.4 |
| Aarhus University, DK | 0.070 | 0.045 | 0.084 | 0.088 | 0.069 | 0.091 | 789599000.0 |
| University of Zürich, CH | 0.058 | 0.050 | 0.083 | 0.038 | 0.041 | 0.079 | 1008015048.7 |
| Technische Universität München, DE | 0.052 | 0.047 | 0.056 | 0.045 | 0.039 | 0.070 | 1095000000.0 |
| University of Copenhagen, DK | 0.051 | 0.040 | 0.070 | 0.038 | 0.039 | 0.071 | 1047874149.0 |
| *Budget Correlation* | *-0.768* | *-0.675* | *-0.761* | *-0.608* | *-0.663* | *-0.735* | |

Table 11.7 Complex Productivity Analysis: Data Envelopment Analysis Results

| University | THE Ranking Position | Eff. Ranking Position | THE Score | Efficiency Score |
|---|---|---|---|---|
| University of Oxford, UK | 1 | 1 | 93.7 | 100.0 |
| University of Cambridge, UK | 2 | 1 | 92.6 | 100.0 |
| Imperial College London, UK | 3 | 1 | 90.6 | 100.0 |
| London School of Economics, UK | 6 | 1 | 73.1 | 100.0 |
| École Polytechnique Fédérale de Lausanne, CH | 7 | 1 | 73.0 | 100.0 |
| Katholieke Universiteit Leuven, BE | 12 | 1 | 66.1 | 100.0 |
| Wageningen University and Research Center, NL | 16 | 1 | 63.2 | 100.0 |
| Delft University of Technology, NL | 19 | 1 | 61.6 | 100.0 |
| Ghent University, BE | 27 | 1 | 58.4 | 100.0 |
| Eindhoven University of Technology, NL | 36 | 1 | 55.6 | 100.0 |
| Maastricht University, NL | 37 | 1 | 55.5 | 100.0 |
| Royal Holloway, University of London, UK | 39 | 1 | 54.9 | 100.0 |
| KTH Royal Institute of Technology, SE | 50 | 1 | 52.9 | 100.0 |
| Universität Basel, CH | 51 | 1 | 52.8 | 100.0 |
| Albert-Ludwigs-Universität Freiburg, DE | 53 | 1 | 52.3 | 100.0 |
| Technical University of Denmark, DK | 56 | 1 | 51.7 | 100.0 |
| École Normale Supérieure de Lyon, FR | 63 | 1 | 49.2 | 100.0 |
| Durham University, UK | 21 | 18 | 60.7 | 98.7 |
| University of Sussex, UK | 34 | 18 | 56.2 | 98.7 |
| University of St Andrews, UK | 31 | 20 | 56.5 | 98.2 |
| Ludwig-Maximilians-Universität München, DE | 9 | 21 | 70.4 | 98.0 |
| University College London, UK | 4 | 22 | 85.5 | 97.5 |
| Georg-August-Universität Göttingen, DE | 15 | 23 | 63.2 | 97.3 |
| Universität Heidelberg, DE | 20 | 24 | 61.4 | 97.2 |
| University of Geneva, CH | 47 | 25 | 53.5 | 97.0 |
| Trinity College Dublin, IR | 33 | 26 | 56.2 | 94.4 |

| | | | | |
|---|---|---|---|---|
| Karolinska Institute, SE | 8 | 27 | 72.4 | 93.6 |
| University of Edinburgh, UK | 5 | 27 | 76.1 | 93.6 |
| University of Twente, NL | 70 | 29 | 47.9 | 93.3 |
| Queen Mary, University of London, UK | 54 | 30 | 52.1 | 92.6 |
| University of Aberdeen, UK | 67 | 31 | 48.8 | 92.3 |
| Utrecht University, NL | 14 | 32 | 64.1 | 92.2 |
| Erasmus University Rotterdam, NL | 17 | 33 | 62.9 | 91.0 |
| Leiden University, NL | 13 | 34 | 65.1 | 90.9 |
| University of Groningen, NL | 24 | 35 | 58.8 | 90.8 |
| Birkbeck, University of London, UK | 74 | 36 | 46.2 | 90.4 |
| University of York, UK | 28 | 37 | 57.1 | 90.3 |
| King's College London, UK | 11 | 38 | 66.2 | 90.2 |
| Université de Lausanne, CH | 45 | 38 | 53.6 | 90.2 |
| University of Vienna, AU | 61 | 40 | 50.2 | 89.4 |
| Karlsruhe Institute of Technology, DE | 57 | 41 | 51.5 | 89.0 |
| University of Bristol, UK | 18 | 42 | 62.5 | 88.7 |
| University of Leicester, UK | 72 | 43 | 46.7 | 87.3 |
| University of East Anglia, UK | 66 | 44 | 48.8 | 86.6 |
| Université Paris-Sud, FR | 26 | 45 | 58.6 | 86.2 |
| University of Zürich, CH | 25 | 46 | 58.8 | 85.1 |
| University of Warwick, UK | 41 | 47 | 54.4 | 85.0 |
| Lancaster University, UK | 55 | 48 | 52.1 | 84.4 |
| Université Joseph Fourier, Grenoble, FR | 68 | 49 | 48.6 | 84.3 |
| VU University Amsterdam, NL | 49 | 50 | 52.9 | 83.7 |
| University of Exeter, UK | 59 | 51 | 51.3 | 83.6 |
| University of Manchester, UK | 10 | 52 | 70.1 | 83.3 |
| University of Amsterdam, NL | 23 | 53 | 60.1 | 82.5 |
| University of Southampton, UK | 46 | 54 | 53.6 | 82.2 |
| RWTH Aachen University, DE | 60 | 55 | 51.1 | 81.7 |
| Radboud University Nijmegen, NL | 42 | 56 | 54.0 | 81.0 |
| University of Glasgow, UK | 48 | 57 | 53.0 | 80.5 |
| Lund University, SE | 22 | 58 | 60.3 | 80.4 |
| University of Reading, UK | 65 | 59 | 48.8 | 80.1 |

| | | | | |
|---|---|---|---|---|
| University of Helsinki, FI | 32 | 60 | 56.4 | 79.8 |
| University College Dublin, IR | 71 | 60 | 47.9 | 79.8 |
| University of Bern, CH | 58 | 62 | 51.5 | 79.3 |
| Technische Universität München, DE | 29 | 63 | 56.8 | 79.0 |
| Aarhus University, DK | 38 | 64 | 55.3 | 78.9 |
| University of Liverpool, UK | 64 | 65 | 49.0 | 78.3 |
| Newcastle University, UK | 69 | 66 | 48.6 | 77.9 |
| University of Copenhagen, DK | 44 | 67 | 53.6 | 77.3 |
| University of Sheffield, UK | 35 | 68 | 56.2 | 77.1 |
| Goethe-Universität Frankfurt, DE | 73 | 69 | 46.4 | 76.3 |
| Université Catholique de Louvain, BE | 62 | 70 | 50.0 | 74.7 |
| University of Nottingham, UK | 40 | 71 | 54.8 | 73.9 |
| Uppsala University, SE | 30 | 72 | 56.6 | 73.4 |
| University of Leeds, UK | 52 | 73 | 52.8 | 71.7 |
| Freie Universität Berlin, DE | 43 | 74 | 53.7 | 71.5 |
| *Correlation (Pearson)* | | *0.398* | | *0.436* |

CARMEN PÉREZ-ESPARRELLS AND EVA M. TORRE

# 12 Fundraising in European Higher Education Institutions: A Strategy for University Enhancement

## The Role of Fundraising in the Global Market of Higher Education

European higher education institutions (HEIs) participate in a 'global market' of higher education with other institutions across the world. Many factors contribute to making higher education the centre of acute competition. Massification and internationalization are two of the most important features, reflected in the boom of global HEI rankings. In this new scenario European HEIs are competing for talent and resources. The identification of opportunities for co-operation with their stakeholders in the private sector, specifically with philanthropic funders, will be a crucial element of the institutional development in European universities.

The European higher education sector is facing problems in relation to financial sustainability: its institutions have to navigate increasing international competition whilst their core public funding is dropping. This situation is leading European universities to diversify their income sources as a risk-mitigation measure. They need to seek new means of raising supplementary private funds in addition to relying on traditional private sources such as student contributions and contracts with business sector (Estermann and Bennetot, 2011).

Therefore, in response to the global financial crisis the funding of European HEIs has started on a path of profound transformation against the background of historical circumstances. This context has led many universities in Europe to diversify their income streams by introducing other fundraising strategies to strengthen the institutional resilience which for a period of time has been attacked by creeping public defunding. Nevertheless, the indispensability of sustainable public funding for the main missions of universities (teaching and research activities) is a fact in Europe.

This chapter focuses on successful fundraising strategies to strengthen institutional resilience. It makes reference to two case studies that belong to different leagues of excellence in the global HEI sector: the British University of Cambridge which is a prestigious university with extensive experience of fundraising, and the Spanish University of Navarra which demonstrates relevant experience in the fundraising field in the Mediterranean region. From this point onwards, the chapter shifts towards a more pragmatic perspective, suggesting a set of basic actions for implementing the theoretical model in less experienced universities and promoting university fundraising.

This chapter is structured as follows: section 2 relates different types of universities and sources of philanthropy to fundraising strategies; section 3 highlights the need to promote fundraising from philanthropic sources in most European universities; section 4 identifies the different factors that integrate a theoretical fundraising model based on good practice in fundraising drawn from the case studies of the University of Cambridge in the United Kingdom and the University of Navarra in Spain; in section 5, first steps in promoting university fundraising are proposed; and finally, section 6 points out the main conclusions of this chapter.

## University Fundraising Models and Funding Strategies in Europe

University fundraising could be defined *'as the search for philanthropic private funding through seeking individuals or organizations that want to share the goals and results of the organization through financial contributions'*

(Pérez-Esparrells and Torre, 2012a). In this sense, it makes reference to non-state financial support that could be considered as a supplementary income stream in order to promote institutional resilience, long term financial robustness and institutional advancement. A fundraising strategy must be a systematic, integrated method developed for a fundraising unit in order to increase the institution's support from its key stakeholders. It comprises communication and marketing, alumni relations and development (Task Force Report to Government, 2004).

Pérez-Esparrells and Torre (2012a) propose a theoretical taxonomy of university fundraising strategies based on the classifications suggested by two of the most important European reports in this field: *Increasing Voluntary Giving to Higher Education* (Task Force Report to Government, 2004); and *Engaging Philanthropy for University Research* (European Commission, 2007). This theoretical taxonomy results in five models of university-donor interaction. Each one of these models aims to obtain a certain type of funding from a particular kind of donor/collaborator and therefore, their implementation requires appropriate (but perhaps differentiated) resources and level of experience. The five models of university-donor interaction are the following:

1. 'Alumni' model which targets small donations from alumni.
2. 'Major Gift' model which is based on the search for major donors.
3. 'Foundation Research' model which is aimed at raising funds for specific research projects.
4. 'Corporation' model which aims to raise philanthropic funds from Major Corporations and Foundations: goals will be shared in common with the university.
5. 'Multi-mode' model which combines the 'Foundation Research' model and the 'Corporation' model.

Given that these five university fundraising models are related to different types of philanthropy and sources of private funds, we propose to classify them as follows:

- 'Alumni' model and 'Major Gift' model are those concerning 'pure' philanthropy and patronage relating to 'friend-raising' activity and university outreach: these are models of university-donor interaction based on informal and/or personal relationships.
- 'Foundation Research', 'Corporation' and 'Multi-mode' models are those relating to the establishment of partnership and sponsorship: these are ultimately models of university-donor interaction based on professional relationships.

Before starting the fundraising activity each HEI must identify which fundraising strategy is the most likely to be successful in their case. Thus, the university leaders and managers with the help of their stakeholders must opt for a specific university fundraising model depending on the characteristics and experience of the university in this field. However, even if for a beginner HEI it is essential to focus its efforts and resources in a single strategy, it is difficult to find cases of universities that have implemented only one of the above-mentioned models because as they increase and consolidate their expertise they tend to address additional fundraising strategies. In other words, universities must invest the timing and the resources dedicated to each model depending on the consolidation stage of their fundraising effort.

But what are the key factors when it comes to deciding which model to choose? That is to say, what would be the best combination of: i) university type; ii) model of university-donor interaction (philanthropy or professional relationships); and iii) fundraising strategy? Below we attempt to answer this question through the analysis of specific examples in Europe:

1. 'Alumni' model: this strategy would be suitable for a small size comprehensive university with its activity focused mainly on teaching and local/regional development. This type of university is often characterized by its strong relationship with students and alumni, making feasible a continuous collection of small donations (voluntary giving) from a large pool of donors assembled through alumni relations fundraising offices or units (Pérez-Esparrells and Torre, 2012a).

For instance: the Università Commerciale Luigi Bocconi in Italy, the Université Catholique de Louvain in Belgium or the University of Navarra (UNAV) in Spain display the characteristics required for this strategy.

2. 'Major Gift' model: larger universities than the above-mentioned are more suitable for the implementation of this strategy in which university leaders must be very active in the creation and maintenance of extensive contacts with wealthy alumni and other potential major donors.

This fundraising strategy is the most common one in the US. In the European case, there are a few examples of universities that have implemented projects funded by major donors. Various examples are found in Germany: Hamburg University (€35 million for the 'Wing Building' project); International University Bremen (SFR 10 million for the 'Jacobs Center of Lifelong Learning' project); Heidelberg University (€13.8 million for building a children's hospital); and Postdam University (more than €50 million for the 'Hasso-Plattner Institute for Software Systems Technology').

3. 'Foundation Research' model: research universities have the potential to address this strategy as they have large groups of individual researchers and professors to apply for grants from research funding bodies.

Several first-class examples of universities with experience of this fundraising strategy are: The Imperial College of Science, Technology and Medicine in the UK; Pierre and Marie Curie University (Paris 6) in France; the University of Zurich in Switzerland; Leiden University, Utrecht University and the Rijksuniversiteit Groningen in the Netherlands.

4. 'Corporation' model: technical universities are well positioned to tackle this fundraising strategy because they already have strong links with enterprises and companies, thanks to their dynamic transfer of knowledge and innovation.

The Chalmers University of Technology in Sweden, the Eidgenössische Technische Hochschule (ETH) Zürich in Switzerland, the Technische Universität Munich in Germany or Delft University of Technology would be good case studies of the implementation of the 'Corporation' model.

5. 'Multi-mode' model: this strategy is very characteristic of world-class universities which are ranked among the top-100 in global rankings and have comprehensive experience in the fundraising field.

Well-known examples of European HEIs that have developed this multi-mode strategy are the University of Cambridge and the University of Oxford in UK.

## The Challenge of Fundraising in European Universities

European universities are undergoing an important process of change to adapt their structures to the new context posed by globalization and the knowledge-based economy. In 2006, the European Commission (COM (2006)/208 final) stated that European universities, over-controlled by governments and weakly funded, are unable to achieve their academic and scientific potential in this environment of growing international competition. Furthermore, in 2011 the European Commission affirmed that European HEIs need to create effective governance and funding mechanisms in support of excellence (COM (2011)/ 1063 final).

As shown by the European University Association (EUA, 2011), European universities are immersed in a context characterized by: (i) decreasing state core funding in relation to universities' total resources; (ii) public funding models based on performance indicators; (iii) greater autonomy of universities in academic and management issues; (iv) and a higher level of accountability. Regarding the education expenditure, the data offered by the OECD (2012) show that on average in 2009 more than 78 per cent of the income of twenty-one European universities came from public resources and in recent years its total amount decreased slowly. Moreover, state funding is often linked to governments' strategies which can be very different from those of the universities.

In this context, European HEIs are in a critical situation, because they cannot rely upon the necessary funding for overall development as world-class universities. Therefore, European universities need to reduce their dependency on public funds by implementing a funding strategy encompassing different private income streams, providing supplementary funds for educational and research purposes and therefore enhancing excellence. In a 'virtuous circle', this leads to greater possibilities of raising funds (Pérez-Esparrells and Torre, 2012b) and is strongly related to internal and external communication strategy.

European universities are continuing the diversification of their additional sources of income. The data from a survey conducted by the EUA in 2011 showed the continuing increase of private income streams in European universities: student contributions, contracts with business sector, philanthropic funding and service-related income. These four variables constitute a growing trend according to the experts and leaders of more than 150 European institutions from twenty-seven countries polled. Moreover, Estermann (2012) pointed out the positive evolution of income streams from non-state funding and funds through alumni donations. Charities and foundations will also increase in the next few years along with contracts from the business sector (Table 12.1).

Table 12.1 Expectations of Income Streams Evolution in European Universities
Source: Estermann (2012).

| Public Funding (state funding) | Expected increase (%) |
|---|---|
| Teaching: national public funding | 43.04% |
| Infrastructures facilities: national public funding | 30.77% |
| Research: national public funding | 28.57% |
| Teaching: regional public funding | 26.53% |
| Infrastructures facilities: regional public funding | 18.18% |
| Research: regional public funding | 16.36% |

| Other funding (non-state funding) | Expected increase (%) |
|---|---|
| EU funds | 74.07% |
| Alumni donations | 67.31% |
| Contracts with business sector | 65.00% |
| International fees | 62.82% |
| Continuing/adult education | 61.25% |
| Charities/Foundations | 56.92% |

Mora and Nugent (1998) highlighted several difficulties for the increase of fundraising in Europe: *lack of tax incentives*, so that in some countries the laws do not concede to the universities the right to maintain their own property. Donations in these cases are converted into gifts to the State and not to the institution; the *philanthropic spirit* is much less pronounced in Europe than in the US; *universities are insufficiently differentiated*: most European universities do not make great efforts to distinguish themselves from each other; students are not encouraged to identify with their own institution. European universities do not treat students as clients to the same extent as those in the US; *little attention is paid to graduates and alumni* who are a key part of the philanthropic process; there is a *lack of institutional fundraising and development offices*; an *atmosphere of academic distrust* prevails towards business and industry and towards the provision of services to society in general; and finally, there is a lack of *organized university sports*.

These factors go far to explain why sponsored fundraising nowadays makes up such a small component of European universities' income structure. According to the EUA (2011), it typically amounts between 3 per cent and 4 per cent of the total university income though with noticeable exceptions. These exist mainly in the UK where some universities generate close to 10 per cent of their budget through philanthropic sources: in some HEIs such as Oxford and Cambridge this rises to over a quarter.

In other words, the fundraising sector has significant potential as a supplementary income stream for universities that has not yet been exploited (The Ross Group and CASE, 2012): some European universities are trying to raise funds from philanthropic sources (foundations, trusts, charities, non-profit organizations, corporate and individual donors, alumni) but with modest results. This is often due to the fact that in order to exploit this potential in terms of funds raised and the return on investment achieved, each HEI needs to design and establish its own long term fundraising strategy. However, this is not necessarily considered as part of the institutional strategy and many HEIs lack a professional fundraising unit or a development office. As Casani, Pérez-Esparrells and Rodriguez-Pomeda (2010) stated, European HEIs need more benchmarks in this domain due to the diversity of legal, institutional, historical, cultural and economic contexts in European countries.

## A University Fundraising Theoretical Model Based on the Case Studies of the University of Cambridge and the University of Navarra

'Good practice' could be defined as case study examples of processes or methodologies that are believed to be more effective at achieving a specific objective (in this case, university fundraising in European HEIs) than any other, and are therefore recommended as a model. Given the eight difficulties identified by Gines-Mora (1998), European HEIs still encounter barriers in implementing a fundraising system, and good practice could shed light on how to address these problems within the sector. Therefore, in this chapter we derive a fundraising theoretical model from the analysis of successful fundraising strategies in two universities that belong to different leagues of excellence in the global HEI sector (top and lower ranking HEIs). In this way, we aim to provide knowledge based on accumulated experience that can be applied by a wide range of universities from diverse backgrounds.

In Europe, it is in the United Kingdom where universities have wider experience in the fundraising field: standing out from others is the University of Cambridge which is usually listed at the very top of global rankings. In fact, in this century it has held the first position among universities from UK and Europe. We choose the University of Cambridge as a case study of a public university in order to analyse how top universities in Europe develop their fundraising strategy: in so doing, we aim to identify those key factors and variables which can be transferred to other European research universities.

The University of Cambridge consists of a 'holding' comprising the following: the university institution (University of Cambridge), thirty-one colleges, the Cambridge Alumni Relations Office (CARO), the alumni office of each one of the thirty-one colleges, the alumni organization 'Cambridge in America', 419 alumni groups throughout 101 countries, and other institutions (e.g. museums, collections, libraries) and foundations (Cambridge University Alumni Relations Office, 2011). The base line of the University of Cambridge is very different from that of any average European university: firstly, because of its international nature; secondly, because of its position in the global rankings and its internationally renowned academic prestige; thirdly, because it is located in one of the European countries with a reasonably well developed philanthropic culture; fourthly, because of its wide experience in the fundraising field; and finally, because of its size.

Broadly speaking, private universities in Europe have some experience in raising funds from private income streams, among them philanthropic funds. In the particular case of Spain, the University of Navarra is linked to the church (therefore, this university is a non-profit institution), and despite not being listed among the first positions in global rankings, it is strongly active in this kind of funding. In fact, the University of Navarra is one of the most prestigious private universities in Spain. It is a very particular case study because of its link with the Business School of IESE (Instituto de Estudios Superiores de la Empresa – which is well positioned in the relevant Business School rankings); moreover, its religious characteristics crucially affect student satisfaction and its relation to stakeholders. In Spain universities have certainly less fundraising experience than in UK; nevertheless, this singular case is an exception and it provides some examples which could be imitated by other medium or small universities.

Despite the different base lines of the University of Cambridge and the University of Navarra, they apply a range of common best practices in fundraising activity (see Pérez-Esparrells and Torre, 2012a: 62–63). After a further analysis of these best practices we propose to condense them into a common code: a first group of intrinsic variables, such as inherent culture and values, a strong sense of belonging to the community, a significant level of internationalization and social outreach; and a second group of communication and marketing variables, for instance, commitment of the institutional leaders to fundraising activities, specific fundraising campaigns, recognition of donors, alumni relations, advertising of tax relief and exemption, etc. There is a possible link between the institutional behaviour and HEIs characteristics as independent variables, impacting on external non-state funding as a dependent variable.

Although no empirical analysis has been made to establish causal relationships underlying all these variables, the fact that these case studies belong to such different institutional backgrounds confers consistency upon our proposed theoretical model which presents the following factors for a hypothetical university:

1. It is necessary that the university creates a brand linked to its image (differentiation, long term goals, outreach, etc.) and a relationship with its social and economic environment and with its students, so that they subsequently become alumni proud of belonging to their alma mater.
2. It is required that the university establishes a professional organization of the fundraising activity co-ordinated by senior management through a fundraising unit (or a development office).
3. The university needs to strengthen its communication actions and to request the involvement in those actions of institutional leadership and the entire university community.

There are also key differences in the fundraising activity carried out by the University of Cambridge and the University of Navarra, the most important being the following. In the first place, while the University of Cambridge fundraising activity from philanthropic sources is highly decentralized and managed by several bodies (a development office of the whole University of Cambridge called CUDO and another development office in each college and other smaller structures), in the University of Navarra this activity is carried out by three organizations. In the second place philanthropic funds raised by the University of Cambridge are meant to finance many kinds of projects such as facilities, research grants, innovative educational initiatives etc., but in the University of Navarra philanthropic funds are meant to finance mainly one type of project (educational and research grants) plus the communication activity of the fundraising units. In its fundraising alumni organization, approximately 56 per cent of the funds raised annually are assigned to educational grants and about 38 per cent are allocated to publishing its magazine (Alumni Universidad de Navarra, 2012). In the third place the University of Cambridge considers a wider range of incentives (such as payroll giving) because the philanthropic system is highly developed in UK.

These three differences are remarkable because we can observe how the centralization or decentralization of fundraising strategies, the diversity or concentration of the activities for raising funds and the type of incentives can have a major influence on the results of the model. In fact, there is a big gap between the two HEIs in the amount raised from philanthropic sources: the University of Cambridge raised £135 million in 2010/2011 (University of Cambridge, 2012); whereas the University of Navarra alumni organization raised approximately €2.7 million in the same academic year. Actually, the results gained by both universities are not comparable, firstly, because the HEIs belong to two different categories: on the one hand the University of Cambridge is a world class 'multinational' institution, while the UNAV is located in a Southern-Mediterranean country and presents a 'domestic' perspective; and, secondly, because of the different size of their total budgets.

## Measures to Foster University Fundraising in European Public Universities

Getting started with fundraising is often the hardest job of all and it requires the investment of considerable time and resources before results are visible. Arguably, most European public universities have no experience in the field, with a few well-known exceptions, and the universities that *have* been pioneers in philanthropy often had to overcome internal resistance, sometimes at the highest level of leadership inside their institutions. A minimum period of two or three years seems to be required, together with appropriate financial and human support, for a fundraising unit to operate properly. In this context, external professional help is very important to boost gifts, grants and other types of donations.

A key point to raising funds from philanthropic sources is to involve the main stakeholders in the university fundraising activity. As shown in Table 12.2, a successful fundraising model needs the university to differentiate itself. HEIs need to be in touch with their external stakeholders, partners, collaborators, sponsors and main donors: alumni, foundations and third sector bodies. Moreover, HEIs must communicate their requests for funds through a range of actions in which the main internal stakeholders are involved.

From the various reports by expert groups analysed previously and from the case studies (University of Cambridge and University of Navarra), we have identified a set of basic actions for implementing the suggested fundraising model in less experienced universities. These actions are classified into two categories: on the one hand, actions implemented by governments and universities aimed at encouraging voluntary action by fostering a social 'culture of giving' through the recommendations from Table 12.3; and on the other hand, actions helping universities to become 'asking' institutions by instilling in their community a 'culture of asking' through the measures adumbrated in Table 12.4.

Table 12.2 Main Higher Education Stakeholders in European Universities and their Function in a Fundraising Strategy
*Note.* Authors' elaboration.

| Type of stakeholder | Stakeholders | Function/Role |
|---|---|---|
| Internal Stakeholders | Faculty and research staff | Fundraisers |
| | HEI's leaders: President, Vice-Chancellor, senior administrators or Rector and Vice-rectors, etc. | Fundraisers<br>Strategic leadership |
| External Stakeholders | Alumni (individuals and organizations), students and other friends | Donors |
| | Central (Federal) Government | Provider of a institutional/legal frame in favour of university fundraising |
| | Regional and Local Governments | Provider of a institutional/legal frame in favour of university fundraising |
| | Research Councils | Partners, collaborators, sponsors and project funders |
| | Patent Offices | Partners, collaborators, sponsors and project funders |
| | Technology centres and Scientific and technological parks | Partners, collaborators, sponsors and project funders |
| | Corporate co-sponsors of research | Partners, collaborators and sponsors |
| | Alliances and consortia | Partners and collaborators |
| | Third sector (foundations, church sponsors, etc.) | Donors |

Table 12.3 First Steps in Promoting University Fundraising: Instilling a 'Culture of Giving'
*Note.* Authors' elaboration.

<table>
<tr><th rowspan="2">Measures from the government</th><th colspan="2">Measures from the university</th></tr>
<tr><th>General measures</th><th>Communication, marketing and public relations strategy: involving alumni and other stakeholders</th></tr>
<tr><td rowspan="2">To take into account fundraising in the agenda for HE funding of the different government levels</td><td rowspan="2">To promote the valorization of knowledge transfer and sharing with society</td><td>Internal and external communication of the university's overall strategy</td></tr>
<tr><td>Internal and external communication of the university's social function/role (outreach or community service)</td></tr>
<tr><td>To reinforce tax incentives for voluntary giving</td><td rowspan="4">To achieve greater involvement of European universities in the (local) environment</td><td>To foster greater differentiation and specialization rewarding the areas of excellence of the institution</td></tr>
<tr><td>To enrol more countries in TGE (Transnational Giving Europe)</td><td>To strengthen alumni's university loyalty and to acknowledge the value that they add to the institution</td></tr>
<tr><td>To establish matched funding schemes</td><td rowspan="2">To build an atmosphere of trust towards university management: transparency and accountability</td></tr>
<tr><td>To promote social awareness of philanthropy (and particularly towards universities)</td></tr>
</table>

As shown in Table 12.3, in order to instil an effective 'culture of giving' within society, European governments and institutions must join forces and work together. On the one hand, European governments ought to underpin their policy work on university fundraising, reinforcing tax incentives for voluntary giving, specifically for those donations directed to universities, as well as simplifying the tax relief claiming system. Moreover, it is also advisable to review what kind of donations benefit from these tax reliefs: for example in Spain, Italy, or other Mediterranean countries, legacies and endowments are not considered.

The tax relief for donations to charitable entities (including universities) applied to the corporate tax is up to 100 per cent in Germany, Great Britain, Luxemburg, Austria, Romania or Hungary, but it is up to 60 per cent in France, 41 per cent in Ireland, 35 per cent in Spain and 12 per cent in Portugal. Furthermore, only in Germany, France and Ireland do individual donors get greater tax relief (applied to the income tax) than corporations (Camps, 2010). Nonetheless, a few exceptions can be found. For instance, compared with other European countries, the UK boasts generous tax incentives for a wide range of gifts, although the system in place is complex and it constitutes a barrier for the small number of wealthy individuals who provide a disproportionate number of donations (Task Force Report to Government, 2004).

Furthermore, the current disparities in tax treatment of donations directed to national or international institutions within Europe are hindering European international philanthropic giving. This is why we consider that enrolment in Transnational Giving Europe (TGE) of those countries that currently are not members will foster international gifts among the European countries. This 'allows donors who are taxpayers in one of the fifteen countries affiliated to TGE, to donate to foreign institutions from countries also belonging to TGE, without sacrificing the tax benefits in their country of tax contribution' (Pérez-Esparrells and Torre, 2012a). The fifteen countries affiliated to TGE are as follows: Belgium, Bulgaria, France, Germany, Hungary, Ireland, Italy, Luxembourg, the Netherlands, Poland, Romania, Slovakia, Slovenia, Switzerland and the UK.

It is also advisable that European Governments establish matched funding schemes to pump-prime the initial investment required to establish professional fundraising offices or development offices (Task Force Report to Government 2004). As a strong case in favour of this proposed measure, the results of the *England Matched Funding Scheme for Voluntary Giving 2008–2011* have shown a general and significant improvement of the fundraising sector outcomes despite the economic recession. Moreover, the benefits of this scheme are expected to be effective for many years to come because they promote the spirit of an 'asking' culture across HEIs and a 'giving' (to HEIs) culture among donors (The Ross Group and CASE, 2012).

On the other hand, universities themselves also are responsible for creating a 'culture of giving'. The measures proposed in Table 12.3 are strongly related to the theoretical model for university fundraising previously proposed in this chapter. In this regard, HEIs must communicate to their stakeholders why it is worth making voluntary donations to them and making their students subsequently donors as proud alumni of their alma mater. In fact, a campaign of communication, marketing and public relations aimed at their internal and external stakeholders must also be implemented in order to increase the social prestige of HEIs by communicating the university's strengths (differentiation and diversification) and its social role (outreach or community service), as well as the transfer of knowledge. As is well known, the most prestigious universities all over the world raise the majority of the private funds for philanthropic funding.

In relation to the particular case of alumni, it is necessary to create among them a 'feeling of belonging' to the institution and to maintain a relationship with them through regular communications, events and services that appeal to their interest. This will help to build and preserve student and alumni loyalty, so that generations of alumni can learn to expect and welcome contact from their universities.

As in Table 12.3, most of the measures proposed in Table 12.4 derive from the theoretical model for university fundraising previously proposed in this chapter. As stated in Table 12.4, since the fundraising effort must be linked to a strategic plan, and must be aimed at achieving the long term goals of the university, creating a successful asking institution needs committed and involved institutional leadership. A successful fundraising strategy requires the allocation of resources and the devotion of academic leaders' time for its design and implementation. Taking responsibility for the realization of the tasks identified in the Expert Group Report (2007) means that they must create a compelling vision, manage the academic priority-setting process, articulate and interpret the case for support, identify prospects, facilitate faculty development partnerships, maintain and advance relationships, and do the asking.

Table 12.4 First Steps in Promoting University Fundraising: Creating an 'Asking Institution'
*Note.* Authors' elaboration

| Strategic measures | Measures from the university: communication, marketing and public relations strategy | |
|---|---|---|
| To involve academic leaders and the entire university community in the university fundraising strategy/activities | All stakeholders | Proactively to strengthen university-alumni/stakeholder relationships |
| | | To maintain regular contact with stakeholders and alumni (long term professional/collaborative relations) |
| To include the fundraising field in the funding strategy of the university | | To promote quantitative and qualitative collaboration between stakeholders and the university |
| To define carefully the timing of every step in the fundraising strategy | | To make it easy and attractive to donate by answering donors' doubts, offering legal advice and tax incentives information |
| | | To recognize and thank donors publicly |
| To professionalize the fundraising activity: fundraising unit/ development office and to ask for professional help when needed | Internal stakeholders | To create (within the university) a culture of the need for educational and research philanthropy |
| | | To promote faculty and other university staff commitment to the fundraising programme |
| | | To build a trust atmosphere towards fundraising programmes and the business world |
| To make it attractive to donate: to develop smart, creative projects | Students and alumni | To collaborate with the alumni organization(s) |
| | | To infuse students and alumni with university values and purposes |
| To allow donatation of restricted and unrestricted funds | | To establish personal and professional relations with students and alumni |
| | | To ask for annual giving |
| | | To ask for operating funds |
| To allocate donations through a Foundation of the university, in order to make donations eligible for as many tax benefits as possible | | To create an up-to-date alumni database |
| | External stakeholders | To collaborate with the university foundation(s) and the companies/organizations related to this/these foundation(s) |
| | | To coordinate the communication strategy of the different university institutions |
| | | To strengthen university relations with companies/organizations participating in lifelong learning programmes |

The fundraising activity must be coordinated by a professional, well-run fundraising unit (or a development office), which should report directly to the academic head of the HEI and operate in a collaborative way with faculties (or Schools), departments and centres, as well as bodies incorporated within the university, such as Foundations and Alumni organizations. The establishment and running of this unit will also improve 'career development opportunities and will lead, over time, to more Development Directors in smaller scale operations having had mid-level experience in a large scale office' (The Ross Group and CASE, 2012).

Supporters' first donations are often small, and can increase over time as a result of a higher involvement in the future of the institution. HEIs need to remain in regular contact with their stakeholders throughout their lives so an environment where asking for donations from them is expected and does not come as a surprise. Furthermore, when possible, HEIs must promote the establishment of long term formal and informal professional relations and other kinds of collaboration with external stakeholders (e.g. volunteerism or counselling): they must foster leaders willing to consider stakeholders' interests and needs.

In other words, HEIs must communicate their requests for funds through a range of actions in which the whole university community is involved. In order to ask effectively, it is necessary to develop attractive, creative projects for educational and research purposes, and to provide information about benefits from the gifts and about the main goals of the university: this is intended to catch donors' interest and increase their willingness to offer support either for general or specific purposes. It is crucial to make it easy and appealing to donate. Donors' doubts must be addressed, offering legal advice and providing information about existing tax benefits applying to donations. It is also essential to acknowledge publicly the importance of all the various stakeholders to the success of the institution, and all private voluntary financial contributions regardless of their amounts. In the case of major donors and sponsors of the university, different means of public recognition should be established, respecting those who wish to remain anonymous.

A university-alumni relations programme has further benefits beyond its impact in fundraising outcomes. As pointed out by the Ross Group

Editorial Board, it also contributes in '[...] many different areas such as marketing (especially for postgraduate programmes), enhancing employability (e.g. alumni helping with placements and work experience) and the student experience (for example through alumni mentoring)' (The Ross Group and CASE, 2012).

These individuals can be segmented by different interests, age and location, for which a comprehensive alumni database is needed. Since the number of alumni varies annually (new and deceased graduates) and since alumni can become 'lost' (e.g. by moving house without informing the university) and then be 'found' again (The Ross Group and CASE, 2012), an effective management of an alumni database requires periodical updating of the number of addressable alumni and their characteristics. An alumni organization could be the agent to reach all the students of the university, asking them annually for small amounts of money in order to support the long term purposes of the institution, as well as identifying prospective major donors among them for the future.

In getting started, external help is very important, either in the case of colleagues or in the case of professional consultants. They can assist: at the beginning of the fundraising process by doing market testing and looking at internal university structures; in the middle of the process by conducting or outsourcing research to identify donors and by helping to train university staff; and at the end by reviewing the whole process (Expert Group Report, 2007).

Finally, to implement all these initiatives and suggestions and to achieve the success on fundraising and income diversification, European universities need to modernize by introducing more progress on governance and autonomy reforms; promoting specialization and stratification of the institutions; enhancing their reputation with more transparency and accountability; boosting international excellence with ambition and realism; attracting talent and strongly reinforcing mobility of staff and students; fostering applied research and transfer of knowledge; and increasing the university-enterprise collaboration for a greater involvement of European universities in economic, social and environmental issues.

## Conclusions

The 2008 global financial crisis has had important funding policy implications for public universities. Most European institutions have suffered a decline in their university budgets in line with the reduction of universities' state funding; but only minor success has been achieved in finding alternative funding, especially from philanthropic sources. Nevertheless, the funding implications of the financial crisis also have strategic implications for universities in the sense of a better balance of sources of control of public European universities (governments vs other external stakeholders such as non-governmental organizations, corporations and individuals): that is to say, this search for greater financial autonomy of universities vis-à-vis governments tips the scale in favour of external stakeholders in the decision making field, becoming less 'public sector-driven' and more 'market-driven'.

But who should start promoting the university fundraising field in European countries? Is it a system-level response or an institutional-level response? We hold the view that both answers are right because a system-level response and an institutional-level response would be complementary. A successful fundraising strategy is not only incumbent upon European HEIs, it is also the business of governments since the existence of public measures supporting university fundraising is essential. As pointed out by the Report of an Expert Group about fundraising by universities from philanthropic sources (Task Force Report to Government, 2004), '*what we need from government is not only tax breaks to donors but also, and maybe even more importantly, the freedom for universities to set their strategies, to recruit the best talents, to design the best programmes and to compete against their counterparts worldwide*.' To do so, European universities need better governance, more autonomy and more incentives in various areas: academic (concerning curricula, programmes, research, etc.); financial (diversification of university income streams, including fundraising); organizational (structure of the university); and staffing (responsibility for recruitment, salaries, etc.).

Initiatives in several European countries represent an important move toward greater government steering of HE systems, fostering university-level responses such as Collaborations, Alliances and Mergers (CAMs) in order to encourage co-operation and economies of scale: this should increase the size and international visibility of European HEIs, thereby fostering a narrow selection of prestigious national universities in some countries (Germany, France and Spain). The universities that took part in the national university excellence programmes and obtained the award got an official hallmark of excellence from the government that endorsed their 'brand' or image and was a signal for the differentiation of those HEIs: this could be a key factor in successful fundraising. Specifically, the universities that were able to get this official hallmark have been able to launch campaigns to recruit talented national and international PhD students and researchers.

Regarding the institutional-level response perspective, most CAMs in Europe are based on public and private funds, and may be the solution for small or middle European HEIs which collaborate, ally or merge with a larger and better positioned university (market-driven) and therefore increase their visibility. There are various examples of European mergers such as: the University of Manchester (UK) and UMIST; Paris Sciences et Lettres (PSL) and the Université de Strasbourg (which reunited three institutions of this area again in 2012); and alliances such as: Limerick Institute of Technology and Tipperary Institute (Ireland), Université de Lausanne and École Polytechnique Fédérale de Lausanne (France) or Universidad Autónoma de Madrid and Centro Superior de Investigaciones Científicas (Spain). Despite these changes and movements to create synergies, in fact, there is a general dearth of European experience on university fundraising in these new mergers and alliances.

Given this background, the next questions to address are the following ones: will these efforts be sufficient to place the above mentioned universities among the Top-20? And what really distinguishes a university located towards the top of the international rankings (e.g. the *Academic Ranking of World Universities* (ARWU)) from other HEIs? A rough analysis of world-class universities shows that the few European universities in the Top-20 international rankings are multinational 'enterprises' demonstrating a broad research intensive activity, and they have a successful institutionally-embedded fundraising strategy: this last characteristic being the one that most European universities and HE systems *lack*.

To sum up, fundraising can be a clear institutional tool to motivate European HEIs to imitate the Top-20 universities or even the Top-50 universities. An enormous cultural change is needed before European universities even begin to approach the might of prestigious US universities or some 'elite' European universities ('Oxbridge') in raising funds from non-state sources.

In a context of increasingly scarce public funding, European HEIs must ensure academic robustness and world-class research through their long term funding and fundraising strategies. A diversification of the universities' income streams to accrue private funds through a more market-driven approach is also an incentive to foster their activities in a competitive world. This will lead to greater university resilience and sustainability in the long term. A new HE social contract is emerging in Europe based on being more competent both in 'asking' and 'giving'. This new culture of social exchange may impact on institutional resilience in due course. However, the revised social contract needs to be legitimated by all HE stakeholders if it is to be institutionalized and normalized. This will require an increased momentum of social learning from all related groups.

## Acknowledgements

We acknowledge the helpful recommendations of Rosalind M.O. Pritchard and Jan Erik Karlsen. We are also grateful to other colleagues of the 34th Annual EAIR Forum who provided useful comments on earlier drafts of this chapter. Obviously, all errors and opinions are our own.

# References

Alumni Universidad de Navarra (2012). Alumni en Cifras. Pamplona: Universidad de Navarra. <http://www.unav.es/alumni/acerca/encifras.html> accessed 27 April 2013.

Cambridge University Alumni Relations Office (2011). Alumni Worldwide Directory 2011 – 2012. Cambridge: University of Cambridge. <http://www.alumni.cam.ac.uk/groups/AWD_2011_web.pdf> accessed 27 April 2013.

Camps, D. (2010). 'Mecenazgo y Fiscalidad aplicada a la Cultura. Desafíos en el Contexto de la Crisis', revista *Opera Actual*, September, 133.

Casani, F., Pérez-Esparrells, C., and Rodríguez-Pomeda, J. (2010). 'Nuevas Estrategias Económicas en la Universidad desde la Responsabilidad Social', *Revista Calidad en la Educación* 33, December, 255–273.

Estermann, T. (2012). European Funding Programmes and the Financial Sustainability of Universities, EUA Funding Forum, Salzburg, June 2012, <http://www.eua.be/Libraries/Funding_Forum/Thomas_ESTERMANN.sflb.ashx> accessed 27 April 2013.

Estermann, T., and Bennetot Pruvot, E.B. (2011). Financially Sustainable Universities II, European Universities diversifying Income Streams. Brussels: European University Association. <http://www.eua.be/Pubs/Financially_Sustainable_Universities_II.pdf> accessed 27 April 2013.

European Commission (2007). Engaging Philanthropy for University Research. Luxembourg: Office for Official Publications of the European Communities. <http://ec.europa.eu/invest-in-research/pdf/download_en/rapport2007_final.pdf> accessed 27 April 2013.

European Commission COM (2006). 208 final. Delivering on the Modernisation Agenda for Universities: Education, Research and Innovation. Brussels: Commission of the European Communities. <http://ec.europa.eu/euraxess/pdf/COM(2006)_208.pdf> accessed 27 April 2013.

European Commission COM (2011). 1063 final. Supporting Growth and Jobs – an Agenda for the Modernisation of Europe's Higher Education Systems. Brussels: European Commission. <http://ec.europa.eu/education/higher-education/doc/com0911_en.pdf> accessed 27 April 2013.

Mora, J-G., and Nugent, M. (1998). 'Seeking New Resources for European Universities: the example of Fundraising in the U.S.', *European Journal of Education*, 33 (1), 113–129.

OECD (2012). *Education at a Glance 2012: OECD Indicators*, Paris: OECD Publishing <http://www.oecd.org/edu/EAG%202012_e-book_EN_200912.pdf>, <http://dx.doi.org/10.1787/eag-2012-en> accessed 27 April 2013.

Pérez-Esparrells, C., and Torre, E.M. (2012a). 'The Challenge of Fundraising in Universities in Europe', *International Journal of Higher Education*, 1 (2), 55–66, <http://dx.doi.org/10.5430/ijhe.v1n2p55> accessed 27 April 2013.

Pérez-Esparrells, C., and Torre, E.M. (2012b). *El Fundraising como una Herramienta complementaria de Financiación Pública de las Universidades Españolas*. Proceedings of XXI Meeting of the Economics of Education Association. Oporto: Portugal.

Task Force Report to Government (2004). *Increasing Voluntary Giving to Higher Education*. UK: Department for Education and Skills. <http://www.bis.gov.uk/assets/biscore/corporate/migratedd/publications/i/increasingvoluntarygivingreport.pdf> accessed 27 April 2013.

The Ross Group and CASE (2012). Ross-CASE Survey Report. London: National Centre for Social Research. <http://www.natcen.ac.uk/rosscasesurvey/findings.html> accessed 27 April 2013.

University of Cambridge (2012). The Cambridge 800th Anniversary Campaign Report 2010–2011.Cambridge: University of Cambridge <http://www.campaign.cam.ac.uk/news/Campaign_Report_10–11.pdf> accessed 27 April 2013.

JAN ERIK KARLSEN

# 13 Backcasting European University Governance 2042+[1]

## Introduction

It is a common vision that the modern society of tomorrow will be 'learning intensive' (Miller, 2006; OECD, 2008; Karlsen and Øverland, 2012). Knowledge, seen as research, innovation and education, will be the lever for both upheaval and progress. However, the thoughts, ideas and images of how this vision will be accomplished differ. Today's images of tomorrow face the constraints of language and uncertainty. Do we presently have the ideas and concepts that will describe the major critical challenges of the role and functions of higher education institutions? We obviously do not know the facts of tomorrow. Our narratives of future universities and their models of governance will be rooted in the present, flavoured by our expectations, hopes and doubts that shape paths to a future. Besides, what are possible, probable, plausible and preferable images of the potential future knowledge society and the place of organized learning within it? In addition to discussing such alternative images of the future, we need to explain the paths that lead to them. So, we need to focus both on the future function of learning/knowledge and on the model of organization: how will the learning take place and what infrastructure will support it?

1 Many thanks to Erik F. Øverland (Freie Universität, Berlin) and Stig Selmer-Anderssen (University of Stavanger) who both assisted in the Future Workshop on which this chapter rests. The author served as instructor and principal moderator of the workshop and its preparatory stages.

This chapter produces an image of future university governance and adaptation, amply illustrated also in the preceding chapters. It presents the relationships between key factors influencing levels and characteristics of university governance policy, and builds on present evidence to identify plausible interventions. Finally the chapter analyses how future characteristics of shared governance might evolve and addresses future responses to such changes.

A point of departure has been to ask whether shared governance and the professional administrators in higher education will be any guarantee for institutional resilience in the longer term perspective. Will the relationship between faculty members and administrators still be contentious? Will there be a continuing expansion in number of administrators and their governance functions? Will there be structural and cultural conflicts – both manifest and latent – and a lack of research on university adaptation in the decades to come? What will be the role of students?

## Methodology and Data

The subsequent empirical material was produced by a class of twenty-five Master's students in a Foresight Management course at the University of Stavanger, Norway, during the Fall semester 2011.[2] They were performing a full day's 'Future Workshop' (Jungk and Müllert, 1987; Apel, 2004; Eickhoff and Geffers, 2006) addressing university governance in 2042+, with the intention of contributing to the experiential basis for this chapter.

2 The students were in their last year of the five year programme in Change Management, and their average age was about twenty-five.

### *Future Workshop*

Following Jungk and Müllert (1987), a Future Workshop has four phases which structured the 2042+ exercise:

1. *Preparation phase*: The method, its rules and the scheduled course of the workshop (in agreement with the participants) is introduced.
2. *Critique phase*: The problem is investigated critically and thoroughly. First of all, brainstorming is performed; then a general and critical question concerning the problem is framed.
3. *Fantasy phase*: All participants try to conceptualize a utopia, drawing an exaggerated picture of future possibilities.
4. *Implementation phase*: The ideas are checked and evaluated in regard to their practicability.

During the *preparation* phase the participants learned why and how such a Future Workshop would be part of their education in foresight management. In addition, prior to the workshop lectures were given and assignments were undertaken on appropriate aspects of foresight. Two background information texts on governance and university futures in 2050 and templates for backcasting and scenario building were issued in advance. The *critique* phase consisted of a lecture on the state-of-the-art of university governance. The present view of this field (e.g. Kehm and Lanzendorf, 2006; de Boer and File, 2009; Paradeise et al., 2009; de Boer et al., 2010; Young and Muller, 2010; Altbach and Salmi, 2011; Paradeise, 2012; Middlehurst and Teixceira, 2012; Amaral et al., 2012; Curaj et al., 2012; Gidley, 2012) was reviewed and applied as a hinterland to identify the broad range of factors that influence university adaptation in a long-term perspective (2042+). The subsequent *fantasy* phase applied creative tools (Paulus and Brown, 2003) and finally a discussion was conducted on events, trends and drivers that could impact on the *implementation* of decisions and outcomes of higher education institution policy.

Two common methods known and used in foresight studies are scenarios and visioning (van der Heijden, 1996; Karlsen and Karlsen 2013). Since forecasting is based on dominant trends this method is unlikely to generate solutions that presuppose the breaking of trends and step changes. Thus, this Future Workshop design was complemented by other foresight methods like brainstorming (Paulus and Brown, 2003) and backcasting (Höjer and Mattson, 2000). As a whole the workshop is a self-steered learning process, in which the visualization of images and change of foresight methods stimulate the process of producing shared knowledge (Karlsen and Karlsen, 2007. By use of foresight methods the workshop participants addressed the challenge of *describing* and *debating* various visions in which knowledge could pave the way to novel university adaptations (European Foresight, 2012).

## *The Qualitative Data*

The methodological idea was to elicit ideas about future university adaptation. The factual point of departure assumed a contemporary shared governance model in most European universities. The most important question to answer was: given that a vision of shared governance in 2042+ is deemed the preferred alternative, how did we arrive there from 2012? Also, when we look back from 2042+ to 2012, which forerunners of this future may be identified at the onset in 2012?

Prior to the workshop, the students had completed assignments about different aspects of foresight analysis; and identified drivers, timelines and significant players that were used as input to elaborate more fully-developed scenarios and storylines on the topic of university resilience and adaptation. Discussion and the exchange of experiences are the core elements of a Future Workshop. The discussions circle around portrayals of alternative futures. An assignment for the students was to deliver an image of the preferred future and a brief 'Vision 2042+'. To achieve this, variables that can have an impact on future higher education policy, for example economic adaptability, scientific progress, novel regulations, opinions and attitudes amongst people etc. were put together in the initial brainstorming exercise.

The students were updated on and discussed a series of challenges, drivers, actors and factors that could influence the European higher education policy scene during the time period from 2012 to 2042+. Such themes comprised global student mobility and study preferences, increased use of digital technologies which presumably will transform the delivery of and access to education, the democratization of and open access to knowledge, the harsh contest of market shares and funding, and the increasing integration and collaboration with both private industry and public sector. Such trends affect the role of universities both as originators, keepers and suppliers of knowledge and were assessed according to their probability and possible consequences or impacts. These aspects were considered to raise awareness that the future could go in very different directions and alert the workshop participants to the potential impact and wider implications of a variety of trends across the board. The different narratives allow users to ask questions, see connections and raise issues that might otherwise not get raised. They provide a context based on plausible outcomes, they are there to explore, not predict, those outcomes, and they aim to challenge current thinking and raise further questions.

In developing scenarios for governance and resilience of universities, relevant driving forces that can influence the situation until 2042+ were included. Drivers are forces in the extramural world that affect the universities, but like individual actors universities cannot easily affect or choose alternative pathways, at least not in the short term perspective. In the scenarios the participants seek the longer term uncertain forces. Arguably, they induce new ideas about the future. Thus they are in accordance with the driving forces that create room for interpretation. No one knows with certainty what the future will be, but everyone can imagine futures. Therefore imaging the uncertain and unthought-of opportunities and options is vital. In short, the participants look for the uncertain, but important and significant driving forces of the adaptation of universities. Thus, the Future Workshop created scenarios illustrating how universities and other higher education institutions in Europe could be organized and governed in 2042+, i.e. in a generation time perspective. One objective was to develop a fourfold scenario matrix, out of which the participants could select one single image or select aspects from all four sub-images as the preferred reference scenario. This would suffice as a basis for policy-building measures for the next generation of higher education institutions.

All points and ideas were recorded concurrently on a computer and shown on a large scale wall screen. During the creative phase the students elaborated a vision for universities in the designated period thirty years from now. As an introduction to this phase three moderators took on different roles, telling different stories about their images of university adaptation and governance. One moderator wore the hat of a high level administrator from the Ministry of Education and Science, another performed as a decision maker in the top management of a university, and the third wore the spectacles of the professors. In such a way, different stories highlighting different modes of reasoning and institutional logic were presented. Then the students were allocated to smaller groups, each dedicated to developing elaborate parts of the possible four-fold scenario matrix on their PCs. Finally, the ideas and images of future governance were checked and a four step backcasting procedure was followed to ensure the achievability of the ideal situational scenario. The bridge between a preferred future (in 2042+) and the perceived present (2012) university adaptation and governance had to be built by examples and action plan elements.

## Foresight as Frame of Reference

Foresight and Future Studies comprise projections or explorations of different potentials and alternatives, based on insights from today's knowledge and expectations of the future. Our perspective on how the future comes about will impact on the enactment of the future itself, as well as on what tools and methods we intend to use. Traditional scenario planning assumes that future is something to which we are reacting, emphasizing 'seeing' and predicting it. In addition, in a Futures Workshop we activate creative imagining and ideas of enactment, such that we may design our own image of the future. If we take for granted that we can plan to react to the future, we may also enact such changes as we prefer. However, action driven by reaction to a prescribed future tends to restrict our freedom of action and limits our opportunities. On the other hand, creative pro-action expands the alternatives (Tevis, 2010: 344). Of course, the potential of our power to create a future is an open ended question.

Foresight is providing a framework for us when trying to image a future of university adaptation. It supports visioning and debating pathways towards our preferred visions. Often foresight studies are open, participative and action oriented activities where participants 'think, debate and shape' their images of the future (EC, 2002). Such a methodology has both strengths and weaknesses. The strengths reside in its focus on how we may understand captivating and plausible probabilities, how various societies and actors anticipate developments and which performative role expectations are pursued; futures as temporal abstractions, narratives and discursive strategies become parts of a social reality. The basic model is depicted in Figure 13.1.

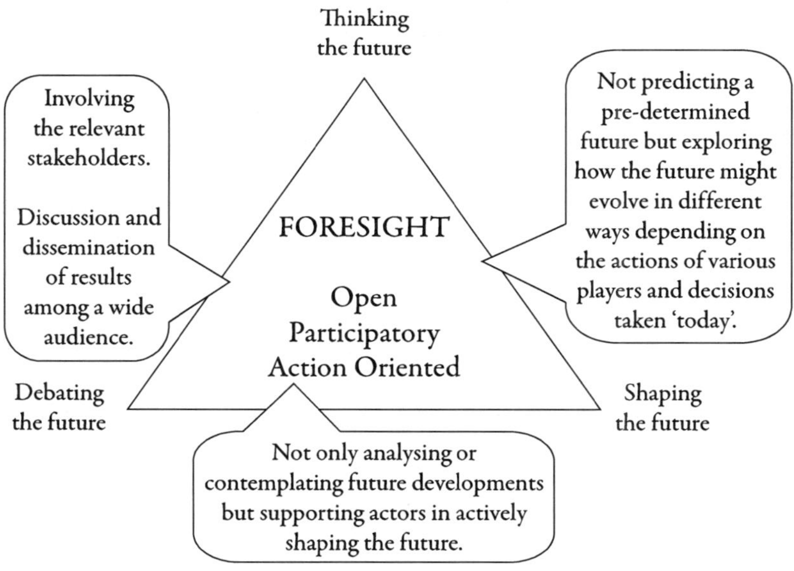


Figure 13.1 The 'Greek Triangle'
Source: Adapted from European Foresight (2012).

Fully fledged foresight exercises draw on the ideas of the 'Greek Triangle', connecting *anticipation* and prospective thoughts (logos), *action* and strategic will (ergo) and *appropriation* or collective mobilization (epithumia). The triangle needs a balance, i.e. it is not enough to think about the future, we need to discuss and share our images as well, and in the end we need to have the power and tools to shape the future. Anticipation may rely on input from domain experts, appropriation means that the stakeholders are vested and the participation is open, while action implies that the actors avoid indecision (Godet, 2006: 17). On the canvas of such triangular thinking, the participants of the Future Workshop set out to think creatively, debate openly and plan strategically the steps towards a preferred future of European higher education institutional governance.

## *Backcasting the Future*

The Future Workshop team decided to include backcasting as tools for the participants. Why backcasting? We are talking about future when we talk about the year 2042+, aren't we? Presumably, any group process where you have to think about the future is difficult. Such difficulties may arise from fear and lack of experience with forward-thinking (Cunha et al., 2006). 'Backmirror/retro analysis' helps us to deal with this fear by designing a new perspective that looks at the past instead of starting with the present. The method is therefore used mostly to carry out qualitative analysis of the thought of the past. Backcasting gives us thought, discussion and action related to normative and desirable scenarios. We create a common vision and need to check whether it is feasible, what implications it has, what potential bottlenecks might happen, and what choices of action we have along the way.

How shall we reach a preferable future? We may design *desirable scenarios* as a basis for strategic action, or we may undertake forecasting or backcasting exercises: all are clearly normative endeavours. Forecasting assumes a closed system, and has a conservative bias because it seeks to predict the future within the limits of existing institutions and patterns. Such forecasting belongs to the 'context of justification; it provides problem-solving within defined limits and terms. Backcasting is looking for possible breaches of invariance, i.e. step changes and other discernible deviations from the current pathways. Knowledge is a social and open process. Hence, we must pick up signals and solutions that can break the trend. Backcasting belongs to the 'context of discovery'; it provides problem structuring of open challenges.

Backcasting starts with defining a desired future and then works backwards to identify policies, programmes and initiatives that will connect the future with the present. It is a method where one imagines the future desired conditions, and where the steps required to achieve these conditions are described. Rather than taking steps that are only a prolongation of the current approach extrapolated into the future, backcasting begins with the end image in mind. Forecasting is ok if we are satisfied with how our organization performs now and want it to continue in this manner. When we need an image of a novel future, then we use backcasting. Possible pathways back to the present are developed, i.e. 'casting back' from the future having a particular time frame in mind. The term 'scenario' covers both the images of the future and the trajectory leading back to the present. The workshop participants applied all three principal ways of looking upon the connection between present and future(s) as depicted in Figure 13.2.

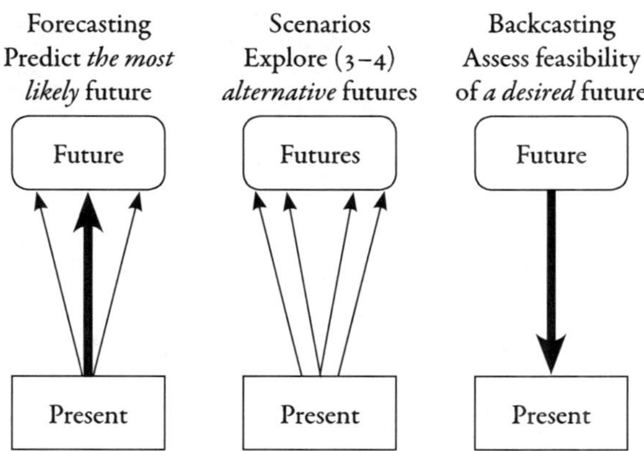


Figure 13.2 Principal Ways of Linking Present and Future

If we want to achieve a particular goal, what steps must we take to get there? This is also the fundamental question of planned organizational change. While forecasting attempts to predict the future based on current trends, backcasting discusses the future from the opposite direction of time (Robinson, 1990). This issue starts with a scenario image, where undesirable futures are discarded, and the desired future image is cultivated. We can use both a scenario cross (long term), a branch tree (medium term) or probability cone (short term) as a method for future pictures. Brainstorming and visioning are also good tools to use in this process.

The participants were asked to address the plausible steps to achieve the visionary situational scenario of 2042+, by applying the backcasting technique (Dreborg, 1996; Höjer and Mattsson, 2000; Karlsen and Øverland, 2010). The objective was to apply the preferred future as described in the situational scenario as a starting point, and then work backwards to identify major events and decisions that generated that image of the future, as depicted in Figure 13.3 below.

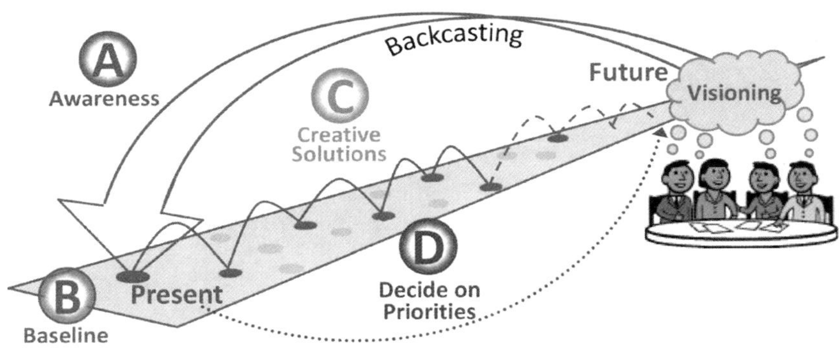


Figure 13.3 Backcasting the Vision 2042+
Source: Adapted from The Natural Step (2012).

This procedure allowed the workshop participants to consider what actions, policies and programmes are needed today that will connect the future to the present. Initially they asked themselves if this image is moving them in the right direction; i.e. towards a plausible and desirable future. Backcasting reminds us that the future is not linear, and can have many alternative outcomes depending on decisions made and the impact of external events on the trajectory of the HEI policy field. The major purpose of this backcasting exercise was to identify possible policies and strategies to reach the future state, and to give plausible explanations to why this future is achievable, not to envisage the estimated timeline of the various steps forward (Popper, 2008: 55). However, each of the actions (creative solutions) we propose will hopefully provide a platform for further improvement, and bring us closer to the future vision.

Let us provide more details on the four steps (A–D) of this backcasting applied to our theme: future adaptation of European universities, as elaborated during the Future Workshop:

## A=AWARENESS AND VISIONING

The initial step of the backcasting exercise was to create awareness, motivation and a 'Vision 2042+' that reflected the thinking of the diverse stakeholders participating in the European higher education sector. The subsequent statement (box) created consensus for the participants. In its condensed form a vision is a sort of a best case scenario, a future that is desired and may lead to a goal statement. Of course, it is a normative statement, loaded with ideology, but with a 30+ year horizon as in this case, visioning also may set a strategy for achieving the goals. Visioning is what it says, imagining a fairly clear and desirable future. A good vision is both realistic and challenging. Too far into the future and it does not create pull. Too close to today and it is just another plan.

> Vision 2042+
>
> Resilient Universities in a
>
> Learning Intensive Society

Visions of future society may be drastically different from today's one; however sometimes it is difficult to avoid designing them as an extrapolation of the present system. Arguably, the visioning should release the group from preconceived limitations and status quo conceptions. A backcasting approach is an appropriate tool for change management, such as describing the development of future governance models of universities. During the Future Workshop the participants applied some supporting concepts in order to reach the vision statement. *Trend* is a gradual change in a particular observed variable, which originates from other, interrelated causes, persists for a long time and covers a certain domain. Trend considers only a specific domain of society, i.e. an observed development in the European way of governing the universities. Relevant trends and megatrends are described by Kekäle in chapter 4. *Transition* covers a long-term, gradual and continuous process of structural societal change. It takes place through mutually reinforcing or contrary developments in technological, economic, ecological and socio-cultural domains. Several such transitions have taken place: the growth in the student population and the massification of higher education; the concurrent growth in the number of universities offering educational tracks of different kinds; and the competition emerging from this structural change, as illustrated by Bakken and Storm in chapter 10. Also new approaches to decision making as described by Selmer-Anderssen in chapter 6 and efficiency aspects discussed by Klumpp in chapter 11 are in our perspective examples of how the shared governance models are reshaped and implemented in the sector. An objective of the backcasting exercise was to analyse aspects of such change management processes.

## B=BASELINE 2012

We may carry out a gap analysis to analyse whether the universities' current situation dictates change, and how such changes can be introduced. As cited, both in the prior section of this chapter and in introductory parts of the book, there is abundant literature on the status quo of university governance. The literature overview also looks at the societal context and organizational culture of universities to understand how to introduce planned change. This allowed the participants of the Future Workshop to identify critical issues related to governance efficiency, their business and environment implications, students' attitudes and preferences, public policies, requirements of a knowledge society, etc. – all drivers for change implying both threats and opportunities.

## C=CREATING CREATIVE SOLUTIONS

Having developed a vision and preliminary ideas about possible actions, the participants were looking backwards from the vision to develop strategies to reach the ideal university position of the situational scenario. This is the real backcasting endeavour: what do we do to achieve the vision? This process prevents participants from developing strategies that can only solve today's problems. Instead they start with the target, and every measure proposed will provide a platform for further improvement.

Scenario building requires distinguishing between a *development* and a *situational* scenario. The former describes the presumed advance from 2012 until 2042+, and the latter encompasses our ideas and images of 2042+. Thus, a structural framework stating the baseline year, the linear time perspective, the intervals, possible inflection points and forerunners and the identified geographical entity had to be described. Besides, the participants needed to distinguish between events, trends and drivers colouring the scenario building efforts. *Events* are seen as present or short term phenomena illuminating what is presently going on around the universities, as described by Hazelkorn in chapter 3. Events are observable, verifiable and we surround ourselves with them daily. *Trends* are short to medium-term forecasts, projections and also hype. How likely are such events to unfold? Trends are likely and verifiable projections, but the development trend may involve violations. *Driving forces* are fundamental influences that drive major developments and are often regarded as unclear and not well documented, described by reference to the present UK situation by Pritchard in chapter 5. Hence, the workshop participants had to take into account relevant driving forces, trends and events that may shape future university governance. What possible pathways are there? When the participants started with the end (Vision 2042+) in mind, they were urged to put forward strategies to obtain appropriate governance and resilience. Each action or measure provided a platform for further improvement and brought them nearer to the ideal situation of the vision.

## D=DECIDE ON PRIORITIES (DOWN TO ACTION!)

After the potential, probable and preferable solutions were clarified in the previous step (C), participants prioritized fastest and cheapest measures for bringing universities to the envisioned target. A tool for step-by-step implementation and action planning of measures was developed and applied by the participants (see Table 13.1). This was meant to help the participants to choose actions that were easy to implement and would give quick results for a university when picking the 'lowest hanging fruit' first. This stage of the backcasting was used to continually assess decisions and actions to see whether they were moving the organization toward the desired outcome identified in the 'A' step (awareness and visioning) in Figure 13.3. This step also incorporated organizational learning and change methods, essential elements to move decision makers into new ways of thinking and working together.

During this phase of the backcasting analysis, the students were asked without any constraints to brainstorm potential solutions to the issues highlighted in the baseline analysis. What are the dependencies of the new 2042+ path? What kind of path breaking activities (i.e. inflection points) could happen in the period 2012–2042+? Which new paths were created? With these questions in mind, the participants looked backwards from the vision to develop strategies for the visionary image of the higher education institutions in a learning intensive society. They began with the end in mind (a different lock-in), moving towards a shared vision, with each action providing a platform for further improvement.

When doing the backcasting, the workshop participants were asked to work their way from the situational vision of 2042+, back to a possible, feasible and recognizable present, as shown in Table 13.1 below.

Table 13.1 Backcasting University Adaptation Actions

| 4. What is possible now? ← | 3. How can this image realistically be achieved? ← | 2. Describe the image with fictional examples. ← | 1. Short version of the chosen future image |
|---|---|---|---|
| When we look back from 2042+ to the present day, what *forerunners* may be described in 2012? | Can we sketch an *action plan*? | *Examples* | Describe a *synopsis* of the resilient university |
| ✓ Increased student influence*<br><br>✓ Increased number of elective subjects<br><br>✓ Saturday exams<br><br>✓ The curriculum is changed according to feedback from students | ✓ Building reputation around the choice of study, model of governance and access<br>✓ High level of ICT proficiency<br>✓ Differential admission requirements<br>✓ More students (50%) at all decision making levels<br>✓ Moderate school fees<br>✓ Increased financial assistance from industry<br>✓ Flexible study progression accepted, even by the Students' Loan Fund.<br>✓ Student payroll potentials | ✓ Optional: on campus or online.<br>✓ Competence-oriented exams: focus on learning outcomes<br>✓ Optional examination and testing schemes<br>✓ Student power is strong(est) in the governance arrangements<br>✓ More flexible forms of learning that can be adapted to different work and life situations | Dream university:<br><br>✓ Building our own degrees<br><br>✓ Balancing practice and theory<br><br>✓ Market orientation<br><br>✓ Lifelong and flexible learning<br><br>✓ Early recruitment/ entrance |

* In 1972 the twenty-one-year-old Gordon Brown, later British prime minister, was elected Vice-Chancellor at the University of Edinburgh. At the election of Vice-Chancellor (Rector) at the University of Oslo in April 2013, a student of twenty-three ran against a well reputed professor. The professor was elected, but the student obtained a 58 per cent share from his student constituency and 29 per cent of the votes across all groups eligible to vote. <http://www.uio.no/om/aktuelt/pressemeldinger/2013/rektorvalresultat.html> accessed 29 April 2013.

The participants started with a brief elaboration of the vision of 2042+ (stage 1) and worked themselves backwards via fictional examples and realistic (but imaged) action plan measures towards what is deemed possible given today's baseline (stage 4). Elements of a 'dream university' were sketched containing a market governance orientation, student autonomy, and continuing alternation between learning and labour. These elements were translated into examples (stage 2) of how the vision could look: e.g. strengthening of student power, focus on learning outcomes, flexible learning sites, etc. An action plan (stage 3) drafted a construction highlighting study programme flexibility, governance model and admission regime, combined with improved financial support to the learners. Finally, some forerunners (signals) of the 2042+ vision of the resilient, dream university were indicated, such as the gradually increasing voice of students in university governance and curricular content, the increasing tendency to arrange exams on afternoons and Saturdays (as experienced at the students' home university) and the expansion of elective subjects into most study programmes.

In a full backcasting sequence, after identifying the opportunities and potential solutions, the participants should usually prioritize the measures that move the policy field fastest toward the preferred situation, while optimizing flexibility as well as maximizing social and economic returns. This foresighting exercise deliberately did not comprise such a detailed planning and implementation stage since the foresight management Master's students are not assumed to be actual decision makers. However, the backcasting ideas produced and illustrated in Table 13.1 above were used as input to the next step in the Futures Workshop, the elaboration of scenario images pertaining to the preferred future vision.

## Creating the Future: The Many Faces of Future Universities

### *From a Vision to a Main Scenario*

As described in chapter 2, prior to the turn of the century a series of articles addressing the university model of the twenty-first century were published. Amongst the more prominent scholarly contributions we found many imaginative models and namings, e.g.: elite-, mega- and niche universities (Inayatullah and Gidley, 2000), learning land, higher education institutions as theme parks and staff as tour guides, mega university, corporate university and academic brokers (Abeles, 1998), ivied halls and virtual malls (Dator, 1998), experience camps and advanced learning networks (Nicholsen, 1998), monophonic university and polyphonic multiversities (Wildman, 1998), just to mention a few of the ideas proposed. Most of these models are quite general, focusing more on the future structure of universities than on the future governance structure and processes. More recent studies (Nasruddin et al., 2012) mention the 'à la carte University' as an emerging prototype.

However, may universities themselves create their future governance model? Among some there is an opinion that 'future' is something that happens to us, rather than something we to a certain degree may bring into being. Any organization is created by its interaction with both intra- and extramural actors. With hindsight, we often try to give rational arguments supporting our organization and its external environment. What challenges and unexpected events can happen in a best or a worst case scenario? An 'objective' environment of an organization is an illusion: it is always socially constructed to serve the purpose of the organization.

Consequently, as a final step the students were asked to construct a main scenario about the situation in 2042+ and the road between today and that year. In doing so they had to include relevant stakeholders and actors as part of the description. The point of departure was the narratives, together with the baseline scenarios and backcasting ideas developed during the workshop. If appropriate, the students could combine mini-scenarios and other ideas to construct the different main images. However, the preferred main scenario would need a storyline, i.e. a narrative that presented the important aspects of the image, including the relationship between driving forces and events of the scenario. The purpose of using this scenario material was to generate ideas regarding what has to be done to reach objectives that they believed we have in common; i.e. creating resilient university institutions to serve knowledge intensive societies.

The workshop participants were split into four groups to work with different parts of a main scenario and to write a brief storyline for each sub-part of the scenario. The two scenario axes, institutional modus and student profile/port of entrance, were chosen from a number of candidate drivers, both due to substantial and methodological considerations. Using a 'foundation' perspective allowed the participants to fill in the four quadrants with 'ideal types' of universities, while a 'scaffold' perspective allowed the axes to be removed in order to develop a more integrated scenario (van't Klooster and van Asselt, 2006: 27–29). The resulting images are depicted in Figure 13.4 below.

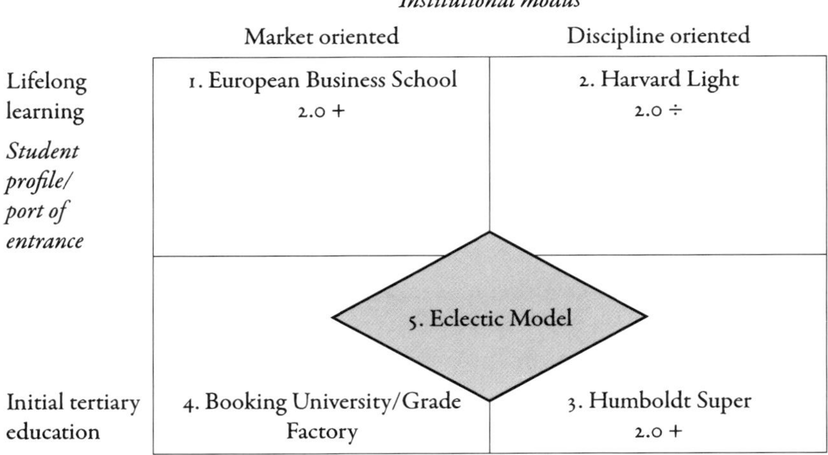


Figure 13.4 University Conceptual Model 2042+

A first storyline describes an image in which the university governance is shaped by students who seek lifelong learning in institutions which are market oriented (quadrant 1). This is a sort of private, *European business school model of tomorrow* in which the student demand (as paying clients) shapes the institutional response. Such universities must defend their reputation, remain flexible and have in-house capacity to monitor the labour market so that their study programmes always are updated and modern. They also need to have an advisory unit to guide the students in their choice of relevant subject combinations. Also, they must be innovative since they are market driven and need to be attractive for their users and stakeholders. Admissions requirements are more experience-based, but the general admission requirements change as well reflecting the differentiated costs of the study programmes. The curricula give increased opportunities for inter-disciplinary work. Students compose their own degrees and are more autonomous and diverse than previously.

A second model describes a *higher education institution* which is discipline oriented, but strives to keep up with the demand from students in a lifelong education scheme (quadrant 2, e.g. called Harvard Light 2.0 ÷). This type of university used to be top ranked, but has not been able to keep up with the global development of discipline orientation and study programme modernization. Its leaders have not been flexible enough and therefore not picked up the signals in the educational market. Also, because of the financial crisis, the loss of public and private sponsors, on which they depend, has made them more vulnerable. They have lost their position on the international ranking scales, mostly due to limited resources and thus less focus on research. As such they are less resilient than before.

The third image supposes that students are entering at an early age into a higher education institution which is *discipline* oriented (quadrant 3, named Humboldt Super 2.0 +). The research in this model is free and independent and the teaching is research based. Studies are characterized by ideals from the more classical Humanities. There is a tight relationship between teacher and student. The university will need insight into prospects of future society which may require brand new disciplines. The basic study model requires four years with different subjects that everyone must take and pass to move on: psychology, philosophy, languages, history, finance, IT, sciences, nanotechnology, sustainability topics, etc. Then the students select a specialization after they have acquired a broad knowledge base. This includes both practical and theoretical themes, like the basic model for nurses' and doctors' education. The leaders of the university must have expertise in foresight management and a strong urge to act to stay ahead of problems and serious, unforeseen challenges. The tasks of governance will overlap so that different persons can have insight and knowledge on a wide range of issues. One hundred per cent state funding supports free admission also for students from other countries. The state treats the university as an autonomous organization that has full rights to determine study content and governance. The internal administration of the university supplies services which take care of all practical tasks so that the professors are dedicated to research and research based teaching. The faculty is reinstated as the most influential source of in-house authority.

The fourth image envisages students entering the universities directly from post-grammar schools to this kind of market oriented, *grade factory* institution (quadrant 4). Students are young and have no prior work experience. They seek more practice in their study programmes, including secondments to public sector or industry. This gives a more diverse student body. Study programmes and curricula are strongly influenced by the interests and needs of extramural stakeholders, in particular demand from the private sector. The model implies that the students are entering with no time gap between post-grammar school and university; however they are quickly out again. Quality may be sacrificed on behalf of efficiency. Such a university should have a mentor scheme and an extensive system for business exchange, a close cooperation with relevant industries, a system for Internet based discussion groups in which students could exchange and reflect on experiences gained when posted in private or public sector as 'stagiaires'. The students should be offered new advisors each semester. Evaluation should take place in practice in collaboration with the supervisor. An industry PhD could serve as a general model for research education.

## *The Storyline of University Governance in 2042+*

With this four-image hinterland, the workshop session developed a fifth model, imaging an eclectic university model embedded in a learning intensive society. This scenario picked elements from the remaining four images, was positioned in the year 2042+ as assumed and located within the European countries. The storyline of the desirable future of European universities in 2042+ runs as in the box below:

> *European University Governance as of 2042+*
>
> Historical development has demonstrated that we have experienced a long term structural shift in the governance of higher education institutions. During the two meagre decades (named 'the academic depression') starting at the turn of the century, the changing need for and attitudes towards academe and academically produced knowledge resulted in a leaner governance model. In fact, the expansion in the number and functions of the 'new professionals', i.e. the well-educated university administrators, eased off. Concurrently, university faculty who feared a novel form of academic capitalism in which the knowledge workers were proletarianized and their social status weakened, experienced global mobilization campaigns spearheaded by the Portuguese professor Irma da Rosa during the 2020s; these neutralized the de-credential trends and tendencies. Higher education was again deemed the most significant gatekeeper for obtaining privileged positions in the stratified labour market and in society as a whole. Academic knowledge paid off.
>
> By the beginning of the 2030s shared governance of universities was based on a global networking model, optimizing disciplinary and institutional division of labour. The learners (formerly called students) defined their own programme of study from across the myriad of courses available at the global university. The Bologna model of 3–2–3 years of study was terminated as society demanded more flexible and tailor-made degrees. Universities included more of their stakeholders (industry, student groups, and local institutions) as co-producers of courses and other knowledge output.

Presently, the provision of and market for flexible, multi-disciplinary learning packages, innovation and research has become larger than ever before. The cleavage between academic superstars and the average teacher 'foot soldiers' that emerged during the decades of the academic depression has faded due to the eLearning revolution. However, programmes and courses matter more than institutions, and this strengthens the positions of the academic entrepreneurs developing novel courses and initiating step-change in research and innovation. Shared governance is practised as a sort of multi-level networking reciprocal commitment in which the professional administrators, faculty and students revolve in the leadership positions.

When we check the backcasting study we performed in 2012 we observe that many of our observations and anticipations turned out to be correct in most aspects. However, the idea that there could be some kind of stable organizational equilibrium model common as a sort of best practice, common to most of the universities, did not materialize.

This storyline is a narrative that presents the important aspects of the situational scenario, including the relationship between driving forces and events of the future image (van der Heijden, 1996). It is written as if it was presented in a science section of a magazine or journal in 2042+, and it focuses on the most highly preferred alternative model; the *resilient university model in a learning intensive society*. Some of these aspects on institutional variation and shared university ideals are elaborated further by Hernes in Chapter 14. He is promoting a model branded a 'super-resilient university'. This resembles what the workshop participants in Figure 4 named 'Humbolt Super 2.0 +'.

## Discussion

### *Some Methodological Considerations*

Foresight, and especially scenario building, is usually considered conducive to strategic reasoning, research processes and policy development (Krawczyk and Slaughter, 2010). Its ultimate success lies in the implementation of foresight insights in policies, strategies and actions (Karlsen et al., 2010). Although the literature on university futures has ample illustrations of trends, drivers and chimerical forms of governance (e.g. Inayatullah and Gidley, 2000; Ughetto, 2007; May, 2011; Curaj et al., 2012; Gidley, 2012), there is seemingly no global consensus on a plausible long term pattern (de Boer and Jongbloed, 2012). Foresight comprises projections or explorations of different futures and alternatives, based on insights from today's knowledge and expectations of the future. Most of these reports and studies, including those on the university future, rely on input from domain experts (Karlsen and Karlsen, 2007). As a contrast, the qualitative data reported in this chapter are produced by Master's students of change and foresight management.

Backcasting is explicitly normative. The preferred future, as stated in the Vision 2042+ and in the Eclectic Model with its embedded governance and institutional resilience aspects, is a consensus based world as seen by the workshop participants. When defining the most preferable future, the workshop participants are neither offering alternative visions nor alternative desirable futures. So, implications of different policies and options for alternatives were not considered, either. The images are meant to stimulate the thinking about the problem at hand: in our case, European higher education institution adaptation. They may be exaggerated or unrealistic in some respects to emphasize different goals, values and trajectories. However, they are neither predictions nor a set of winner options.

Foresight carried out along the lines presented in this chapter also demonstrates an integrated and creative use of path theories in which path dependency analyses occurs, path breaking activities are demonstrated and new paths are created (Karlsen and Øverland, 2012). In the case of a university foresight analysis, it is evidently a gap between the complexity of future options and the analytical tools applied to map these future aspects. Furthermore, foresight analysis offers no consensus on an appropriate methodological balance between the qualitative and quantitative approaches. The lack of a common and approved methodology originates, at least partly, from the inherent ontological and epistemic characteristics of qualitative and quantitative methods. They differ when it comes to capturing the complexity of issues addressed in most foresight exercises (Karlsen and Karlsen, 2013). Still, having all these precautions in mind and proposing ways out of a seemingly locked situation, a participative Future Workshop is a good starting point to develop images of a European university future, based on informed and evidence based knowledge from the field. In this context, the Master's students are domain experts as good as anyone.

### *When Does the Future Start?*

In times of rapid and deep societal change it may be necessary to produce, not only analyses of the threats but also of the opportunities for the higher education sector. For that purpose we will need images of the preferred vision, and discussion about the possible options, as well as ideas about how a sought after future can be planned and created. So, the future starts when the Future Workshop commences, or whenever we start thinking about it (Schwartz, 1991; Young and Muller, 2010; Tevis, 2010).

In the view of the workshop participants European universities are undergoing radical transformation in terms of governance, financial modus and societal role. Arguably, they state that today's European (and Western) university role models will not prevail. The predominantly publicly funded, broad spectrum teaching and research university, having a large (and increasing) in-house back office, is out of date. Even today's most prominent ideal types (cf. chapter 2) and role models have to be changed in order to be more robust and viable. Some universities (e.g. 'Humboldt Super 2.0 +') may still be oriented towards traditional disciplines and broad-based academic fields; however they may re-create their governance and relationship to all major stakeholders. Others (e.g. 'Grade Factories') may rethink and reshape the education and research market, targeting particular student groups and customers to deliver tailor made services, also implying a more flexible and lean governance model. These two models will focus upon young students entering straight from post-primary school, but they will keep them for different lengths of study. The concept of lifelong learning represents another perspective on the role of education in society. Learning is supposed to be increasing in demand throughout the life span of an individual, since many of the established curricula have short expiration dates thus requiring retraining, and because the whole working population is becoming 'greyer' and needs upgrading of its skills and competencies. The 'European Business School 2.0 +' is seen as such a transformer of the higher education sector, which creates a more seamless web with other sectors, mainly in the business sector, but also supplies knowledge that meets the demand in the leisure market or in the increasing older population. Finally, some excellent present-day providers of research, education and value added services (e.g. 'Harvard Light 2.0 ÷') will not be able to defend their position and global ranking, despite their orientation towards the lifelong market segment and their tradition of being discipline oriented. They will simply prove unviable since they have not converted their in-house governance sufficiently to deliver their services to an elite higher education market segment. Lack of resilience and anticipation has blind-folded these institutions and rendered them unable to read the early warnings of new market signals.

Of course, applying a two-fold scenario axes method restricts the imaging to four models. However, the foresight students also introduced a fifth category, an 'Eclectic Model' picking the appropriate elements from each of the four principal types, when needed. The fact of having increased resilience and anticipation as a stimulus to a collective mindfulness, also suggests that future universities do not necessarily have to be utterly loyal to their prior governance history in order to adapt to changing times. Change they would arguably have to, but they could do it more pragmatically and flexibly. There might be lessons to learn from all principal models: the hybrid (eclectic) organization may still be named a university, but the mode of operation is constantly in flux. The leadership of the university has to choose an appropriate strategy to achieve both flexibility and the capability to improvise when necessary (Weick, 1998).

Arguably, the social contract of higher education institutions has to be reshaped. Most certainly, as societal institutions universities will survive. However, they may have to adjust their governance models more swiftly than before to the changing endogenous and exogenous actors and factors. The growth in university administration is presumably close to its vertex at present. Observing a cumulative proletarianization of faculty and other members of academe as discussed in previous chapters of this book, we may expect a new wave of private for-profit higher education institutions. They may either re-instigate the autonomy and the power of academic teachers and researchers or be cheap and exploitative of both staff and students. We may also see new niche university institutions being established and organized as academic partnerships like today's law firms or private medical centres. This upsurge of private, smaller, high quality universities may be a response to the assumed decline in status and market appeal from the more established university 'top dogs', as discussed in the case of the private 'Harvard Light 2.0 ÷' model.

## Conclusion

Given the drivers of change impacting on the European university sector, the participants in the Future Workshop expected significant reshaping of university models during the next generation. However, today's broad-based teaching and research institution model was not postulated to be the 'steady as she goes' generic future shape. Arguably, European universities have not changed much since their inception; however, longevity is no guarantee for permanence in the eyes of the workshop participants. Rather, the Master's students opted for increased flexibility, resilience and viability through a 'pick-and-mix' model serving students via different routes and having different institutional modalities.

The participants did not distinguish between universities of different sizes, belonging to or excluded from partnerships or mergers. They did not differentiate between general universities or specialized universities, or between those who are developing towards teaching only or those who are targeted upon long term research programmes. However, some general implications for both universities and policymakers sprang from the discussion of the ideal university types. Most important is the need to sustain and possibly improve academic excellence, including relevant, high quality teaching and research. Academe presumably improves with age, but this does not replace the need for talent management and recruitment. The future academic university workforce will need to deliver appropriate productivity and support new governance models. The workshop participants assumed the existence of increasingly competitive and consumer driven higher education markets indicating that both the academic and administrative employees will have to extend their market skills and capabilities. Also, change management and speed-to-market has to be addressed. The California based company Coursera offers in 2013 to several million students free courses, developed and delivered by international elite universities (e.g. Columbia and more than sixty others in the same league) as 'massive open online course' (MOOCs). The universities are offered 15 per cent of the turnover plus 20 per cent of the profit (<http://en.wikipedia.org/wiki/Coursera>). Arguably, universities will have to be first-to-market with new teaching and research programmes such as MOOCs where the lectures, net based assignments and discussion groups are connected into a unified and global system. Also, the relationship with government will have to change from being mainly focused on funding, to a dialogue or possibly a partnership based on innovation and value creation. From such a perspective a change from shared governance to multi-level governance might be in sight. Crellin (2010: 80) argues that shared governance has to be re-infused with new meaning and definition if it is to prevail as a navigating instrument for the higher education sector in the stormy waters to come.

In many ways universities are delivering a public good; however knowledge is increasingly often created in contested and private sector markets. Thus, it is not an easy task for government to instigate policy for the higher education sector entering into a learning intensive society. However, universities will most probably be the prime suppliers of talents, new insights and ideas as well as intellectual property needed for a future high performing, high reliability economy. European policy makers will have to present a well legitimized public policy, making clear the essential role of the universities in the modernization of society. Developing visions and different scenarios for the next generation might be an instrumental way to illuminate what the best practices of the universities will be and in what ways policy could affect the output from the higher education sector. Also, the desirability of and market share of the more established public universities and new private entrants must be addressed. Is there an optimal mix between non-profit public and private for-profit universities? What kind of regulation would be necessary in order to obtain academic excellence and high teaching quality for both non- and for-profit universities? In most European countries universities are claiming student fees to secure their funding, but as of yet there is seemingly no equilibrium state between prices and demand. Pricing policy and flexibility will have to be discussed and adjusted to macro-economic and social conditions, not just left to the market forces of supply and demand. In short, future European university adaptation calls for resilience and anticipation, as well as novel and flexible models of intra- and extramural collaboration.

## References

Abeles, T.P. (1998). 'The Academy in a Wired World', *Futures*, 30 (7), 603–613.

Altbach, P., and Salmi, J. (eds) (2011). *The Road to Academic Excellence. The Making of World-Class Research Universities.* Washington, D.C.: The World Bank.

Amaral, A., Tavares, O., and Santos, C. (2012). 'Higher Education Reforms in Europe: a Comparative Perspective of New Legal Frameworks in Europe', In A. Curaj, P. Scott, L. Vlasceanu, and L. Wilson (eds), *European Higher Education at the Crossroads: Between the Bologna Process and National Reforms*, pp. 655–673. Dordrecht: Springer.

Apel, H. (2004). 'The Future Workshop'. Deutsches Institut für Erwachsenbildung. Available at: <http://en.wikipedia.org/wiki/Future_workshop> accessed 23 February 2012. Archived by WebCite® at <http://www.webcitation.org/65fMKiKWC>.

Crellin, M.A. (2010). 'The Future of Shared Governance'. *New Directions for Higher Education*, No. 151, Fall 2010:71–81. Available from: Wiley Online Library (wileyonlinelibrary.com). DOI:10.1002/he.402. Accessed 24 January 2013.

Cunha, M.P., Palma, P., and Costa, N.G. (2006). 'Fear of Foresight: Knowledge and Ignorance in Organizational Foresight', *Futures*, 38 (8), 942–955.

Curaj, A., Scott, P., Vlasceanu, L., and Wilson, L. (2012). *European Higher Education at the Crossroads. Between the Bologna Process and National Reforms.* Dordrecht: Springer Science + Business Media.

Dator, J. (1998). 'The Futures of Universities. Ivied Halls, Virtual Malls, or Theme Parks?', *Futures*, 30 (7), 615–623.

de Boer, H., and File, J. (2009). *Higher Education Governance Reforms Across Europe.* Brussels: ESMU.

de Boer, H., Enders, J., File, J., and Jongbloed, B. (2010). *Governance Reform. Progress in Higher Education Reform Across Europe*: Vol. 1. Executive Summary Main Report. Brussels: European Commission.

de Boer, H. F,. and Jongbloed, B.W.A. (2012). 'A Cross-National Comparison of Higher Education Markets in Western Europe'. In A. Curaj et al. (eds), *European Higher Education at the Crossroads: Between the Bologna Process and National Reforms.* Volume 2, pp. 553–572. Dordrecht, Heidelberg, New York: Springer.

Dreborg, K. (1996). 'The Essence of Backcasting', *Futures*, 28 (9), 813–828.

Eickhoff, P., and Geffers, S.G. (2006). 'Power of Imagination Studio – A Further Development of the Future Workshop Concept', Chapter 26. In P. Holman, T. Devane, and S. Cady (eds), *The Change Handbook – The Definitive Resource on Today's Best Methods for Engaging Whole Systems* (2nd edn), pp. 267–272. San Francisco: Berrett Kohler Publishers.

European Commission, Directorate-General for Research (2002). *Thinking, Debating and Shaping the Future: Foresight for Europe. Final Report Prepared by a High Level Expert Group.* <ftp://ftp.cordis.lu/pub/foresight/docs/for_hleg_final_report_en.pdf> accessed 23 January 2013.

European Foresight (2012). 'What is Foresight?' Available from: <http://forera.jrc.ec.europa.eu/> accessed 25 February 2012. Archived by WebCite® at <http://www.webcitation.org/65iVRMHK2.>

Gidley, J.M. (2012). 'Evolution of Education: From Weak Signals to Rich Imaginaries of Educational Futures', *Futures* 44 (1), 46–54.

Godet, M. (2006). *Creating Futures. Scenario Planning as a Strategic Management Tool.* London: Economica.

Höjer. M., and Mattsson, L. (2000). 'Determinism and Backcasting in Future Studies', *Futures*, 32 (7), 613–634.

Inayatullah, S., and Gidley, J. (2000). 'Forces Shaping University Futures', In J. Gidley, and S. Inayatullah (eds), *The University in Transformation: Global Perspectives on the Futures of the University*, pp. 1–14. Westport Ct.: Bergin and Garvey.

Jungk, R., and Müllert, N. (1987). *Future Workshops: How to Create Desirable Futures*. London: Institute for Social Inventions.

Karlsen, J.E., and Karlsen, H. (2007). 'Expert Groups as Production Units for Shared Knowledge in Energy Foresights', *Foresight*, 9 (1), 37–49.

Karlsen, J.E., Øverland, E.F., and Karlsen, H. (2010). 'Sociological Contributions to Futures' Theory Building', *Foresight*, 12 (3), 59–72.

Karlsen, J.E., and Øverland, E.F. (2010). *Carpe Futurum*. Oslo: Cappelen Academic Press.

Karlsen, J.E., and Øverland, E.F. (2012). 'Promoting Diversity in Long-term Policy Development: The SMARTT Case of Norway', *Journal of Futures Studies*, 16 (3), 63–78.

Karlsen, J.E., and Karlsen, H. (2013). 'Classification of Tools and Approaches Applicable in Foresight Studies'. In M. Giaoutzi, and Sapio, B. (eds), *Recent Developments in Foresight Methodologies*, pp. 27–52. London: Springer.

Kehm, B.M., and Lanzendorf, U. (2006). *Reforming University Governance. Changing Conditions for Research in Four European Countries*. Bonn: Lemmens.

Krawczyk, E., and Slaughter, R. (2010). 'New Generations of Futures Methods', *Futures* 42 (1), 75–82.

May, G.H. (2011). 'Education: Time to Rethink the Industrial Model?' *Journal of Futures Studies*, 16 (1), 101–108.

Middlehurst, R., and Teixeira, P. (2012). 'Governance Within the EHEA: Dynamic Trends, Common Challenges and National Particularities'. In A. Curaj et al. (eds), *European Higher Education at the Crossroads: Between the Bologna Process and National Reforms*, pp. 527–551. Dordrecht: Springer.

Miller, R. (2006). 'Futures Literacy: a Hybrid Strategic Scenario Method', *Futures* 39 (3), 341–362.

Nasruddin, E., Bustami, R., and Inayatullah, S. (2012). 'Transformative Foresight: Universiti Sains Malaysia Leads the Way'. *Futures* 44 (1), 36–45.

Nicholson, P.A. (1998). 'Higher Education in the Year 2030', *Futures*, 30 (7), 725–729.

OECD (2008). *Tertiary Education for the Knowledge Society. OECD Thematic Review of Tertiary Education*. Paris: OECD.

Paradeise, C., Ferlie, E., Bleiklie, I., and Reale, E. (eds) (2009). *University Governance. Western European Comparative Perspectives*. Dordrecht: Springer.

Paradeise, C. (2012). 'Tools and Implementation for a New Governance of Universities. Understanding Variability Between and Within Countries'. In A. Curaj et al. (eds), *European Higher Education at the Crossroads: Between the Bologna Process and National Reforms*, pp. 573–598. Dordrecht: Springer.

Paulus, P.B., and Brown, V.R. (2003). 'Enhancing Ideational Creativity in Groups'. In P.B. Paulus, and B.A. Nijstad (eds), *Group Creativity: Innovation through Collaboration*, pp. 110–136. Oxford, UK: Oxford University Press.

Popper, R. (2008). 'Foresight Methodology'. In L. Georghiou, J.C. Harper, M. Keenan, I. Miles, and R. Popper (eds), *The Handbook of Technology Foresight*, pp. 44–88. Cheltenham, UK: Edward Elgar.

Robinson, J. (1990). 'Futures Under Glass: a Recipe for People Who Hate to Predict', *Futures*, 22 (8), 820–842.

Schwartz, P. (1991). *The Art of the Long View: Planning for the Future in an Uncertain World*. New York: Currency Doubleday.

Tevis, R.E. (2010). 'Creating the Future: Goal-oriented Scenario Planning', *Futures*, 42 (4), 337–344.

The Natural Step (2012). 'Applying the ABCD Method'. Available at: <http://www.naturalstep.org/en/abcd-process>accessed: 21 February 2012. Archived by WebCite® at: <http://www.webcitation.org/65cCRQf2n>.

Ughetto, E. (2007). 'Foresight as a Triple Helix of Industry, University, and Government Relations', *Foresight*, 9 (5), 14–22.

Van't Klooster, S.A., and van Asselt, M.B.A. (2006). 'Practising the Scenario-axes Technique', *Futures*, 38 (1), 15–30.

van der Heijden, K. (1996). *Scenarios: the Art of Strategic Conversation*. Chichester, England: Wiley.

Young, M., and Muller, J. (2010). 'Three Educational Scenarios for the Future: Lessons From the Sociology of Knowledge', *European Journal of Education*, 45 (1), Part I, 11–27.

Weick, K. (1998). 'Improvisation as a Mindset for Organizational Analysis', *Organization Science*, 9 (5), 543–555.

Wildman, P. (1998). 'From the Monophonic University to Polyphonic Multiversities', *Futures*, 30 (7), 625–633.

GUDMUND HERNES

# 14 Super-Resilient Organizations

To assess the success of organisms as well as organizations, one may use a simple criterion – a Darwinian one. And by that criterion, institutions of higher education have been very successful – indeed, among the most successful of all times:

- *Survival*: Universities are old – and they have endured a millennium from the first that was established as an association of students in Bologna in 1088 and the second as a guild of teachers in Paris about 1150. From them we still borrow academic titles such as *Bachelor* and *Master*. But the origins of universities are even older if we include institutions such as Greek Academies in antiquity or The House of Wisdom in Baghdad during the Islamic Golden Age.
- *Proliferation*: Institutions of higher education have spread more widely, indeed have become ubiquitous. They are found on all continents and in all countries with the same general morphology or characteristic form. Or put even more sharply: universities have become universal.
- *Multiplication*: The number of institutions of higher education is growing all the time. There are thousands of them and the number increases with every passing year. Whatever else they may be, they are no endangered species.
- *Expansion*: Universities have grown in size – some are even called *megaversities* with tens of thousands of students. The University of Bologna now has more than 90,000 – far greater than the population of the city when it was first founded. And many universities endeavour to grow beyond their current size. Their staffs have been increasing – including administrative and non-academic cadres.

- *Femininization*: From universities being bastions of male supremacy, women are becoming an increasing proportion of students and staff. This is a global phenomenon. In Norway, to take but one example, about two thirds of those who enrol as students are now women. They are in the majority not just at the Bachelor level, but also at the Master level.
- *Diversification*: The composition of students and staff has become more varied. Not only have women markedly increased their presence – so have minorities and students of slender means. Students and staff have become more diverse
- *Academization*: More fields of knowledge have been added to university studies and research. In the last century new fields such as sociology, meteorology and informatics were added. New fields have also arisen by combining old ones, such as molecular biology or bioinformatics. And professions have to enhance their status by building an academic fundament on which to base their expertise, such as nursing science or media studies.
- *Internationalization*: Where previously at universities dialects from the same nation were the norm, one can now hear the mother tongues from many nations. This in turn has led to a movement to facilitate interaction, notably by more teaching taking place in what has become the *lingua franca* of universities, English. Admittedly there were different nationals also at medieval Bologna – those who came from the other side of the mountains were called *ultramontano* – and Latin was the language of scholars. And, until 1811, Norwegians who wanted a university degree enrolled at the University of Copenhagen. Yet clearly there was nothing on the scope and scale of present day migration of students. After the Second World War the United States set up the Fulbright programme. In 1987 the European Union established the Erasmus programme which now encompasses more than 4,000 institutions of higher education in more than thirty countries – and so far has recruited about 2.5 million students. China has become the single greatest country of recruitment for foreign students in the

USA – in 2009/ 2010 nearly 130,000.[1] Put differently: students are increasing globetrotters and the community of scholars is becoming a global meritocracy. Universities look for their status in international rankings and take pride if their professors receive international awards such as the Nobel Prize, the Fields medal or other awards for outstanding discoveries.

- *Networking*: Higher education institutions are decreasingly standalone entities. They not only link scholars who can be traced by citations or conferences. They also enter different kinds of collaborative networks. Some are old, such as the Rhodes Scholarships for selected foreign students at the University of Oxford; some are quite new such as the recent consortia for online education. Many universities have also established subsidiaries abroad: e.g. the New York University Abu Dhabi.

The broad result is this: in earlier times the human condition was more determined by nature and the environment and less by socially constructed conditions – nature was something you adapted to. Now the environment is more and more something we change – the substances, the forces and the species of nature are something we analyse, interpret, modify and use. Our environment is more and more determined by knowledge. Indeed, it becomes increasingly difficult to talk of research and the environment of research as two distinct matters – our environment is more and more a result of research, whether it is the food that we eat or the latest version of Windows we use for our PowerPoint presentations. As a consequence the status of higher education institutions has risen. Indeed modern societies are a university product. This can be illustrated by different types of indicators.

Over the last century the proportion of a nation's resources that goes into higher education and research has increased – even if the economic crisis of the last several years has led to cuts even in places that have lauded themselves for the quality of their institutions, such as Great Britain or

1 See <http://www.petersons.com/college-search/international-student-college-enrollment-statistics-china.aspx> accessed 29 April 2013.

California. When firms and corporations want to signal that they are cutting edge and have an intellectual environment characterized by energetic exchange of ideas and innovation, then they borrow the 'university' name. Apple and Google call their headquarters 'campus' – and they have copied the informality and professionalism of university life rather than the staid style of corporate boardrooms. It should also be added that several of the largest global companies emerged from universities – again one could use Apple and Google, or Facebook and Twitter as examples. Universities are the places where the future is made. Clearly this is also the reason why so many firms stay close to a real university campus – after all: new products are embodied ideas.

So institutions of higher educations are key institutions in the modern ecosystem producing the concepts and theories that are translated into innovations both economic and organizational. To take just one illustration: The drones that are increasingly used by the military and the police are but airborne knowledge.

Indeed, one could argue that the essence of modernity is the university. Universities particularly during the last two centuries have provided the nexus between research and the remaking of inherited ways of doing things. They have installed themselves in different social environments, they have transcended boundaries between political systems and they have survived shifting regimes. Our modern societies are a university product, the outcome of a long series of academic contributions – from the classical physics of Professor Isaac Newton or the modern physics of Professor Niels Bohr, from the classical economics of Professor Adam Smith to the neoclassical economics of Professor Kenneth Arrow, from the classical bacteriology of Professors Koch and Pasteur to the modern molecular biology of Professors Watson and Crick. So hardly any other institution has been as been as adaptive and resilient whilst still maintaining its core structure and functioning. Hence the question is why.

## The Sources of Success

The first and obvious answer is encapsulated in Francis Bacon's dictum: knowledge is power. The dual purposes of universities have been to transmit learning and advance science. And they have devised methods for achieving both – i.e. for maintaining and imparting a body of knowledge as well as constantly transforming it by the scientific method.

That knowledge is power, of course, was discovered by the wielders of power. Hence universities increasingly came to educate the 'King's servants', so to speak, i.e. the professionals that would help govern the realm in all key areas based on certified skills. Kings and farmers had to know the variations of the seasons to get food from the earth and tax from crops. The King's servants had to be educated to organized life itself in so many ways, from time-keeping to book-keeping. Observations about celestial motions could be translated into calendars and could keep track of the periods of the year; the laws of physics could be used for navigation, calculus for determining the trajectories of cannon balls. Mathematics was translated for the engineering of bridges and cathedrals and for estimating the length of meridians. Lawyers became the drafters of Constitutions and royal decrees; the polyglots who mastered languages became the interlocutors who made diplomacy possible. The servants of the King, those who manned civil service and military ranks, officials and officers, were all in some way linked to universities and the knowledge they produced. And of course Kings also needed to influence the hearts and minds of the people. Theologians built belief systems, became the interpreters of norms which organized the lives of ordinary people through rituals for birth, marriage and death. As the Roman Church was challenged, theologians were increasingly trained at universities. Another impetus for universities was the knowledge they could provide to ameliorate private and public health – such as the germ theory of disease in the nineteenth century. Academics also advanced the idea that the health and growth of whole economies could be influenced – one only needs to mention the many contributions from Professor Adam Smith to Professor John Maynard Keynes.

So from the sixteenth century a big shift took place in *the organization of knowledge*. What had been disparate and muddled pursuits, such as alchemy mixed with magic and abracadabra, became organized into bodies of thought *with whole new paradigms*. Examples are Keplerian astronomy, Newtonian physics, the periodic system in chemistry or the new branches of mathematics. Academic research, paradoxically, became simultaneously more abstract, more experimental and more applied – there really was no opposition between the three. It was discovered that nothing is as practical as a good theory. This development accelerated in the nineteenth and the twentieth centuries.

At the same time there was a shift between the two key components of the activities of universities – the transmission of learning and the advancement of knowledge: new knowledge and the capacity to produce it have become all the more important, not just to be academically recognized, but also as a key ingredient in teaching and, moreover, as an input to society and its economy, from agriculture to industry. Academics and professors moved beyond being servants of the state or the king – they also became the inventors of products and processes that became the basis for whole new industries, e.g. the dyes or aspirin of Bayer AG or the mineral fertilizer produced by Norsk Hydro by a process of nitrogen fixation invented by Professor Kristian Birkeland. Organizational innovations can also be mentioned in this context, e.g. the managerialism that grew out of the Harvard Business School during the period between the two world wars under the leadership of Professor Elton Mayo.

The basic point is this: in everything with which humans surround themselves, in their cars and in their kitchens, in their communications and in their health care, the component of knowledge is increasing. Most of us could whittle a passable wooden spoon using a sheath knife. None of us could by ourselves make the plastic spoon we get when we buy a tub of ice-cream. A typewriter was built around a mechanical technology that is fairly easy to understand; few of us master the innards of a PC. A very large part of this knowledge, that is so ubiquitous that we barely reflect upon it, emanates from universities and professional education at universities.

*In sum*: more and more of the products we consume, the practical solutions we adopt and the services we pick are based on knowledge our grandparents did not have. My grandparents were born in a society without telephone – in fact, they never owned one, my parents were born in a society without radio, I was born in a society without TV, my son was born in a society without PC and Internet.

What about the governance of institutions of higher education?

The most striking feature is that most of them have the same morphology. They consist of professors and students, there are lectures and courses and exams. They have broadly the same degree structure – BA, MA and PhD. The similarity is so great that exchanges of personnel are relatively simple: acquiring qualifications at one provides acceptable knowledge for another. Accreditation makes for transferability. Clearly this has in recent years been further facilitated by the Bologna Process – the ministerial meetings and accords between European countries to introduce common standards for higher education qualifications. It has resulted in the European Higher Education Area and the Lisbon Recognition Convention. Indeed, scholars belong to the same broad global community, buttressed by international professional organizations and journals which aspire to keep the same standards. Yet there are of course differences between countries and institutions. This variation provides information, i.e. opportunities for research.

## The Four Stages of University Technology

One can also argue that higher education institutions have gone through the same historical progression. Schematically one can distinguish between four stages based on different technologies for transmitting learning and acquiring knowledge.

The first was the *lecture* – i.e. oral communication and argumentation. It was based on the idea that most knowledge was embedded in individuals and could be passed on from person to person, from the lectern to the auditorium where the listeners could learn. Students could also take notes to store the imparted knowledge, and later on transport it, quote from it and build on it. What was presented could be explored by dialogue in colloquia, and controversial points could be disputed and challenged. Indeed, the *trivium* – the first part of a liberal arts education in medieval and renaissance universities – consisting of grammar, logic and rhetoric, was also a preparation for the acquisition and presentation of learning. The *disputas* or defence for doctoral thesis is an outgrowth of this early oral technology, yet still a key element in the maintenance of academic standards.

The second technology was the *book*. Clearly universities had scrolls, scriptures and treatises hand written by scholars and copied by scribes. But it was only the Gutenbergian revolution of the fifteenth century, making possible the printing of books and pamphlets by removable and reusable type, that made books available for ordinary students, first at libraries and later as individual possessions. The printed book allowed both for reproduction, massification and transportation of knowledge – knowledge was on a fully new scale liberated from person, time and place. And it was the harbinger of democratization, i.e. spread of knowledge at a lower cost with broader diffusion over longer distances. In this way the printed book also promoted internationalization. In time the process of printing facilitated scientific publishing which became a catalyst if not a catapult for the scientific revolution. Printing also provided the technology for scientific journals – periodicals where observations, calculations, experiments and research results could be reported. Their history dates back to 1665 when the French *Journal des sçavans* (later *savans*) and the English *Philosophical Transactions of the Royal Society* were both first issued. Journals made it possible not just to diffuse scientific and scholarly articles, but also to use them for training and – not least – to challenge what had been submitted in earlier issues. Hence publishing became an integral part of the scientific process, for establishing priority, for quality control, for keeping a permanent scientific record and for diffusing new ideas.

The third technology was the establishment of scientific *laboratories* – i.e. specialized technical workrooms or facilities with instruments and machines for carrying out systematic testing and measurements under controlled conditions. They can differ in design according to their purpose: an anatomical laboratory for medical studies, a chemical laboratory for testing, an arboretum or greenhouse for botanical or zoological experiments, etc. Laboratories became an essential part of universities and critical for many fields of study, particularly in the sciences. They also provided the testing ground for the experiments which became more and more fundamental to the whole scientific enterprise. It is important to note that the later technologies did not displace the earlier ones, but added to them. They became complementary and interblended: The results from a laboratory experiment could be presented first orally in a seminar, then in a journal or book – or provide the findings and substance for a dissertation to be defended in a doctoral oral dispute.

The fourth stage of university technologies is the present one where *information-communication technology* (ICT) has permeated all aspects of university life, from training and research to administration. ICT is not an additive technology; it is transformative in the sense that it restructures the intellectual and social relations of universities. The key aspects of this transformation are the following.

*Data generation and collection* have gone through a quantum leap. Data are logged in real time, whether it is weather satellites recording meteorological data, chemical processes that are continuously monitored by machines, complex sensors tracing the subatomic particles in high-energy accelerators, traffic flows registered in cities, purchase decisions filed on the internet, neuroimaging or brain scans (PET or MRI) stored on servers or the evolution of social networks mapped from Facebook. We have entered the era of *big data*.

Secondly these data are stored in big *server farms* which allow multiple users to have access to them. The rudimentary versions go back to the 1960s, but again there has been a dramatic increase in scale and scope.

Thirdly, new methods of *data mining* have been developed, both in terms of the techniques and models used for analysis as well as the speed and capacity of the computers doing the mining. This also allows for analysis and feedback in real time, such as we privately know from Amazon's 'Recommendations for you' – the algorithm of your ever shifting profile based on past behaviour.

For institutions of higher education the development of the *new modes of communication* has taken place over the last twenty-five years, starting with connections between academic computers in the so-called Bit-net between CUNY and Yale in 1981. This has morphed into the Internet with a large number of universities and other academic nodes, allowing for not just exchange of data, but also for use of library services, downloading of articles and exchanges of manuscripts.

The most prominent, indeed awesome, example of combining all these technologies is probably the Large Hadron Collider, which lies in a tunnel of twenty seven kilometres between France and Switzerland near Geneva. It has been built by more than 10,000 scientists, and when in use produces unprecedented amounts of data – tens of petabytes per year and which is analysed by a computer network connecting more than 170 computer centres in thirty-six countries.[2] In other words: the new technology has changed not just what is studied and how it is done but also the sociology of collaboration between institutions of higher learning.

ICT has also restructured the *dissemination* of knowledge. There are online journals and new forms of visualization: E-publishing and open access are new catchwords. However, this also has generated new problems and pitfalls: for example plagiarism and academic fraud can become easier. Indeed, universities now routinely check their students' papers and theses for plagiarism and their tests for cheating.[3]

Another snare of the new technology is its fatal attraction to distraction: students who surf the net or interact with friends on Facebook during lectures, or professors who are tempted by colleagues or bloggers to become instantly available on the screen. The online life can make heavy demands on attention and focus.

So where does this last stage of technology for higher education institutions leave us?

2 See for example <http://home.web.cern.ch/about> accessed 29 April 2013.

3 See Charlotte Haug (2013), 'The Downside of Open-Access Publishing', *The New England Journal of Medicine*, 368: 791–793, 28 February, DOI: 10.1056/NEJMp1214750; and see, for example, Erin Zlomek (2013), 'B-Schools Use Turnitin Software to Crack Down on Plagiarism', *BusinessWeek*, 18 April, <http://www.businessweek.com/articles/2013-04-18/b-schools-use-turnitin-software-to-crack-down-on-plagiarism> accessed 29 April 2013.

## Variations on a Theme

Above I have outlined the historical success and the developmental stages of higher education. The institutions have much the same history and morphology – yet there are different strains. Some of the dimensions along which they vary are the following

- *Institutional autonomy* relative to the state. Some are not just state financed; the state also adopts the laws and regulations by which they are governed.
- *Internal governance*, e.g. whether they are, simply put, *presidential*, with power and discretion lodged in a Chancellor or President with considerable personal leeway for decisions on policy as well as the appointment of subordinates, or whether they are *collegial* in the sense that professors more or less rule the institution, e.g. by peer choice of a Rector and of Deans, with regular meetings in academic bodies which can make binding decisions by vote, etc. Clearly there are also many mixed forms, as well as variations in the extent to which non-academic staff and students have a say in the running of the university.
- *The mix between public and private universities*. Over the last decades the number of private institutions has increased on many continents, e.g. in Africa.[4] There are also private institutions that derive part of their funding from the state.
- Institutions of higher education *vary in the level of the highest degree that they grant* – there is a whole range from community colleges to PhD-granting universities.
- Institutions vary in the *scope of subject fields they encompass*, ranging from basically all-encompassing large universities to specialized schools for agriculture, technology, business, etc.

4 N.V. Varghese (2013), 'Private Higher Education: The Global Surge and Indian Concerns', in *India Infrastructure Report 2012: Private Sector in Education*, London and New Delhi: Routledge (Taylor and Francis Group), IDFC, pp. 145–156.

- Institutions of higher education can have different *institutional, ethnic, linguistic and religious affiliation*, e.g. military academies, French speaking universities or catholic colleges.
- *The main sources of funding* vary greatly, with purely state funding at one end to overwhelmingly private funding at the other, and mixed forms based on land-grants, tuition, donations or returns on patents, etc.

If one distinguishes between two levels of governance – at the level of the institution and the level of the national system one can therefore conclude that there is no strict unitary or universal model. Moreover, the way the institutions work depends on the system in which they are embedded.

## *Institutional Variation – Shared Ideals*

In spite of the variation in university organization and governance and the systemic differences between countries in the way higher education is structured and financed, one can argue that there are a set of constituting principles for higher education institutions. Basically they express the ideal of academic freedom as the precondition for the discovery and dissemination of knowledge.[5] They are generally attributed to Karl Wilhelm von Humboldt when he was in charge of establishing the University of Berlin around 1810, and they are encapsulated in his terms *Lernfreiheit*

5 See Thorsten Nybom (2003), 'The Humboldt Legacy: Reflections on the Past, Present, and Future of the European University', *Higher Education Policy*, 16 (2), 141–159, <http://www.palgrave-journals.com/hep/journal/v16/n2/full/8300013a.html> accessed 29 April 2013. See also Terence Karran (2009), 'Academic Freedom in Europe: Time for a Magna Charta?' *Higher Education Policy*, 22 (2), 163–189, <http://www.palgrave-journals.com/hep/journal/v22/n2/full/hep20092a.html#bib32> accessed 29 April 2013. Karran has an excellent and dense summary in *Academic Freedom: Why do we need a Magna Charta?* Higher Education Research Group Seminar, University of Oxford, 1 December 2009, <http://eprints.lincoln.ac.uk/2133/>.

and *Lehrfreiheit*.[6] They express the fundamental rights of students and professor for a university to function

Students and professors alike are encompassed by *Lernfreiheit* – that they should be 'free to take their own road to the truth'.[7] They should be enabled to pursue knowledge according to their own preferences, both what to study and how to go about it. For students it implies the freedom to choose courses or transfer from one university to another in the pursuit of learning. Students should have the opportunity to discover what they did not know – including discovering what they did not know was in them and how it can be developed. Hence it is contrary to indoctrination. This also has an implication at the institutional level. If *Lehrfreiheit* is to be real, universities have the responsibility to maintain fields of knowledge even if there is a drop in student interest. The freedom to learn cannot be maintained just by demand – the institutions of higher education must also maintain the supply. Hence universities have to be the defenders of knowledge for which there is little current demand – also in the interest of future generations that have not yet expressed any demand.

For professors especially *Lernfreiheit* entails *the right to 'learn about'* in the sense that they must have the liberty to carry out *research of their own choosing*. The moral imperative for the faculty of a university is that it should be dedicated to seeking the knowledge they themselves deem important or intriguing, unencumbered by external constraints. Institutionally professors should not be driven by the need for remuneration or immediate practical utility, but have autonomy in their choice of topics for research and the methods employed. They should be motivated by the intrinsic interest of a topic, not by the outlook for profit or by the principle that 'he who pays the fiddler calls the tune'. In higher education the supreme reward is collegial recognition and prestige derived from original contributions and novel discoveries, by untangling unsolved problems or by giving a new direction for research.

6 For an excellent exposition, see R.M.O. Pritchard (1990). *The End of Elitism? The Democratization of the West German University System* (New York, Oxford: Berg). See especially Chapter 2 on *Lernfreiheit* and *Lehrfreiheit*, pp. 45 ff.

7 Ibid.: 45.

Finally professors should have *Lehrfreiheit* – the opportunity to teach without any extraneous impositions or control. This entails academic autonomy in setting the curriculum, assignments for students, etc. with no strings attached. Preferably students should learn about current research, indeed from current research by themselves taking part in it. In short, universities or professors should not be held to any orthodoxy.

To buttress these principles various organizational measures have been introduced. They encompass funding independent of external requirements, autonomy of the governing bodies at universities, tenure of faculty so that they cannot be fired for deviant or controversial opinions, international exchange programmes like ERASMUS to allow and encourage student mobility, the emphasis upon research-based teaching and training, etc.

Principles of academic freedom have been embodied in the Constitution of some countries, e.g. Greece or Spain, and also in important international norm-setting conventions, such as the *World Declaration on Higher Education for the Twenty-First Century: Vision and Action*, adopted by UNESCO in 1998.

This does not mean that the principles of academic freedom have been solidly lodged in all countries. Indeed, in many places they are challenged, subverted or breached. Historically there have been setbacks as well as advances. Yet the Humboldtian ideals are in a sense a global gold standard against which institutions of higher education are measured and held accountable. They serve as a tacit injunction for institutions of higher education, e.g. in the sense that they should transmit learning by advancing knowledge, integrate education with the experience of research and encourage productive contemplation and informed action. In particular they should foster the capacity for asking fresh questions, the imagination to connect dots by interdisciplinary interaction, alertness and serendipity. The broader agenda of a university is to foster a public spirit, responsible citizenship and accountability to the broader community, indeed, humanity.

## *Present Challenges for University Governance*

Hence one could argue that the key question for university governance is this: how to advance the Humboldtian agenda in today's rapidly changing environment where one size does not fit all?

We can seek an answer in going back to the Darwinian process we started with. The first observation then is that universities are still evolving. They are all the time trying new adaptations. They experiment, they change and they mutate. Along with successes, there are also strains – and some of the strains come from the very expansion of institutions of higher education. They are subject to new selective pressures. Therefore it would be a mistake to pose the questions of institutional governance as if their environment and ecology were constant. Indeed, they are caught in cross-pressures and crosswinds. So which are the most important trends and central tensions they face?

The first challenge in many countries is a *shrinking support from the public purse* – in one word: austerity. This is partly a result of the present recession, which is the worst since the Great Depression. It has hit universities all over the world. To take but one example: the California two tier university system with a stellar reputation had its budget slashed by 20 per cent in 2011. Students had to pay a 26 per cent higher tuition for less service.[8] But also in many other institutions of higher education scholarships are down, tuition is up requiring more outside work for students. Courses have been cut, class sizes increased and the number of teaching assistants curtailed. Many institutions have also adopted a policy for internal distribution of 'money follows the student', which means that whole disciplines have been cut. A key question is therefore how unpredictable support affects planning, whether quality is falling and whether the lost ground will be recovered.[9]

8 See 'California Cuts Weigh Heavily on Its Colleges', *The New York Times*, 8 July 2011, <http://www.nytimes.com/2011/07/09/us/09uc.html?pagewanted=all> accessed 29 April 2013.

9 In the case of California it must, however, be mentioned that in the Fall of 2012 voters approved a proposition to raise taxes and use most of them for education – including

Another important trend is the globalization of institutions of higher education and *expansion of subsidiaries* – indeed, some talk of the 'Global Networked University', e.g. the above mentioned New York University Abu Dhabi – NYUAD. The business idea is to make all the resources available to global students. There are many examples of such global expansion. Johns Hopkins University has established itself in Nanjing, and in Hong Kong alone there are more than fifty UK providers of university courses, among them Coventry, Edinburgh, Glyndwr, Sheffield – and offers from other Western universities as well.[10]

Before 2000 *university rankings* were mainly restricted to the US. Since then there has been a proliferation of both national and international rankings of institutions of higher education. Among the best known global rankings are the Shanghai Jiao Tong Academic Ranking of World Universities which began in 2003, followed by the Spanish Webometrics and the Times Higher Education World University Ranking in 2004.[11] There are also rankings of more specialized institutions, such as the Financial Times' 'Global MBA Ranking'.[12] These rankings provide new metrics which makes it increasingly simple to get information on performance and quality. But they may also opportunistically affect research agendas and even the internal policies and organization of institutions who aim to improve their rank by a kind of global academic one-upmanship. This impacts on research agendas and student recruitment: altogether the rankings tend to make for a more global branding and hierarchization of academic institutions. It is an interesting question whether the proliferation of college and university rankings have their influence most at the level of university Presidents and Rectors rather than at the level of professors.

---

higher education. See, 'Resurrecting California's Public Universities', *The New York Times*, 30 March 2013, <http://www.nytimes.com/2013/03/31/opinion/sunday/resurrecting-californias-public-universities.html> accessed 29 April 2013.

10 See, for example, 'Your Guide to Postgraduate Study in Hong Kong – Other Providers', *South China Morning Post*, 11 August 2012, <http://www.scmp.com/node/572035> accessed 29 April 2013.

11 For a quick overview, see 'College and University Rankings', *Wikipedia*.

12 See <http://rankings.ft.com/businessschoolrankings/global-mba-ranking-2013>.

Yet another trend in present day globalization is the fact that an ever increasing percentage of students and professors are foreign born rather than nationals. This is probably more the case at the top ranked institutions than at the middle or lower levels – those at the top are more attractive to academic globetrotters.

International students apply to foreign universities both to study with eminent professors but also because they value a top level academic brand name. So the migration of both students and professors – footloose cosmopolitans – contribute to the internationalization of academic culture. To use but one illustration: the total number of international students enrolled in the US increased to an all-time high of 764,495 in 2011–2012, an increase of 6 per cent from the year before.[13] The number of international scholars working at US universities and colleges – as professors, researchers, instructors – rose to an all-time high of 115,000 in 2010, up from 86,000 in 2001. Some of the same flows can be observed for other countries, such as Great Britain or Australia. The effect is a brain drain from poorer countries, though one can also observe the reverse process, e.g. when about 60 per cent of PhDs in the technological fields in Norway are earned by foreign students, most of whom return home after completion.

## *The Challenges of the Fourth Stage of University Technologies*

However, the greatest challenge to higher education institutions is the fourth stage of technological change discussed above – i.e. the transformative ICT technology and the effects of what can be called disruptive digitalization. The challenge it poses could, sharply put, be stated as a question: *is a university first and foremost a place or a site?*

There are now several institutions which call themselves universities which are primarily net based. For example the British Open University was established in 1969 and has over the years used a wide range of methods for

13 For statistics, see Institute for International Education, <http://www.iie.org/en/Research-and-Publications/Open-Doors> accessed 29 April 2013.

distance learning which has evolved with technology, featuring broadcasts by the BBC, DVDs and increasingly Internet video, including moderated forums. In the US the for-profit University of Phoenix has students in more than 100 locations and online programmes for students around the world. Other examples of e-learning can be found at the Kahn Academy, WorldWideLearn or easily accessible courses from iTunes University.

Over the last few years there have been important new developments. On 30 August 2012, Stanford University created a Vice Provost for Online Learning: 'a landmark step in its commitment to bring new teaching and learning methods to Stanford students – and to students around the world – in response to the requirements and potential of the 21st century'. It was heralded as a restructuring of the university to ensure 'pedagogical agility and rigor in the face of global, economic and social transformations'. The primary commitment was to use technology to improve existing classes for on-campus Stanford students, but also to 'offer new learning opportunities to millions of people, both in the United States and around the world'.[14] In the Fall term of 2012 fifteen courses were offered.

What this means is that teaching is separated from the class-room – the first of the technologies of universities mentioned above. Yet in a sense it can bring the teacher closer to students in front of their screens than to students at the back of the auditorium.

The new technology means that international academic superstars can lecture and teach millions. Stanford in 2012 organized a ten-week course on App-development for the iPhone and iPad which was downloaded ten million times. So access can be open, equal – and transnational. With the new technology it is also possible to enrich lectures with on-screen dynamic illustrations. Courses can be designed with quizzes for instant feedback and even customized monitoring. This, clearly, can enhance traditional class-teaching as well. However, there is a loss of face-to-face contact or the personal tutoring, the contact between professor and student or among students.

14 See 'Stanford takes landmark step in online learning, appoints new vice provost', Stanford Report, 30 August 2012, <http://news.stanford.edu/news/2012/august/online-learning-office-083012.html>accessed 29 April 2013.

But then again: the generation of students is coming of age now is adept at and adapted to online interaction, e.g. conversation in groups by video-streaming via Skype or similar applications. Already it is easy to enrich online teaching with online colloquia. Indeed, the iTunes university has already gone interactive, with class discussions among participants and study groups where students can chat, ask questions and work out problems together. And students give feedback to providers by commenting, evaluating and ranking courses.

The benefit of on-line courses is first of all that they can lower tuition – there is no room and board required. Many courses are also free. For example in January 2012 it was reported that iTunes University had had 700 million downloads of lectures, course materials, instructional videos and reading lists.[15]

Several institutions have launched low-cost web-based education or 'MOOCs' – Massive Open Online Courses. Their purpose is to organize open access courses with large-scale interactive participation. Students can download and use traditional course materials such as books, readings, assignments and tests. But students, teachers and teaching assistants are provided with a platform for interaction, videoconferencing, blogging and commenting. The courses are participatory and allow students to connect, collaborate and engage with each other around shared materials. They can ask questions and get answers from their peers. The videos are generally shorter than the traditional academic lecture of forty-five minutes – often ten-minute chunks which are accompanied by quizzes with immediate feedback. So they can check whether the topic of the chunk is mastered. The videos allow illustrations which are more difficult to manage in traditional classes. Students can serve as free helpers who can guide others, like in a virtual seminar. Groups can be organized so that students learn from each other, grade themselves or each other. Since there are so many participants, the quizzes and tests provide feedback also for those who have produced the videos – if many make the same mistake, the material can be

15 See Apple Press Info, 19 January 2012, <http://www.apple.com/pr/library/2012/01/19Apple-Unveils-All-New-iTunes-U-App-for-iPad-iPhone-iPod-touch.html> accessed 29 April 2013.

corrected and improved. Students who participate can motivate each other and some maintain a virtual network after completing a course.[16] A key advantage of MOOCs is that they can be downloaded and studied where one wants when one wants, on a PC, on an iPad or on a mobile phone.

Already consortia of universities are making MOOCs available, e.g. the for-profit *Udacity*, or *edX* founded by Harvard and MIT and *Coursera* which is a company that works with universities to make their courses in the sciences, humanities and social sciences available online. The new technology raises many intriguing legal issues – e.g. who owns the courses, should professors receive extra pay for successful courses etc.

Again we are likely to see a Darwinian process unfold. The present stage is one of experimentation and innovation. Surely best practice will be found, selected and spread. The key questions are: How will institutions of higher education respond to this new and disruptive technology? What systems of governance will be most appropriate when teachers are on line and on video with students not on campus? How will old universities develop and integrate new online courses? Which types of institutions of higher education will be most adversely affected – will it be those who are primarily focused on teaching rather than research? Will teaching and curricula become more standardized globally? Will there be different styles of teaching in different disciplines? Will the competitive edge that nations have vary across fields of study? Which courses and style of teaching will students find most attractive? To what extent will interactivity be a selling point? Will the ephemeral networks that students establish in one course solidify and remain a source of motivation, encouragement and collegiality for another? Will those who have taken one course recruit others? Will the style of teaching and training learn from gaming, for example? What types of activities do not easily lend themselves to online courses – e.g. to learn chemistry one has to do some real shaking of test-tubes. Which teaching regime works best? What design triggers extra effort? What can

16 There are several introductions to MOOCs on YouTube; see, for example, David Glance, 'MOOCs and the end of universities', <http://www.youtube.com/watch?v=Mw9nvV4nvtY> accessed 29 April 2013.

make students overcome their own inertia and surpass themselves? How can professors be enticed to contribute beyond the call of duty? Clearly these are important questions for research – and for action.

## Reasons for Optimism

The questions are many – and there are some grounds for worry. Indeed, one can ask whether information technology could mean the end of the universities as we know them. So let me end on some optimistic notes.

For nearly a thousand years universities and institutions of higher education have been among the most successful of organizations – they have adapted to new technology, changed their mode of operation as well as their mode of governance. They have been exposed to shocks and disturbances – yet they have recovered from setbacks. They have, in one word, been resilient and have maintained their original purposes – to transmit learning and advance knowledge.

I would argue that they are more than resilient organizations: they have themselves produced and triggered innovations that have drastically altered their own environment. As stated at the outset the university is at the heart of modernity. The fourth technology that is now disruptive as well as daunting – ICT – is also to a large extent a university product which feeds back to the way universities will function, can function and must function. This is probably best illustrated in the name 'Silicon Valley': the place where the new digital world contrived at universities has changed their own environment as well as changed the environment and adaptive strategies of other types of organizations. Organisms that are able to adapt and rebound from a challenging environment which *they themselves have produced*, could be called *super-resilient organizations*.

And universities are super-resilient for three important reasons.

The first is this: resources of all kinds are unequally distributed around the world – arable land, minerals, hydroelectric power, oil, water. But there is one resource that is more equally distributed than any other: human talent. *Wherever there are people, there is talent!* It is a resource that not only can be used – it can be developed, and institutions of higher education are the places where it is most advanced.

The second resource is this. At universities there are always more questions than answers. There are always more problems than current solutions. Or put differently: *Universities will never run out of important things to do because we will never run out of ignorance.* That is why the university is a universal institution. It is also universal in the sense that it serves as a bridge between the pillars of knowledge.[17] Indeed, the idea of a university is best imagined as an architrave, i.e. the beam that rests horizontally on the columns in a Greek temple. The task of a university is not just to construct the pillars of knowledge in different disciplines, but also to put in place and maintain the knowledge that joins them.

And more than anything this is what should unite all disciplines: not just to foster knowledge and learning, but also to generate the emotional joys of intellectual work: to learn something new almost every day, and every now and then discover something new. This is the third resource that can be tapped.

Hence if I were to compress the mission of a university into a simple formula, it would be this: its task is to foster *lifelong obsessions* for students and staff. Because it is the obsession of posing and solving problems, small and large, that can fill a life with meaning and imbue ordinary weekdays with passion and drive.

17 This in a sense corresponds to the old idea of the unity of knowledge. Cf. Pritchard, op. cit., p. 41.

# Notes on Contributors

PÅL BAKKEN works as Senior Adviser at the Norwegian Agency for Quality Assurance in Education (NOKUT).

LISE DEGN is a PhD student at the Danish Centre for Studies in Research and Research Policy in the Department of Political Science, at Aarhus University.

GEORGE GORDON is Emeritus Professor in Educational Enhancement at the University of Strathclyde in Glasgow.

ELLEN HAZELKORN is Vice President of Research and Enterprise and Dean of the Graduate Research School at the Dublin Institute of Technology.

GUDMUND HERNES is a researcher at the Fafo Institute in Oslo, and a professor at the Norwegian School of Management.

MARIA HINFELAAR has been President of Limerick Institute of Technology since 2004.

JAN ERIK KARLSEN is Emeritus Professor of Change Management/ Industrial Economics at the University of Stavanger.

JOUNI KEKÄLE is Human Resources Director at the University of Eastern Finland (UEF). He is also a professor and an advisor to the Rector at the UEF.

MICHAEL O'CONNELL is Vice-President for Strategy and External Affairs at Limerick Institute of Technology.

MATTHIAS KLUMPP is Senior Researcher at the University of Duisburg-Essen (HELENA Research Group) and Professor of Business Administration, Logistics and Service Industries at FOM University of Applied Sciences, Essen.

CARMEN PÉREZ-ESPARRELLS is Associate Professor in Applied Economics and Pro Vice-Chancellor for Innovation at the Universidad Autónoma de Madrid.

ROSALIND M.O. PRITCHARD is Professor of Education at the University of Ulster.

STIG A. SELMER-ANDERSSEN manages the Quality Office in the Institutional Development Unit in the University of Stavanger's Department of Finance and Governance.

INGRID STORM is a Marston Research Associate at the University of Manchester's Institute for Social Change; she was formerly employed at the Norwegian Agency for Quality Assurance in Education (NOKUT).

EVA M. TORRE is Technical Expert at the governing body which represents society within the Universidad Autónoma de Madrid (the so-called Consejo Social) and a PhD student at the same university.

CELIA WHITCHURCH is Senior Lecturer in Higher Education at the Institute of Education, University of London.

# Index


academic
drift 263, 269
excellence 48
management 192
academization 381
access 122–124
accountability 67–68, 77–78, 93, 106, 108, 110, 328, 337, 342
adaptation 2
university adaptation 6, 13, 17–48
adaptive institutions 38, 213
adaptiveness 3
age cohorts 95, 99
ageing 97, 101, 104
agenda setters 10, 206–208
'Aimhigher' 123, 141
alliances 139, 239
alternative providers of higher education 128–130
alumni 325–327, 329–330, 332–337, 339–342
amalgamate 250
amalgamation 250, 255
annualized contract(s) 217
anticipation 19, 356
appropriation 356
Arts, Humanities and the Social Sciences 119, 140
attention 150–151, 154–156
audit 166–167, 175–176
authorities 149–189
awareness 358–359

backcasting 349, 356
bailouts 98
bank crisis 110
baseline 360
basic funding 91, 94, 100
benefit package(s) 217
best practice 332–333
binary system 261, 263
binary HE system 240, 246–247, 254, 256
Bologna process 125
British Academy 125
Browne, Lord 119, 138–139
budget cuts 92

Cable, Vince 127
campus of international excellence 344
career(s) 221, 228, 230
career development 228
career pathway(s) 229
case study 324, 326–328, 331–335
cautious adaptation 233
Central Bank 99
change
incremental 29–30
strategic 29–30
change management 244–245, 256
changing youth cultures 93
Charnes-Cooper transformation 311
choice 150–157, 160–165, 182–188
coalition 31, 118, 128
Coalition of Conservatives and Liberal Democrats 118, 128
collaboration 239, 242, 247–249, 253, 255–258

collaboration, alliances and mergers (CAMs) 239–247, 249–250, 252–253, 255, 344
College of Law 128
communication 325, 329, 333–334, 337, 339–340
competition 117
competitive 242–243, 245, 246, 250–251, 256–257
competitiveness 7, 30, 57, 64, 107, 139, 239, 245, 249, 261
comprehensive university 326
computer programme 155
conceptual
  model 47, 156, 182
  scaffolding 48
configuration 241, 249
consolidation 239, 241, 253
consortium 221–222
constitutive logic 25
context
  of discovery 38
  of justification 38
contract(s) 214, 215, 217–218, 221, 224, 227, 229, 231
co-ordinators 10, 205–208
'core and margin' system 119
Council of Validating Universities 127
counter-megatrends 109
culture of asking 335, 339–341, 345
culture of giving 335, 337–339
Curnock 124

data envelopment analysis 288–289, 294–295
decision making 149–158, 166, 173, 177–178
  unit 308–310
decline
  in part-time entrants 121
  in postgraduate students 121
demography 91, 95
Denmark 6, 191–192, 201
Department for Business, Innovation and Skills (BIS) 123
Department Heads 10, 191–192, 194, 197–199, 201–202, 204–208
development office 325–326, 330–331, 333, 335, 338, 340–341
differentiation 330, 335, 339
disadvantaged students 75, 122–123
discourse 64, 106
diseconomies of scale 299, 301
'disjointed incrementalism' 138
distribution politics 93, 106
diversification 117, 138–139, 329, 339, 342–343, 345, 381
diversity 125
donations 325–326, 329–330, 335, 337, 338–341
dream university 364
driving forces 353, 361
dual management structure 35

eclectic model 366
economic crisis 53–55, 66, 69–70, 79–80, 91
economies of scale 140, 242, 299–301, 344
edtech 34
education exports 133
educational
  diversity 267
  markets 91, 118
  technology 91
e-education market 102
effectiveness, 117, 134
efficiency 117
  effectiveness trade off *see* ETTO
eLearning 92, 101–102, 105, 109
elite 53, 71, 73–76, 79–80, 375
employee partnership 220, 221

employment contract(s)218
employment package(s) 224
employment practice(s) 214
employment proposition 227
energy 152–153, 159–160, 186–189
environment, 116–117
ETTO principle 117, 134, 302
  efficiency thoroughness trade off 117, 134, 141, 302
Euro crisis 92, 98–99, 123
European Business School 2.0+ 373
European Higher Education Area (EHEA) 56
European Research Area (ERA) 56
European Stability Mechanism 99
EU Youth Strategy 103
excellence 324, 328–329, 331, 337, 342, 344
expansion 381
  of subsidiaries 396
extramural 28, 31, 45, 353, 365

faint signals 42, 116
feminization 381
financial base 91, 98
financial viability 47–48
Finland 141
flexible 218
flexibility 4
flying faculty 231
foresight analysis 351
'for profit' HEIs 129
Fortran 188
forward-thinking 356
Foundation Degrees 128
four stages of university technology 387
frames of reference 354
functional-historicist structure 47
funding mechanisms 91, 94, 328
funding models 106
funding packages 99
funding strategy 329, 340
fundraising 323–345
fundraising strategy 324–328, 331–332, 334–335, 339, 340, 343
further education 126–128
futures
  plausible 349
  possible 349
  probable 349
  preferable 349, 356
future images 355, 357
future studies 354
Future Workshop 350

Garbage Can Model 149–189
gender 124
global
  economic crisis 53–55, 69–70, 80
  financial crisis 54, 56, 58, 65
  rankings 59, 63, 69
global competitiveness 59, 68
globalization 53–54, 70, 77, 80
governance 149, 156, 171–172, 177
  anticipatory governance 45
  distributed governance 23
  good governance 36
  governance game 32
  governance model 21, 241, 247–248, 253
  governance triangle 26
  institutional governance 19, 242, 243, 245
  shared governance 254, 350
  university governance 19, 349
grade factory 368
Greek Triangle 355–356

Harkin Report 129
'harm absorber' 9, 140
Harvard Light 2.0 ÷ 373
HEFCE *see* Higher Education Funding Council for England

HEIs
Higher education institutions 367
Higher Education Act of 2004 123
higher education efficiency 283–321
Higher Education Funding Council for England (HEFCE) 126-, 130, 140, 213
higher education reform 191–193
higher tariff institutions 122
homogenization 139
Horizon *2020* 100, 101
Hotson, Howard 118
House of Lords 126, 130
Humboldt 392
Humboldt Super 2.0+ 372

ideal type 26
ideational institutionalism 194–196
identity construction 197, 207–208
immigration 95, 109
incentives 233
incorporation 249–250, 255, 257
innovation 327, 334
institutes of technology (IOTs) 240, 241, 247, 250–255
institutional
accreditation 264
advancement 323, 325
autonomy 168, 391
capability 2
drift 262, 270, 273–274
hierarchy 264
innovation 18
leadership 333, 335–336, 339
mergers 265, 272–274
type 25
uniqueness 48
variation 370, 392
institutional changes
adaptation 29
re-creation 29
re-orientation 29
tuning 29
institutional isomorphism 269
coercive isomorphism 269, 272, 274
competitive isomorphism 269, 272, 274
mimetic processes 269, 272, 274, 278
normative pressures 269
institutional-level response 343
internal culture 107, 197
internal diversification 267
internal governance 391
internationalization 381
international students 133
intramural 27, 45, 167–168, 365
investment bankers 98, 111
Ireland 55, 64–67, 69, 123
Ivy League Colleges 123

Joint Information Systems Committee 223
Joint Negotiating Committee for Higher Education Staff 224

knowledge
economy 54, 58, 64
exchange 214, 219, 229–230
'knowledge production workers' 43

'latent pathogens' 2, 136
leadership 29, 240, 242–247, 256–257
learning intensive society 370
lifelong learning 97, 109, 373
Limerick Institute of Technology 239–257
Lisbon Agenda 56, 59
local managers 231, 233
London Metropolitan University (LMU) 132–133, 139

Lord Browne of Madingley 119

management 328, 333, 337, 342
    practice 198, 205, 207
    reform 192
    relationships 225
managerial instruments 157, 166, 176
market
    market-driven 343–345
    market logic 106
    marketing 325, 333, 337, 339–340, 342
massification 94, 95
matched funding schemes 337–338
megatrends 14, 47, 92–111
mergers 239, 241–245, 249, 250–251, 253–255
    incidental mergers 242, 245, 256–257, 273–274
    policy-induced mergers 242–243, 245, 257, 273–274
migration 65, 115, 126, 132, 382, 397
'Million Plus Group' 132
mimetic processes 269, 272, 274
mindfulness 175
    capability mindfulness 38
    collective mindfulness 40, 42
    institutional mindfulness 38
    processes of mindfulness 39
model
    fundraising theoretical model 331, 333, 335, 339
    Garbage Can Model 149–189
    Multiple Streams 155
    organizational 149, 150, 156, 166, 177–178, 233
    Organizational Resilience Theoretical Framework 173–175
    Overlap Model 170
    university-donor interaction 325–328
modern languages 125
MOOCs 399
morale 215, 231
motivation 215
multi-authority system 28, 149–189
multiplication 381
Multiple Streams theory 155

National Scholarship Programme 123
neoliberalism 116
networking 381
new higher education professionals 170, 178
non-state funding 329–330, 333
normative pressures 269, 272, 274
Norway 159, 166–167, 175–178

OECD scenarios 95, 105
Office
    for Fair Access (OFFA) 123, 130, 139–140
    of the Auditor General 159, 166–167, 169, 171, 175–178
    of the Independent Adjudicator 130, 136
one-off payment(s) 214
open access 353
open systems 104
Open Method of Coordination (OMC) 157
operational environment 91
optimal size 299
organization of knowledge 386
organizational
    change 29
    identity 10, 208
    resistance 29
    sclerosis, 116
Organizational Resilience Theoretical Framework 173–175
organized anarchy 151, 162, 167, 175

output
  output indicators 285, 287–290
outreach
outsourcing 213, 222, 326, 333, 337, 339
Overlap Model 170
overseas campus(es) 231

paradox 173–177
participation 356
partnership 216, 219–221, 225, 229, 233, 326, 339
path theories 371
patronage 326
performance and productivity measurement 286–289
performance related pay 217, 231
philanthropic funds 323, 325, 329, 332–335, 343
philanthropy 324–326, 330, 332, 334–335, 337–338, 340
policy trade-offs 55, 69, 79
population changes 93
portfolio 214, 219–220, 229–231
post-1992 HEIs, 132
prestige 332, 339
private
  degree courses 129
  funding 323–325, 339, 341, 344–345
  HEIs 128, 140
  income streams 329, 332
  universities 140
programme rationalization 139
proliferation 381
psychological contract 224
public finances 98
public funding 96, 98, 104, 109, 110
public relations 337, 339–340
public sector-driven 343

quality 54, 59, 62–64, 66–69, 71, 74, 77, 79–80
Quality Assurance Agency (QAA) 135
'Quality Reform' 264
quasi-market 141

ranking 323, 328, 331–332, 344
rationalization 241, 245, 248, 250, 252, 256–257
regional clusters 241, 251–253, 256–257
relevance 107, 108, 110
research 54–57, 59–62, 64–72, 76, 78–80, 214–215, 218–220, 222, 227, 228–231, 327
research oriented universities 261
research productivity 12, 283, 299
research university 70, 80, 372
resilience 2, 115–116, 124, 149–150, 172–175, 215, 232–234
  institutional 3, 17, 142
  operational 175
  strategic 175
  super-resilient organizations 381
  university resilience 17
resourcefulness 3
retention 217
reward package(s) 220
rewards 215, 228, 233–234
robustness 3, 38
Russell Group 131

scenario 352
  axes 373
  building 361
  development 361
  situational 361
scholarship 218, 222, 228–231
self-organization 4
senior management team 219, 221, 225, 231
sensemaking 191, 193–199, 201, 203, 207
  processes 10, 191, 193–202, 204–206
  strategy 200, 203, 205–206
Shannon Consortium 247–249, 252–257

shared services 213, 223
shielders 10, 205–206, 208
short term applications 107
shrinking support 395
simulation 163–171
'sisu' 3
slack 174–175
sources of income 391
sovereign debt 93, 98, 106
sponsorship 326, 330, 335–336, 341
staffing model(s) 215
staffing practice(s) 230–231
stakeholder 149, 157–158, 162–163, 177–178, 323, 325–326, 332, 335–337, 339–341, 343, 345
state intervention 142
steering core 243–246, 254–257
steering mechanism 100
STEM
  subjects 125
story line 352, 367
Strategic Innovation Fund 248
strategic positioning 242, 245, 247, 257
strategic resilience 175
strategy 29, 331, 337
  decay 135
stratification 75, 76, 80
stress 136–137
structural changes 42, 106
student
  experience 213, 222
  mobility 96, 280, 353, 394
  protest UK 120
  recruitment 120–124
Student Loans Company 129
survival 381
Sutton Trust 121–122, 139
Swiss Cheese Model 135
system-level response 343
system restructuring 70

tax incentives 330, 333, 337–338, 340–341, 343
tax revenues 97, 98
teaching 214–215, 218–219, 221–222, 226, 228–231
  teaching technologies 48, 92
team 214, 217–219, 221–222, 224–227, 230–231
technical university 327
technological universities 241, 251
Thatcher, Margaret 118
'The 1994 Group' 134
'The Women's Library' 142
third space 170
timeline comparisons 291
Times Higher Education World University Rankings 396
  2011–2012 134
  2012–2013 134, 290
top up fees 139
transfer of knowledge 327, 339, 342
transition 360
Transparency Approach to Costing 135
trend 360–361
'trickle-down' economics 79
tuition fees 119
two-year degrees 125
typology
  of governance models 25
  of institutional change 29

UCAS 122, 125, 138
UCU 139
  Report 124, 138
UK Border Agency (UKBA) 132–133, 140
UK entry figures 2012 121
universities
  private 391
  public 391
Universities and Colleges Admissions Service 121

Universities Founding Council 139
Universities of Norway 159, 166–167, 175–178
UniversitiesUK 129, 213
university
  adaptation 47, 363
  colleges 261, 263
  elites 375
  fundraising 324–329, 337, 343
  leadership 29
  management 200, 204, 206–207
  rankings 396
'University Alliance' 132
University and College Union 129, 137
University of
  Cambridge 324, 328, 331–335
  Maastricht 123
  Navarra 324, 327, 331–335
  Oslo 167
University Visitor 136
variety 117
Vice-Chancellors 9, 23, 136, 215–216, 227
visioning 359
visions 24
voluntary giving 325–326, 337–338, 340

Warwick University 109, 118
weak signals *see* faint signals
  early warnings 42
White Paper (UK, 2011) 119, 139
Workforce 214, 235
workload model(s) 218, 226
world-class university 70–71, 79–80, 328–329, 344–345

youth culture 93, 102, 105

'zero trauma', 115